Foundations of
Predictive
Analytics

Chapman & Hall/CRC
Data Mining and Knowledge Discovery Series

SERIES EDITOR
Vipin Kumar
University of Minnesota
Department of Computer Science and Engineering
Minneapolis, Minnesota, U.S.A

AIMS AND SCOPE

This series aims to capture new developments and applications in data mining and knowledge discovery, while summarizing the computational tools and techniques useful in data analysis. This series encourages the integration of mathematical, statistical, and computational methods and techniques through the publication of a broad range of textbooks, reference works, and handbooks. The inclusion of concrete examples and applications is highly encouraged. The scope of the series includes, but is not limited to, titles in the areas of data mining and knowledge discovery methods and applications, modeling, algorithms, theory and foundations, data and knowledge visualization, data mining systems and tools, and privacy and security issues.

PUBLISHED TITLES

UNDERSTANDING COMPLEX DATASETS:
DATA MINING WITH MATRIX DECOMPOSITIONS
David Skillicorn

COMPUTATIONAL METHODS OF FEATURE SELECTION
Huan Liu and Hiroshi Motoda

CONSTRAINED CLUSTERING: ADVANCES IN ALGORITHMS, THEORY, AND APPLICATIONS
Sugato Basu, Ian Davidson, and Kiri L. Wagstaff

KNOWLEDGE DISCOVERY FOR COUNTERTERRORISM AND LAW ENFORCEMENT
David Skillicorn

MULTIMEDIA DATA MINING: A SYSTEMATIC INTRODUCTION TO CONCEPTS AND THEORY
Zhongfei Zhang and Ruofei Zhang

NEXT GENERATION OF DATA MINING
Hillol Kargupta, Jiawei Han, Philip S. Yu, Rajeev Motwani, and Vipin Kumar

DATA MINING FOR DESIGN AND MARKETING
Yukio Ohsawa and Katsutoshi Yada

THE TOP TEN ALGORITHMS IN DATA MINING
Xindong Wu and Vipin Kumar

GEOGRAPHIC DATA MINING AND KNOWLEDGE DISCOVERY, SECOND EDITION
Harvey J. Miller and Jiawei Han

TEXT MINING: CLASSIFICATION, CLUSTERING, AND APPLICATIONS
Ashok N. Srivastava and Mehran Sahami

BIOLOGICAL DATA MINING
Jake Y. Chen and Stefano Lonardi

Foundations of Predictive Analytics

James Wu

Stephen Coggeshall

CRC Press
Taylor & Francis Group
Boca Raton London New York

CRC Press is an imprint of the
Taylor & Francis Group, an **Informa** business

A CHAPMAN & HALL BOOK

CRC Press
Taylor & Francis Group
6000 Broken Sound Parkway NW, Suite 300
Boca Raton, FL 33487-2742

Version Date: 20120119

International Standard Book Number: 978-1-4398-6946-8 (Hardback)

Library of Congress Cataloging-in-Publication Data

Wu, James, 1965-
    Foundations of predictive analytics / James Wu, Stephen Coggeshall.
       p. cm. -- (Chapman & Hall/CRC data mining and knowledge discovery series)
    Includes bibliographical references and index.
    ISBN 978-1-4398-6946-8 (hardback : acid-free paper)
    1. Data mining. 2. Predictive control--Mathematical models. 3. Automatic control. I. Coggeshall, Stephen. II. Title.

QA76.9.D343W83 2012
006.3'12--dc23

2011049779

Visit the Taylor & Francis Web site at
http://www.taylorandfrancis.com

and the CRC Press Web site at
http://www.crcpress.com

Contents

List of Figures

List of Tables

Preface

This text is a summary of techniques of data analysis and modeling that the authors have encountered and used in our two decades of experience practicing the art of applied data mining across many different fields. The authors have worked in this field together and separately for many large and small companies, including the Los Alamos National Laboratory, Bank One (JPMorgan Chase), Morgan Stanley, and the startups of the Center for Adaptive Systems Applications (CASA), the Los Alamos Computational Group, and ID Analytics. We have applied these techniques to traditional and nontraditional problems in a wide range of areas including consumer behavior modeling (credit, fraud, marketing), consumer products, stock forecasting, fund analysis, asset allocation, and equity and fixed income options pricing.

This book provides the necessary information for understanding the common techniques for exploratory data analysis and modeling. It also explains the details of the algorithms behind these techniques, including underlying assumptions and mathematical formulations. It is the authors' opinion that in order to apply different techniques to different problems appropriately, it is essential to understand the assumptions and theory behind each technique.

It is recognized that this work is far from a complete treatise on the subject. Many excellent additional texts exist on the popular subjects and it was not a goal for this present text to be a complete compilation. Rather, this text contains various discussions on many practical subjects that are frequently missing from other texts, as well as details on some subjects that are not often or easily found. Thus this text makes an excellent supplemental and referential resource for the practitioners of these subjects. This text is self-contained in that it provides a step-by-step derivation explicitly for each topic from the underlying assumptions to the final conclusions.

We hope the readers will enjoy reading and using this text, and will find it to be helpful to better understand the various subjects treated here. You can find the software package (DataMinerXL library for building predictive models) and more information on the topics of modeling at the author's website: www.DataMinerXL.com.

We would appreciate receiving your suggestions and comments at the contact at www.DataMinerXL.com.

Chapter 1

Introduction

In this book we cover the essentials of the foundations of statistical modeling. We begin with the concepts and properties of statistical distributions, and describe important properties of the various frequently encountered distributions as well as some of the more exotic but useful ones. We have an extensive section on matrix properties that are fundamental to many of the algorithmic techniques we use in modeling. This includes sections on unusual yet useful methods to split complex calculations and to iterate with the inclusion/exclusion of specific data points. We describe the characteristics of the most common modeling frameworks, both linear and nonlinear. Time series or forecasting models have certain idiosyncrasies that are sufficiently special so we devote a chapter to these methods.

There is description of how and why to prepare the data for statistical modeling, including much discussion on practical approaches. We discuss the variety of goodness measures and how and when they are applied. There is a section on optimization methods which are required for many of the training algorithms. We also have description on some of the less well-known topics such as multidimensional scaling, Dempster–Shafer Theory, and some practical discussion about simulation and reject inference.

1.1   What Is a Model?

In its most general definition, a model is a representation of something. It could be a static model that just "sits there" or it could be a dynamic model that represents some kind of process. Examples of static models include a woman walking down a fashion runway wearing some new designer clothes, and she represents how a person would look wearing these clothes. A model of the atom is a conceptual representation of a nucleus with tightly bound protons and neutrons surrounded by a cloud of electrons in various complex orbital shells. A model airplane is typically a smaller and simpler representation of the real object. Examples of dynamic models might be a set of equations that describe how fluid flows through passageways, traffic flowing in cities, stock values rising and falling in time.

Models are usually simpler representations of more complicated systems.

1

We build models to help us understand what is going on, how things interact, or to predict what may happen as things change or evolve. Models could be physical objects or algorithms (a set of rules and/or equations). For algorithmic models they could be first principles or statistical. For first principle models we examine a system and write down a set of rules/equations that describe the essence of the system, ignoring complicating details that are less important. The first principles models could be differential equations that describe a dynamical system or they could be a set of evolutional rules that are written down from expert knowledge of the system's processes.

We are guided in modeling by observing the real system to be modeled. We do our best to understand the important elements of the system, what features characterize the system, what changes, what are the possible dependencies, and what are the important characteristics we are interested in. This observation guides us in constructing the model, either through the first principles or in building a statistical model. Sometimes the process is so complex or unknown that we cannot begin to write down first principles equations, but our observations are sufficient that we have many data examples of the system to be modeled. In these cases we can build a statistical model. The remainder of this book will deal with issues around such statistical modeling.

1.2   What Is a Statistical Model?

A statistical model is typically a set of equations with adjustable parameters that we "train" using the many data observations. Invariably we have an overdetermined system, where we have many more data examples than adjustable parameters, and we desire the "best" set of parameters that allow our equations to fit the data as best as possible. The structure of the equations can be very simple or very complex. It could be a simple linear combination of parameters times system characteristics, or it could be a highly complex nonlinear combination of characteristics and parameters. Our modeling task has several components: (1) a set of equations/rules with adjustable parameters, (2) a set of data that entails examples of the system that we are trying to model, (3) a concept of goodness of fit to the data, and (4) a set of rules that tells us how to adjust the parameters to increase the goodness of the model fit.

The set of parameter-adjusting rules are usually obtained from the goodness of fit measure, often differentiating an objective function with respect to the fitting parameters and setting it to zero, thus finding the set of parameters that are at least locally optimal. One can consider the objective function as a model error surface that floats above a hyperplane of the parameter space, and our desire is to find the minimum of this error surface in this hyperplane. If the error surface is simple we may have an easy-to-find location with the global minimum over the set of all possible parameter values. This is the case with linear regression using a mean square error objective, where the error surface is a paraboloid over the hyperplane of the set of parameters. Often, however, this fitting surface is complex and has multiple local valleys in which we can be trapped as we traverse the hyperplane of possible parameters in search of the minimum. Many techniques exist to help us avoid getting trapped in these local minima regions, such as gradient search with momentum, simulated annealing where the step size starts off large and decreases, or genetic algorithms. The more complex the model, the more complex the fitting surface, and the more likely we need to be careful about local versus global minima.

1.3   The Modeling Process

The process of building a model is a blend of both science and art, as are most endeavors. There is a straightforward formulaic process that we follow, and at each step we are guided by intuition and experience. Here are the basic steps in building a statistical model:

1. **Define the goals.** What are we trying to achieve? What is the outcome we are trying to predict? Under what situations will the model be used and for what purposes? Understand what will determine a good model.

2. **Gather data.** What data is available, in what form, with what quality? How many records (we use the term record interchangeably with data point) will we have? What fields (or model inputs) might be available? How far back in time does the data go, and how relevant are the older records? Generally, modelers want as much data as possible.

3. **Decide the model structure.** Should we do a linear regression, logistic regression, or a nonlinear model, and if so, which kind? What time frames and/or populations should be used for model development and validation? What are the inputs, the output(s), and the measure of goodness? A good approach might be to try a simple linear model as a baseline and then try various nonlinear models to see if one can do better. Choices of model structure require experience and deep knowledge of the strengths and weaknesses of each technique. Important characteristics to consider in the choice of technique include continuous or categorical (classification) output, number of records, likely dimensionality, and amount of data noise.

4. **Prepare the data.** Assemble the data records into the appropriate form for the model. Encode the data into inputs, using expert knowledge as much as possible. Appropriately normalize the numerical data and encode

the categorical data fields. Examine distributions for appropriateness and take care of outliers. Separate data into the desired training, testing, and validation sets.

5. **Variable selection and elimination.** In this step, which may or may not be associated with candidate models, variables are examined for the importance to the models and selected or eliminated. Some variable selection methods are stand alone (filters) and others (wrappers) are integrated with a particular model methodology. Generally in this step a list of candidate good variables rank ordered by importance is decided.

6. **Build candidate models.** Begin building models and assessing the model goodness. We may begin with baseline linear models and then try to improve using more complex nonlinear models. In this and all phases it is important to keep in mind the environment in which the model will be implemented.

7. **Finalize the model.** Select among the candidates the most appropriate model to be implemented. Document the model as needed.

8. **Implementation and monitoring.** Here the model is embedded into the necessary system process, and monitoring steps are built to examine the model performance in ongoing use.

1.4 Modeling Pitfalls

There are many possible traps and difficulties in the model building process. Here we list a few in each of the above-mentioned modeling steps:

1. **Define the goals—pitfalls.** Lack of clarity around problem definition. Problems being defined too narrowly. Sometimes a larger, more important problem can be solved, broader than the one specifically being targeted. Lack of understanding how and where the model will be used. Sometimes key data will not be available for the model when implemented.

2. **Gather data—pitfalls.** Using data too old or otherwise not relevant going forward. Not excluding records of types that will not be seen by the model when implemented. Not considering additional key data sources (features/inputs) or data sets (records) that might be available.

3. **Decide the model structure—pitfalls.** Using too simple a model (rarely a problem). Using too complex a model (more often a problem). Using

a modeling methodology that is not appropriate for the nature of the data (sizes, dimensions, noise...).

4. **Prepare the data—pitfalls.** Not cleaning or considering outliers (some techniques are robust to outliers; many are not). Not properly scaling data. Inefficient encoding of categorical variables. Not eliminating fields that will not be available or will be different going forward. Not giving enough thought to building special expert variables. Not recognizing inherent data bias, including not having data from important categories of records.

5. **Variable selection and elimination—pitfalls.** Relying on only linear variable selection or compression techniques (e.g., PCA). Too much reliance on simply eliminating correlated variables. Not examining all model inputs (distributions, outliers). Keeping too many variables, making it hard for modeling, interpretation, implementation, or model maintenance. Target leakage, where the output value to be predicted is inadvertently and inappropriately hiding in one of the input variables. (Important note—Look carefully and skeptically at any variables that seem to be TOO good in the model.)

6. **Build candidate models—pitfalls.** Going deep on a single specialized technique instead of at first trying a broad spectrum of methods. Not doing a simple linear model as a baseline. Not doing proper training/testing as one examines candidate models. Overfitting.

7. **Finalize the model—pitfalls.** Not rebuilding the final model optimally using all the appropriate data. Improperly selecting the final model without consideration to some implementation constraints. Lack of proper model documentation.

8. **Implementation and monitoring—pitfalls.** Errors in the implementation process: data input streams, variable encodings, algorithm mistakes, simple bugs around special cases. Not monitoring model ongoing performance (inputs, outputs, predictive power).

1.5   Characteristics of Good Modelers

Good modelers can come from a wide range of technical backgrounds. They typically have an undergraduate and a graduate degree in any one of a handful of scientific disciplines, including computer science, mathematics, statistics, engineering, and physics. Physicists make some of the best modelers because of the rigorous applied mathematical exposure, and the trained ability to eliminate all but the essential nature of a problem. Applied mathematicians have built up a repertoire of the tools needed for modeling and are not afraid of jumping into any new algorithmic technology. Engineers, like physicists, have a keen sense of what is essential to the system being modeled. Statisticians are awash in the foundations of the tools underlying most of the modeling techniques. Anyone with any of these backgrounds has the essential baseline skills to become a good modeler.

What are the characteristics that are important to be a good modeler?

1. **Technical competence**. Mastery of the advanced math and statistics fundamentals, such as those found in this book. Very good programming skills since everything is done in software, and one needs the ability to quickly and efficiently code one's new ideas. These are the basic tools of the trade. A bonus is experience with very large, messy data sets. Given these as backgrounds, good modelers will have complete in-depth understanding of every modeling technique they are using rather than just running some commercial software. This deep understanding is the only way one can make good choices between possible techniques and allow the possible modifications of existing algorithms.

2. **Curiosity**. The best modelers are those who are innately curious. They drill into something that just does not look or feel right. If there is something that they do not completely understand they dig deeper to find out what is going on. Frequently the best results come from inadvertent discoveries while chasing a vague feeling around a mystery.

3. **Common sense and perspective**. One needs the ability to drill deep without losing sight of the big picture. A good modeler is constantly making appropriate judgments about what is more and less important, focusing the pursuit in the directions that provide the most overall value without plunging down a rabbit hole.

4. **Passion for data**. The best modelers have an unbridled passion for everything about data—lots and lots of data. One can never get enough data. Never say no to data. One needs to understand everything about the data: where it came from, where it will come from, the quality, robustness, and stability of the data. A lot of effort needs to go into data cleansing, standardizing and organizing. A good data steward will build libraries of data for present and future uses. Data is the lifeblood of statistical model builders. It is the foundation of all our models and everything we do. It is better to use basic techniques on good data sets than to use complex, sophisticated techniques on poor quality data.

5. **Tenacity**. There are many processes involved in good model building and it is important to do each step well without cutting corners. It is tempting to jump around in the model searching process while sometimes a more rigorous, organized search method is appropriate. Tenacity is also an important part in the curiosity characteristic in the chasing down of loose ends.

6. **Creativity**. Always be questioning your modeling technique. Is it the most appropriate for your particular problem and data set? Look for possible modifications of the algorithms that might help, for example, model training rules, data weighting, fuzzifying rather than using sharp boundaries. Don't be afraid to modify algorithms based on need or hunches. Watch for the possibility of broadening of the problem objective to some higher-order goal that may be of more use.

7. **Communication skills**. A useful characteristic for modelers is the ability to explain the essence of the model to nontechnical people. This would include aspects such as what inputs are used, what is the output modeled, what are the strengths, weaknesses, and performance of the model, the nature of the algorithmic structure, the training and testing process, and opinions about robustness and stability based on various statistical tests. A desired skill is to be able to explain complex processes in clear, concise nontechnical language. This requires complete understanding of all the underlying aspects and details of the model, data, and process.

8. **Ability to work in teams**. Modelers are frequently required to work in teams, where a complex modeling task is divided up into subtasks. Ability to work well together with good cooperation, communication, and helping each other is very important.

1.6   The Future of Predictive Analytics

Statistical modeling is a booming field. There is an explosion of data everywhere, being collected more and more around ever-increasing and ubiquitous monitoring of many processes. Data continues to grow and hardware is successfully struggling to keep up, both in processing power and large volume data repositories. New data repository structures have evolved, for example the MapReduce/Hadoop paradigm. Cloud data storage and computing is growing, particularly in problems that can be separable, using distributed processes. Data sizes of terabytes are now the norm. Predictive Analytics is an exciting and growing field!

Data can be broadly categorized as either structured or unstructured. Structured data has well-defined and delimited fields, and this is the usual type of data used in statistical modeling. More often now we have the need to incorporate unstructured data, such as free text, speech, sound, pictures and video. These formats require sophisticated encoding techniques, and many currently exists and more continue to emerge. Generally we reduce these unstructured data sets to structured fields through these specialized data encoding methodologies that are particular to the characteristics of the unstructured data and the particular problem to be modeled. It is likely that we will need to deal more and more with these unstructured data in the future.

Statistical modeling can also be divided into two broad categories: search and prediction. For search problems we try to identify categories of data and then match search requests with the appropriate data records. In prediction problems we try to estimate a functional relationship, so we can provide an output to a set of inputs. These prediction statistical models are in general the types of modeling problems that are considered in this text.

Chapter 2

Properties of Statistical Distributions

This chapter presents common distributions widely used in data analysis and modeling. Fully understanding these distributions is key to understanding the underlying assumptions about the distributions of data. The next chapter will discuss various aspects of matrix theory, which is a convenient vehicle to formulate many of these types of problems.

The basic distributions found in data analysis begin with the simplest, the uniform distribution, then the most common, the normal distribution, then a wide variety of special distributions that are commonly found in many aspects of data analysis from consumer modeling and finance to operations research. Many of these distributions are fundamental to standard statistical tests of data relevance (chi-squared, Student's t...). For example, the non-central chi-squared distribution is found to be important in the solution of interest rate models in finance.

The central limit theorem is used explicitly or implicitly throughout statistical analysis and is core to examining statistical properties of compound phenomenon.

First a word about naming conventions. To make a clear differentiation between density functions, distribution functions, and cumulative density/distribution functions we will use the convention of a probability distribution function (pdf) as the density function, and when we integrate over some domain we have the cumulative distribution function (cdf).

2.1 Fundamental Distributions

2.1.1 Uniform Distribution

The simplest distribution is the uniform distribution over the interval from zero to one, $U(0, 1)$. Its pdf is

$$u(x) = \begin{cases} 1 & \text{if } x \in (0,\, 1) \\ 0 & \text{otherwise.} \end{cases} \tag{2.1}$$

Most modern computer languages provide random number generators for the uniform distribution. It can be used to generate random variables with other distributions and we will discuss this in a later section of this chapter, when we discuss random number generators.

2.1.2　Details of the Normal (Gaussian) Distribution

The most common distribution is the normal distribution, also known as the Gaussian distribution or a bell-shaped curve. Because of its central importance in all statistical modeling we describe here a fairly extensive set of fundamental properties and characteristics. The normal distribution $N[\mu, \sigma^2]$, with mean μ and variance σ^2, is

$$\varphi\left(x, \mu, \sigma^2\right) = \frac{1}{\sqrt{2\pi\sigma^2}} e^{-\frac{(x-\mu)^2}{2\sigma^2}}. \tag{2.2}$$

The standard normal distribution, $N[0, 1]$, has zero mean and unit standard deviation,

$$\varphi(x) = \frac{1}{\sqrt{2\pi}} e^{-x^2/2}. \tag{2.3}$$

Its cumulative distribution function (cdf) is

$$\Phi(x) = \frac{1}{\sqrt{2\pi}} \int_{-\infty}^{x} e^{-t^2/2} dt. \tag{2.4}$$

It can be expressed in terms of the complementary error function

$$\Phi(x) = 1 - \tfrac{1}{2}\mathrm{erfc}\left(x/\sqrt{2}\right), \tag{2.5}$$

or in terms of the error function

$$\Phi(x) = \tfrac{1}{2} + \tfrac{1}{2}\mathrm{erf}\left(x/\sqrt{2}\right), \tag{2.6}$$

where

$$\mathrm{erfc}(x) = \frac{2}{\sqrt{\pi}} \int_{x}^{\infty} e^{-t^2} dt \quad \text{and} \quad \mathrm{erf}(x) = \frac{2}{\sqrt{\pi}} \int_{0}^{x} e^{-t^2} dt \tag{2.7}$$

are the complementary error function and the error function, respectively, and they satisfy $\mathrm{erf}(x) + \mathrm{erfc}(x) = 1$.

Asymptotic Expansion of the Normal Distribution

The asymptotic expansion of $\Phi(x)$ is

$$\Phi(x) \sim -\varphi(x) \left[\frac{1}{x} - \frac{1}{x^3} + \frac{1\cdot3}{x^5} + ... + (-1)^k \frac{(2k-1)!!}{x^{2k+1}} \right] \quad x < 0 \tag{2.8}$$

and

$$1 - \Phi(x) \sim \varphi(x) \left[\frac{1}{x} - \frac{1}{x^3} + \frac{1\cdot3}{x^5} + ... + (-1)^k \frac{(2k-1)!!}{x^{2k+1}} \right] \quad x > 0. \tag{2.9}$$

The right-hand side overestimates if k is even and underestimates if k is odd. The leading order approximation is

$$\begin{aligned}
\Phi(x) &\sim -\tfrac{1}{x}\varphi(x) & x \to -\infty \\
\Phi(x) &\sim 1 - \tfrac{1}{x}\varphi(x) & x \to \infty.
\end{aligned} \tag{2.10}$$

We can directly work on the integration to obtain the asymptotic expansion. For $x < 0$ we have

$$\begin{aligned}
\Phi(x) &= \tfrac{1}{\sqrt{2\pi}}\int_{-\infty}^{x} e^{-t^2/2}dt \\
&= \tfrac{1}{\sqrt{2\pi}}\int_{-\infty}^{0} e^{-(x+t)^2/2}dt \\
&= \tfrac{e^{-x^2/2}}{\sqrt{2\pi}}\int_{-\infty}^{0} e^{-(xt+t^2/2)}dt \\
&= \tfrac{e^{-x^2/2}}{\sqrt{2\pi}}\tfrac{1}{-x}\int_{0}^{\infty} e^{-\left(t+\frac{t^2}{2x^2}\right)}dt \\
&= -\tfrac{1}{x}\varphi(x)\,I(x),
\end{aligned} \tag{2.11}$$

where

$$I(x) = \int_{0}^{\infty} e^{-\left(t+\frac{t^2}{2x^2}\right)}dt. \tag{2.12}$$

Clearly it is easy to see that $I(-\infty) = \int_{0}^{\infty} e^{-t}dt = 1$. The higher-order terms are

$$\begin{aligned}
I(x) &= \sum_{k=0}^{\infty}\int_{0}^{\infty} e^{-t}\tfrac{1}{k!}\left(\tfrac{-t^2}{2x^2}\right)^k dt \\
&= \sum_{k=0}^{\infty}\tfrac{(-1)^k}{k!}\left(\tfrac{1}{2x^2}\right)^k\int_{0}^{\infty} e^{-t}t^{2k}dt \\
&= \sum_{k=0}^{\infty}\tfrac{(-1)^k}{k!}\left(\tfrac{1}{2x^2}\right)^k(2k)! \\
&= \sum_{k=0}^{\infty}(-1)^k\tfrac{(2k-1)!!}{x^{2k}}.
\end{aligned} \tag{2.13}$$

Therefore we have

$$\Phi(x) = -\frac{1}{x}\varphi(x)\sum_{k=0}^{\infty}(-1)^k\frac{(2k-1)!!}{x^{2k}}, \qquad x < 0. \tag{2.14}$$

The Multivariate Normal Distribution

Some integrals related to the Gaussian distribution are useful. The first one is the normalization

$$\int_{-\infty}^{\infty} dx\, e^{-x^2} = \sqrt{\pi}. \tag{2.15}$$

Let a be a positive real number. Through transformation of the x variable we have

$$\int_{-\infty}^{\infty} dx\, e^{-ax^2} = (\pi/a)^{1/2} \tag{2.16}$$

and

$$\int_{-\infty}^{\infty} dx\, e^{-(ax^2+bx)} = (\pi/a)^{1/2}\, e^{b^2/(4a)}. \tag{2.17}$$

Also handy is

$$\int_{-\infty}^{\infty} dx\, x e^{-(ax^2+bx)} = -\frac{b}{2a}\, (\pi/a)^{1/2}\, e^{b^2/(4a)}. \tag{2.18}$$

Another useful related integral that is not easy to find is

$$I_n(a) = \int_0^{\infty} dx\, x^n e^{-ax^2}, \quad a > 0. \tag{2.19}$$

This branches depending on whether or not n is even or odd:

$$I_{2n}(a) = \frac{(2n-1)!\sqrt{\pi}}{2^{2n}(n-1)!}a^{-(n+1/2)} \quad \text{and} \quad I_{2n+1}(a) = \frac{1}{2}n!\,a^{-(n+1)}. \tag{2.20}$$

The generalization to p-dimensional integration is straightforward. If we let A be an $n \times n$ positive definite and symmetric square matrix and B a p-dimensional vector, we have

$$\int_{-\infty}^{\infty} d^P x\, e^{-\frac{1}{2}x^T A x + B^T x} = \left(\frac{(2\pi)^p}{\det A}\right)^{1/2} e^{\frac{1}{2}B^T A^{-1}B} \tag{2.21}$$

and

$$\int_{-\infty}^{\infty} d^P x\, x_i x_j\, e^{-\frac{1}{2}x^T A x} = \left(\frac{(2\pi)^p}{\det A}\right)^{1/2} (A^{-1})_{ij}. \tag{2.22}$$

Distributions can easily be extended into higher dimensions. In a p-dimensional space, the multi-dimensional normal distribution function, $N[\mu, \Sigma]$, is

$$f(x) = \frac{1}{(2\pi)^{p/2}(\det \Sigma)^{1/2}} e^{-\frac{1}{2}(x-\mu)^T \Sigma^{-1}(x-\mu)}, \tag{2.23}$$

where the mean μ now is a vector and the standard deviation now is the covariance matrix Σ. If $x \sim N[\mu, \Sigma]$ (read this as "x is a random variable distributed as $N[\mu, \Sigma]$"), then any linear combinations of x, $Ax+b$, are normally distributed. Note that

$$E[Ax] = A\,E[x] = A\mu \tag{2.24}$$

and

$$\text{var}[Ax] = A\,\text{var}[x]A^T = A\Sigma A^T. \tag{2.25}$$

Here $E[x]$ is the expectation of x and var$[x]$ is the variance of x. We have

$$E[Ax + b] = A\mu + b \tag{2.26}$$

and

$$\text{var}[Ax + b] = A\Sigma A^T. \tag{2.27}$$

We therefore have

$$Ax + b \sim N[A\mu + b, A\Sigma A^T]. \tag{2.28}$$

Here we give a proof that the linear combination of the normally distributed variables is normally distributed. Since the characteristic function (discussed in Section 2.10) uniquely determines a distribution function, we can use it to prove that variables have a normal distribution. Letting $y = Ax + b$, its characteristic function is

$$\begin{aligned}
E\left[e^{ik^T y}\right] &= E\left[e^{ik^T(Ax+b)}\right] = E\left[e^{i(A^T k)^T x + ik^T b}\right] \\
&= e^{i(A^T k)^T \mu - \frac{1}{2}(A^T k)^T \Sigma(A^T k) + ik^T b} \\
&= e^{ik^T(A\mu+b) - \frac{1}{2}k^T(A\Sigma A^T)k}.
\end{aligned} \tag{2.29}$$

Therefore y is normally distributed:

$$y \sim N[A\mu + b, A\Sigma A^T]. \tag{2.30}$$

As a special case, if $x \sim N[0, I]$ and A is a square matrix, and $AA^T = 1$, then $Ax \sim N[0, I]$.

Given a collection of $x_i \sim N[\mu_i, \sigma_i^2]$, $i = 1, 2, ..., n$ and they are independent of each other, then $(x_1, x_2, ..., x_n) \sim N[\mu, \Sigma]$, where $\mu = (\mu_1, \mu_2, ..., \mu_n)^T$ and $\Sigma = \text{diag}(\sigma_1^2, \sigma_2^2, ..., \sigma_n^2)$. Let $y = \sum_{i=1}^{n} x_i$, i.e., $A = (1, 1, ..., 1)$ and $b = 0$, then we have

$$y = \sum_{i=1}^{n} x_i \sim N\left[\sum_{i=1}^{n} \mu_i, \sum_{i=1}^{n} \sigma_i^2\right]. \tag{2.31}$$

If we partition the x-space into separate regions we can identify several properties. Let the partitions of x and the covariance matrix be

$$x - \mu = \begin{bmatrix} x_1 - \mu_1 \\ x_2 - \mu_2 \end{bmatrix} \quad \text{and} \quad \Sigma = \begin{bmatrix} \Sigma_{11} & \Sigma_{12} \\ \Sigma_{21} & \Sigma_{22} \end{bmatrix}, \tag{2.32}$$

with dimensions p_1 for x_1 and p_2 for x_2. By direct integration we can prove that the marginal distribution of a multiple normal distribution is normal, namely,

$$\int d^{p_2} x_2 f(x_1, x_2) = \frac{1}{(2\pi)^{p_1/2}(\det \Sigma_{11})^{1/2}} e^{-\frac{1}{2}(x_1 - \mu_1)^T \Sigma_{11}^{-1}(x_1 - \mu_1)}. \tag{2.33}$$

In general, the pdf $f_p(x)$ can be expressed as the product of $f_{p_1}(x_1)$ and $f_{p_2}(x_2)$. The determinant and inverse of the covariance matrix are

$$\det \Sigma = \det \Sigma_{11} \cdot \det \left(\Sigma_{22} - \Sigma_{21}\Sigma_{11}^{-1}\Sigma_{12} \right), \tag{2.34}$$

$$\begin{bmatrix} \Sigma_{11} & \Sigma_{12} \\ \Sigma_{21} & \Sigma_{22} \end{bmatrix}^{-1} = \begin{bmatrix} \Sigma_{11}^{-1}\left(1 + \Sigma_{12}F_2\Sigma_{21}\Sigma_{11}^{-1}\right) & -\Sigma_{11}^{-1}\Sigma_{12}F_2 \\ -F_2\Sigma_{21}\Sigma_{11}^{-1} & F_2 \end{bmatrix} \tag{2.35}$$

where $F_2 = \left(\Sigma_{22} - \Sigma_{21}\Sigma_{11}^{-1}\Sigma_{12} \right)^{-1}$ (see Sections 3.4 and 3.5). We then have

$$(x - \mu)^T\Sigma^{-1}(x - \mu) = (x_1 - \mu_1)^T\Sigma_{11}^{-1}(x_1 - \mu_1)$$
$$+\left(x_2 - \mu_2 - \Sigma_{21}\Sigma_{11}^{-1}(x_1 - \mu_1)\right)^T\left(\Sigma_{22} - \Sigma_{21}\Sigma_{11}^{-1}\Sigma_{12}\right)^{-1} \tag{2.36}$$
$$\left(x_2 - \mu_2 - \Sigma_{21}\Sigma_{11}^{-1}(x_1 - \mu_1)\right).$$

Therefore we have

$$f_p(x_1, x_2) = f_{p_1}(x_1, \mu_1, \Sigma_{11}) \cdot f_{p_2}(x_2, \mu_2 + \Sigma_{21}\Sigma_{11}^{-1}(x_1 - \mu_1), \Sigma_{22} - \Sigma_{21}\Sigma_{11}^{-1}\Sigma_{12}). \tag{2.37}$$

By symmetry, these results also hold when exchanging indices 1 and 2. From this expression it is very easy to see that the marginal distribution of a normal distribution is a normal distribution.

Note that the conditional distribution is

$$\begin{aligned} f(x_2|x_1) &= f_p(x_1, x_2)/f_{p_1}(x_1, \mu_1, \Sigma_{11}) \\ &= f_{p_2}(x_2, \mu_2 + \Sigma_{21}\Sigma_{11}^{-1}(x_1 - \mu_1), \Sigma_{22} - \Sigma_{21}\Sigma_{11}^{-1}\Sigma_{12}). \end{aligned} \tag{2.38}$$

Therefore the conditional distribution of a normal distribution is still a normal distribution.

What is the relationship between $E[x_1|x_2]$ and $E[x_1]$? Note that

$$E[x_1|x_2] = \int x_1 f(x_1|x_2)dx_1 = \int x_1 f(x_1, x_2)/f(x_2)dx_1. \tag{2.39}$$

In general there is no closed form for this integration, but for the Gaussian distribution we do have an explicit form. Note that the conditional distribution is still a Gaussian distribution

$$f(x_1|x_2) = f\left(x_1, \mu_1 + \rho\sigma_1/\sigma_2(x_2 - \mu_2), \sigma_1^2(1 - \rho^2)\right). \tag{2.40}$$

We have

$$\begin{aligned} E[x_1|x_2] &= \int x_1 f\left(x_1, \mu_1 + \rho\frac{\sigma_1}{\sigma_2}(x_2 - \mu_2), \sigma_1^2(1 - \rho^2)\right) dx_1 \\ &= \mu_1 + \rho\frac{\sigma_1}{\sigma_2}(x_2 - \mu_2). \end{aligned} \tag{2.41}$$

We can rewrite this as

$$E[x_1|x_2] = E[x_1] + \frac{\text{Cov}(x_1, x_2)}{\text{Var}(x_2)}(x_2 - E[x_2]). \tag{2.42}$$

For multi-dimensional distributions, we have

$$f(x_1|x_2) = f\left(x_1, \mu_1 + \Sigma_{12}\Sigma_{22}^{-1}(x_2 - \mu_2), \Sigma_{11} - \Sigma_{12}\Sigma_{22}^{-1}\Sigma_{21}\right). \tag{2.43}$$

Then

$$\begin{aligned}
E[x_1|x_2] &= \int x_1 f\left(x_1, \mu_1 + \Sigma_{12}\Sigma_{22}^{-1}(x_2 - \mu_2), \Sigma_{11} - \Sigma_{12}\Sigma_{22}^{-1}\Sigma_{21}\right) dx_1 \\
&= \mu_1 + \Sigma_{12}\Sigma_{22}^{-1}(x_2 - \mu_2).
\end{aligned} \tag{2.44}$$

We have

$$E[x_1|x_2] = E[x_1] + \Sigma_{12}\Sigma_{22}^{-1}(x_2 - E[x_2]). \tag{2.45}$$

If Σ is a full rank, then the term in the exponential in the multiple normal distribution function can be rewritten as

$$(x - \mu)^T \Sigma^{-1}(x - \mu) = \left[\Sigma^{-1/2}(x - \mu)\right]^T \left[\Sigma^{-1/2}(x - \mu)\right]. \tag{2.46}$$

Here $\Sigma^{-1/2}$ is defined such that $\left(\Sigma^{1/2}\right)\left(\Sigma^{-1/2}\right) = \Sigma^{-1}$. We have $E\left[\Sigma^{-1/2}(x - \mu)\right] = 0$ and

$$\text{var}\left[\Sigma^{-1/2}(x - \mu)\right] = \Sigma^{-1/2} \text{var}\left[x - \mu\right] \Sigma^{-1/2} = \Sigma^{-1/2}\Sigma\Sigma^{-1/2} = I. \tag{2.47}$$

Therefore we have $\Sigma^{-1/2}(x - \mu) \sim N[0, I]$. Since all the components of the vector have a standard normal distribution and are linearly independent, we have

$$(x - \mu)^T \Sigma^{-1}(x - \mu) \sim \chi^2[p], \tag{2.48}$$

where $\chi^2[p]$ is the chi-squared distribution with p degrees of freedom.

Let A be a symmetric idempotent matrix (A is symmetric and $A^2 = A$). Its eigenvalues must be either 1 or 0. If $x \sim N[0, I]$, we have

$$x^T A x = x^T U \Lambda U^T x = \sum_{j=1}^{J} y_j^2, \tag{2.49}$$

where $y = U^T x \sim N[0, I]$, U is some unitary matrix, Λ is a diagonal matrix of eigenvalues, and J is the number of 1s of the eigenvalues of A. Therefore

$$x^T A x \sim \chi^2[\text{Tr}(A)]. \tag{2.50}$$

The Bivariate Normal Distribution

Let's examine the bivariate normal distribution in more detail. With $p = 2$, the covariance matrix is

$$\Sigma = \begin{bmatrix} \sigma_1^2 & \rho\sigma_1\sigma_2 \\ \rho\sigma_1\sigma_2 & \sigma_2^2 \end{bmatrix} \tag{2.51}$$

and its inverse is

$$\Sigma^{-1} = \frac{1}{\sigma_1^2\sigma_2^2(1-\rho^2)}\begin{bmatrix} \sigma_2^2 & -\rho\sigma_1\sigma_2 \\ -\rho\sigma_1\sigma_2 & \sigma_1^2 \end{bmatrix}. \tag{2.52}$$

The explicit form of the pdf is

$$f(x_1, x_2) = \frac{1}{2\pi\sqrt{\sigma_1^2\sigma_2^2(1-\rho^2)}} e^{-\frac{1}{2(1-\rho^2)}\left(\frac{(x_1-\mu_1)^2}{\sigma_1^2}+\frac{(x_2-\mu_2)^2}{\sigma_2^2}-2\rho\frac{(x_1-\mu_1)(x_2-\mu_2)}{\sigma_1\sigma_2}\right)}. \tag{2.53}$$

Note that we can express this pdf as a product of two distribution functions:

$$\begin{aligned} f(x_1, x_2) &= \frac{1}{2\pi\sqrt{\sigma_1^2\sigma_2^2(1-\rho^2)}} e^{-\frac{1}{2(1-\rho^2)}\left(\frac{(x_1-\mu_1)^2}{\sigma_1^2}+\frac{(x_2-\mu_2)^2}{\sigma_2^2}-2\rho\frac{(x_1-\mu_1)(x_2-\mu_2)}{\sigma_1\sigma_2}\right)} \\ &= \frac{1}{\sqrt{2\pi\sigma_1^2}} e^{-\frac{(x_1-\mu_1)^2}{2\sigma_1^2}} \cdot \frac{1}{\sqrt{2\pi\sigma_2^2(1-\rho^2)}} e^{-\frac{1}{2\sigma_2^2(1-\rho^2)}\left(x_2-\mu_2-\rho\frac{\sigma_2}{\sigma_1}(x_1-\mu_1)\right)^2} \\ &= f\left(x_1, \mu_1, \sigma_1^2\right) \cdot f\left(x_2, \mu_2 + \rho\frac{\sigma_2}{\sigma_1}(x_1-\mu_1), \sigma_2^2(1-\rho^2)\right). \end{aligned} \tag{2.54}$$

By symmetry, we also have

$$f(x_1, x_2) = f\left(x_2, \mu_2, \sigma_2^2\right) \cdot f\left(x_1, \mu_1 + \rho\frac{\sigma_1}{\sigma_2}(x_2-\mu_2), \sigma_1^2(1-\rho^2)\right). \tag{2.55}$$

For a general two-dimensional distribution, it can be expressed in terms of a marginal distribution and a conditional distribution:

$$f(x_1, x_2) = f(x_1)f(x_2|x_1) \tag{2.56}$$

and

$$f(x_1, x_2) = f(x_2)f(x_1|x_2). \tag{2.57}$$

When $\mu_1 = \mu_2 = 0$, $\sigma_1 = \sigma_2 = 1$, this becomes

$$f(x_1, x_2) = \frac{1}{2\pi\sqrt{1-\rho^2}} e^{-\frac{1}{2(1-\rho^2)}\left(x_1^2+x_2^2-2\rho\,x_1 x_2\right)}. \tag{2.58}$$

The cdf is

$$\begin{aligned} \Phi[a, b, \rho] &= \int_{-\infty}^{a} dx_1 \int_{-\infty}^{b} dx_2 f(x_1, x_2) \\ &= \frac{\sqrt{1-\rho^2}}{\pi} \int_{-\infty}^{a'} dx_1 \int_{-\infty}^{b'} dx_2\, e^{-(x_1^2+x_2^2-2\rho\,x_1 x_2)}, \end{aligned} \tag{2.59}$$

where

$$a' = \frac{a}{\sqrt{2(1-\rho^2)}}, \qquad b' = \frac{b}{\sqrt{2(1-\rho^2)}}. \tag{2.60}$$

Drezner (1978) provides an approximation for the case of $a \leq 0, b \leq 0, \rho \leq 0$:

$$\Phi[a, b, \rho] \approx \frac{\sqrt{1-\rho^2}}{\pi} \left(\sum_{i,j=1}^{4} A_i A_j f(B_i, B_j) \right), \tag{2.61}$$

where

$$f(x, y) = e^{a'(2x-a')+b'(2y-b')+2\rho(x-a')(y-b')}, \tag{2.62}$$

and

$$A_1 = 0.3253030, \quad A_2 = 0.4211071, \quad A_3 = 0.1334425, \quad A_4 = 0.006374323;$$
$$B_1 = 0.1337764, \quad B_2 = 0.6243247, \quad B_3 = 1.3425378, \quad B_4 = 2.2626645.$$

For any a, b, ρ, we have the following useful equalities:

$$\Phi[a, b, \rho] = \Phi[b, a, \rho],$$
$$\Phi[a, b, \rho] = \Phi[a] - \Phi[a, -b, -\rho],$$
$$\Phi[a, b, \rho] = \Phi[b] - \Phi[-a, b, -\rho], \tag{2.63}$$
$$\Phi[a, b, \rho] = \Phi[a] + \Phi[b] - 1 + \Phi[-a, -b, \rho].$$

The proof of these equalities is straightforward by changing the sign of the variables in the integral. When $a \neq 0, b \neq 0$, we have the equality

$$\Phi[a, b, \rho] = \Phi\left[a, 0, \frac{(a\rho-b)\mathrm{sgn}(a)}{\sqrt{a^2+b^2-\rho ab}}\right] + \Phi\left[b, 0, \frac{(b\rho-a)\mathrm{sgn}(b)}{\sqrt{a^2+b^2-\rho ab}}\right]$$
$$- \frac{1-\mathrm{sgn}(a)\mathrm{sgn}(b)}{4}. \tag{2.64}$$

Using the approximation expression for the case of $a \leq 0, b \leq 0, \rho \leq 0$ shown above, we can use the above equalities to get the cdf for any signs of a, b, ρ. As an example, let's prove the above equality when $a > 0, b > 0$:

$$\Phi[a, b, \rho] = \Phi\left[a, 0, \frac{a\rho-b}{\sqrt{a^2+b^2-\rho ab}}\right] + \Phi\left[b, 0, \frac{b\rho-a}{\sqrt{a^2+b^2-\rho ab}}\right]. \tag{2.65}$$

First cut the integration area into two areas using the line from $(0,0)$ to (a,b). For the bottom area, define two variables as

$$y_1 = x_1, \quad y_2 = \frac{ax_2 - bx_1}{\sqrt{a^2+b^2-\rho ab}}. \tag{2.66}$$

The integration in the bottom area becomes $\Phi[a, 0, \rho_1]$, where

$$\rho_1 = \mathrm{Cov}(y_1, y_2) = \frac{a\rho - b}{\sqrt{a^2+b^2-\rho ab}}. \tag{2.67}$$

For the upper area, define two variables as

$$y_1 = \frac{-ax_2 + bx_1}{\sqrt{a^2 + b^2 - \rho ab}}, \quad y_2 = x_2. \tag{2.68}$$

The integration in the upper area becomes $\Phi[b, 0, \rho_2]$, where

$$\rho_2 = \mathrm{Cov}(y_1, y_2) = \frac{b\rho - a}{\sqrt{a^2 + b^2 - \rho ab}}. \tag{2.69}$$

For the other cases of different signs of a, b, ρ, we can prove the equality using this result of this particular special case and the equalities shown above.

Let's look at the limiting cases of the bivariate cdf of a normal distribution, when $\rho = 1$ and $\rho = -1$. When $\rho = 1$, then $x_1 = x_2$. We have

$$\begin{aligned}
\Phi[a, b, \rho = 1] &= P[x_1 < a, \, x_2 < b] = P[x_1 < a, \, x_1 < b] \\
&= P[x_1 < \min(a, b)] = \Phi[\min(a, b)].
\end{aligned} \tag{2.70}$$

When $\rho = -1$, then $x_1 = -x_2$. We have

$$\begin{aligned}
\Phi[a, b, \rho = -1] &= P[x_1 < a, \, x_2 < b] \\
&= P[x_1 < a, \, -x_1 < b] \\
&= P[x_1 < a, \, x_1 > -b] \\
&= P[-b < x_1 < a] \\
&= \max(0, \, \Phi[a] - \Phi[-b]).
\end{aligned} \tag{2.71}$$

Finally, let's establish a Taylor expansion of the probability density function of the bivariate normal distribution with respect to ρ. The pdf is

$$f(x_1, x_2, \rho) = \frac{1}{2\pi\sqrt{1 - \rho^2}} e^{-\frac{1}{2(1 - \rho^2)}(x_1^2 + x_2^2 - 2\rho x_1 x_2)}. \tag{2.72}$$

Its Taylor expansion with respect to ρ is

$$f(x_1, x_2, \rho) = f(x_1, x_2, 0) \sum_{n=0}^{\infty} \frac{\rho^n}{n!} \mathrm{He}_n(x_1) \mathrm{He}_n(x_2), \tag{2.73}$$

where $\mathrm{He}_n(x)$ is the Chebyshev–Hermite polynomial, a modified version of the Hermite polynomial. Refer to Section 2.10 for details. The first attempt to prove this expansion is by directly expanding in a Taylor series

$$f(x_1, x_2, \rho) = \sum_{n=0}^{\infty} \frac{\rho^n}{n!} \frac{d^n f(x_1, x_2, \rho)}{d\rho^n} \bigg|_{\rho=0}. \tag{2.74}$$

After working out the first and second derivatives you will realize that it is cumbersome to work on the higher-order derivatives with respect to ρ. Alternatively, we can more easily work on its characteristic function. Noting that

$$E\left[e^{ik_1x_1+ik_2x_2}\right] = e^{-\frac{1}{2}\left(k_1^2+k_2^2+2\rho k_1 k_2\right)}, \tag{2.75}$$

we have from the inverse Fourier transform

$$f(x_1,x_2,\rho) = \frac{1}{(2\pi)^2}\int dk_1 dk_2 e^{-\frac{1}{2}\left(k_1^2+k_2^2+2\rho k_1 k_2\right)}e^{-ik_1x_1-ik_2x_2}$$

$$= \sum_{n=0}^{\infty}\frac{\rho^n}{n!}\frac{1}{(2\pi)^2}\int dk_1 dk_2 e^{-\frac{1}{2}\left(k_1^2+k_2^2\right)-ik_1x_1-ik_2x_2}(-k_1k_2)^n$$

$$= \sum_{n=0}^{\infty}\frac{\rho^n}{n!}\left[\frac{1}{2\pi}\int dk_1 e^{-\frac{1}{2}k_1^2-ik_1x_1}(ik_1)^n\right]\cdot\left[\frac{1}{2\pi}\int dk_2 e^{-\frac{1}{2}k_2^2-ik_2x_2}(ik_2)^n\right]. \tag{2.76}$$

From (2.306), we have

$$\frac{1}{2\pi}\int dk\, e^{-\frac{1}{2}k^2-ikx}(ik)^n = \varphi(x)\mathrm{He}_n(x). \tag{2.77}$$

Finally, we have

$$f(x_1,x_2,\rho) = f(x_1,x_2,0)\sum_{n=0}^{\infty}\frac{\rho^n}{n!}\mathrm{He}_n(x_1)\mathrm{He}_n(x_2). \tag{2.78}$$

2.1.3 Lognormal Distribution

Let $\varphi(y)$ be the normal distribution $N[\mu,\sigma^2]$. Let $y = \ln x$ and y satisfies the normal distribution, then x satisfies the lognormal distribution. Note that $\varphi(y)dy = \varphi(\ln x)d(\ln x) = \varphi(\ln x)/x\,dx = f(x)dx$. Therefore the density function of the lognormal distribution, $LN[\mu,\sigma^2]$, is

$$f(x) = \frac{\varphi(\ln x)}{x} = \frac{1}{\sqrt{2\pi\sigma^2}x}e^{-\frac{(\ln x-\mu)^2}{2\sigma^2}}. \tag{2.79}$$

Let's calculate the mean and variance of the lognormal distribution. The first two moments are

$$E[x] = \int_0^\infty f(x)x\,dx = \int_{-\infty}^\infty \varphi(x)e^x dx \tag{2.80}$$

$$E[x^2] = \int_0^\infty f(x)x^2 dx = \int_{-\infty}^\infty \varphi(x)e^{2x}dx. \tag{2.81}$$

Here we used $dx = e^{\ln x}d(\ln x)$. Note that

$$\int_{-\infty}^\infty \varphi(x)e^{\alpha x}dx = \int_{-\infty}^\infty \frac{1}{\sqrt{2\pi\sigma^2}}e^{-\frac{1}{2\sigma^2}\left[(x-\mu-\sigma^2\alpha)^2-2\mu\sigma^2\alpha-\sigma^4\alpha^2\right]}dx$$

$$= e^{\mu\alpha+\sigma^2\alpha^2/2}. \tag{2.82}$$

Therefore the mean and variance of this lognormal distribution are

$$\theta = e^{\mu + \sigma^2/2}, \quad \lambda^2 = e^{2\mu + \sigma^2}(e^{\sigma^2} - 1). \tag{2.83}$$

The reverse relationship between (μ, σ^2) and (θ, λ^2) is

$$\mu = \ln\theta - \tfrac{1}{2}\ln\left(1 + \lambda^2/\theta^2\right), \quad \sigma^2 = \ln\left(1 + \lambda^2/\theta^2\right). \tag{2.84}$$

Note that if $x_i \sim LN[\mu_i, \sigma_i^2]$ then $\ln x_i \sim N[\mu_i, \sigma_i^2]$, and we have

$$\ln x = \ln x_1 + \ln x_2 \sim N[\mu_1 + \mu_2, \sigma_1^2 + \sigma_2^2]. \tag{2.85}$$

Therefore, we have

$$x = x_1 x_2 \sim LN[\mu_1 + \mu_2, \sigma_1^2 + \sigma_2^2]. \tag{2.86}$$

Since if $x \sim LN[\mu, \sigma^2]$ then $r \ln x \sim N[r\mu, r^2\sigma^2]$, and we have $x^r \sim LN[r\mu, r^2\sigma^2]$. Let $x_1 \sim LN[\mu_1, \sigma_1^2]$, $x_2 \sim LN[\mu_2, \sigma_2^2]$ and they are correlated. We can write them as

$$x_1 = e^{\mu_1 + \sigma_1\varepsilon_1}, x_2 = e^{\mu_2 + \sigma_2\varepsilon_2}, E[\varepsilon_1\varepsilon_2] = \rho, \tag{2.87}$$

where each of ε_1 and ε_2 follows a standard normal distribution. Then we have

$$
\begin{aligned}
E[x_1 x_2] &= E\left[e^{\mu_1 + \mu_2 + \sigma_1\varepsilon_1 + \sigma_2\varepsilon_2}\right] \\
&= e^{\mu_1 + \mu_2 + \frac{1}{2}\text{Var}(\sigma_1\varepsilon_1 + \sigma_2\varepsilon_2)} \\
&= e^{\mu_1 + \mu_2 + \frac{1}{2}\sigma_1^2 + \frac{1}{2}\sigma_2^2 + \rho\sigma_1\sigma_2}.
\end{aligned}
\tag{2.88}
$$

This can be rewritten concisely for any two lognormal distributed variables:

$$E[x_1 x_2] = E[x_1]E[x_2]\, e^{\rho\sigma_1\sigma_2}. \tag{2.89}$$

The correlation between x_1 and x_2 is

$$\rho(x_1, x_2) = \frac{\text{Cov}(x_1, x_2)}{\sqrt{\text{Var}(x_1)\,\text{Var}(x_2)}} = \frac{e^{\rho\sigma_1\sigma_2} - 1}{\sqrt{\left(e^{\sigma_1^2} - 1\right)\left(e^{\sigma_2^2} - 1\right)}}. \tag{2.90}$$

2.1.4 Γ Distribution

The probability density function of the $\Gamma(\alpha, \beta)$ ($\alpha > 0$, $\beta > 0$) distribution is defined by

$$f(x) = \frac{\beta^\alpha}{\Gamma(\alpha)} x^{\alpha - 1} e^{-\beta x} \quad x > 0. \tag{2.91}$$

The mean and variance are

$$\mu = E[x] = \alpha/\beta \quad \text{and} \quad \sigma^2 = \text{Var}[x] = \alpha/\beta^2. \tag{2.92}$$

The Γ distribution is additive with respect to α and has the following property: if $x_1 \sim \Gamma(\alpha_1, \beta)$, $x_2 \sim \Gamma(\alpha_2, \beta)$, then $x_1 + x_2 \sim \Gamma(\alpha_1 + \alpha_2, \beta)$. Note that the probability distribution function of $x_1 + x_2$ is

$$g(x) = \int_0^x f(x_1)f(x - x_1)dx_1. \qquad (2.93)$$

By performing the integration directly we can easily prove this property. The n-order moment of the Γ distribution is

$$
\begin{aligned}
E[x^n] &= \int_0^\infty x^n f(x)dx \\
&= \int_0^\infty \frac{\beta^\alpha}{\Gamma(\alpha)} x^{\alpha+n-1} e^{-\beta x} dx \\
&= \frac{1}{\beta^\alpha} \frac{\Gamma(\alpha+n)}{\Gamma(\alpha)} \\
&= \frac{1}{\beta^\alpha} \alpha(\alpha+1)...(\alpha+n-1).
\end{aligned} \qquad (2.94)
$$

Thus the first four moments are

$$
\begin{aligned}
E[x] &= \alpha/\beta, \\
E[x^2] &= \alpha(\alpha+1)/\beta^2, \\
E[x^3] &= \alpha(\alpha+1)(\alpha+2)/\beta^3, \\
E[x^4] &= \alpha(\alpha+1)(\alpha+2)(\alpha+3)/\beta^4.
\end{aligned} \qquad (2.95)
$$

The following integrals are useful:

$$
\begin{aligned}
E[e^{\gamma x}] &= \int_0^\infty \frac{\beta^\alpha}{\Gamma(\alpha)} x^{\alpha-1} e^{-(\beta-\gamma)x} dx \\
&= \frac{\beta^\alpha}{(\beta-\gamma)^\alpha} \\
&= (1 - \gamma/\beta)^{-\alpha},
\end{aligned} \qquad (2.96)
$$

$$
\begin{aligned}
E_{x>\delta}[e^{\gamma x}] &= \int_\delta^\infty \frac{\beta^\alpha}{\Gamma(\alpha)} x^{\alpha-1} e^{-(\beta-\gamma)x} dx \\
&= \frac{\beta^\alpha}{(\beta-\gamma)^\alpha} \int_{(\beta-\delta)\delta}^\infty \frac{1}{\Gamma(\alpha)} t^{\alpha-1} e^{-t} dt \\
&= (1 - \gamma/\beta)^{-\alpha} Q\left(\alpha, (\beta-\gamma)\delta\right),
\end{aligned} \qquad (2.97)
$$

$$E_{x<\delta}[e^{\gamma x}] = (1 - \gamma/\beta)^{-\alpha} P\left(\alpha, (\beta-\gamma)\delta\right), \qquad (2.98)$$

where $P(a, x)$ is the incomplete gamma function and $Q(a, x)$ is the complementary incomplete gamma function. Explicitly, the incomplete gamma function is expressed as

$$P(a, x) = \frac{1}{\Gamma(a)} \int_0^x t^{a-1} e^{-t} dt \qquad (2.99)$$

with $P(a, 0) = 0$ and $P(a, \infty) = 1$. Its complement function is $Q(a, x) = 1 - P(a, x)$.

Let γ be a complex number. We still can evaluate the following expectation

$$
\begin{aligned}
E[e^{\gamma x}] &= \int_0^\infty \frac{\beta^\alpha}{\Gamma(\alpha)} x^{\alpha-1} e^{-(\beta-\gamma)x} dx \\
&= \frac{\beta^\alpha}{(\beta-\gamma)^\alpha} \int_0^{(\beta-\gamma)\infty} \frac{1}{\Gamma(\alpha)} z^{\alpha-1} e^{-z} dz.
\end{aligned}
\tag{2.100}
$$

As long as $(\beta - \gamma)$ is in the first or fourth quadrants in the complex plane, namely $\mathrm{Re}(\beta - \gamma) > 0$, we have

$$
\int_0^{(\beta-\gamma)\infty} z^{\alpha-1} e^{-z} dz = \Gamma(\alpha).
\tag{2.101}
$$

We have

$$
E[e^{\gamma x}] = (1 - \gamma/\beta)^{-\alpha}, \qquad \mathrm{Re}(\beta - \gamma) > 0.
\tag{2.102}
$$

2.1.5   Chi-Squared Distribution

The chi-squared distribution with n degrees of freedom, $\chi^2(n)$, is defined by the sum of the squares of n standard normal distributions,

$$
\chi^2(n) \sim X_1^2 + X_2^2 + \cdots X_n^2,
\tag{2.103}
$$

where each variable X_i $(i = 1, 2, ..., n)$ is independently drawn from a standard normal distribution. When $n = 1$, the distribution of y from a $\chi^2(1)$ distribution has the property $f(y)dy = \varphi(x)dx + \varphi(-x)dx$. This leads to $f(y) = \varphi(\sqrt{y})/\sqrt{y}$. Therefore we have

$$
f(x) = \frac{1}{2^{1/2}\Gamma(1/2)} x^{-1/2} e^{-x/2}.
\tag{2.104}
$$

This is a Γ distribution, and we have $\chi^2(1) \sim \Gamma(1/2, 1/2)$.

From the property of Γ distributions we have $\chi^2(n) \sim \Gamma(n/2, 1/2)$. Therefore the probability density function is

$$
f(x) = \frac{1}{2^{n/2}\Gamma(n/2)} x^{n/2-1} e^{-x/2},
\tag{2.105}
$$

and its cumulative distribution function is

$$
P(\chi^2|n) \equiv \int_0^{x^2} f(x)dx = P(n/2, \chi^2/2),
\tag{2.106}
$$

where $P(a, x)$ is the incomplete gamma function.

The chi-square test is widely used to measure the similarity of two groups of populations as described in the following. Suppose we have two groups of populations, Group 1 and Group 2, and each member of each group falls into one of two possible categories. Let us consider the 2×2 cross-table:

actual	1	2	Total
1	n_{11}	n_{12}	n_{1+}
2	n_{21}	n_{22}	n_{2+}
Total	n_{+1}	n_{+2}	n

expected	1	2	Total
1	m_{11}	m_{12}	n_{1+}
2	m_{21}	m_{22}	n_{2+}
Total	n_{+1}	n_{+2}	n

where each row is one of the two groups and each column is one of the two categories. The Pearson's chi-square measure is defined by

$$\chi_P^2 = \sum_{i=1}^{2} \sum_{j=1}^{2} (n_{ij} - m_{ij})^2 / m_{ij}, \qquad (2.107)$$

where $m_{ij} = n_{i+}n_{+j}/n$. Noting that $(n_{ij} - m_{ij})^2 = (n_{11}n_{22} - n_{12}n_{21})^2/n^2$ and is independent of i and j, and

$$\sum_{i=1}^{2} \sum_{j=1}^{2} \frac{1}{m_{ij}} = \frac{n^3}{n_{1+}n_{2+}n_{+1}n_{+2}}, \qquad (2.108)$$

we have

$$\chi_P^2 = n \cdot \left[\frac{(n_{11}n_{22} - n_{12}n_{21})^2}{n_{1+}n_{2+}n_{+1}n_{+2}} \right]. \qquad (2.109)$$

Let's consider the correlation for two binary variables x and y. There are four possible combinations of (x, y) as shown in the following table:

	$Y:0$	$Y:1$	Total
$X:0$	n_{00}	n_{01}	n_{0+}
$X:1$	n_{10}	n_{11}	n_{1+}
Total	n_{+0}	n_{+1}	n

Then the correlation between x and y is

$$
\begin{aligned}
\rho &= \frac{\mathrm{Cov}(x,y)}{\sqrt{\mathrm{Var}(x)\,\mathrm{Var}(y)}} \\
&= \frac{E[xy] - E[x]E[y]}{\sqrt{\left(E[x^2] - (E[x])^2\right)\left(E[y^2] - (E[y])^2\right)}} \\
&= \frac{\frac{n_{11}}{n} - \frac{n_{1+}}{n} \cdot \frac{n_{+1}}{n}}{\sqrt{\frac{n_{1+}}{n}\left(1 - \frac{n_{1+}}{n}\right)\frac{n_{+1}}{n}\left(1 - \frac{n_{+1}}{n}\right)}} \\
&= \frac{n_{00}n_{11} - n_{10}n_{01}}{\sqrt{n_{0+}n_{1+}n_{+0}n_{+1}}}.
\end{aligned}
\qquad (2.110)
$$

Therefore we have $\chi_P^2 = n \cdot \rho^2$.

Of special interest are two limiting cases. When $n_{00} \to \infty$, we have $\rho = \frac{n_{11}}{\sqrt{n_{1+}n_{+1}}}$. When $n_{00} \to 0$, we have $\rho = -\sqrt{\frac{n_{10}n_{01}}{n_{1+}n_{+1}}}$.

Let's consider two groups of populations with total members C_1 and C_2, where each member is one of two possible types, which we can generically call "good" and "bad." There are data points with goods/bads within each population.

	Good	Bad	Total
Group 1	G_1	B_1	C_1
Group 2	G_2	B_2	C_2
Total	G	B	n

The chi-squared measure may be rewritten as

$$\chi_P^2 = n \cdot \left[\frac{C_1 \cdot C_2}{G \cdot B} \cdot (r_1 - r_2)^2 \right], \qquad (2.111)$$

where r_1 and r_2 are bad rates in each of the groups 1 and 2, respectively: $r_i = B_i/(B_i + G_i), i = 1, 2$. This formula explicitly shows the relationship between the chi-square measure and the difference of bad rates in two populations.

Consider now two groups where each member can be any of K different types. Let us consider the following $2 \times K$ cross-tables:

actual	1	2	...	K	Total
1	n_{11}	n_{12}	...	n_{1K}	n_{1+}
2	n_{21}	n_{22}	...	n_{2K}	n_{2+}
Total	n_{+1}	n_{+2}	...	n_{+K}	n

and

expected	1	2	...	K	Total
1	m_{11}	m_{12}	...	m_{1K}	n_{1+}
2	m_{21}	m_{22}	...	m_{2K}	n_{2+}
Total	n_{+1}	n_{+2}	...	n_{+K}	n

The Pearson's chi-square measure is defined in this case by

$$\chi_P^2 = \sum_{i=1}^{2} \sum_{j=1}^{K} (n_{ij} - m_{ij})^2 / m_{ij}, \qquad (2.112)$$

where $m_{ij} = n_{i+}n_{+j}/n$. Noting that $n_{ij} - m_{ij} = n_{i+}n_{\bar{i}+}/n(p_i(j) - p_{\bar{i}}(j))^2$ and $p_i(j) = n_{ij}/n_{i+}$, we have

$$\chi_P^2 = n_{1+}n_{2+} \sum_{j=1}^{K} [p_1(j) - p_2(j)]^2 / n_{+j}. \qquad (2.113)$$

As a special case, if the population only has two different categories ($K = 2$), we arrive at the same result as obtained above.

Consider the distribution of the following function:

$$y = \frac{1}{\sqrt{x/n}}, \qquad (2.114)$$

where x is from a chi-squared distribution. The distribution function of y is

$$h(y) = f(x)\,|1/y'| = f(x)2n/y^3 = \frac{2\,(n/2)^{n/2}}{\Gamma\,(n/2)}y^{-(n+1)}e^{-n/(2y^2)}. \qquad (2.115)$$

By performing the integration explicitly, we find

$$\int_0^\infty y^2 h(y)\,dy = n/(n-2). \qquad (2.116)$$

2.1.6 Non-Central Chi-Squared Distribution

Let $x_i \sim N[\mu_i, 1]$, $i = 1, 2, ..., n$ be n independent normal distributions. In this case the distributions are not standard normal in that each has its own mean μ_i. Let $W = \sum_{i=1}^n x_i^2$. W is a non-central chi-squared distribution

$$W \sim \chi_n^2(\lambda), \qquad \lambda = \sum_{i=1}^n \mu_i^2. \qquad (2.117)$$

It will be shown below that the distribution depends on λ, not on the individual μ_is. We define a vector $x = [x_1, x_2, ..., x_n]^T$. We have $x \sim N[\mu, I]$, $\mu = [\mu_1, \mu_2, ..., \mu_n]^T$, and $W = x^T x$. It is always possible to find an orthogonal matrix A such that $A\mu = [\sqrt{\lambda}, 0, ..., 0]^T$, where the first component is the only non-zero component. Defining $y = Ax$, we have $y = Ax \sim N[A\mu, AIA^T] = N[A\mu, I]$ and $W = x^T x = y^T y$. Therefore W can be expressed as $W = U + V$, where $U \sim \chi_1^2(\lambda)$, $V \sim \chi_{n-1}^2$. Therefore the non-central chi-squared distribution only depends on λ, not on the individual μ_is.

Noting that the normal distribution $N[\sqrt{\lambda}, 1]$ is $f(x) = e^{-(x-\sqrt{\lambda})^2/2}/\sqrt{2\pi}$, we have the distribution of U

$$
\begin{aligned}
f_U(x) &= \frac{f(\sqrt{x}) + f(-\sqrt{x})}{2\sqrt{x}} \\
&= \frac{1}{2^{1/2}\Gamma(1/2)}x^{-1/2}e^{-x/2}\,e^{-\lambda/2}\cosh(\sqrt{\lambda x}).
\end{aligned} \qquad (2.118)
$$

It is clear that when $\lambda = 0$, $f_U(x)$ leads to $\chi^2(1)$.

Given the distribution of U and V, the distribution of W is the convolution of U and V as

$$
\begin{aligned}
f_W(x) &= \int_0^x f_U(x_1)f_V(x - x_1)dx_1 \\
&= \left(\frac{e^{-x/2}}{2^{n/2}\Gamma(1/2)\Gamma((n-1)/2)}\right)\,e^{-\lambda/2}\int_0^x x_1^{-1/2}(x - x_1)^{(n-1)/2-1}\cosh(\sqrt{\lambda x_1})\,dx_1 \\
&= \left(\frac{x^{(n-2)/2}e^{-x/2}}{2^{n/2}\Gamma(n/2)}\right)\left(e^{-\lambda/2}\sum_{i=0}^\infty \frac{(\lambda x)^i}{(2i)!}\frac{B(i+1/2,(n-1)/2)}{B(1/2,(n-1)/2)}\right) \\
&= \left(\frac{x^{(n-2)/2}e^{-x/2}}{2^{n/2}\Gamma(n/2)}\right)\left(e^{-\lambda/2}\sum_{i=0}^\infty \frac{(\lambda x/2)^i\Gamma(n/2)}{2^i\,i!\,\Gamma(i+n/2)}\right).
\end{aligned}
$$

$$(2.119)$$

Here we have used the equality $\Gamma(i+1/2) = \frac{(2i)!}{4^i\,i!}\Gamma(1/2)$. Note that the first term is the density function of the chi-squared distribution, χ_n^2, and the second term is

$$e^{\frac{\lambda}{2}} \sum_{i=0}^{\infty} \frac{(\lambda x/2)^i \Gamma(\frac{n}{2})}{2^i\, i!\, \Gamma(i+\frac{n}{2})} = e^{-\frac{\lambda}{2}}\left[1 + \frac{1}{n}\left(\frac{\lambda x}{2}\right) + \frac{1}{n(n+2)\,2!}\left(\frac{\lambda x}{2}\right)^2 + \cdots\right].$$

(2.120)

Rearranging the terms, we have

$$f_W(x) = \sum_{i=0}^{\infty} \left(\frac{(\lambda/2)^i}{i!} e^{-\lambda/2}\right)\left(\frac{x^{(n+2i-2)/2} e^{-x/2}}{2^{(n+2i)/2}\Gamma\left((n+2i)/2\right)}\right).$$

(2.121)

The first term is the Poisson distribution $\pi(\lambda/2)$ and the second term is χ_{n+2i}^2. Therefore the non-central chi-squared distribution is a weighted sum of chi-squared distributions. From this form of the non-central chi-squared distribution it can be seen that it is similar to the modified Bessel function of the first kind of order ν:

$$I_\nu(x) = (x/2)^\nu \sum_{k=0}^{\infty} \frac{(x/2)^{2k}}{k!\,\Gamma(\nu+k+1)}.$$

(2.122)

When ν is an integer, $I_\nu(x) = I_{-\nu}(x)$. Actually, the non-central chi-squared distribution can be expressed in terms of Bessel functions as

$$f_{n,\lambda}(x) = \frac{1}{2} e^{-(\lambda+x)/2}\,(x/\lambda)^{\nu/2}\,I_\nu(\sqrt{\lambda x}), \quad \nu = (n-2)/2.$$

(2.123)

From the definition of a non-central chi-squared distribution, n is a positive integer. However, we can use this expression as a definition for any real number n to extend to nonintegral values of n. Noting that the function is close to symmetric by exchanging λ and x, we have

$$\left(\frac{x}{\lambda}\right)^{-\nu}\frac{1}{2} e^{-\frac{1}{2}(\lambda+x)}\left(\frac{x}{\lambda}\right)^{\frac{\nu}{2}} I_\nu(\sqrt{\lambda x}) = \frac{1}{2} e^{-\frac{1}{2}(\lambda+x)}\left(\frac{x}{\lambda}\right)^{-\frac{\nu}{2}} I_{-\nu}(\sqrt{\lambda x}),$$

(2.124)

when ν is an integer. This leads to

$$x^{(2-n)/2} f_{n,\lambda}(x) = \lambda^{(2-n)/2} f_{4-n,\lambda}(x), \quad n \text{ is even.}$$

(2.125)

Let the cumulative distribution function be

$$\chi^2(a,b,c) = \int_0^a f_{b,c}(x)\,dx.$$

(2.126)

Define

$$g(n,x) = \frac{1}{\Gamma(n)} x^{n-1} e^{-x},$$

(2.127)

$$Q(n,x) = \int_x^{\infty} g(n,t)\,dt = \frac{1}{\Gamma(n)} \int_x^{\infty} t^{n-1} e^{-t}\,dt,$$

(2.128)

with the following properties:

$$Q(n, x) = Q(n - 1, x) + g(n, x), \tag{2.129}$$

$$Q(1, x) = g(1, x), \tag{2.130}$$

$$Q(n, x) = \sum_{i=1}^{n} g(i, t), \tag{2.131}$$

$$Q(\infty, x) = 1. \tag{2.132}$$

We then have

$$
\begin{aligned}
1 - \chi^2(a, b, c) &= \int_a^\infty f_{b,c}(x)\, dx \\
&= \sum_{i=1}^{\infty} g\left(i, \tfrac{c}{2}\right) Q\left(\tfrac{b+2(i-1)}{2}, \tfrac{a}{2}\right) \\
&= \sum_{i=1}^{\infty} g\left(i, \tfrac{c}{2}\right) \sum_{j=1}^{(b-2+2i)/2} g\left(j, \tfrac{a}{2}\right) \\
&= \sum_{i=1}^{\infty} \sum_{j=1}^{\infty} g\left(i, \tfrac{c}{2}\right) g\left(j, \tfrac{a}{2}\right) \theta\left(\tfrac{b-2}{2} + i + \tfrac{1}{2} - j\right),
\end{aligned} \tag{2.133}
$$

where $\theta(x)$ is the Heaviside step function whose value is 1 for $x > 0$ and 0 for $x < 0$. By switching the indices i and j, we have

$$
\begin{aligned}
1 - \chi^2(a, b, c) &= \sum_{i=1}^{\infty} \sum_{j=1}^{\infty} g\left(i, \tfrac{a}{2}\right) g\left(j, \tfrac{c}{2}\right) \theta\left(\tfrac{b-2}{2} + j + \tfrac{1}{2} - i\right) \\
&= \sum_{i=1}^{\infty} \sum_{j=1}^{\infty} g\left(i, \tfrac{a}{2}\right) g\left(j, \tfrac{c}{2}\right) \left[1 - \theta\left(-\tfrac{b-2}{2} - j - \tfrac{1}{2} + i\right)\right] \\
&= 1 - \sum_{i=1}^{\infty} \sum_{j=1}^{\infty} g\left(i, \tfrac{a}{2}\right) g\left(j, \tfrac{c}{2}\right) \theta\left(\tfrac{-b+2-2}{2} + i + \tfrac{1}{2} - j\right) \\
&= 1 - \left[1 - \chi^2(c, 2 - b, a)\right].
\end{aligned} \tag{2.134}
$$

Therefore we have

$$\chi^2(a, b, c) + \chi^2(c, 2 - b, a) = 1, \quad b \text{ is an integer.} \tag{2.135}$$

Sankaran (1959) derived an approximation of the non-central chi-squared distribution when n and λ are large. Let $x \sim \chi_n^2(\lambda)$,

$$\left(\frac{x}{n + \lambda}\right)^h \sim N[\mu, \sigma^2] \tag{2.136}$$

where

$$\mu = 1 - hp\left[1 - h + \frac{1}{2}(2 - h)mp\right], \quad \sigma^2 = h^2 2p(1 + mp), \tag{2.137}$$

and

$$h = 1 - \frac{2}{3}\frac{(n+\lambda)(n+3\lambda)}{(n+2\lambda)^2},$$

$$m = (h-1)(1-3h), \tag{2.138}$$

$$p = \frac{n+2\lambda}{(n+\lambda)^2}.$$

Therefore

$$
\begin{aligned}
\chi^2(z, n, \lambda) &= \Pr[x < z] = \Pr\left[\left(\frac{x}{n+\lambda}\right)^h < \left(\frac{z}{n+\lambda}\right)^h\right] \\
&= \Phi\left[\frac{\left(\frac{z}{n+\lambda}\right)^h - \mu}{\sigma}\right] \\
&= \Phi\left[\frac{\left(\frac{z}{n+\lambda}\right)^h - 1 + hp\left[1 - h + \frac{1}{2}h(2-h)mp\right]}{h\sqrt{2p(1+mp)}}\right].
\end{aligned}
\tag{2.139}
$$

2.1.7 Student's t-Distribution

If $z \sim N[0, 1]$, $x \sim \chi^2[n]$, and z is independent of x, then the ratio

$$t[n] = \frac{z}{\sqrt{x/n}} \tag{2.140}$$

has a t-distribution with n degrees of freedom. The explicit expression of the t-distribution function is

$$f(t, n) = \frac{1}{\sqrt{n}B(n/2, 1/2)}\left(1 + t^2/n\right)^{-(n+1)/2}. \tag{2.141}$$

Here $B(a, b)$ is the beta function

$$B(a, b) \equiv \int_0^1 t^{a-1}(1-t)^{b-1}dt, \tag{2.142}$$

which is related to the gamma function by

$$B(a, b) = \frac{\Gamma(a) \cdot \Gamma(b)}{\Gamma(a+b)}. \tag{2.143}$$

When n goes to infinity, $f(t, n)$ goes to standard normal distribution. This can be readily verified using Stirling's formula (see Appendix A.4). Alternatively, considering (2.233) from Section 2.2, we can be convinced that the t-distribution indeed goes to standard normal distribution when n approaches to infinite.

The cumulative distribution function of the t-distribution is:

$$\text{prob\_t}(x, n) \equiv \int_{-\infty}^{x} f(t, n)dt = \begin{cases} 1 - \frac{1}{2}I_{\left(\frac{n}{n+x^2}\right)}\left(\frac{n}{2}, \frac{1}{2}\right) & x \geq 0, \\ \frac{1}{2}I_{\left(\frac{n}{n+x^2}\right)}\left(\frac{n}{2}, \frac{1}{2}\right) & x < 0, \end{cases} \tag{2.144}$$

where I is the incomplete beta function defined by

$$I_x(a,b) \equiv \frac{1}{B(a,b)} \int_0^x t^{a-1}(1-t)^{b-1} dt,$$ (2.145)

with the symmetric property $I_x(a,b) = 1 - I_{1-x}(b,a)$.

The t-distribution is used to test the difference of means between two populations. If the variances s^2 are the same, the t-test is

$$t = \frac{\bar{x}_1 - \bar{x}_2}{s\sqrt{1/n_1 + 1/n_2}}.$$ (2.146)

If the variances are not the same, the Smith-Satterthwaite (Welch-Satterthwaite) t-test is commonly used:

$$t = \frac{\bar{x}_1 - \bar{x}_2 - \Delta_0}{\sqrt{s_1^2/n_1 + s_2^2/n_2}}.$$ (2.147)

Here Δ_0 is a user-selected tolerance amount for the comparison of the two means. The degree of freedom, df, is estimated by

$$df = \frac{\left(s_1^2/n_1 + s_2^2/n_2\right)^2}{\left(s_1^2/n_1\right)^2 / (n_1 - 1) + \left(s_2^2/n_2\right)^2 / (n_2 - 1)}.$$ (2.148)

2.1.8 Multivariate t-Distribution

Let $z \sim N[0, \Sigma]$, $\Sigma = [n \times n]$ be a covariance matrix, $x \sim \chi^2[k]$, and z and x are independent. The multivariate t-distribution is defined as

$$t = \frac{z}{\sqrt{x/k}}.$$ (2.149)

Each component of t is a t-distribution if each component of z is a standard normal distribution:

$$t_i = \frac{z_i}{\sqrt{x/k}}, \quad i = 1, 2, ..., n.$$ (2.150)

Let $h(y)$ be the distribution of $y = \frac{1}{\sqrt{x/k}}$. We have

$$f(t) = \int_{-\infty}^{\infty} \frac{1}{y^n} f_Z(t/y) \, h(y) \, dy.$$ (2.151)

Note that

$$\begin{aligned}\frac{1}{y^n} f_Z(t/y) &= \frac{1}{y^n} \frac{1}{(2\pi)^{n/2}(\det\Sigma)^{1/2}} e^{-\frac{1}{2}(t/y)^T \Sigma^{-1}(t/y)} \\ &= \frac{1}{(2\pi)^{n/2}(\det(y^2\Sigma))^{1/2}} e^{-\frac{1}{2}t^T(y^2\Sigma)^{-1}t} \\ &= f(t, 0, y^2\Sigma).\end{aligned}$$ (2.152)

We have

$$f(t) = \int_{-\infty}^{\infty} f(t, 0, y^2 \Sigma) \, h(y) \, dy. \tag{2.153}$$

Therefore we have $E[t] = 0$, and

$$
\begin{aligned}
(\mathrm{Var}[t])_{ij} &= E[t_i t_j] \\
&= \int_{-\infty}^{\infty} t_i t_j \, f(t, 0, y^2 \Sigma) \, h(y) \, dy \, dt \\
&= \int_{-\infty}^{\infty} y^2 \Sigma_{ij} \, h(y) \, dy \\
&= \frac{k}{k-2} \Sigma_{ij}.
\end{aligned}
\tag{2.154}
$$

Here we have used a property of the distribution of $h(y)$ shown in (2.116) in the section on the chi-squared distribution.

By performing the transformation $(z_1, \, ..., \, z_n, x) \to (t_1, \, ..., \, t_n, x)$, the Jacobian determinant is $|\partial(t_1, \, ..., \, t_n, x) / \partial(z_1, \, ..., \, z_n, x)| = (k/x)^{n/2}$. We have

$$f_{T_1, \, ..., \, T_n, X}(t_1, \, ..., \, t_n, x) = f_{Z_1, \, ..., \, Z_n, X}(z_1, \, ..., \, z_n, x) \, (x/k)^{n/2}. \tag{2.155}$$

By performing the integration over x using the explicit expressions of the normal and chi-squared distributions, and using the equality

$$\int_0^\infty x^{\alpha-1} e^{-\beta x} \, dx = \Gamma(\alpha)/\beta^\alpha, \tag{2.156}$$

we can reach the following probability density function of $t = (t_1, \, ..., \, t_n)^T$:

$$f(t) = \frac{\Gamma\left((n+k)/2\right)}{\Gamma\left(k/2\right)} \cdot \frac{1}{(\pi k)^{n/2} \, (\det \Sigma)^{1/2}} \left[\frac{t^T \Sigma^{-1} t}{k} + 1 \right]^{-(n+k)/2}. \tag{2.157}$$

Let's consider the bivariate t-distribution ($n = 2$), when the covariance matrix is

$$\Sigma = \begin{bmatrix} 1 & \rho \\ \rho & 1 \end{bmatrix}. \tag{2.158}$$

We have

$$f(t_1, t_2) = \frac{1}{2\pi \sqrt{1-\rho^2}} \left[\frac{t_1^2 + t_2^2 - 2\rho t_1 t_2}{k(1-\rho^2)} + 1 \right]^{-(k+2)/2}. \tag{2.159}$$

It can be seen from the definition or can be verified from direct integration that the marginal distributions for the bivariate t-distribution are t-distributions. The following integration is useful for performing the integration over t_1 or t_2:

$$\int_{-\infty}^{\infty} \frac{1}{(x^2 + a^2)^\alpha} \, dx = a^{-2\alpha+1} \, B\left(\alpha - 1/2, 1/2\right), \tag{2.160}$$

with B the beta function.

2.1.9   F-Distribution

If $x_1 \sim \chi^2[n_1]$ and $x_2 \sim \chi^2[n_2]$, and x_1 and x_2 are independent, then the ratio

$$F[n_1, n_2] = \frac{x_1/n_1}{x_2/n_2} \qquad (2.161)$$

has the F-distribution with n_1 and n_2 degrees of freedom. The explicit expression of the F-distribution is:

$$f(x, n_1, n_2) = \frac{(n_1/n_2)^{n_1/2}}{B(n_1/2, n_2/2)} x^{(n_1-2)/2}(1 + n_1 x/n_2)^{-(n_1+n_2)/2}, \qquad (2.162)$$

for $x \geq 0$. The cumulative distribution function of the F-distribution is

$$\text{prob\_f}(x, n_1, n_2) \equiv \int_0^x f(t, n_1, n_2) dt = \begin{cases} I\left(\frac{n_1 x}{n_2 + n_1 x}\right)\left(\frac{n_1}{2}, \frac{n_2}{2}\right) & x \geq 0 \\ 0 & x < 0 \end{cases}$$
$$(2.163)$$

where I is the incomplete beta function. It is clear to see that if $x \sim t[n]$, then $x^2 \sim F[1, n]$ and vice versa. Therefore the F-distribution is related to the t-distribution through

$$1 - \text{prob\_f}(x^2, 1, n) = 2\left[1 - \text{prob\_t}(|x|, n)\right]. \qquad (2.164)$$

2.1.10   Binomial Distribution

The probability distribution function of the binomial distribution, $b(n, p)$, is

$$f(x) = C_n^x p^x (1 - p)^{n-x}, \qquad x = 0, 1, ..., n. \qquad (2.165)$$

By direct but lengthy calculation, the mean and variance are

$$\mu = np \quad \text{and} \quad \sigma^2 = np(1 - p). \qquad (2.166)$$

When n is large and k is small, the binomial distribution tends to the Poisson distribution

$$\lim_{n \to \infty} C_n^k p^k (1 - p)^{n-k} = \frac{\lambda^k e^{-\lambda}}{k!}, \qquad \lambda = np. \qquad (2.167)$$

Using Stirling's formula

$$\lim_{n \to \infty} \frac{n!}{\sqrt{2n\pi}(n/e)^n} = 1, \qquad (2.168)$$

we have

$$C_n^k = \frac{n!}{k!(n-k)!} \approx \frac{n^k}{k!} \qquad (2.169)$$

when n is large and k is small. Therefore

$$\lim_{n \to \infty} C_n^k p^k (1 - p)^{n-k} = \lim_{n \to \infty} \frac{n^k}{k!} p^k (1 - p)^{n-k} = \frac{\lambda^k e^{-\lambda}}{k!}. \qquad (2.170)$$

Consider a random variable x with distribution

$$x = \begin{cases} 1 & \text{with probability } p \\ 0 & \text{with probability } 1-p \end{cases} \tag{2.171}$$

Its mean and variance are $\mu = p$, $\sigma^2 = p(1-p)$. According to the central limit theorem, we have

$$\frac{x_1 + x_2 + ... + x_n - np}{\sqrt{np(1-p)}} \sim N[0,1], \tag{2.172}$$

or

$$\frac{j - np}{\sqrt{np(1-p)}} \sim N[0,1]. \tag{2.173}$$

Here j is the number of 1s from x_1 to x_n. Note that $\sum_{j=a}^{n} C_n^j p^j q^{n-j}$ is the probability of $j \geq a$, and we have

$$\sum_{j=a}^{n} C_n^j p^j q^{n-j} \approx \Phi\left(\frac{np - a + 1}{\sqrt{np(1-p)}}\right). \tag{2.174}$$

This approximation can be used in proving that the option formula in the binomial tree approaches the Black–Scholes formula when the number of time steps goes to infinity.

2.1.11 Poisson Distribution

The probability density function of the Poisson distribution is

$$p(k; \lambda) = \frac{\lambda^k e^{-\lambda}}{k!}, \quad k = 0, 1, 2, ... \tag{2.175}$$

The mean and variance are

$$\mu = E[k] = \lambda \quad \text{and} \quad \sigma^2 = \text{Var}[k] = \lambda. \tag{2.176}$$

2.1.12 Exponential Distribution

The probability density function of the exponential distribution with a parameter λ is

$$f(x) = \frac{1}{\lambda} e^{-x/\lambda}, \quad x \geq 0. \tag{2.177}$$

Its mean and variance are

$$\mu = E[x] = \lambda \quad \text{and} \quad \sigma^2 = \text{Var}[x] = \lambda^2. \tag{2.178}$$

2.1.13 Geometric Distribution

Let's assume that there are two outcomes (A or B) for each trial with the probability of A being p. What is the distribution of the number of trials to get the first A? It is clear that

$$P(k) = p(1-p)^{k-1}, \quad k = 1, 2, ... \qquad (2.179)$$

We have $\sum_{k=1}^{\infty} P(k) = 1$. Let $q = 1 - p$. Note that

$$\sum_{k=1}^{\infty} k\, q^{k-1} = \frac{d}{dq} \sum_{k=1}^{\infty} q^k = \frac{d}{dq}\left(\frac{q}{1-q}\right) = \frac{1}{(1-q)^2}, \qquad (2.180)$$

$$\sum_{k=1}^{\infty} k^2 q^{k-1} = \frac{d}{dq} \sum_{k=1}^{\infty} k q^k = \frac{d}{dq}\left(\frac{q}{(1-q)^2}\right) = \frac{1+q}{(1-q)^3}. \qquad (2.181)$$

We have

$$\mu = \sum_{k=1}^{\infty} P(k)k = 1/p \qquad (2.182)$$

and

$$\sigma^2 = \sum_{k=1}^{\infty} P(k)k^2 - \left(\sum_{k=1}^{\infty} P(k)k\right)^2 = (1-p)/p^2 \qquad (2.183)$$

as the mean and variance.

2.1.14 Hypergeometric Distribution

There are N balls in a box, of which M balls are red. Now we pick n ($n \le M$) balls without replacement. What is the distribution of the number of red balls we get? It is clear that

$$P(k) = \frac{C_M^k C_{N-M}^{n-k}}{C_N^n}, \quad k = 0, 1, ..., n. \qquad (2.184)$$

Expanding both sides of the following equality, respectively,

$$(x+1)^{n_1}(x+1)^{n_2} = (x+1)^{n_1+n_2} \qquad (2.185)$$

leads to

$$\sum_{k_1=0}^{k} C_{n_1}^{k_1} C_{n_2}^{k-k_1} = C_{n_1+n_2}^{k}. \qquad (2.186)$$

Therefore we have $\sum_{k=0}^{n} P(k) = 1$. Noting that

$$k C_M^k = M C_{M-1}^{k-1},$$
$$k^2 C_M^k = M(M-1)C_{M-2}^{k-2} + M C_{M-1}^{k-1}, \qquad (2.187)$$

we have

$$\mu = \frac{nM}{N} \quad \text{and} \quad \sigma^2 = \frac{nM}{N}\frac{(N-M)(N-n)}{N(N-1)}. \qquad (2.188)$$

2.1.15 Negative Binomial Distribution

The negative binomial distribution is also called the Pascal distribution. It is a generalization of the geometric distribution. Let's assume that there are two outcomes (A or B) for each trial with the probability of A being p. What is the distribution of the number of trials to get the first r A's? It is clear that

$$P_r(k) = C_{k-1}^{r-1} p^r (1-p)^{k-r}, \quad k = r, r+1, ... \tag{2.189}$$

Note that

$$
\begin{aligned}
\sum_{k=r}^{\infty} C_{k-1}^{r-1} q^{k-r} &= \sum_{k=r}^{\infty} \frac{1}{(r-1)!} \frac{d^{r-1}}{dq^{r-1}} \left(q^{k-1} \right) \\
&= \frac{1}{(r-1)!} \frac{d^{r-1}}{dq^{r-1}} \left(\frac{q^{r-1}}{1-q} \right) \\
&= \frac{1}{(r-1)!} \frac{d^{r-1}}{dq^{r-1}} \left(\frac{(q-1+1)^{r-1}}{1-q} \right) \\
&= \frac{1}{(r-1)!} \frac{d^{r-1}}{dq^{r-1}} \left(\frac{1}{1-q} + \text{a polynomial of } (q-1) \text{ of order } (r-2) \right) \\
&= \frac{1}{(r-1)!} \frac{d^{r-1}}{dq^{r-1}} \left(\frac{1}{1-q} \right) \\
&= \frac{1}{(1-q)^r} .
\end{aligned}
\tag{2.190}
$$

Therefore we have $\sum_{k=1}^{\infty} P_k(k) = 1$. Note that

$$P_r(k)k = \frac{r}{p} P_{r+1}(k+1), \tag{2.191}$$

$$P_r(k)k^2 = \frac{r}{p} P_{r+1}(k+1)(k+1-1) = \frac{r(r+1)}{p^2} P_{r+2}(k+2) - \frac{r}{p} P_{r+1}(k+1). \tag{2.192}$$

We have

$$\sum_{k=r}^{\infty} P_r(k)k = r/p, \tag{2.193}$$

$$\sum_{k=r}^{\infty} P_r(k)k^2 = r(r+1)/p^2 - r/p. \tag{2.194}$$

Therefore

$$\mu = \sum_{k=r}^{\infty} P_r(k)k = r/p, \tag{2.195}$$

$$\sigma^2 = \sum_{k=r}^{\infty} P_r(k)k^2 - \left(\sum_{k=r}^{\infty} P_r(k)k \right)^2 = r(1-p)/p^2. \tag{2.196}$$

2.1.16 Inverse Gaussian (IG) Distribution

Consider a Brownian motion with a drift

$$x_t = \theta t + \sigma z_t, \quad z_t = \sqrt{t}\,\varepsilon. \tag{2.197}$$

Define t_α to be the first passage time for a fixed level $\alpha > 0$, namely $t_\alpha = \min\{0 < t < \infty \,|\, x_t = \alpha\}$. Therefore the distribution function is

$$
\begin{aligned}
P(t_\alpha < t) &= P(M_t > \alpha) \\
&= 1 - P(M_t < \alpha) \\
&= 1 - N\left(\frac{\alpha - \theta t}{\sigma\sqrt{t}}\right) + e^{\frac{2\theta\alpha}{\sigma^2}} N\left(\frac{-\alpha - \theta t}{\sigma\sqrt{t}}\right) \\
&= N\left(\sqrt{\lambda/t}\,(t/\mu - 1)\right) + e^{2\lambda/\mu} N\left(-\sqrt{\lambda/t}\,(t/\mu + 1)\right) \\
&\sim IG(\mu, \lambda),
\end{aligned}
\tag{2.198}
$$

where $\lambda > 0, \mu > 0, t > 0$ and $\lambda = \alpha^2/\sigma^2$, $\mu = \alpha/\theta$. The probability density function is

$$
\begin{aligned}
f(t) &= \frac{dP(t_\alpha < t)}{dt} \\
&= \varphi\left(\sqrt{\lambda/t}\,(t/\mu - 1)\right)\left(\sqrt{\lambda}\,t^{-3/2}\right) \\
&= \sqrt{\frac{\lambda}{2\pi t^3}}\,e^{-\frac{\lambda(t-\mu)^2}{2\mu^2 t}} \\
&\sim IG(\mu, \lambda).
\end{aligned}
\tag{2.199}
$$

By using the following integration[1]

$$\int_0^\infty e^{-at^2 - b/t^2}\,dt = \frac{1}{2}\sqrt{\pi/a}\,e^{-2\sqrt{ab}}, \tag{2.200}$$

the characteristic function is

$$E\left[e^{iux}\right] = e^{\lambda/\mu\left(1 - \sqrt{1 - iu2\mu^2/\lambda}\right)}. \tag{2.201}$$

If $x \sim IG(\mu, \lambda)$, we have

$$E\left[e^{iucx}\right] = e^{\lambda/\mu\left(1 - \sqrt{1 - iuc2\mu^2/\lambda}\right)} = e^{c\lambda/(c\mu)\left(1 - \sqrt{1 - iu2(c\mu)^2/(c\lambda)}\right)}. \tag{2.202}$$

Thus $cx \sim IG(c\mu, c\lambda)$. By direct integration we can verify that

$$\int_0^\infty f(x)dx = \sqrt{\frac{\lambda}{2\pi}}\,2e^{\frac{\lambda}{\mu}}\int_0^\infty e^{-\frac{\lambda}{2}t^2 - \frac{\lambda}{2\mu^2}\frac{1}{t^2}}\,dt. \tag{2.203}$$

By using the integration shown above, we have $\int_0^\infty f(x)dx = 1$.

---

[1]By changing variable $y = \sqrt{a}\,x - \sqrt{b}/x$, we can easily carry out this integration.

The first moment is

$$\int_0^\infty x f(x) dx = \sqrt{\frac{\lambda}{2\pi}} 2 e^{\frac{\lambda}{\mu}} \int_0^\infty e^{-\frac{\lambda}{2\mu^2}t^2 - \frac{\lambda}{2}\frac{1}{t^2}} dt = \mu. \tag{2.204}$$

Here we have used the same integration shown above. Noting that

$$\int_0^\infty t^2 e^{-at^2 - b/t^2} dt = \frac{1}{4}\sqrt{\pi/a^3}\left(1 + 2\sqrt{ab}\right)e^{-2\sqrt{ab}}, \tag{2.205}$$

we have

$$\int_0^\infty x^2 f(x) dx = \sqrt{\frac{\lambda}{2\pi}} 2 e^{\frac{\lambda}{\mu}} \int_0^\infty t^2 e^{-\frac{\lambda}{2\mu^2}t^2 - \frac{\lambda}{2}\frac{1}{t^2}} dt = \mu^2 + \mu^3/\lambda. \tag{2.206}$$

Therefore we have

$$E[x] = \mu \quad \text{and} \quad \text{Var}[x] = \mu^3/\lambda. \tag{2.207}$$

2.1.17 Normal Inverse Gaussian (NIG) Distribution

If a random variable conditional to another random variable with an inverse Gaussian distribution is a normal distribution, then it is distributed as a normal inverse Gaussian distribution. Explicitly, if x is a normal inverse Gaussian distribution the following conditions hold:

$$\begin{aligned} x|y &\sim N[\mu + \beta y, y], \\ y &\sim IG(a, b). \end{aligned} \tag{2.208}$$

We will choose a and b such that the distribution function of x has a simple form. The distribution function of x is

$$\begin{aligned} f_X(x) &= \int_0^\infty dy\, f_N(x, \mu + \beta y, y) f_{IG}(y, a, b) \\ &= \int_0^\infty dy\, \frac{1}{\sqrt{2\pi y}} e^{-\frac{(x-\mu-\beta y)^2}{2y}} \sqrt{\frac{b}{2\pi y^3}} e^{-\frac{b(y-a)^2}{2a^2 y}} \\ &= \frac{\sqrt{b}}{\pi} e^{\beta(x-\mu)+b/a} \frac{\sqrt{\beta^2 + b/a^2}}{\sqrt{(x-\mu)^2 + b}} K_1\left(\sqrt{(x-\mu)^2 + b} \cdot \sqrt{\beta^2 + b/a^2}\right). \end{aligned} \tag{2.209}$$

Here we used

$$\int_0^\infty dx\, e^{-\alpha x - \beta/x} = \sqrt{4\beta/\alpha}\, K_1(2\sqrt{\alpha\beta}), \tag{2.210}$$

where K_1 denotes a modified Bessel function of the second order. By choosing a and b as $a = \delta/\gamma$, $b = \delta^2$, we have

$$f_X(x) = \frac{\alpha\delta}{\pi} e^{\beta(x-\mu)+\delta\gamma} \frac{K_1\left(\alpha\sqrt{(x-\mu)^2 + \delta^2}\right)}{\sqrt{(x-\mu)^2 + \delta^2}}. \tag{2.211}$$

We denote the NIG distribution as $x \sim NIG(\alpha, \beta, \mu, \delta)$ with four parameters and its density function is a convolution from a normal distribution and an IG distribution:

$$x|y \sim N[\mu + \beta y, y],$$
$$y \sim IG\left(\delta/\gamma, \delta^2\right), \quad \gamma = \sqrt{\alpha^2 - \beta^2}, \tag{2.212}$$

$$f_X(x) = \int_0^\infty dy \, f_N(x, \mu + \beta y, y) f_{IG}(y, \delta/\gamma, \delta^2). \tag{2.213}$$

Since $f_X(x)$ is a convolution of a normal distribution and an IG distribution, it is easy to see $\int_{-\infty}^\infty f(x)dx = 1$. Noting that

$$
\begin{aligned}
\int_{-\infty}^\infty x f(x)dx &= \int_{-\infty}^\infty dx \int_0^\infty dy \, x \, f_N(x, \mu + \beta y, y) f_{IG}(y, \delta/\gamma, \delta^2) \\
&= \int_0^\infty dy \, (\mu + \beta y) f_{IG}(y, \delta/\gamma, \delta^2) \\
&= \mu + \beta \delta/\gamma,
\end{aligned}
\tag{2.214}
$$

and

$$
\begin{aligned}
\int_{-\infty}^\infty x^2 f(x)dx &= \int_{-\infty}^\infty dx \int_0^\infty dy \, x^2 f_N(x, \mu + \beta y, y) f_{IG}(y, \delta/\gamma, \delta^2) \\
&= \int_0^\infty dy \left((\mu + \beta y)^2 + y \right) f_{IG}(y, \delta/\gamma, \delta^2) \\
&= \mu^2 + 2\mu\beta\delta/\gamma + \delta/\gamma + \beta^2\delta^2/\gamma^2 + \beta^2\delta/\gamma^3,
\end{aligned}
\tag{2.215}
$$

we have

$$E[x] = \mu + \beta\delta/\gamma \quad \text{and} \quad \text{Var}[x] = \delta\alpha^2/\gamma^3. \tag{2.216}$$

From the characteristic function of the IG, the characteristic function of the NIG is

$$
\begin{aligned}
E\left[e^{iux}\right] &= \int_{-\infty}^\infty dx \, e^{iux} \int_0^\infty dy \, f_N(x, \mu + \beta y, y) f_{IG}(y, \delta/\gamma, \delta^2) \\
&= \int_0^\infty e^{iu(\mu + \beta y) - \frac{1}{2}u^2 y} f_{IG}(y, \delta/\gamma, \delta^2) \, dy \\
&= e^{i\mu u + \delta\gamma - \delta\sqrt{\alpha^2 - (\beta + iu)^2}}.
\end{aligned}
\tag{2.217}
$$

Since the exponential part of the characteristic function is a linear function of μ, δ, the NIG distribution is additive with respect to μ, δ. Namely, If $x_1 \sim NIG(\alpha, \beta, \mu_1, \delta_1)$ and $x_2 \sim NIG(\alpha, \beta, \mu_2, \delta_2)$, then

$$x_1 + x_2 \sim NIG(\alpha, \beta, \mu_1 + \mu_2, \delta_1 + \delta_2). \tag{2.218}$$

Note that, if $x \sim NIG(\alpha, \beta, \mu, \delta)$,

$$
\begin{aligned}
E\left[e^{iucx}\right] &= e^{ic\mu u + \delta\gamma - \delta\sqrt{\alpha^2 - (\beta + icu)^2}} \\
&= e^{i(c\mu)u + (c\delta)(\gamma/c) - (c\delta)\sqrt{(\alpha/c)^2 - (\beta/c + iu)^2}}.
\end{aligned}
\tag{2.219}
$$

Therefore we have

$$cx \sim NIG\left(\alpha/c, \beta/c, c\mu, c\delta\right). \tag{2.220}$$

2.2 Central Limit Theorem

Let $x_1, x_2, ..., x_n$ be a random sample from a distribution with mean μ and variance σ^2 and that they are independent of each other. Then we have

$$\mu_x = E[x_1 + x_2 + ... + x_n] = n\,\mu,$$

$$\sigma_x^2 = E[(x_1 + x_2 + ... + x_n - n\,\mu)^2] = n\,\sigma^2. \tag{2.221}$$

Therefore the following random variable has mean 0 and standard deviation 1:

$$x = \frac{x_1 + x_2 + ... + x_n - n\,\mu}{\sqrt{n}\,\sigma}. \tag{2.222}$$

In general, it does not satisfy the normal distribution. However, when n is big, it approaches a standard normal distribution

$$x = \frac{x_1 + x_2 + ... + x_n - n\,\mu}{\sqrt{n}\,\sigma} \sim N[0, 1]. \tag{2.223}$$

This is the central limit theorem. This result is very general and (remarkably) does not depend on the underlying distribution of x_i.

Here we give a simple proof by using the characteristic function. The characteristic function of x is

$$E\left[e^{itx}\right] = E\left[e^{it\,\frac{x_1 + x_2 + ... + x_n - n\,\mu}{\sqrt{n}\,\sigma}}\right] = \left(E\left[e^{it\,\frac{x_1 - \mu}{\sqrt{n}\,\sigma}}\right]\right)^n. \tag{2.224}$$

Noting that

$$\begin{aligned}
E\left[e^{it\,\frac{x_1-\mu}{\sqrt{n}\,\sigma}}\right] &= E\left[1 + it\,\frac{x_1-\mu}{\sqrt{n}\,\sigma} + \frac{1}{2}\left(it\,\frac{x_1-\mu}{\sqrt{n}\,\sigma}\right)^2 + o\left(\frac{1}{n}\right)\right] \\
&= 1 - t^2/(2n) + o\,(1/n),
\end{aligned} \tag{2.225}$$

and

$$\lim_{n\to\infty}\,(1 + a(n)/n)^n = e^{\lim_{n\to\infty} a(n)}, \tag{2.226}$$

we have

$$E\left[e^{itx}\right] = \lim_{n\to\infty}\,\left(1 - t^2/(2n) + o\,(1/n)\right)^n = e^{-t^2/2}. \tag{2.227}$$

This is the same characteristic function of the standard normal distribution. Therefore

$$x = \frac{x_1 + x_2 + ... + x_n - n\,\mu}{\sqrt{n}\,\sigma} \sim N[0, 1] \tag{2.228}$$

when n is large.

Let's consider a special case when the underlying distribution is a standard normal distribution. Let $\chi^2(n)$ be the chi-square distribution:

$$\chi^2(n) \sim x_1^2 + x_2^2 + \ldots + x_n^2. \tag{2.229}$$

We have:

$$\mu = E[\chi^2(n)] = n, \quad \sigma^2 = \text{Var}[\chi^2(n)] = 2n. \tag{2.230}$$

Let

$$x = \chi^2(n)/n = \left(x_1^2 + x_1^2 + \ldots + x_n^2\right)/n. \tag{2.231}$$

We have

$$\mu = E[\chi^2(n)/n] = 1, \quad \sigma^2 = \text{Var}[\chi^2(n)/n] = 2/n. \tag{2.232}$$

Therefore we have

$$\lim_{n \to \infty} \chi^2(n)/n = \lim_{n \to \infty} N[1, 2/n] = 1. \tag{2.233}$$

When n approaches infinity, the normal distribution becomes infinitely narrow and we can regard this random variable as 1. This is the basis of Ito's lemma which is widely used in financial mathematics.

This result can also be derived by using the Stirling formula explicitly. From the chi-square distribution, the distribution function of a random variable $x = \chi^2(n)/n$ is

$$
\begin{aligned}
f(x) &= n \frac{1}{2^{n/2}\Gamma(n/2)} (nx)^{n/2-1} e^{-nx/2} \\
&\approx n \frac{n/2}{2^{n/2}(n/2)^{n/2}e^{-n/2}\sqrt{2\pi n/2}} (nx)^{n/2-1} e^{-nx/2} \\
&= \frac{1}{\sqrt{2\pi 2/n}} x^{n/2-1} e^{-n(x-1)/2} \\
&\approx \frac{1}{\sqrt{2\pi 2/n}} e^{-(x-1)-\frac{1}{2}(n/2-1)(x-1)^2} \\
&\approx \frac{1}{\sqrt{2\pi 2/n}} e^{-\frac{(x-1)^2}{2(2/n)}} \\
&\sim N[1, 2/n].
\end{aligned}
\tag{2.234}
$$

In the second equality, we have used the Stirling formula. Noting that $\ln(1 + x) \approx x - \frac{1}{2}x^2$ when $x \sim 0$, we have $x \approx e^{x-1-\frac{1}{2}(x-1)^2}$ when $x \sim 1$. This approximation is used in the fourth equality above. This is a concrete example of the central limit theorem.

2.3   Estimate of Mean, Variance, Skewness, and Kurtosis from Sample Data

Given a set of data, some of the first questions we can ask are basic descriptions of the distribution, including the various moments. The mean is the first moment and the variance the second. The third and fourth moments are the skewness and the kurtosis.

The population variance is defined as $\sigma^2 = E[(x - \mu)^2]$. The sample variance is calculated as

$$s^2 = \frac{1}{n-1} \sum_{i=1}^{n} (x_i - \bar{x})^2. \tag{2.235}$$

The population skewness is defined as $E[(x - \mu)^3]/\sigma^3$. It measures the asymmetry of the distribution around its mean. It can be estimated from a data sample as

$$\text{Skewness} = \frac{n}{(n-1)(n-2)} \sum_{i=1}^{n} (x_i - \bar{x})^3/s^3. \tag{2.236}$$

The population kurtosis is defined as $E[(x - \mu)^4]/\sigma^4 - 3$. For a normal distribution, it is zero (one of the reasons for the "-3" in the kurtosis definition). Kurtosis measures the relative peakedness or flatness of a given distribution compared to a normal distribution. It can be estimated from a sample data through

$$\text{Kurtosis} = \frac{n(n+1)}{(n-1)(n-2)(n-3)} \sum_{i=1}^{n} (x_i - \bar{x})^4/s^4 - \frac{3(n-1)^2}{(n-2)(n-3)}. \tag{2.237}$$

There are other forms of sample kurtosis and more discussion can be found in Sheskin (2000).

2.4   Estimate of the Standard Deviation of the Sample Mean

Let x_1, x_2, ..., x_n be random samples from a distribution with mean μ and variance σ^2 and that they are independent of each other. The sample mean is

$$\bar{x} = (x_1 + x_2 + \ldots + x_n)/n. \tag{2.238}$$

Then the expectation value and variance of the mean are:

$$E[\bar{x}] = \mu \quad \text{and} \quad \text{Var}[\bar{x}] = \sigma^2/n. \tag{2.239}$$

Let $x_1, x_2, ..., x_n$ and $y_1, y_2, ..., y_n$ be two sets of random samples from the same distribution with mean μ and variance σ^2, the sample means are

$$\bar{x} = (x_1 + x_2 + ... + x_n)/n, \quad \bar{y} = (y_1 + y_2 + ... + y_n)/n. \qquad (2.240)$$

If we let $\bar{V} = (\bar{x} + \bar{y})/2$, we have $E[\bar{V}] = \mu$,

$$\text{Var}[\bar{V}] = \left(\text{Var}[\bar{x}] + \text{Var}[\bar{y}] + 2\text{Cov}(\bar{x}, \bar{y})\right)/4. \qquad (2.241)$$

If $x_1, x_2, ..., x_n$ and $y_1, y_2, ..., y_n$ are independent of each other, then

$$\text{Var}[\bar{V}] = \left(\text{Var}[\bar{x}] + \text{Var}[\bar{y}]\right)/4 = \sigma^2/(2n). \qquad (2.242)$$

As expected, it is the same variance as when the random sample size is $2n$. If $x_1, x_2, ..., x_n$ and $y_1, y_2, ..., y_n$ are correlated with[2] $\text{Corr}(\bar{x}, \bar{y}) = \rho$, then

$$\text{Var}[\bar{V}] = (1 + \rho)\,\sigma^2/(2n). \qquad (2.243)$$

If $\rho < 0$, then

$$\text{Var}[\bar{V}] < \sigma^2/(2n). \qquad (2.244)$$

This shows that the variance from $2n$ samples with negative correlation is less than the variance from $2n$ independent samples. In the antithetic variate method, one of the variance reduction techniques in Monte Carlo simulation, and the second set of random samples is selected such that it is negatively correlated with the first set of random samples. This special selection will reduce the variance of the estimated value given the same sample size.

2.5 (Pseudo) Random Number Generators

In the next section we will describe the Mersenne twister pseudorandom number generator for generating the uniform distribution. In many instances we desire a set of random numbers drawn from a distribution $f(x)$ other than a uniform distribution. How do we generate such a set given complete knowledge of the desired distribution?

The uniform distribution can be used to generate random variables that have other distributions. Let $f(x)$ be a distribution function and $F(x)$ be its cumulative distribution function. We are looking for the mapping from the uniform distribution to $x : u \to x$, such that $du = f(x)dx$. We have $u = F(x)$. Therefore the random number with this distribution is $x = F^{-1}(u)$, where u is a random number from $U(0, 1)$. For some functions there are closed forms for the inverse of cumulative distribution. However for some functions there is no closed form of function and other techniques, generally numerical integration, are required to generate the desired set of random numbers.

---

[2]We can sample $y_1, y_2, ..., y_n$ such that $\text{Corr}(x_i, y_j) = \rho\delta_{ij}$, $(i, j = 0, 1, ..., n)$. Then $\text{Cov}(\bar{x}, \bar{y}) = 1/n^2 \sum_{i=0, j=0}^{n} \text{Cov}(x_i, y_j) = \rho\sigma^2/n$. This leads to $\text{Corr}(\bar{x}, \bar{y}) = \rho$.

2.5.1 Mersenne Twister Pseudorandom Number Generator

The random numbers of the uniform distribution can be generated by the Mersenne twister, which is a pseudorandom number generator developed by Matsumoto and Nishimura. Mersenne twister MT19937 is the random number generator of period $2^{19937} - 1$. More details of the algorithm can be found on the web page of Matsumoto and Nishimura or the Wikipedia page on the Mersenne twister.

We have implemented MT19937 pseudorandom number generator in the function "*matrix_random()*" in DataMinerXL. See Appendix B for all functions in DataMinerXL.

2.5.2 Box–Muller Transform for Generating a Normal Distribution

Since there is no analytical expression for the cumulative normal distribution, the method of using the inverse of the cumulative distribution is not feasible to get the random number. Consider the two-dimensional mapping: $(u, v) \to (x, y)$, where u and v are the random numbers from $U(0, 1)$ and x and y are the random numbers from the standard normal distribution $N[0, 1]$. We have $dudv = f(x, y)dxdy$ via the Jacobian.

Note that with the variable transformations $x = r\cos\theta$ and $y = r\sin\theta$, we have

$$\left(\frac{1}{\sqrt{2\pi}}e^{-\frac{x^2}{2}}\right) \cdot \left(\frac{1}{\sqrt{2\pi}}e^{-\frac{y^2}{2}}\right) dxdy = d\left(-e^{-\frac{r^2}{2}}\right) \cdot d\left(\frac{\theta}{2\pi}\right). \qquad (2.245)$$

Therefore we have $\theta = 2\pi v$ and $r = \sqrt{-2\ln(1-u)}$. Since the distribution of u and $(1-u)$ are the same, we have the following convenient formula to generate two random numbers with standard normal distribution $N[0, 1]$:

$$\begin{aligned} x &= \sqrt{-2\ln u}\cos(2\pi v) \\ y &= \sqrt{-2\ln u}\sin(2\pi v) \end{aligned} \qquad (2.246)$$

where u and v are from $U(0, 1)$. Random numbers with the distribution $N[\mu, \sigma^2]$ can be generated by

$$\begin{aligned} x &= \mu + \sigma\sqrt{-2\ln u}\cos(2\pi v) \\ y &= \mu + \sigma\sqrt{-2\ln u}\sin(2\pi v). \end{aligned} \qquad (2.247)$$

This is called the Box–Muller transform. To use this methodology to generate a set of random numbers with distribution $N[\mu, \sigma^2]$ one simply generates many random number pairs u and v from a uniform distribution $U(0, 1)$, and then uses the above formula to transform to x and y pairs, which have the distribution $N[\mu, \sigma^2]$. We can use similar concepts to build processes for generating many other common distributions.

2.6 Transformation of a Distribution Function

Let the probability density function of a random variable x be $f(x)$. Is it possible to transform this distribution function $f(x)$ into another distribution function $g(y)$? The answer is yes. If we let $f(x)\,dx = g(y)\,dy$, we have $F(x) = G(y)$. The desired transformation is

$$y(x) = G^{-1}(F(x)). \tag{2.248}$$

For example, if we want to transform the distribution into the uniform distribution, we have $y(x) = F(x)$. If we want to transform the distribution into the normal distribution, we have $y(x) = \Phi^{-1}(F(x))$.

2.7 Distribution of a Function of Random Variables

Let x_1, x_2 be two random variables, and y_1, y_2 be functions of x_1, x_2. We have

$$f(x_1,\, x_2)dx_1 dx_2 = g(y_1,\, y_2)dy_1 dy_2. \tag{2.249}$$

We then have the distribution of y_1, y_2 in terms of the distribution of x_1, x_2:

$$g(y_1,\, y_2) = f(x_1,\, x_2)\,|\partial x/\partial y|. \tag{2.250}$$

This is true for any number of random variables

$$g(y_1,\, y_2,\, ...,\, y_n) = f(x_1,\, x_2,\, ...,\, x_n)\,|\partial x/\partial y|. \tag{2.251}$$

The univariate distribution of y_1 can be obtained from integration over y_2:

$$g(y_1) = \int_{-\infty}^{\infty} g(y_1,\, y_2)dy_2. \tag{2.252}$$

As examples, the t-distribution and F-distribution can be obtained using the following transformations: $(z,\, x) \to (t,\, y)$ where

$$t = \frac{z}{\sqrt{x/n}},\, y = x \tag{2.253}$$

for the t-distribution, and $(x_1,\, x_2) \to (F,\, y)$ where

$$F = \frac{x_1/n_1}{x_2/n_2},\quad y = x_2 \tag{2.254}$$

for the F-distribution. The integrations involved to reach the t-distribution and F-distribution are straightforward.

Let's discuss some common functions of random variables.

2.7.1 $Z = X + Y$

Consider the transformation $(x, y) \rightarrow (x, z)$ where $z = x + y$. For this transformation the Jacobian determinant is $|\partial(x, z)/\partial(x, y)| = 1$. Therefore $f_{X,Z}(x, z) = f_{X,Y}(x, y)$. The distribution of Z is

$$
\begin{aligned}
f_Z(z) &= \int_{-\infty}^{\infty} f_{X,Z}(x, z) dx \\
&= \int_{-\infty}^{\infty} f_{X,Y}(x, z - x) dx.
\end{aligned}
\tag{2.255}
$$

If X and Y are independent, we have

$$
\begin{aligned}
f_Z(z) &= \int_{-\infty}^{\infty} f_X(x) f_Y(z - x) dx \\
&= \int_{-\infty}^{\infty} f_X(z - x) f_Y(x) dx.
\end{aligned}
\tag{2.256}
$$

This is the convolution of the distributions of X and Y.

2.7.2 $Z = X \cdot Y$

Consider the transformation $(x, y) \rightarrow (x, z)$ where $z = xy$. For this transformation the Jacobian determinant is $|\partial(x, z)/\partial(x, y)| = x$. Therefore

$$
f_{X,Z}(x, z) = \frac{1}{|x|} f_{X,Y}(x, y).
\tag{2.257}
$$

The distribution of Z is

$$
\begin{aligned}
f_Z(z) &= \int_{-\infty}^{\infty} f_{X,Z}(x, z) dx \\
&= \int_{-\infty}^{\infty} \frac{1}{|x|} f_{X,Y}(x, z/x) \, dx \\
&= \int_{-\infty}^{\infty} \frac{1}{|y|} f_{X,Y}(z/y, y) \, dy \quad \text{(by symmetry)}.
\end{aligned}
\tag{2.258}
$$

If X and Y are independent, we have

$$
\begin{aligned}
f_Z(z) &= \int_{-\infty}^{\infty} \frac{1}{|x|} f_X(x) f_Y(z/x) \, dx \\
&= \int_{-\infty}^{\infty} \frac{1}{|y|} f_X(z/y) f_Y(y) \, dy.
\end{aligned}
\tag{2.259}
$$

2.7.3 $(Z_1, Z_2, ..., Z_n) = (X_1, X_2, ..., X_n) \cdot Y$

Consider the transformation $(x_1, x_2, ..., x_n, y) \rightarrow (z_1, z_2, ..., z_n, y)$. Here the Jacobian determinant is $|\partial(z, y)/\partial(x, y)| = y^n$. Therefore

$$
f_{Z,Y}(z, y) = \frac{1}{|y^n|} f_{X,Y}(x, y).
\tag{2.260}
$$

The distribution of Z is

$$
\begin{aligned}
f_Z(z) &= \int_{-\infty}^{\infty} f_{Z,Y}(z, y) dy \\
&= \int_{-\infty}^{\infty} \frac{1}{|y^n|} f_{X,Y}(z/y, y) dy.
\end{aligned}
\tag{2.261}
$$

If X and Y are independent, we have

$$f_Z(z) = \int_{-\infty}^{\infty} \frac{1}{|y^n|} f_X(z/y) f_Y(y) \, dy. \tag{2.262}$$

2.7.4 $Z = X/Y$

Consider the transformation $(x, y) \to (z, y)$ where $z = x/y$. The Jacobian determinant is $|\partial(z, y)/\partial(x, y)| = 1/y$. Then the distribution of Z is

$$\begin{aligned} f_Z(z) &= \int_{-\infty}^{\infty} f_{Z,Y}(z, y) dy \\ &= \int_{-\infty}^{\infty} |y| f_{X,Y}(yz, y) \, dy. \end{aligned} \tag{2.263}$$

If X and Y are independent, we have

$$f_Z(z) = \int_{-\infty}^{\infty} |y| f_X(yz) f_Y(y) \, dy. \tag{2.264}$$

2.7.5 $Z = \max(X, Y)$

Note that

$$P[Z < z] = P[\max(X, Y) < z] = P[X < z, Y < z]. \tag{2.265}$$

If X and Y are independent, we have

$$F_Z(z) = F_X(z) F_Y(z). \tag{2.266}$$

Thus the distribution of Z is

$$f_Z(z) = f_X(z) F_Y(z) + F_X(z) f_Y(z). \tag{2.267}$$

2.7.6 $Z = \min(X, Y)$

Note that

$$\begin{aligned} P[Z < z] &= 1 - P[Z > z] \\ &= 1 - P[\min(X, Y) > z] \\ &= 1 - P[X > z, Y > z]. \end{aligned} \tag{2.268}$$

If X and Y are independent, we have

$$F_Z(z) = 1 - [1 - F_X(z)] [1 - F_Y(z)]. \tag{2.269}$$

Thus the distribution of Z is

$$f_Z(z) = f_X(z) [1 - F_Y(z)] + f_Y(z) [1 - F_X(z)]. \tag{2.270}$$

2.8 Moment Generating Function

Let $f(x)$ be the distribution density function. Then the moment generating function is

$$M_X(t) = E[e^{tx}] = \int_{-\infty}^{\infty} e^{tx} f(x) dx = \int_{-\infty}^{\infty} \left[1 + tx + \frac{t^2 x^2}{2!} + ... \right] f(x) dx. \tag{2.271}$$

The rth-order moment can be obtained from this moment generating function through

$$m_r = E[x^r] = \frac{d^r M_X(t)}{dt^r} \bigg|_{t=0}. \tag{2.272}$$

If $X = X_1 + ... + X_n$ and X_i are all independent, then

$$M_X(t) = \int_{-\infty}^{\infty} e^{tx} f_1(x_1) ... f_n(x_n) dx_1 ... dx_n = M_{X_1}(t) ... M_{X_n}(t). \tag{2.273}$$

Let us consider several important distributions in the next few sections.

2.8.1 Moment Generating Function of Binomial Distribution

The distribution function is

$$f(x) = C_n^x p^x (1-p)^{n-x}, \ x = 0, 1, ..., n. \tag{2.274}$$

By direct (lengthy) calculation, we have

$$\mu = np, \quad \sigma^2 = np(1-p). \tag{2.275}$$

But it is much easier to arrive at this result by using the moment generating function, $M_X(t)$:

$$M_X(t) = \sum_{x=0}^{n} e^{tx} p^x (1-p)^{n-x} = (e^t p + 1 - p)^n. \tag{2.276}$$

Here the integral over all possible values in the distribution is replaced by an infinite sum over all possible discrete values. Therefore

$$\frac{dM_X(t)}{dt} = n(e^t p + 1 - p)^{n-1} e^t p, \tag{2.277}$$

$$\frac{d^2 M_X(t)}{dt^2} = n(n-1)(e^t p + 1 - p)^{n-2} e^{2t} p^2 + n(e^t p + 1 - p)^{n-1} e^t p. \tag{2.278}$$

Thus, $m_1 = np$, $m_2 = n(n-1)p^2 + np$.

2.8.2 Moment Generating Function of Normal Distribution

For the normal distribution the moment generating function is

$$M_X(t) = \int_{-\infty}^{\infty} e^{tx} \varphi(\mu, \sigma) dx = e^{\mu t + \frac{1}{2}\sigma^2 t^2}. \tag{2.279}$$

Its first and second derivatives are

$$\frac{dM_X(t)}{dt} = e^{\mu t + \frac{1}{2}\sigma^2 t^2} (\mu + \sigma^2 t), \tag{2.280}$$

$$\frac{d^2 M_X(t)}{dt^2} = e^{\mu t + \frac{1}{2}\sigma^2 t^2} (\mu + \sigma^2 t)^2 + e^{\mu t + \frac{1}{2}\sigma^2 t^2} \sigma^2. \tag{2.281}$$

Therefore we have

$$m_1 = \mu, \quad m_2 = \mu^2 + \sigma^2. \tag{2.282}$$

2.8.3 Moment Generating Function of the Γ Distribution

For the gamma distribution, $\Gamma(\alpha, \beta)$ $(\alpha > 0, \beta > 0)$, the moment generating function is

$$
\begin{aligned}
M_X(t) &= \int_0^{\infty} e^{tx} \frac{\beta^\alpha}{\Gamma(\alpha)} x^{\alpha-1} e^{-\beta x} dx \\
&= \frac{\beta^\alpha}{(\beta-t)^\alpha} \int_0^{\infty} \frac{(\beta-t)^\alpha}{\Gamma(\alpha)} x^{\alpha-1} e^{-(\beta-t)x} dx \\
&= \frac{1}{(1-t/\beta)^\alpha}.
\end{aligned}
\tag{2.283}
$$

2.8.4 Moment Generating Function of Chi-Square Distribution

If X is the $\chi^2(1)$ distribution, then

$$M_X(t) = \int_{-\infty}^{\infty} e^{t x^2} \varphi(0, 1) dx = (1 - 2t)^{-1/2}. \tag{2.284}$$

If X is the $\chi^2(n)$ distribution, we have

$$M_X(t) = (1 - 2t)^{-n/2}, \tag{2.285}$$

$$\frac{dM_X(t)}{dt} = n (1 - 2t)^{-n/2-1}, \tag{2.286}$$

$$\frac{d^2 M_X(t)}{dt^2} = n(n + 2) (1 - 2t)^{-n/2-2}. \tag{2.287}$$

Thus for the $\chi^2(n)$ distribution, $m_1 = n$, $m_2 = n(n+2)$. Therefore, we have $\mu = n$, $\sigma^2 = 2n$.

2.8.5　Moment Generating Function of the Poisson Distribution

The moment generating function of the Poisson distribution is

$$M_K(t) = E[e^{tk}] = \sum_{k=0}^{\infty} e^{tk} P(k) = \sum_{k=0}^{\infty} e^{tk} \lambda^k e^{-\lambda}/k! = e^{\lambda(e^t - 1)}, \qquad (2.288)$$

Therefore

$$\frac{dM_k(t)}{dt} = e^{\lambda(e^t - 1)} \lambda e^t$$

$$\frac{d^2 M_k(t)}{dt^2} = e^{\lambda(e^t - 1)} \left[(\lambda e^t)^2 + \lambda e^t \right]. \qquad (2.289)$$

Thus $m_1 = \lambda$, $m_2 = \lambda^2 + \lambda$. We have $\mu = \lambda$, $\sigma^2 = \lambda$.

2.9　Cumulant Generating Function

The centered moments, μ_r, and non-centered moments, m_r, are defined by

$$\mu_r = E[(x - \mu)^r], \quad m_r = E[x^r], \quad r = 0, 1, ... \qquad (2.290)$$

where $\mu = E[x]$. The moment generating function generates the moments in the following expression:

$$M_X(t) = E[e^{tx}] = \sum_{r=0}^{\infty} E\left[x^r t^r / r!\right] = \sum_{r=0}^{\infty} m_r t^r / r!. \qquad (2.291)$$

The cumulant generating function is defined by the logarithm of the moment generating function

$$\ln M_X(t) = \ln E[e^{tx}] = \ln \left(\sum_{r=0}^{\infty} m_r t^r / r! \right) = \sum_{r=0}^{\infty} k_r t^r / r!. \qquad (2.292)$$

Here k_r is the rth cumulant.

Noting that the moment generating function of the normal distribution is $M_X(t) = e^{\mu t + \frac{1}{2}\sigma^2 t^2}$, the cumulants of the normal distribution are

$$k_1 = \mu,$$

$$k_2 = \sigma^2, \qquad (2.293)$$

$$k_r = 0, \quad r = 3, 4, ...$$

It is clear that μ_r, m_r, and k_r are related. The following relationships can be established.

1. μ_r in terms of m_r:

$$\mu_0 = 1$$

$$\mu_1 = 0$$

$$\mu_2 = E[(x - \mu)^2] = m_2 - m_1^2 \qquad (2.294)$$

$$\mu_3 = E[(x - \mu)^3] = m_3 - 3m_2m_1 + 2m_1^3$$

$$\mu_4 = E[(x - \mu)^4] = m_4 - 4m_3m_1 + 6m_2m_1^2 - 3m_1^4$$

2. m_r in terms of μ_r:

$$m_0 = 1$$

$$m_1 = \mu$$

$$m_2 = E[x^2] = \mu_2 + \mu^2 \qquad (2.295)$$

$$m_3 = E[x^3] = \mu_3 + 3\mu_2\mu + \mu^3$$

$$m_4 = E[x^4] = \mu_4 + 4\mu_3\mu + 6\mu_2\mu^2 + \mu^4$$

3. k_r in terms of m_r:

Using $\ln(1+x) = x - \frac{1}{2}x^2 + \frac{1}{3}x^3 + \dots$ to expand the LHS of the following equality:

$$\ln\left(\sum_{r=0}^{\infty} m_r t^r / r!\right) = \sum_{r=0}^{\infty} k_r t^r / r!, \qquad (2.296)$$

we can establish the relations of k_r in terms of m_r:

$$k_0 = 0$$

$$k_1 = m_1$$

$$k_2 = m_2 - m_1^2 \qquad (2.297)$$

$$k_3 = m_3 - 3m_1m_2 + 2m_1^3$$

$$k_4 = m_4 - 3m_2^2 - 4m_1m_3 + 12m_1^2m_2 - 6m_1^4$$

4. k_r in terms of μ_r:

$$k_0 = 0$$

$$k_1 = \mu$$

$$k_2 = \mu_2 \qquad (2.298)$$

$$k_3 = \mu_3$$

$$k_4 = \mu_4 - 3\mu_2^2$$

2.10   Characteristic Function

Let $f(x)$ be the probability distribution function of a random variable x. The expected value of any function $g(x)$ is given by

$$E\left[g(x)\right] = \int dx\, g(x) f(x). \tag{2.299}$$

The expected value of the function $e^{ik^T x}$, where k and x are both vectors, is

$$E\left[e^{ik^T x}\right] = \int dx\, e^{ik^T x} f(x), \tag{2.300}$$

and is called the characteristic function of the distribution function. We can also recognize that it is the Fourier transform. It is often more convenient to work with the characteristic function of a probability distribution function.

For a one-dimensional distribution $f(x)$, let $f(k)$ be its Fourier transform. Then the inverse Fourier transform is

$$f(x) = \frac{1}{2\pi} \int e^{-ikx} f(k)\, dk. \tag{2.301}$$

Taking the derivative $D = d/dx$ on both sides, we have

$$(-D)^n f(x) = \frac{1}{2\pi} \int e^{-ikx} (ik)^n f(k)\, dk. \tag{2.302}$$

For any function $g(x)$, we have

$$g(-D)f(x) = \frac{1}{2\pi} \int e^{-ikx} g(ik) f(k)\, dk. \tag{2.303}$$

We conclude that if $f(k)$ is the Fourier transform of $f(x)$, then $(ik)^n f(k)$ is the Fourier transform of $(-D)^n f(x)$. In general for any function $g(x)$, $g(ik)f(k)$ is the Fourier transform of $g(-D)f(x)$.

As an example, for the standard normal distribution, the characteristic function is

$$E\left[e^{ikx}\right] = e^{-\frac{1}{2}k^2}. \tag{2.304}$$

Then we have

$$\varphi(x) = \frac{1}{2\pi} \int e^{-ikx} e^{-\frac{1}{2}k^2}\, dk. \tag{2.305}$$

Taking the derivative $D = d/dx$ on both sides leads to

$$(-D)^n \varphi(x) = \frac{1}{2\pi} \int e^{-ikx} (ik)^n e^{-\frac{1}{2}k^2}\, dk. \tag{2.306}$$

The Chebyshev–Hermite polynomials, $\text{He}_n(x)$, are defined as

$$(-D)^n \varphi(x) = \varphi(x) \text{He}_n(x). \tag{2.307}$$

Explicitly

$$\text{He}_n(x) = e^{x^2/2} (-1)^n \frac{d^n}{dx^n} e^{-x^2/2}, \tag{2.308}$$

with the property

$$D\left(\varphi(x) \text{He}_n(x)\right) = -\varphi(x) \text{He}_{n+1}(x). \tag{2.309}$$

The first seven polynomials are

$$\text{He}_0(x) = 1 \qquad\qquad \text{He}_1(x) = x$$

$$\text{He}_2(x) = x^2 - 1 \qquad\qquad \text{He}_3(x) = x^3 - 3x$$

$$\text{He}_4(x) = x^4 - 6x^2 + 3 \qquad\qquad \text{He}_5(x) = x^5 - 10x^3 + 15x$$

$$\text{He}_6(x) = x^6 - 15x^4 + 45x^2 - 15$$

2.10.1 Relationship between Cumulative Function and Characteristic Function

Let's establish the following relationship between the cumulative distribution and the characteristic function:

$$\int_k^\infty f(x)dx = \frac{1}{2} + \frac{1}{\pi} \int_0^\infty \text{Re}\left[\frac{e^{-iuk}\varphi(u)}{iu}\right] du. \tag{2.310}$$

Replacing the distribution function in terms of its characteristic function, we have

$$\begin{aligned}
\int_k^\infty f(x)dx &= \frac{1}{2\pi} \int_k^\infty dx \int_{-\infty}^\infty du \varphi(u) e^{-iux} \\
&= \frac{1}{2\pi} \int_{-\infty}^\infty du \varphi(u) \frac{e^{-iu\infty} - e^{-iuk}}{-iu}.
\end{aligned} \tag{2.311}$$

Letting $g(u) = \varphi(u)e^{-iuk}/(iu)$, we have $g^*(u) = g(-u)$. Then we have

$$\int_k^\infty f(x)dx = -\frac{1}{2\pi} \int_{-\infty}^\infty \text{Re}\left[\varphi(u)\frac{e^{-iu\infty}}{iu}\right] du + \frac{1}{\pi} \int_0^\infty \text{Re}\left[\varphi(u)\frac{e^{-iuk}}{iu}\right] du. \tag{2.312}$$

The first term is

$$\begin{aligned}
I &= \lim_{k\to\infty} \left\{ -\frac{1}{2\pi} \int_{-\infty}^\infty \text{Re}\left[E[e^{iux}]\frac{e^{-iuk}}{iu}\right] du \right\} \\
&= \lim_{k\to\infty} \left\{ -\frac{1}{2\pi} \int_{-\infty}^\infty \text{Re}\left[E\left(\frac{e^{iu(x-k)}}{iu}\right)\right] du \right\} \\
&= \lim_{k\to\infty} \left\{ -\frac{1}{2\pi} \int_{-\infty}^\infty E\left[\frac{\sin(u(x-k))}{u}\right] du \right\} \\
&= \frac{1}{2\pi} \int_{-\infty}^\infty E\left[\pi\delta(u)\right] du \\
&= \frac{1}{2}.
\end{aligned} \tag{2.313}$$

Therefore we have

$$\int_k^\infty f(x)dx = \frac{1}{2} + \frac{1}{\pi}\int_0^\infty \mathrm{Re}\left[\varphi(u)\frac{e^{-iuk}}{iu}\right]du. \qquad (2.314)$$

2.10.2 Characteristic Function of Normal Distribution

When $f(x)$ is a normal distribution, $N[\mu, \Sigma]$, by performing the integration, we have

$$E\left[e^{ik^T x}\right] = e^{ik^T\mu - \frac{1}{2}k^T\Sigma k}. \qquad (2.315)$$

Since the Fourier transform is unique, we can calculate the characteristic function of a distribution to prove or disprove that it is a normal distribution. However we cannot do this by calculating the moment generating functions, since the moment generating functions do not determine a distribution uniquely.

2.10.3 Characteristic Function of Γ Distribution

Let the gamma distribution be $\Gamma(\alpha, \beta)$ ($\alpha > 0$, $\beta > 0$). Its density function is

$$f(x) = \frac{\beta^\alpha}{\Gamma(\alpha)}x^{\alpha-1}e^{-\beta x}, \quad x > 0. \qquad (2.316)$$

The characteristic function is

$$\begin{aligned}
E\left[e^{ikx}\right] &= \int_0^\infty \frac{\beta^\alpha}{\Gamma(\alpha)}x^{\alpha-1}e^{-\beta x + ikx}dx \\
&= \frac{\beta^\alpha}{(\beta-ik)^\alpha\Gamma(\alpha)}\int_0^\infty (\beta-ik)^\alpha x^{\alpha-1}e^{-(\beta-ik)x}dx \\
&= \frac{1}{(1-ik/\beta)^\alpha\Gamma(\alpha)}\int_0^\infty [(1-ik/\beta)x]^{\alpha-1}e^{-(1-ik/\beta)x}d(1-ik/\beta)x \\
&= \frac{1}{(1-ik/\beta)^\alpha\Gamma(\alpha)}I,
\end{aligned} \qquad (2.317)$$

where $I = \int_l z^{\alpha-1}e^{-z}dz$. The integral path, l, is a line from the origin to $Re^{i\alpha}$, $R \to \infty$, $|\alpha| < \pi/2$, an infinite far point in the first or fourth quadrants. Changing the contour of the integration we have

$$\begin{aligned}
I &= \int_l z^{\alpha-1}e^{-z}dz \\
&= \int_0^\infty z^{\alpha-1}e^{-z}dz + \int_{C_R} z^{\alpha-1}e^{-z}dz - \int_{C_r} z^{\alpha-1}e^{-z}dz \qquad (2.318) \\
&= \Gamma(\alpha) + \int_{C_R} z^{\alpha-1}e^{-z}dz - \int_{C_r} z^{\alpha-1}e^{-z}dz.
\end{aligned}$$

Note that

$$\begin{aligned}
\left|\int_{C_R} z^{\alpha-1}e^{-z}dz\right| &\leq \int_{C_R} \left|z^{\alpha-1}\right|\cdot\left|e^{-z}\right|\cdot|dz| \\
&= \int_{C_R} R^\alpha e^{-R\cos\theta}d\theta \leq \int_{C_R} R^\alpha e^{-R\cos\alpha}d\theta \qquad (2.319) \\
&= R^\alpha e^{-R\cos\alpha}\alpha \overset{R\to\infty}{\to} 0,
\end{aligned}$$

and similarly

$$\left| \int_{C_r} z^{\alpha-1} e^{-z} dz \right| \le r^\alpha e^{-r \cos \alpha} \alpha \overset{r \to 0}{\to} 0. \tag{2.320}$$

We have

$$I = \int_l z^{\alpha-1} e^{-z} dz = \Gamma(\alpha). \tag{2.321}$$

Therefore we have

$$E\left[e^{ikx}\right] = \frac{1}{(1 - ik/\beta)^\alpha}. \tag{2.322}$$

Let $x_1 \sim \Gamma(\alpha_1, \beta)$, $x_2 \sim \Gamma(\alpha_2, \beta)$, then the characteristic function for $x = x_1 + x_2$ is

$$
\begin{aligned}
E\left[e^{ik(x_1+x_2)}\right] &= E\left[e^{ikx_1}\right] \cdot E\left[e^{ikx_2}\right] \\
&= \frac{1}{(1-ik/\beta)^{\alpha_1}} \cdot \frac{1}{(1-ik/\beta)^{\alpha_2}} \\
&= \frac{1}{(1-ik/\beta)^{\alpha_1+\alpha_2}}.
\end{aligned} \tag{2.323}
$$

This leads to

$$x = x_1 + x_2 \sim \Gamma(\alpha_1 + \alpha_2, \beta). \tag{2.324}$$

Let $x_1 \sim \Gamma(\alpha, \beta_1)$, $x_2 \sim \Gamma(\alpha, \beta_2)$, then the characteristic function for $x = x_1 + x_2$ is

$$
\begin{aligned}
E\left[e^{ik(x_1+x_2)}\right] &= E\left[e^{ikx_1}\right] \cdot E\left[e^{ikx_2}\right] \\
&= \frac{1}{(1-ik/\beta_1)^\alpha} \cdot \frac{1}{(1-ik/\beta_2)^\alpha} \\
&= \frac{1}{[1-ik(1/\beta_1+1/\beta_2)-k^2/(\beta_1\beta_2)]^\alpha},
\end{aligned} \tag{2.325}
$$

and the characteristic function for $x = x_1 - x_2$ is

$$
\begin{aligned}
E\left[e^{ik(x_1-x_2)}\right] &= E\left[e^{ikx_1}\right] \cdot E\left[e^{-ikx_2}\right] \\
&= \frac{1}{(1-ik/\beta_1)^\alpha} \cdot \frac{1}{(1+ik/\beta_2)^\alpha} \\
&= \frac{1}{[1-ik(1/\beta_1-1/\beta_2)+k^2/(\beta_1\beta_2)]^\alpha}.
\end{aligned} \tag{2.326}
$$

2.11 Chebyshev's Inequality

Note that

$$
\begin{aligned}
\text{Var}[x] &= \int_{-\infty}^{\infty} f(x)(x-\mu)^2 dx \\
&\ge \int_{-\infty}^{\mu-k} f(x)(x-\mu)^2 dx + \int_{\mu+k}^{\infty} f(x)(x-\mu)^2 dx \\
&\ge k^2 \int_{-\infty}^{\mu-k} f(x)dx + k^2 \int_{\mu+k}^{\infty} f(x)dx \\
&\ge k^2 P\left[x \mid |x-\mu| \ge k\right].
\end{aligned} \tag{2.327}
$$

Therefore we have

$$P\left[x \mid |x - E[x]| \geq k\right] \leq \mathrm{Var}[x]/k^2. \tag{2.328}$$

This is known as Chebyshev's inequality, and it shows that most data points in a sample lie close to the mean. More precisely, it states that no more than $1/k^2$ of the data points can be more than k standard deviations from the mean.

2.12   Markov's Inequality

Let x be a nonnegative random variable, with $\mu = E[x]$. Then for any positive constant a we have

$$
\begin{aligned}
\mu &= \int_0^\infty f(x)x\,dx \\
&= \int_0^a f(x)x\,dx + \int_a^\infty f(x)x\,dx \\
&\geq \int_a^\infty f(x)a\,dx \\
&= a\,P\left[x > a\right].
\end{aligned}
\tag{2.329}
$$

Therefore we have

$$P\left[x > a\right] \leq \mu/a. \tag{2.330}$$

2.13   Gram–Charlier Series

For any distribution $f(x)$, the moment generating function $f(t)$ is

$$f(t) = E[e^{itx}] = e^{\sum_{r=1}^{\infty} k_r \frac{(it)^r}{r!}}. \tag{2.331}$$

Let $\varphi(t)$ be the moment generating function of the normal distribution:

$$\varphi(t) = E[e^{itx}] = e^{\sum_{r=1}^{\infty} \alpha_r \frac{(it)^r}{r!}}. \tag{2.332}$$

We have

$$f(t) = e^{\sum_{r=1}^{\infty} (k_r - \alpha_r)\frac{(it)^r}{r!}} \varphi(t). \tag{2.333}$$

Then we have from (2.303),

$$f(x) = e^{\sum_{r=1}^{\infty} (k_r - \alpha_r)\frac{(-D)^r}{r!}} \varphi(x). \tag{2.334}$$

Selecting $\mu = k_1$, $\sigma^2 = k_2$, $\varphi(x) = \varphi(x, \mu, \sigma^2)$, we have

$$f(x) = e^{\sum\limits_{r=3}^{\infty} k_r \frac{(-D)^r}{r!}} \varphi(x, \mu, \sigma^2). \qquad (2.335)$$

The first three terms are

$$f(x) = \left(1 + \frac{k_3}{3!\sigma^3} \text{He}_3\left(\frac{x-\mu}{\sigma}\right) + \frac{k_4}{4!\sigma^4} \text{He}_4\left(\frac{x-\mu}{\sigma}\right)\right) \varphi(x, \mu, \sigma^2), \qquad (2.336)$$

where $\text{He}_n(x)(n = 0, 1, 2, ...)$ are Chebyshev–Hermite polynomials (refer to Section 2.10 on the characteristic function for details). The higher order of the Gram–Charlier series can be found in the paper by Blinnikov and Moessner (1998).

2.14 Edgeworth Expansion

Let x_1, x_2, ..., x_n be a random sample from a distribution with mean μ and variance σ^2, and that they are independent of each other. The following random variable has mean 0 and variance 1:

$$x = \frac{x_1 + x_2 + ... + x_n - n\mu}{\sqrt{n}\,\sigma}. \qquad (2.337)$$

The central limit theorem tells that when n is big, it approaches a standard normal distribution. The Edgeworth expansion tells how closely it approaches the normal distribution when n is finite. Following the same setting as in Section 2.2 on the central limit theorem, taking the Taylor expansion and keeping the terms up to the fourth order of moments, we have

$$E\left[e^{it\frac{x_1-\mu}{\sigma\sqrt{n}}}\right] = E\left[1 + it\frac{x_1-\mu}{\sigma\sqrt{n}} + \frac{(it)^2}{2}\left(\frac{x_1-\mu}{\sigma\sqrt{n}}\right)^2 + \frac{(it)^3}{6}\left(\frac{x_1-\mu}{\sigma\sqrt{n}}\right)^3\right.$$
$$\left. + \frac{(it)^4}{24}\left(\frac{x_1-\mu}{\sigma\sqrt{n}}\right)^4 + o\left(\frac{1}{n^2}\right)\right] = 1 - \frac{t^2}{2n} + \frac{(it)^3\mu_3}{6n^{3/2}} + \frac{(it)^4\mu_4}{24n^2} + o\left(\frac{1}{n^2}\right).$$
$$(2.338)$$

Here $\mu_3 = E\left[(x_1 - \mu)^3/\sigma^3\right]$ and $\mu_4 = E\left[(x_1 - \mu)^4/\sigma^4\right]$ are centered moments. Using

$$\left[1 + \frac{a}{n} + \frac{b}{n^{3/2}} + \frac{c}{n^2} + o\left(\frac{1}{n^2}\right)\right]^n = e^a\left[1 + \frac{b}{n^{1/2}} + \frac{c - (a^2 - b^2)/2}{n}\right] + o\left(\frac{1}{n}\right), \qquad (2.339)$$

we have

$$E\left[e^{itx}\right] = \left(E\left[e^{it\frac{x_1-\mu}{\sigma\sqrt{n}}}\right]\right)^n$$
$$= e^{-t^2/2}\left[1 + \frac{(it)^3\mu_3}{6\,n^{1/2}} + \frac{(it)^4(\mu_4-3)}{24\,n} + \frac{(it)^6\mu_3^2}{72\,n}\right] + o\left(\frac{1}{n}\right). \qquad (2.340)$$

Therefore

$$f(x) = \left[1 + \frac{\mu_3(-D)^3}{6\,n^{1/2}} + \frac{(\mu_4 - 3)(-D)^4}{24\,n} + \frac{\mu_3^2(-D)^6}{72\,n} \right] \varphi(x) + o\left(\frac{1}{n}\right).$$
(2.341)

Noting that $(-D)^n \varphi(x) = \varphi(x)\mathrm{He}_n(x)$ and $\mathrm{He}_n(x)$ is the Chebyshev–Hermite polynomial, we have

$$f(x) = \varphi(x) \left[1 + \frac{\mu_3}{6\,n^{1/2}}\mathrm{He}_3(x) + \frac{(\mu_4 - 3)}{24\,n}\mathrm{He}_4(x) + \frac{\mu_3^2}{72\,n}\mathrm{He}_6(x) \right] + o\left(\frac{1}{n}\right).$$
(2.342)

Using $D\left(\varphi(x)\mathrm{He}_n(x)\right) = -\varphi(x)\mathrm{He}_{n+1}(x)$, we have

$$F(x) = \Phi(x) - \varphi(x) \left[\frac{\mu_3}{6\,n^{1/2}}\mathrm{He}_2(x) + \frac{(\mu_4 - 3)}{24\,n}\mathrm{He}_3(x) + \frac{\mu_3^2}{72\,n}\mathrm{He}_5(x) \right] + o\left(\frac{1}{n}\right).$$
(2.343)

Let $n = 1$. The Edgeworth expansion up to the fourth moments is

$$F(x) = \Phi(x) - \varphi(x) \left[\frac{\mu_3}{6}\mathrm{He}_2(x) + \frac{(\mu_4 - 3)}{24}\mathrm{He}_3(x) + \frac{\mu_3^2}{72}\mathrm{He}_5(x) \right].$$
(2.344)

The higher order of the Edgeworth expansion can be found in the paper by Blinnikov and Moessner (1998).

2.15   Cornish–Fisher Expansion

The main reference of this section is the paper by Jaschke (2002). Before going into this expansion we introduce the Lagrange inversion theorem.

2.15.1   Lagrange Inversion Theorem

Consider a function: $s \to t = t(s)$ defined by the implicit expression $t = c + s \cdot h(t)$, where c is a constant and $h(t)$ is analytic at $t = c$. It is clear to see that $t(0) = c$. We can prove that:

$$\left. \frac{d^r}{ds^r} f(t(s)) \right|_{s=0} = \left. \frac{d^{r-1}}{dt^{r-1}} \left(f' h^r \right)(t) \right|_{t=c}.$$
(2.345)

Then the Taylor expansion around zero is

$$f(t) = f(t(s)) = f(t(0)) + \sum_{r=1}^{\infty} \frac{s^r}{r!} \left[\left. \frac{d^r}{ds^r} f(t(s)) \right|_{s=0} \right].$$
(2.346)

Then we have

$$f(t) = f(c) + \sum_{r=1}^{\infty} \frac{s^r}{r!} D_t^{r-1} \left[f' \cdot h^r \right] (c),$$ (2.347)

which is the Lagrange inversion theorem.

2.15.2 Cornish–Fisher Expansion

The Cornish–Fisher expansion, published in Cornish and Fisher (1937), is a formula for approximating quantiles of a random variable based only on the first few cumulants of the probability distribution function. In finance it is often used for calculating value-at-risk, which is the integral of a small part of the right-hand-side tail of a distribution. The value at risk is a convenient estimate of the exposure to unlikely tail events. Detailed discussion on this topic can be found in *RiskMetrics Technical Document* by Zangari et al. (1996).

The Cornish–Fisher expansion relates two percentiles of two distribution functions. Let us consider two distributions Φ and F. We look at two points z and x such that $\Phi(z) = \alpha$, $\Phi(x) = \beta$, $F(x) = \alpha$. Noting that $z \to \alpha \to x \to \beta$, we have

$$\beta - \alpha = \Phi(x) - F(x) = (\Phi - F) \circ \Phi^{-1}(\beta) = h(\beta).$$ (2.348)

We then find that $\beta = \alpha + h(\beta)$. Using the Lagrange inversion theorem and setting $s = 1$ and $f = \Phi^{-1}$, we have

$$\Phi^{-1}(\beta) = \Phi^{-1}(\alpha) + \sum_{r=1}^{\infty} \frac{1}{r!} D_\alpha^{r-1} \left[(\Phi^{-1})' \left[(\Phi - F) \circ \Phi^{-1} \right]^r \right] (\alpha).$$ (2.349)

Noting that $[\Phi^{-1}(\alpha)]' = 1/[\Phi'(z)] = 1/\varphi(z)$, we have

$$x = z + \sum_{r=1}^{\infty} \frac{1}{r!} D_\alpha^{r-1} \left[(\Phi - F)^r / \varphi \circ \Phi^{-1} \right] [\Phi(z)].$$ (2.350)

Note that

$$\frac{d^{r-1}}{d\alpha^{r-1}} \left[a^r \cdot \varphi^{r-1} \right] = D_{(r-1)} a^r,$$ (2.351)

where

$$D_{(r)} = \left(D_z + \frac{\varphi'}{\varphi} \right) \left(D_z + 2\frac{\varphi'}{\varphi} \right) \cdots \left(D_z + r\frac{\varphi'}{\varphi} \right)$$ (2.352)

and $D_0 = 1$. Finally, we have the Cornish–Fisher expansion:

$$x = z + \sum_{r=1}^{\infty} \frac{1}{r!} D_{(r-1)} \left[a^r \right] (z), \quad a = (\Phi - F)/\varphi.$$ (2.353)

From the Edgeworth expansion in Section 2.14 we have the expansion for $a(z) = (\Phi(z) - F(z))/\varphi(z)$,

$$a(z) = \frac{\mu_3}{6\, n^{1/2}} \mathrm{He}_2(z) + \frac{(\mu_4 - 3)}{24\, n} \mathrm{He}_3(z) + \frac{\mu_3^2}{72\, n} \mathrm{He}_5(z) + o\left(\frac{1}{n} \right).$$ (2.354)

Then the Cornish–Fisher expansion is

$$x = z + a(z) + \frac{1}{2!}(D_z - z)a^2(z) + \frac{1}{3!}(D_z - z)(D_z - 2z)a^3(z) + \cdots. \quad (2.355)$$

Substituting $a(z)$ into this equation and only keeping the terms up to the order of $1/n$, we have

$$x = z + \frac{\mu_3}{6\,n^{1/2}}\mathrm{He}_2(z) + \frac{(\mu_4 - 3)}{24\,n}\mathrm{He}_3(z) + \frac{\mu_3^2}{72\,n}\mathrm{He}_5(z) + \frac{\mu_3^2}{72\,n}(D_z - z)\mathrm{He}_2^2(z). \quad (2.356)$$

Noting that $\mathrm{He}_5(z) + (D_z - z)\mathrm{He}_2^2(z) = -4z^3 + 10z$, we have

$$x = z + \frac{\mu_3}{6\,n^{1/2}}\mathrm{He}_2(z) + \frac{(\mu_4 - 3)}{24\,n}\mathrm{He}_3(z) - \frac{\mu_3^2}{36\,n}(2z^3 - 5z), \quad (2.357)$$

or explicitly, we have

$$x = z + \frac{\mu_3}{6\,n^{1/2}}(z^2 - 1) + \frac{(\mu_4 - 3)}{24\,n}(z^3 - 3z) - \frac{\mu_3^2}{36\,n}(2z^3 - 5z). \quad (2.358)$$

Let $n = 1$. We have the Cornish–Fisher expansion up to the first three terms:

$$x = z + \frac{\mu_3}{6}(z^2 - 1) + \frac{(\mu_4 - 3)}{24}(z^3 - 3z) - \frac{\mu_3^2}{36}(2z^3 - 5z). \quad (2.359)$$

2.16   Copula Functions

For any random variable x, we can define another random variable U in terms of its cdf $F(x)$, where $u = F(x)$. Note that $du = f(x)\,dx$, where $f(x)$ is the distribution function. We have $f_U(u) = 1$, $u \in [0, 1]$, namely u is a uniform random variable. Explicitly we have

$$F_U(u) = P[U < u] = P[F_X(X) < u] = P[X < F_X^{-1}(u)] = F_X(F_X^{-1}(u)) = u. \quad (2.360)$$

This shows that u is a uniform distribution in $[0, 1]$.

In general, for a multivariate distribution, $f(x_1, x_2, ..., x_n)$, its copula function is defined as

$$C(u_1, u_2, ..., u_n) = F(F_1^{-1}(u_1), F_2^{-1}(u_2), ..., F_n^{-1}(u_n)), \quad (2.361)$$

or

$$F(x_1, x_2, ..., x_n) = C(F_1(x_1), F_2(x_2), ..., F_n(x_n)). \quad (2.362)$$

It can also be interpreted as

$$
\begin{aligned}
C(u_1, u_2, ..., u_n) &= F(F_1^{-1}(u_1), F_2^{-1}(u_2), \cdots, F_n^{-1}(u_n)) \\
&= P\left[X_1 < F_1^{-1}(u_1), X_2 < F_2^{-1}(u_2), \cdots, X_n < F_n^{-1}(u_n)\right] \\
&= P\left[F_1(X_1) < u_1, F_2(X_2) < u_2, \cdots, F_n(X_n) < u_n\right] \\
&= P\left[U_1 < u_1, U_2 < u_2, \cdots, U_n < u_n\right].
\end{aligned}
\tag{2.363}
$$

Therefore $C(u_1, u_2, ..., u_n)$ is a cdf of $(u_1, u_2, ..., u_n)$. Its pdf is

$$
c(u_1, u_2, ..., u_n) = \frac{\partial^n}{\partial u_1 \partial u_2 \cdots \partial u_n} C(u_1, u_2, ..., u_n).
\tag{2.364}
$$

Note that

$$
\begin{aligned}
f(x_1, x_2, ..., x_n) &= \frac{\partial^n}{\partial x_1 \partial x_2 \cdots \partial x_n} F(x_1, x_2, ..., x_n) \\
&= \frac{\partial^n}{\partial u_1 \partial u_2 \cdots \partial u_n} C(F_1(x_1), F_2(x_2), ..., F_n(x_n)) f_1(x_1) f_2(x_2)...f_n(x_n) \\
&= c(F_1(x_1), F_2(x_2), ..., F_n(x_n)) f_1(x_1) f_2(x_2)...f_n(x_n).
\end{aligned}
\tag{2.365}
$$

Therefore the joint multivariate distribution function can be constructed from the marginal distributions and the pdf of the copula function. This shows that the density of the copula function measures the dependency of variables. The probability density function of the copula function is

$$
c(F_1(x_1), F_2(x_2), ..., F_n(x_n)) = \frac{f(x_1, x_2, ..., x_n)}{f_1(x_1) f_2(x_2)...f_n(x_n)}.
\tag{2.366}
$$

Let's look at some properties of the copula functions:

$$
\begin{aligned}
C(0, u_2) &= F(F_1^{-1}(0), F_2^{-1}(u_2)) = 0, \\
C(u_1, 0) &= F(F_1^{-1}(u_1), F_2^{-1}(0)) = 0, \\
C(1, u_2) &= F(F_1^{-1}(1), F_2^{-1}(u_2)) = F_2(F_2^{-1}(u_2)) = u_2, \\
C(u_1, 1) &= F(F_1^{-1}(u_1), F_2^{-1}(1)) = F_1(F_1^{-1}(u_1)) = u_1.
\end{aligned}
\tag{2.367}
$$

Let $X_1 = X_2$, then $F_1(x) = F_2(x)$.

$$
\begin{aligned}
C(u_1, u_2) &= P\left[U_1 < u_1, U_1 < u_2\right] \\
&= P\left[U_1 < \min(u_1, u_2)\right] \\
&= \min(u_1, u_2).
\end{aligned}
\tag{2.368}
$$

In a similar way, if $X_1 = X_2 = ... = X_n$, we have

$$
C(u_1, u_2, \cdots, u_n) = \min(u_1, u_2, \cdots, u_n).
\tag{2.369}
$$

Let $X_1 = -X_2$, then $F_1(x_1) = P[X_1 < x_1] = P[-X_2 < -x_2] = 1 - F_2(x_2)$, namely $U_1 + U_2 = 1$. We have

$$
\begin{aligned}
C(u_1, u_2) &= P[U_1 < u_1, U_2 < u_2] \\
&= P[U_1 < u_1, 1 - U_1 < u_2] \\
&= P[1 - u_2 < U_1 < u_1] \\
&= \max(u_1 + u_2 - 1, 0).
\end{aligned}
\tag{2.370}
$$

Let X_1, X_2 be independent, then U_1, U_2 are independent. We have

$$
\begin{aligned}
C(u_1, u_2) &= P[U_1 < u_1, U_2 < u_2] \\
&= P[U_1 < u_1]\, P[U_1 < u_1] \\
&= u_1 u_2.
\end{aligned}
\tag{2.371}
$$

In a similar way, if $X_1, X_2, ..., X_n$ are all independent of one another, we have

$$
C(u_1, u_2, \cdots u_n) = u_1 u_2 \cdots u_n.
\tag{2.372}
$$

Let $X_1 = X_2^3$. Then $F_{X^3}(X^3) = F_X(X)$, $U_1 = F_{X^3}(X^3) = F_X(X) = U_2$, and we have

$$
\begin{aligned}
C(u_1, u_2) &= P[U_1 < u_1, U_1 < u_2] \\
&= P[U_1 < \min(u_1, u_2)] \\
&= \min(u_1, u_2).
\end{aligned}
\tag{2.373}
$$

Therefore the copula function does not change (is invariant) under a monotonic transformation.

Let's define three functions as:

$$
\begin{aligned}
C^+(u_1, u_2, \cdots, u_n) &= \min(u_1, u_2, \cdots, u_n), \\
C^-(u_1, u_2, \cdots, u_n) &= \max(u_1 + u_2 + \cdots + u_n + 1 - n, 0), \\
C^\perp(u_1, u_2, \cdots, u_n) &= u_1 u_2 \cdots u_n.
\end{aligned}
\tag{2.374}
$$

With these definitions we find the following inequality is satisfied:

$$
C^+(u_1, u_2, \cdots, u_n) \le C^\perp(u_1, u_2, \cdots, u_n) \le C^+(u_1, u_2, \cdots, u_n).
\tag{2.375}
$$

In the following we will introduce some common copula functions.

2.16.1   Gaussian Copula

For the Gaussian distribution, the Gaussian copula does not have a closed form expression. The probability density function of the copula function can be obtained by using the expression of multivariate normal distribution and defining $\Sigma_d = \text{diag}(\Sigma) = \text{diag}(\sigma_1^2, \sigma_2^2, ..., \sigma_n^2)$:

$$
\begin{aligned}
c(u_1, u_2, ..., u_n) &= \frac{f(x_1, x_2, ..., x_n)}{f_1(x_1) f_2(x_2) ... f_n(x_n)} \\
&= \frac{(\det \Sigma_d)^{1/2}}{(\det \Sigma)^{1/2}} e^{-\frac{1}{2}(x-\mu)^T (\Sigma^{-1} - (\Sigma_d)^{-1})(x-\mu)}.
\end{aligned}
\tag{2.376}
$$

When the distribution of each component is a standard normal distribution, we have

$$
c(u_1, u_2, ..., u_n) = \frac{1}{(\det \Sigma)^{1/2}} e^{-\frac{1}{2} x^T (\Sigma^{-1} - 1) x}.
\tag{2.377}
$$

The bivariate Gaussian copula function is

$$
C(u_1, u_2) = \Phi\left(\Phi^{-1}(u_1), \Phi^{-1}(u_2), \rho\right),
\tag{2.378}
$$

and explicitly it is

$$
C(u_1, u_2) = \int_{-\infty}^{\Phi^{-1}(u_1)} \int_{-\infty}^{\Phi^{-1}(u_2)} \frac{1}{2\pi\sqrt{1-\rho^2}} e^{-\frac{x_1^2 + x_2^2 - 2\rho x_1 x_2}{2(1-\rho^2)}} \, dx_1 dx_2.
\tag{2.379}
$$

2.16.2 *t*-Copula

The multivariate *t*-distribution is defined as

$$
t = \frac{z}{\sqrt{x/k}},
\tag{2.380}
$$

where $z \sim N[0, \Sigma]$, $\Sigma = [n \times n]$ is a covariance matrix, $x \sim \chi^2[k]$, and z and x are independent. Using the expression of the multivariate *t*-distribution and the *t*-distribution, we have

$$
\begin{aligned}
c(u_1, u_2, ..., u_n) &= \frac{f(x_1, x_2, ..., x_n)}{f_1(x_1) f_2(x_2) ... f_n(x_n)} \\
&= (\det \Sigma)^{-1/2} \frac{\Gamma((n+k)/2)}{\Gamma(k/2)} \cdot \left[\frac{\Gamma(k/2)}{\Gamma((k+1)/2)}\right]^n \cdot \frac{\left(t^T \Sigma^{-1} t/k + 1\right)^{-(k+n)/2}}{\prod\limits_{i=1}^{n} \left(t_i^2/k + 1\right)^{-(k+1)/2}}.
\end{aligned}
\tag{2.381}
$$

For the bivariate *t*-distribution, the *t*-copula is

$$
C(u_1, u_2) = T_{2,k}\left(T_k^{-1}(u_1), T_k^{-1}(u_2), \rho\right),
\tag{2.382}
$$

and explicitly it is

$$
C(u_1, u_2) = \int_{-\infty}^{t_n^{-1}(u_1)} \int_{-\infty}^{t_n^{-1}(u_2)} \frac{1}{2\pi\sqrt{1-\rho^2}} \left[\frac{t_1^2 + t_2^2 - 2\rho t_1 t_2}{k(1-\rho^2)} + 1\right]^{-\frac{k+2}{2}} dt_1 dt_2.
\tag{2.383}
$$

2.16.3   Archimedean Copula

The Archimedean copula is generated by a function

$$\phi : [0,1] \to [0,\infty] \tag{2.384}$$

satisfying

$$\phi'(u) < 0, \quad \phi''(u) > 0, \quad \phi(1) = 0. \tag{2.385}$$

The associated copula is

$$C(u_1, u_2) = \phi^{[-1]}(\phi(u_1) + \phi(u_2)), \tag{2.386}$$

where $\phi^{[-1]}(t)$ is the pseudo-inverse of the function $\phi(u)$:

$$\phi^{[-1]}(t) = \begin{cases} \phi^{-1}(t) & 0 \le t \le \phi(0) \\ 0 & t > \phi(0). \end{cases} \tag{2.387}$$

As an example of the Archimedean copula, let's look at the Clayton family of copula functions generated by the following function:

$$\phi(u) = (u^{-\theta} - 1)/\theta, \quad \theta \in [-1, \infty]\backslash\{0\}, \tag{2.388}$$

$$\phi'(u) = -u^{-\theta-1}, \quad \phi''(u) = (\theta+1)\, u^{-\theta-2}. \tag{2.389}$$

Its inverse function is

$$\phi^{-1}(t) = (1 + \theta\,\phi)^{-1/\theta}. \tag{2.390}$$

Therefore the generated copula function is

$$C_\theta(u_1, u_2) = \left[\max\left(u_1^{-\theta} + u_2^{-\theta} - 1, 0\right) \right]^{-1/\theta}. \tag{2.391}$$

Taking various limits on the parameter θ, we have

$$\begin{aligned} C_{\theta=-1}(u_1, u_2) &= C^-(u_1, u_2), \\ C_{\theta\to 0}(u_1, u_2) &= C^{\perp}(u_1, u_2), \\ C_{\theta\to\infty}(u_1, u_2) &= C^+(u_1, u_2). \end{aligned} \tag{2.392}$$

Chapter 3

Important Matrix Relationships

The use of matrices is a convenient vehicle to formulate many data modeling techniques. The full understanding of underlying properties of matrices is key to understanding the formulation of many modeling techniques.

In this chapter we describe a variety of fundamental and advanced methodologies for matrix manipulation and techniques. Some of these topics are difficult to find in alternative treatises of this subject.

We have developed a suite of matrix operation functions in the DataMinerXL add-in for Microsoft Excel. Refer to Appendix B.17 for a list of the matrix operation functions in the DataMinerXL library.

3.1 Pseudo-Inverse of a Matrix

When we write a matrix as $A = [m \times n]$, we mean that matrix A has m rows and n columns. Consider a set of linear equations

$$Ax = b, \tag{3.1}$$

where $A = [m \times n]$, $x = [n \times 1]$, $b = [m \times 1]$. We have m equations and n unknown variables.

Let us consider the case $m < n$, where the number of equations is less than the number of unknown variables. In general, for this underdetermined case, there exists more than one solution vector x. Observing that $AA^T(AA^T)^{-1} = 1$ if AA^T is not singular, one solution is

$$x = A^T(AA^T)^{-1}b. \tag{3.2}$$

It can be shown that its norm is the minimum among all solutions. Considering the following minimization problem,

$$\text{minimize } \|x\|^2 \text{ subject to } Ax = b, \tag{3.3}$$

we construct the Lagrange multiplier (refer to Section 9.1)

$$z = \frac{1}{2}x^T x - \lambda^T (Ax - b). \tag{3.4}$$

We find the same result as above. Defining $A^+ = A^T(AA^T)^{-1}$, we have $AA^+ = 1$. It can be readily shown that A^+ satisfies the following four properties:

1. $AA^+A = A$.

2. $A^+AA^+ = A^+$.

3. AA^+ is symmetric.

4. A^+A is symmetric.

This is the so-called pseudo-inverse of matrix A.

If $m > n$, then there are more equations than the number of variables (overdetermined). This is the case for almost all data mining/machine learning problems. In general, there is no exact solution satisfying this set of equations. But we can find a "best fit" solution that best matches the overdetermined data with a whatever fitting objective function that represents the fitting error we would like to choose. A commonly used error function is the least squares measurement, which sums the squares of the deviation in the values of b only. A nice feature of this particular least squares error function is that one can take the derivative with respect to the unknowns, x, set it to zero, and derive a closed form solution of the exact best fit for the unknowns x:

$$x = (A^TA)^{-1}A^Tb. \tag{3.5}$$

Define $A^+ = (A^TA)^{-1}A^T$, we have $A^+A = 1$. It is easy to verify that A^+ satisfies the above-mentioned four properties.

In general, for any matrix A, there is a unique matrix A^+ satisfying these four requirements. "*matrix_pinv()*" computes the pseudo-inverse of a matrix (see Appendix B.17 for other matrix functions). Here are some examples:

$$\begin{bmatrix} 1 & 1 \\ 1 & 1 \end{bmatrix}^+ = \begin{bmatrix} 0.25 & 0.25 \\ 0.25 & 0.25 \end{bmatrix},$$

$$\begin{bmatrix} 1 & 2 \\ 3 & 4 \\ 5 & 6 \end{bmatrix}^+ = \begin{bmatrix} -1.3333 & -0.3333 & 0.6667 \\ 1.0833 & 0.3333 & -0.4167 \end{bmatrix},$$

$$\begin{bmatrix} 1 & 3 & 5 \\ 2 & 4 & 6 \end{bmatrix}^+ = \begin{bmatrix} -1.3333 & 1.0833 \\ -0.3333 & 0.3333 \\ 0.6667 & -0.4167 \end{bmatrix}.$$

3.2 A Lemma of Matrix Inversion

We introduce a lemma around matrix inversion:

$$(1 + AB)^{-1} = 1 - A(1 + BA)^{-1}B, \tag{3.6}$$

where the dimensions of matrices are: $A = [n \times m]$, $B = [m \times n]$. It can easily be directly verified by multiplication. One way to intuitively see how to come up with this equation is to expand the matrix on the left-hand side of the equation in Taylor series symbolically,

$$(1 + AB)^{-1} = 1 - AB + (AB)^2 - \cdots = 1 - A\Big(1 - BA + (BA)^2 + \cdots\Big)B$$

$$= 1 - A(1 + BA)^{-1}B.$$

$$(3.7)$$

By using this lemma it is straightforward to derive the following more general lemma of matrix inversion:

$$(A + BCD)^{-1} = A^{-1} - A^{-1}B(DA^{-1}B + C^{-1})^{-1}DA^{-1}, \qquad (3.8)$$

where the dimensions of matrices are: $A = [n \times n]$, $B = [n \times m]$, $C = [m \times m]$, $D = [m \times n]$. This formula can also be explicitly verified by multiplication.

Let's consider special cases. Let $A = [n \times n]$, $B = [n \times m]$, and $C = [m \times n]$. We have:

$$(A + BC)^{-1} = A^{-1} - A^{-1}B(1 + CA^{-1}B)^{-1}CA^{-1} \qquad (3.9)$$

Let A be a square matrix and u and v be two column vectors, namely, $A = [n \times n]$, $u = [n \times 1]$, and $v = [n \times 1]$. We have

$$(A + uv^T)^{-1} = A^{-1} - \frac{A^{-1}uv^TA^{-1}}{1 + v^TA^{-1}u}. \qquad (3.10)$$

There is an interesting application of this lemma for solving least squared regression when we obtain incremental data observations and would like to update the model. We will discuss this in Section 4.2.4 on incremental regression.

We can establish and prove a relationship of determinants between the updated matrix and original matrix:

$$\det(A + uv^T) = \det A \cdot (1 + v^TA^{-1}u). \qquad (3.11)$$

To prove this relationship first consider a special case where A is a diagonal matrix. In this case, explicitly working out the determinant, we find

$$\det(A + uv^T) = \prod_{i=1}^{n} a_i \cdot \Big(1 + \sum_{i=1}^{n} u_i v_i / a_i\Big), \qquad (3.12)$$

where $a_i, i = 1, 2, ..., n$, are diagonal elements of the matrix A. In general, however, A is not a diagonal matrix. By using singular value decomposition (SVD), discussed in Section 3.7, and writing $A = UWV^T$ where W is a diagonal matrix, along with the above diagonal case, we have

$$
\begin{aligned}
\det(A + uv^T) &= \det(UWV^T + uv^T) \\
&= \det(U)\det(V)\det\left(W + (U^T u)(V^T v)^T\right) \\
&= \det(U)\det(V)\det(W)\left(1 + (V^T v)^T W^{-1}(U^T u)\right) \\
&= \det(A)\left(1 + v^T A^{-1} u\right).
\end{aligned}
\tag{3.13}
$$

3.3   Identity for a Matrix Determinant

Noting that the determinant of a matrix can be expressed in terms of its cofactors, and the matrix inverse can also be expressed in terms of the matrix's cofactors, we can establish the following identity:

$$
\frac{1}{\det A}\frac{\partial \det A}{\partial x} = \sum_{i,j} A_{ij}^{-1}\frac{\partial A_{ji}}{\partial x} = Tr\left(A^{-1}\frac{\partial A}{\partial x}\right).
\tag{3.14}
$$

3.4   Inversion of Partitioned Matrix

Let A be a square matrix with its partition as

$$
A = \begin{bmatrix} A_{11} & A_{12} \\ A_{21} & A_{22} \end{bmatrix},
\tag{3.15}
$$

where A_{11} and A_{22} are square matrices. By the Gauss–Jordan elimination, its inversion is

$$
A^{-1} = \begin{bmatrix} A_{11}^{-1}\left(1 + A_{12}F_2 A_{21}A_{11}^{-1}\right) & -A_{11}^{-1}A_{12}F_2 \\ -F_2 A_{21}A_{11}^{-1} & F_2 \end{bmatrix},
\tag{3.16}
$$

where $F_2 = \left(A_{22} - A_{21}A_{11}^{-1}A_{12}\right)^{-1}$. By symmetry we also have

$$
A^{-1} = \begin{bmatrix} F_1 & -F_1 A_{12}A_{22}^{-1} \\ -A_{22}^{-1}A_{21}F_1 & A_{22}^{-1}\left(1 + A_{21}F_1 A_{12}A_{22}^{-1}\right) \end{bmatrix},
\tag{3.17}
$$

where $F_1 = \left(A_{11} - A_{12}A_{22}^{-1}A_{21}\right)^{-1}$. Alternatively, both of these results can be verified by direct matrix multiplication.

3.5 Determinant of Partitioned Matrix

Let A be a square matrix with its partition as

$$A = \begin{bmatrix} A_{11} & A_{12} \\ A_{21} & A_{22} \end{bmatrix}, \tag{3.18}$$

where A_{11} and A_{22} are square matrices. By using the Gauss–Jordan elimination, we have

$$\det \begin{bmatrix} A_{11} & A_{12} \\ A_{21} & A_{22} \end{bmatrix} = \det \begin{bmatrix} A_{11} & A_{12} \\ 0 & A_{22} - A_{21} A_{11}^{-1} A_{12} \end{bmatrix}. \tag{3.19}$$

Therefore we have

$$\det A = \det A_{11} \cdot \det \left(A_{22} - A_{21} A_{11}^{-1} A_{12} \right). \tag{3.20}$$

One interesting result on the determinant of the inverse matrix is

$$\det A^{-1} = (\det A_{11})^{-1} \cdot \det \left(A^{-1} \right)_{22}. \tag{3.21}$$

By symmetry we have the following equations:

$$\det A = \det A_{22} \cdot \det \left(A_{11} - A_{12} A_{22}^{-1} A_{21} \right) \tag{3.22}$$

and

$$\det A^{-1} = (\det A_{22})^{-1} \cdot \det \left(A^{-1} \right)_{11}. \tag{3.23}$$

3.6 Matrix Sweep and Partial Correlation

Let $A = [m \times n]$ be a general matrix (not necessarily square) with a partition denoted as

$$A = \begin{bmatrix} R & S \\ T & U \end{bmatrix}, \tag{3.24}$$

where R is a square matrix. By using the Gauss–Jordan elimination, we can transform the matrix R into an identity matrix, i.e.,

$$\underset{m \times m}{\begin{bmatrix} R^{-1} & 0 \\ -TR^{-1} & 1 \end{bmatrix}} \cdot \underset{m \times n}{\begin{bmatrix} R & S \\ T & U \end{bmatrix}} = \underset{m \times n}{\begin{bmatrix} 1 & R^{-1}S \\ 0 & U - TR^{-1}S \end{bmatrix}}. \tag{3.25}$$

We define the sweep of matrix of A with respect to R as

$$\text{sweep}(A,\, R) = \begin{bmatrix} R^{-1} & R^{-1}S \\ -TR^{-1} & U - TR^{-1}S \end{bmatrix}. \tag{3.26}$$

It can be proven that the sweep operation has the property

$$\text{sweep}(\text{sweep}(A,\, R),\, R) = A, \tag{3.27}$$

and a sequential property

$$\text{sweep}(\text{sweep}(A,\, R_1),\, R_2) = \text{sweep}(A,\, (R_1, R_2)). \tag{3.28}$$

There is no order of pivot elements. That is,

$$\text{sweep}(A,\, (R_1, R_2)) = \text{sweep}(A,\, (R_2, R_1)). \tag{3.29}$$

One interesting application of the sweep of a matrix is in linear regression. Let A be the covariance matrix:

$$A = \begin{bmatrix} X^T X & X^T Y \\ Y^T X & Y^T Y \end{bmatrix}, \tag{3.30}$$

where X and Y are centered (zero means).

If X is partitioned as $X = \begin{bmatrix} X_1 & X_2 \end{bmatrix}$, then the matrix A becomes

$$A = \begin{bmatrix} X_1^T X_1 & X_1^T X_2 & X_1^T Y \\ X_2^T X_1 & X_2^T X_2 & X_2^T Y \\ Y^T X_1 & Y^T X_2 & Y^T Y \end{bmatrix}, \tag{3.31}$$

and its sweep with respect to X_1 is

$$\text{sweep}(A,\, X_1) = \begin{bmatrix} (X_1^T X_1)^{-1} & (X_1^T X_1)^{-1} X_1^T X_2 & (X_1^T X_1)^{-1} X_1^T Y \\ -X_2^T X_1 (X_1^T X_1)^{-1} & X_{2*}^T X_{2*} & X_{2*}^T Y_* \\ -Y^T X_1 (X_1^T X_1)^{-1} & Y_*^T X_{2*} & Y_*^T Y_* \end{bmatrix} \tag{3.32}$$

where $X_{2*} = M_1 X_2$, $Y_* = M_1 Y$, $M_1 = 1 - X_1(X_1^T X_1)^{-1} X_1^T$. The matrix M_1 has the property $M_1^2 = M_1$ (M_1 is idempotent). Now the partial correlation between X_2 and Y can be read from the sweep matrix, $\text{sweep}(A, X_1)$:

$$r_{*yx_2}^2 = \frac{\left(x_{2*}^T y_*\right)^2}{(y_*^T y_*) \cdot \left(x_{2*}^T x_{2*}\right)}. \tag{3.33}$$

It is extremely convenient to use the sweep matrix in iterative variable selection in linear regression:

$$t_{x_2}^2 = \left(\frac{r_{*yx_2}^2}{1 - r_{*yx_2}^2}\right) \cdot (n - k - 1). \tag{3.34}$$

3.7   Singular Value Decomposition (SVD)

Let $A = [m \times n]$ be any matrix. Note that $AA^T = [m \times m]$ and $A^T A = [n \times n]$ are both Hermitian matrices and also have the same eigenvalues. We have

$$AA^T u_i = \lambda_i u_i, \tag{3.35}$$

and $u_i^T u_j = \delta_{ij}$, $(i, j = 1, 2, ..., m)$. Also

$$A^T A v_i = \lambda_i v_i, \tag{3.36}$$

and $v_i^T v_j = \delta_{ij}$, $(i, j = 1, 2, ..., n)$. Since $\mathrm{rank}(A^T A) = \mathrm{rank}(AA^T) = \mathrm{rank}(A) \leq \min(m, n)$, some of the eigenvalues may be zero, but the eigenvectors are not zero. Note that

$$AA^T (A v_i) = \lambda_i (A v_i), \tag{3.37}$$

so $A v_i$ is an eigenvector of AA^T with eigenvalue λ_i. Therefore $A v_i$ and one of the us, labeled as u_i without loss of generality, are the same vector up to a normalization factor. By choosing the sign of vectors of u_i and v_i, we have

$$A v_i = w_i u_i \tag{3.38}$$

and $w_i \geq 0$, where $w_i = \sqrt{\lambda_i}$. We have

$$u_i^T A v_j = w_i \delta_{ij}. \tag{3.39}$$

Constructing unitary matrices U and V in terms of u_i and v_i as column vectors, respectively, and a diagonal matrix W using the w_is, we can rewrite this as $U^T A V = W$, or

$$\begin{array}{ccccc} A & = & U & W & V^T \\ m \times n & & m \times m & m \times n & n \times n \end{array} \tag{3.40}$$

In this form the dimension of W is the same as A. This can be rewritten by appending zero row vectors and column vectors as

$$\begin{array}{ccccc} A & = & U & W & V^T. \\ m \times n & & m \times n & n \times n & n \times n \end{array} \tag{3.41}$$

In this form the dimension of U is the same as A. Actually, if r is the number of non-zero eigenvalues, then A can be written as

$$\begin{array}{ccccc} A & = & U & W & V^T. \\ m \times n & & m \times r & r \times r & r \times n \end{array} \tag{3.42}$$

This is the singular value decomposition (SVD) for any matrix A. This decomposition holds for all m and n and is unique up to permutation of columns of U, V, and W. It can be written as[1]

$$A = \sum_l w_l u_l v_l^T, \tag{3.43}$$

where w_l is the diagonal element of W, and u_l and v_l are the column vectors of the matrices U and V, respectively.

We have implemented a function "*matrix_svd()*" in DatatMinerXL, which decomposes any matrix in terms of SVD. See Appendix B.17 for other matrix functions in the DataMinerXL library. Here we give two examples of SVD:

$$\begin{bmatrix} 1 & 2 \\ 3 & 4 \\ 5 & 6 \end{bmatrix} = \begin{bmatrix} 0.2298 & 0.8835 \\ 0.5247 & 0.2408 \\ 0.8196 & -0.4019 \end{bmatrix} \times \begin{bmatrix} 9.5255 & 0 \\ 0 & 0.5143 \end{bmatrix} \times \begin{bmatrix} 0.6196 & 0.7849 \\ -0.7849 & 0.6196 \end{bmatrix}$$

and

$$\begin{bmatrix} 1 & 3 & 5 \\ 2 & 4 & 6 \end{bmatrix} = \begin{bmatrix} -0.6196 & -0.7849 & 0 \\ -0.7849 & 0.6196 & 0 \end{bmatrix} \times \begin{bmatrix} 9.5255 & 0 & 0 \\ 0 & 0.5143 & 0 \\ 0 & 0 & 0 \end{bmatrix}$$
$$\times \begin{bmatrix} -0.2298 & -0.5247 & -0.8196 \\ 0.8835 & 0.2408 & -0.4019 \\ 0.4082 & -0.8165 & 0.4082 \end{bmatrix}.$$

Without loss of generality, assume that $m \geq n$,

$$A = UWV^T. \tag{3.44}$$

Here A and W have the same dimension. We have

$$AA^T = UWW^T U^T \tag{3.45}$$

and

$$A^T A = VW^T WV^T. \tag{3.46}$$

Here

$$WW^T = \text{diag}\left(\lambda_1^2, \cdots, \lambda_n^2, 0\right), \qquad W^T W = \text{diag}\left(\lambda_1^2, \cdots, \lambda_n^2\right). \tag{3.47}$$

If R_1 and R_2 are non-singular square matrices, we have the following property for any matrix A:

$$\text{rank}(R_1 A) = \text{rank}(AR_2) = \text{rank}(A). \tag{3.48}$$

---

[1] $AB^T = \sum_k a_k b_k^T$ and $ABC^T = \sum_{kl} a_k B_{kl} c_l^T$, where a_k, b_k, and c_k are the column vectors of matrices A, B, and C, respectively. This can be proved directly by matrix multiplication. As a special case, if W is a diagonal matrix with diagonal element w_l, we have $AWB^T = \sum_l w_l a_l b_l^T$.

From this property, the ranks for A, A^T, AA^T, A^TA are all the same. We have

$$\det(AA^T + 1) = \prod_{i=1}^{n} (1 + \lambda_i^2), \quad \text{and}$$

$$\det(A^TA + 1) = \prod_{i=1}^{n} (1 + \lambda_i^2). \tag{3.49}$$

Therefore we have

$$\det(AA^T + 1) = \det(A^TA + 1). \tag{3.50}$$

The pseudo-inverse of matrix A is

$$A^+ = VW^{-1}U^T, \tag{3.51}$$

where the diagonal elements of W^{-1} are assigned to be zero if the corresponding diagonal element of W is zero. It can be proven that the four requirements of the pseudo-inverse of a matrix shown in last section are satisfied.

If A is a normal matrix, namely $AA^T = A^TA$, we have that u_i and v_i are the same up to a sign. Therefore each of the columns of the matrices U and V are the same up to a sign. If A is a normal and positive definite matrix, then $U = V$, and the SVD is equivalent to a diagonalization of the matrix A. Consider an example: $A = \text{diag}(2, -3)$. Its SVD is

$$\underset{A}{\begin{bmatrix} 2 & 0 \\ 0 & -3 \end{bmatrix}} = \underset{U}{\begin{bmatrix} 0 & -1 \\ -1 & 0 \end{bmatrix}} \cdot \underset{W}{\begin{bmatrix} 3 & 0 \\ 0 & 2 \end{bmatrix}} \cdot \underset{V^T}{\begin{bmatrix} 0 & 1 \\ -1 & 0 \end{bmatrix}}. \tag{3.52}$$

Note that $U \neq V$ because A is not positive definite even though it is a normal matrix. As a special case, if A is symmetric, then it is a normal matrix and can be diagonalizd, but its eigenvalues may be negative. Only if the matrix is symmetric and positive definite will all the eigenvalues be positive, and the matrix diagonalization will be the same as the singular value decomposition.

3.8 Diagonalization of a Matrix

In this section we will discuss a very general theorem about a normal matrix. A matrix is normal if $AA^H = A^HA$, where $A^H = (A^T)^*$ is the conjugate transpose, called the Hermitian conjugate of matrix A. A matrix is unitary if its inverse equals its Hermitian conjugate: $Q^HQ = QQ^H = I$.

Theorem 3.1 (diagonalization theorem): *A matrix A is normal if and only if there exists a unitary matrix Q, satisfying the condition*

$$Q^HAQ = D, \tag{3.53}$$

and D is a diagonal matrix.

In order to prove this theorem we need to introduce the following related propositions.

Proposition 3.1 (the Householder matrix): *For a given vector, there exists a Householder matrix to transform the vector in the direction of the first axis.*

Proof 3.1 *The conclusion is very obvious since in the vector space you can do a transformation to rotate the vector into the first axis. For any given vector u, we can construct a Householder matrix P as*

$$P = 1 - 2\frac{u\,u^H}{u^H u}. \tag{3.54}$$

Note that $P^H = P$ and $P^H P = 1$, so P is both Hermitian and a unitary matrix. For any vector x, we can find a vector u such that Px is in the first axis:

$$P x = \lambda e_1, \tag{3.55}$$

where $e_1 = (1, 0, \cdots, 0)^T$. Namely

$$\left(1 - 2\frac{u\,u^H}{u^H u}\right) x = \lambda e_1. \tag{3.56}$$

We have $|\lambda|^2 = x^H x$. By choosing λ appropriately we have

$$u = x - \lambda e_1. \tag{3.57}$$

Proposition 3.2 (the QR factorization theorem): *Any matrix A can be expressed in the form*

$$A = Q\,R \tag{3.58}$$

where $A = [m \times n]$, $Q = [m \times m]$, and $R = [m \times n]$ and Q is a unitary matrix and R is an upper triangular matrix.

Proof 3.2 *Considering the vector formed by the first column of matrix A we can construct a Householder matrix Q_1 to transform this column vector into a vector with the first entry nonzero and all the others zero. Considering now the second column vector in A without the first row we construct another such Householder matrix Q_2. Continuing we can construct such a series of matrices Q_i so that the product of the Q matrices, appropriately dimensionally expanded, will produce an upper triangle matrix R. The product of the Q's is unitary, so $Q^T Q = I$, giving $A = Q^T R$. We can relabel Q^T as Q.*

Proposition 3.3: *If $A = [n \times n]$, $B = [p \times p]$, $X = [n \times p]$ and*

$$AX = XB \tag{3.59}$$

and $p \leq n$ and $\operatorname{rank}(X) = p$, then there exists a unitary matrix Q such that

$$Q^H AQ = T = \begin{bmatrix} T_{11} & T_{12} \\ 0 & T_{22} \end{bmatrix} . \begin{matrix} p \\ n-p \end{matrix}$$
$$\begin{matrix} p & n-p \end{matrix}$$

(3.60)

Proof 3.3 *From the factorization theorem we have*

$$X = Q \begin{bmatrix} R_1 \\ 0 \end{bmatrix}$$

(3.61)

where R_1 is a $[p \times p]$ matrix. If $AX = XB$ then we have

$$Q^H AQ \begin{bmatrix} R_1 \\ 0 \end{bmatrix} = \begin{bmatrix} R_1 B \\ 0 \end{bmatrix} .$$

(3.62)

We can see the left lower block of the matrix $Q^H AQ$ is zero.

Proposition 3.4 (Schur's decomposition): *For any matrix A, there exists a unitary matrix Q such that*

$$Q^H AQ = T = D + N,$$

(3.63)

where $D = \operatorname{diag}(\lambda_1, \lambda_2, \cdots, \lambda_n)$ and N is a strictly upper triangular matrix. λ_i $(i = 1, 2, \cdots, n)$ are the eigenvalues of the matrix A.

Proof 3.4 *Let $Ax = \lambda x$. According to Proposition 3.3 there exists a unitary matrix U such that*

$$U^H AU = T = \begin{bmatrix} \lambda & \omega^H \\ 0 & C \end{bmatrix} . \begin{matrix} 1 \\ n-1 \end{matrix}$$
$$\begin{matrix} 1 & n-1 \end{matrix}$$

(3.64)

By induction, if it is true for $n - 1$, then C can be written as

$$V^H CV = \hat{V},$$

(3.65)

where $\hat{V}$ is an upper triangular matrix. Therefore we have

$$\begin{bmatrix} \lambda & \omega^H \\ 0 & C \end{bmatrix} = \begin{bmatrix} 1 & 0 \\ 0 & V \end{bmatrix} . \begin{bmatrix} \lambda & \omega^H V \\ 0 & \hat{V} \end{bmatrix} . \begin{bmatrix} 1 & 0 \\ 0 & V^H \end{bmatrix} .$$

(3.66)

Let $Q = U \cdot \operatorname{diag}(1, V)$. We have

$$Q^H AQ = \begin{bmatrix} \lambda & \omega^H V \\ 0 & \hat{V} \end{bmatrix}$$

(3.67)

and thus an upper triangular matrix.

Proposition 3.5: *If a triangular matrix is normal, then it is a diagonal matrix.*

Proof 3.5 *The proof is straightforward by working out the matrix multiplication explicitly.*

After introduction of the above five propositions now we are ready to prove the theorem about a normal matrix.

$$Q^H A Q = D \quad \Rightarrow \quad A A^H = A^H A. \tag{3.68}$$

If $Q^H A Q = D$, then $A = Q D Q^H$ and $A^H = Q D^H Q^H$. We have

$$A A^H = Q D D^H Q^H \tag{3.69}$$

and

$$A^H A = Q D^H D Q^H. \tag{3.70}$$

Since D is diagonal we have

$$A A^H = A^H A. \tag{3.71}$$

So A is normal.

$$A A^H = A^H A \quad \Rightarrow \quad Q^H A Q = D. \tag{3.72}$$

According to the Schur's decomposition we have $Q^H A Q = T$, where T is an upper triangular matrix. If A is normal then T is normal. According to Proposition 3.5, T is diagonal.

Alternatively, the diagonalization theorem can be proved by constructing a Hermitian matrix. First we prove a proposition about Hermitian matrix:

Proposition 3.6: *Any Hermitian matrix can be diagonalized.*

Proof 3.6 *Let $A = [n \times n]$ be a square and Hermitian matrix. We can find n eigenvectors as*

$$A u_i = \lambda_i u_i \quad (i = 1, 2, ..., n). \tag{3.73}$$

Note that

$$u_i^H A u_j = \lambda_j u_i^H u_j = \lambda_i^* u_i^H u_j, \tag{3.74}$$

its eigenvalues are real and $u_i^H u_j = \delta_{ij}$. By stacking eigenvectors, we have

$$A [u_1, u_2, ..., u_n] = [u_1, u_2, ..., u_n] \cdot \mathrm{diag}\,(\lambda_1, \lambda_2, \cdots, \lambda_n). \tag{3.75}$$

Therefore we have a unitary matrix $U = [u_1, u_2, ..., u_n]$ such that $AU = U\Lambda$ or

$$U^H A U = \Lambda. \tag{3.76}$$

This proves the proposition.

Let $A = [n \times n]$ be a normal matrix. We have $AA^H = A^H A$. These two matrices have the same eigenvectors:

$$AA^H u_i = \lambda_i u_i \tag{3.77}$$

and

$$A^H A u_i = \lambda_i u_i, \quad (i = 1, 2, ..., n), \tag{3.78}$$

where $u_i^H u_j = \delta_{ij}$. Note that $AA^H(A u_i) = \lambda_i(A u_i)$, $A u_i$ is also an unnormalized eigenvector of AA^H with the same eigenvalue. We have

$$A u_i = d_i u_i. \tag{3.79}$$

Stacking eigenvectors into a matrix U and constructing a diagonal matrix

$$D = \mathrm{diag}(d_1, d_2, ..., d_n), \tag{3.80}$$

we have

$$U^H A U = D. \tag{3.81}$$

We conclude that a normal matrix can be diagonalized.

3.9 Spectral Decomposition of a Positive Semi-Definite Matrix

Let A be a symmetric positive semi-definite matrix, we have n eigenvalues and corresponding eigenvectors, λ_i and p_i,

$$A p_i = \lambda_i p_i, \quad i = 1, 2, \cdots, n, \tag{3.82}$$

and $p_i^T p_j = \delta_{ij}$. Define a matrix $U = [p_1, p_2, \cdots, p_n]$, whose columns are the eigenvectors, and a diagonal matrix composed of the eigenvalues, $\Lambda = \mathrm{diag}(\lambda_1, \lambda_2, \cdots, \lambda_n)$. We have $U^T U = UU^T = 1$. Therefore

$$A = U\Lambda U^T = \sum_{i=1}^{n} \lambda_i p_i p_i^T. \tag{3.83}$$

This is called the spectral decomposition of a positive semi-definite matrix. If we let $V = U\Lambda^{1/2}$, we have

$$A = VV^T. \tag{3.84}$$

If A is a symmetric idempotent matrix ($AA = A$ and $A^T = A$), then its eigenvalues are either 1 or 0. If we let J be the number of 1s of its eigenvalues, we have

$$J = \mathrm{rank}(A) = \mathrm{Tr}(A). \tag{3.85}$$

Let's give an example of the spectral decomposition for a 2 by 2 correlation matrix

$$A = \begin{bmatrix} 1 & \rho \\ \rho & 1 \end{bmatrix}. \tag{3.86}$$

The two eigenvalues are $\lambda_{1,2} = 1 \pm \rho$ and two corresponding eigenvectors are

$$p_1 = \frac{1}{\sqrt{2}} \begin{bmatrix} 1 \\ 1 \end{bmatrix}, \quad p_2 = \frac{1}{\sqrt{2}} \begin{bmatrix} 1 \\ -1 \end{bmatrix}. \tag{3.87}$$

The matrices U and V are

$$U = \frac{1}{\sqrt{2}} \begin{bmatrix} 1 & 1 \\ 1 & -1 \end{bmatrix}, \tag{3.88}$$

$$V = \frac{1}{\sqrt{2}} \begin{bmatrix} \sqrt{1+\rho} & \sqrt{1-\rho} \\ \sqrt{1+\rho} & -\sqrt{1-\rho} \end{bmatrix}. \tag{3.89}$$

The spectral decomposition is

$$\begin{bmatrix} \rho & 1 \\ 1 & \rho \end{bmatrix} = \frac{1}{\sqrt{2}} \begin{bmatrix} 1 & 1 \\ 1 & -1 \end{bmatrix} \cdot \begin{bmatrix} 1+\rho & 0 \\ 0 & 1-\rho \end{bmatrix} \cdot \frac{1}{\sqrt{2}} \begin{bmatrix} 1 & 1 \\ 1 & -1 \end{bmatrix}. \tag{3.90}$$

The matrix is the multiplication of its squared root matrix and transpose matrix,

$$\begin{bmatrix} \rho & 1 \\ 1 & \rho \end{bmatrix} = \frac{1}{\sqrt{2}} \begin{bmatrix} \sqrt{1+\rho} & \sqrt{1-\rho} \\ \sqrt{1+\rho} & -\sqrt{1-\rho} \end{bmatrix} \cdot \frac{1}{\sqrt{2}} \begin{bmatrix} \sqrt{1+\rho} & \sqrt{1+\rho} \\ \sqrt{1-\rho} & -\sqrt{1-\rho} \end{bmatrix}. \tag{3.91}$$

There are multiple ways to express the matrix in terms of its squared root matrix. The Cholesky decomposition, discussed in Section 3.12, is another example.

3.10 Normalization in Vector Space

Let x_i $(i = 1, 2, \cdots, n)$ be n independent vectors in a vector space. The dimension of the underlying vector space could be larger than n. If these n vectors are linearly independent then we can find a set of n vectors, t_i $(i = 1, 2, \cdots, n)$, that are the linear combination of x_i such that $t_i^T t_j = \delta_{ij}$ $(i, j = 1, 2, \cdots n)$. Let $(t_1, t_2, \cdots, t_n) = (x_1, x_2, \cdots, x_n)A$, or $T = XA$, where A is an $n \times n$ matrix. We have $T^T T = A^T(X^T X)A = I$. Therefore we have $AA^T = (X^T X)^{-1}$. Since $X^T X$ is a positive definite matrix, according to the spectral decomposition we have $X^T X = U\Lambda U^T$. The inverse of the cross product is

$$(X^T X)^{-1} = U\Lambda^{-1}U^T = U\Lambda^{-1/2}\left(U\Lambda^{-1/2}\right)^T, \tag{3.92}$$

and we have

$$A = U \Lambda^{-1/2}. \tag{3.93}$$

3.11 Conjugate Decomposition of a Symmetric Definite Matrix

Let A be an $n \times n$ positive definite matrix. Then there exist n vectors p_i $(i = 1, 2, \cdots, n)$ such that

$$p_i^T A p_j = \delta_{ij}, \quad i, j = 1, 2, \cdots n. \tag{3.94}$$

The vectors p_i $(i = 1, 2, \cdots, n)$ are the conjugate vectors with respect to the matrix A. By the spectral decomposition of matrix A, we can rewrite

$$
\begin{aligned}
p_i^T A p_j &= p_i^T \left(U \Lambda U^T \right) p_j = p_i^T \left(\Lambda^{1/2} U^T \right)^T \left(\Lambda^{1/2} U^T \right) p_j \\
&= \left(\Lambda^{1/2} U^T p_i \right)^T \left(\Lambda^{1/2} U^T p_j \right).
\end{aligned} \tag{3.95}
$$

Let $\Lambda^{1/2} U^T p_i = e_i$, where $e_i^T e_j = \delta_{ij}$. We then have

$$p_i = U \Lambda^{-1/2} e_i. \tag{3.96}$$

3.12 Cholesky Decomposition

In this section we describe how to simulate a set of multivariate normal random variables with the given covariance matrix Σ. Let $Y = AX$ and $\text{cov}(X) = I$. We have $\text{cov}(Y) = A \text{cov}(X) A^T = A A^T$. Therefore the problem is to find a matrix A such that $\Sigma = A A^T$. If Σ is positive definite then there is a solution. Let's consider an example with three variables. Intuitively, we may construct the vectors from independent normal random variables like

$$
\begin{aligned}
y_1 &= a_{11} x_1 \\
y_2 &= a_{21} x_1 + a_{22} x_2 \\
y_3 &= a_{31} x_1 + a_{32} x_2 + a_{33} x_3
\end{aligned} \tag{3.97}
$$

or

$$A = \begin{bmatrix} a_{11} & 0 & 0 \\ a_{21} & a_{22} & 0 \\ a_{31} & a_{32} & a_{33} \end{bmatrix}. \tag{3.98}$$

Therefore we have

$$
\begin{bmatrix} s_{11} & s_{12} & s_{13} \\ s_{21} & s_{22} & s_{23} \\ s_{31} & s_{32} & s_{33} \end{bmatrix} = \begin{bmatrix} a_{11} & 0 & 0 \\ a_{21} & a_{22} & 0 \\ a_{31} & a_{32} & a_{33} \end{bmatrix} \cdot \begin{bmatrix} a_{11} & a_{21} & a_{31} \\ 0 & a_{22} & a_{32} \\ 0 & 0 & a_{33} \end{bmatrix}, \tag{3.99}
$$

or explicitly

$$
\begin{bmatrix} s_{11} & s_{12} & s_{13} \\ s_{21} & s_{22} & s_{23} \\ s_{31} & s_{32} & s_{33} \end{bmatrix} = \begin{bmatrix} a_{11}^2 & a_{11}a_{21} & a_{11}a_{31} \\ a_{11}a_{21} & a_{21}^2 + a_{22}^2 & a_{31}a_{21} + a_{32}a_{22} \\ a_{11}a_{31} & a_{31}a_{21} + a_{32}a_{22} & a_{31}^2 + a_{32}^2 + a_{33}^2 \end{bmatrix}. \tag{3.100}
$$

Since the matrix is symmetric, we only need to look at the low triangle. The solution is

1. $a_{11} = \sqrt{s_{11}}$

2. $a_{21} = \frac{s_{21}}{a_{11}}$

3. $a_{22} = \sqrt{s_{22} - a_{21}^2}$

4. $a_{31} = \frac{s_{31}}{a_{11}}$

5. $a_{32} = \frac{1}{a_{22}}(s_{32} - a_{31}\,a_{21})$

6. $a_{33} = \sqrt{s_{33} - a_{31}^2 - a_{32}^2}$.

The order of the evaluation is shown in the following matrix:

$$
\begin{bmatrix} 1 & & \\ 2 & 3 & \\ 4 & 5 & 6 \end{bmatrix}. \tag{3.101}
$$

In general, the recursive equations are

$$
a_{ii} = \left(s_{ii} - \sum_{k=1}^{i-1} a_{ik}^2 \right)^{1/2},
$$

$$
a_{ij} = \frac{1}{a_{jj}} \left(s_{ij} - \sum_{k=1}^{j-1} a_{ik}a_{jk} \right)^{1/2}, \quad j = 1, 2, \cdots, i-1. \tag{3.102}
$$

The order of evaluation is row by row for the lower triangle.

As an example, the Cholesky decomposition for a 2 by 2 covariance matrix is

$$
\begin{bmatrix} \sigma_{11} & \sigma_{12} \\ \sigma_{21} & \sigma_{22} \end{bmatrix} = \begin{bmatrix} \sigma_1 & 0 \\ \rho\sigma_2 & \sigma_2\sqrt{1-\rho^2} \end{bmatrix} \cdot \begin{bmatrix} \sigma_1 & \rho\sigma_2 \\ 0 & \sigma_2\sqrt{1-\rho^2} \end{bmatrix}. \tag{3.103}
$$

For a 3 by 3 correlation matrix

$$\rho = \begin{bmatrix} 1 & \rho_{12} & \rho_{13} \\ \rho_{12} & 1 & \rho_{23} \\ \rho_{13} & \rho_{23} & 1 \end{bmatrix}, \tag{3.104}$$

the Cholesky decomposition is

$$A = \begin{bmatrix} 1 & 0 & 0 \\ \rho_{12} & \sqrt{1-\rho_{12}^2} & 0 \\ \rho_{13} & \frac{\rho_{23}-\rho_{12}\rho_{13}}{\sqrt{1-\rho_{12}^2}} & \sqrt{1-\rho_{13}^2 - \frac{(\rho_{23}-\rho_{12}\rho_{13})^2}{1-\rho_{12}^2}} \end{bmatrix}. \tag{3.105}$$

For example, for a matrix

$$\Sigma = \begin{bmatrix} 1 & 0.3 & 0.4 & 0.6 \\ 0.3 & 1 & 0.5 & 0.7 \\ 0.4 & 0.5 & 1 & 0.8 \\ 0.6 & 0.7 & 0.8 & 1 \end{bmatrix}$$

using "*matrix_chol()*" (see Appendix B.17 for other matrix functions), we find its Cholesky decomposition as $\Sigma = AA^T$, where A is

$$A = \begin{bmatrix} 1.0000 & 0 & 0 & 0 \\ 0.3000 & 0.9539 & 0 & 0 \\ 0.4000 & 0.3983 & 0.8254 & 0 \\ 0.6000 & 0.5451 & 0.4154 & 0.4127 \end{bmatrix}.$$

The Cholesky decomposition is a special decomposition in the form of

$$\Sigma = AA^T. \tag{3.106}$$

The decomposition in the form of $\Sigma = AA^T$ is not unique. Let $A = A'R$, then $AA^T = A'RR^T A'^T$. If we choose R such that $RR^T = 1$, we have $AA^T = A'A'^T$. For example, from the spectral decomposition discussed in Section 3.9 we have

$$\Sigma = U\Lambda U^T = U\Lambda^{1/2}\left(U\Lambda^{1/2}\right)^T = A'A'^T \tag{3.107}$$

where $A' = U\Lambda^{1/2}$.

The Cholesky decomposition is well defined only if the matrix Σ is positive definite. If Σ is only positive semi-definite, the Cholesky decomposition will fail and we can use the spectral decomposition as shown above.

3.13   Cauchy–Schwartz Inequality

The Cauchy–Schwartz inequality is stated as follows: let b and d be any two vectors, then

$$\left(b^T d\right)^2 \leq \left(b^T b\right) \cdot \left(d^T d\right) \tag{3.108}$$

with equality if and only if $b = cd$ for some constant c.

This inequality can be easily shown by defining a function $f(\lambda) = b - \lambda d$, and then finding the minimum value of $f^2(\lambda)$.

From this inequality, we have a bounded range for the inner product of two vectors in high-dimensional space:

$$- |b| \cdot |d| \leq b^T d \leq |b| \cdot |d| . \tag{3.109}$$

Therefore there exists an angle θ such that

$$b^T d = |b| \cdot |d| \cos \theta. \tag{3.110}$$

The angle θ is the angle between the two vectors in a high-dimensional space.

In the same manner, if b and d are two random variables, by constructing

$$f(\lambda) = E[(b - \lambda d)^2], \tag{3.111}$$

we can show that

$$[E(b\,d)]^2 \leq E(b^2)\, E(d^2). \tag{3.112}$$

Similarly, we have

$$[E\,(|bd|)]^2 \leq E\left(b^2\right)\, E\left(d^2\right). \tag{3.113}$$

Proposition 3.7: *If B is a positive definite matrix and b and d are any two vectors, we have*

$$\left(b^T d\right)^2 \leq \left(b^T B b\right) \cdot \left(d^T B^{-1} d\right) \tag{3.114}$$

with equality if and only if $d = cBb$ for some constant c.

This proposition can be proved by using the square root of the matrix B and using the Cauchy–Schwartz inequality. From this proposition we have the following proposition.

Proposition 3.8: *Let B be a positive definite matrix and d be a given vector. Then for any arbitrary non-zero vector x, we have*

$$\frac{\left(x^T d\right)^2}{x^T B x} \leq d^T B^{-1} d \tag{3.115}$$

with the maximum attained when $x = cB^{-1}d$ for some constant c.

3.14 Relationship of Correlation among Three Variables

Let us consider three vectors in a high-dimensional space. If the first and the second are almost parallel and the first and the third are almost parallel, then we can argue that the second and the third are almost parallel. What are the minimum and maximum correlation of vector pairs (2, 3) given the correlations of (1, 2) and (1, 3)? Consider the correlation matrix:

$$A = \begin{bmatrix} 1 & \rho_{12} & \rho_{13} \\ \rho_{12} & 1 & \rho_{23} \\ \rho_{13} & \rho_{23} & 1 \end{bmatrix}, \tag{3.116}$$

with the determinant $\det A = 1 - \rho_{12}^2 - \rho_{13}^2 - \rho_{23}^2 + 2\rho_{12}\rho_{13}\rho_{23}$. Since A is a positive semi-definite matrix, then $\det A = \prod_i \lambda_i \geq 0$, where λ_i $(i = 1, 2, 3)$ are the eigenvalues of the matrix A. It leads to

$$\rho_{12}^2 + \rho_{13}^2 + \rho_{23}^2 - 2\rho_{12}\rho_{13}\rho_{23} \leq 1, \tag{3.117}$$

or more explicitly

$$\rho_{12}\rho_{13} - \sqrt{(1 - \rho_{12}^2)(1 - \rho_{13}^2)} \leq \rho_{23} \leq \rho_{12}\rho_{13} + \sqrt{(1 - \rho_{12}^2)(1 - \rho_{13}^2)}. \tag{3.118}$$

If we let $\rho_{12} = \cos\alpha$, $\rho_{13} = \cos\beta$, $\rho_{23} = \cos\gamma$, we have

$$\cos(\alpha + \beta) \leq \cos\gamma \leq \cos(\alpha - \beta). \tag{3.119}$$

It is easy to see this relation geometrically. The equality also holds when three vectors are in the same plane; that is when the dimensionality can be reduced.

Chapter 4

Linear Modeling and Regression

The most common data modeling methods are regressions, both linear and logistic. It is likely that 90% or more of real world applications of data mining end up with a relatively simple regression as the final model, typically after very careful data preparation, encoding, and creation of variables. There are many kinds of regression: both linear, logistic and nonlinear, each with strengths and weaknesses. Many regressions are purely linear, some only slightly nonlinear, and others completely nonlinear. Most multivariate regressions consider each independent variable separately and do not allow for nonlinear interaction among independent variables. Treatment of nonlinearities and interactions can be done through careful encoding of independent variables such as binning or univariate or multivariate mapping to nonlinear functions. Once this mapping has been done one can then do a linear regression using these new functions as independent variables.

We can state our problem as that of finding a best fitting function for a set of data. We can think of this as fitting a modeling function that contains a number of free, adjustable parameters so that we get a "best fit." We do this by building an objective function and then deriving a mathematical procedure to set or adjust these free parameters so that our fitting function is this "best fit." This fitting function in a modeling exercise is usually a functional relationship between a large set of independent variables and this single independent variable. We typically have an overdetermined problem because we are given a large set of data that consists of many example records, each record consisting of a vector of independent variables followed by a single dependent variable. The problem is overdetermined because we have many, many more data records than we have free parameters in our fitting function, and our modeling problem becomes that of finding the best set of values for these free parameters using the mathematical procedure around optimizing our objective function.

The fitting problem is also sometimes described in terms of finding the best fitting function in the form of a probability distribution function that most likely represents a collection of data. Again, we set up a candidate probability function that contains a set of free parameters that are adjusted by some mathematical procedure to optimize a chosen objective function. This alternative viewpoint motivates a second common approach to fitting a function using many data records, that of a maximum likelihood estimator (MLE). The MLE is a function that has the statistical property of optimally fitting the data given the selected form of the MLE. In this approach we write down a Maximum Likelihood Function which we seek to optimize. For calculational ease we frequently optimize the log of this likelihood function, which also solves our problem because of the monotonic relationship between a function and the log of that function.

There are several reasons why regressions are so commonly used. First, they are generally straightforward both to understand and compute. The mean square error (MSE) objective function, being quadratic in the fitting parameters, has a closed-form linear solution obtained by differentiating the MSE with respect to the unknown parameters and setting the derivatives to zero. The resulting system of equations is easily solved through linear manipulations and can be solved via a matrix inversion. Frequently the matrix is close to singular, and many regression solutions are built around safely inverting the data matrix (SVD, ridge regression, conjugate gradient, PCR, PLS, etc.).

Before we go into details for each regression method, in this first section we discuss some issues common for all regression models, including tests on significance of variables and parameter estimation. We discuss these in the contexts of least square estimation (LSE) and maximum likelihood estimation (MLE). For more extended references on regressions, refer to the texts by Greene (1997), Johnson and Wichern (1992), and Monahan (2001).

4.1   Properties of Maximum Likelihood Estimators

Consider a situation where we are trying to fit a function using information from discrete data points. We can parameterize a fitting function f using a set of to-be-determined parameters θ. We look for a criterion to select a best set of fitting parameters θ. A popular methodology to select this parameter set is the use of a maximum likelihood. To proceed, we define a likelihood function L, which is a function of all the independent variables and the parameters θ.

Under a regularity condition, the maximum likelihood estimator has the following property of asymptotic normality:

$$\hat{\theta} \xrightarrow{a} N[\theta, I^{-1}(\theta)] \text{ where } I(\theta) = -E\left[\frac{\partial^2 \ln L}{\partial\theta\partial\theta}\right], \tag{4.1}$$

where $I(\theta)$ is called the information matrix.

Here we sketch the proof of this property. First we state a lemma: for any density function $f(x, \theta)$ with parameters θ, under a regularity condition, we have the following results:

$$E\left[\frac{\partial \ln f(x, \theta)}{\partial\theta_i}\right] = 0 \tag{4.2}$$

and

$$E\left[\frac{\partial^2 \ln f(x,\theta)}{\partial\theta_i\partial\theta_j}\right] + E\left[\frac{\partial \ln f(x,\theta)}{\partial\theta_i} \cdot \frac{\partial \ln f(x,\theta)}{\partial\theta_j}\right] = 0. \tag{4.3}$$

These can be easily proved by noting the following:

$$\frac{\partial \ln f(x,\theta)}{\partial\theta_i} = \frac{1}{f(x,\theta)}\frac{\partial f(x,\theta)}{\partial\theta_i} \tag{4.4}$$

and

$$\begin{aligned}\frac{\partial^2 \ln f(x,\theta)}{\partial\theta_i\partial\theta_j} &= -\frac{1}{f^2(x,\theta)}\frac{\partial f(x,\theta)}{\partial\theta_i}\frac{\partial f(x,\theta)}{\partial\theta_j} + \frac{1}{f(x,\theta)}\frac{\partial^2 f(x,\theta)}{\partial\theta_i\partial\theta_j}\\ &= -\frac{\partial \ln f(x,\theta)}{\partial\theta_i}\frac{\partial \ln f(x,\theta)}{\partial\theta_j} + \frac{1}{f(x,\theta)}\frac{\partial^2 f(x,\theta)}{\partial\theta_i\partial\theta_j}\end{aligned} \tag{4.5}$$

Therefore

$$E\left[\frac{\partial \ln f(x,\theta)}{\partial\theta_i}\right] = \int \frac{\partial f(x,\theta)}{\partial\theta_i}dx = \frac{\partial}{\partial\theta_i}\int f(x,\theta)dx = 0 \tag{4.6}$$

and

$$\begin{aligned}E\left[\frac{\partial^2 \ln f(x,\theta)}{\partial\theta_i\partial\theta_j} + \frac{\partial \ln f(x,\theta)}{\partial\theta_i}\frac{\partial \ln f(x,\theta)}{\partial\theta_j}\right] &= \int \frac{\partial^2 f(x,\theta)}{\partial\theta_i\partial\theta_j}dx\\ &= \frac{\partial^2}{\partial\theta_i\partial\theta_j}\int f(x,\theta)dx = 0.\end{aligned} \tag{4.7}$$

In the above we only used one regularity condition—that the order of differentiation and integration can be switched.

The likelihood function and log-likelihood function are defined as

$$L(x,\theta) = \prod_{i=1}^{n} f(x_i,\theta), \tag{4.8}$$

$$\ln L(x,\theta) = \sum_{i=1}^{n} \ln f(x_i,\theta). \tag{4.9}$$

The first derivative and Hessian matrix are

$$g = \frac{\partial \ln L(x,\theta)}{\partial\theta} = \sum_{i=1}^{n} \frac{\partial \ln f(x_i,\theta)}{\partial\theta} = \sum_{i=1}^{n} g_i, \tag{4.10}$$

$$H = \frac{\partial^2 \ln L(x,\theta)}{\partial\theta\partial\theta} = \sum_{i=1}^{n} \frac{\partial^2 \ln f(x_i,\theta)}{\partial\theta\partial\theta} = \sum_{i=1}^{n} H_i. \tag{4.11}$$

Then we have

$$E[g_i] = \int \frac{\partial \ln f(x,\theta)}{\partial\theta}f(x,\theta)dx = \frac{\partial}{\partial\theta}\int f(x,\theta)dx = 0 \tag{4.12}$$

and

$$\text{Var}[g_i] = E[g_i g_i^T] = \int \frac{\partial \ln f(x,\theta)}{\partial\theta}\frac{\partial \ln f(x,\theta)}{\partial\theta}f(x,\theta)dx. \tag{4.13}$$

Noting that $\frac{\partial \ln f}{\partial \theta} \frac{\partial \ln f}{\partial \theta} f = \frac{\partial^2 f}{\partial \theta \partial \theta} - \frac{\partial^2 \ln f}{\partial \theta \partial \theta} f$, we have

$$\text{Var}[g_i] = -E\left(\frac{\partial^2 \ln f(x, \theta)}{\partial \theta \partial \theta}\right) = -E[H_i]. \tag{4.14}$$

Taking a Taylor expansion around the true value (θ_0) we have

$$g(\hat{\theta}) = g(\theta_0) + H(\theta_0)(\hat{\theta} - \theta_0), \tag{4.15}$$

and noting that $g(\hat{\theta}) = 0$, we have

$$\hat{\theta} - \theta_0 = -H^{-1}(\theta_0)\, g(\theta_0). \tag{4.16}$$

Note that g and H are calculated from n observed data points and when n is large enough we can apply the central limit theorem to get the asymptotic behavior. We have

$$E[g] = \sum_{i=1}^{n} E[g_i] = 0. \tag{4.17}$$

Since g_i $(i = 1, 2, ..., n)$ are all independent, we have

$$\text{Var}[g] = \sum_{i=1}^{n} \text{Var}[g_i] = -\sum_{i=1}^{n} E[H_i] = -E[H]. \tag{4.18}$$

Therefore under a large sample limit we have

$$\frac{1}{n} H(\theta_0) \to \frac{1}{n} E[H(\theta_0)], \tag{4.19}$$

$$\frac{1}{n} g(\theta_0) \to N\left[0, -\frac{1}{n^2} E[H(\theta_0)]\right]. \tag{4.20}$$

Finally we have

$$\hat{\theta} - \theta_0 \to N\left[0, -\{E[H(\theta_0)]\}^{-1}\right]. \tag{4.21}$$

Namely

$$\hat{\theta} \to N\left[\theta_0, I^{-1}(\theta_0)\right] \tag{4.22}$$

where $I(\theta_0) = -E[H(\theta_0)]$ is the information matrix. Therefore

$$E[\hat{\theta}] = \theta_0, \qquad \text{Var}[\hat{\theta}] = I^{-1}(\theta_0). \tag{4.23}$$

Next, we consider how to measure the significance of variables. Let's consider three models:

1. Model M_0: with no variables

2. Model M_s: with s variables $(x_1, x_2, ..., x_s)$

3. Model M_t: with t $(t > s)$ variables $(x_1, x_2, ..., x_s, x_{s+1}, ..., x_t)$.

By comparing the models M_0 and M_s we can test the significance of the variables $(x_1, x_2, ..., x_s)$ overall. If the model M_s is significantly better than the model M_0, then $(x_1, x_2, ..., x_s)$ overall are significant to the model performance. By comparing M_s and M_t we can test the significance of the $(t - s)$ variables $(x_{s+1}, x_{s+2}, ..., x_t)$. If the latter is much better than the former, the additional $(t - s)$ variables are significant to the model performance.

Let us consider a more general problem to test the significance of variables. We consider the following hypothesis test:

$$H_0 : c(\theta) = q. \tag{4.24}$$

Let R be the number of restrictions imposed in this test. The model comparisons discussed above are just some of the special linear cases. There are many hypothesis tests, and we will discuss three common tests.

4.1.1 Likelihood Ratio Test

Let L be the likelihood function without restriction and L_R be the likelihood function with a restriction. We then have $L_R \leq L$. Define a likelihood ratio $\lambda = L_R/L$, so $0 \leq \lambda \leq 1$. If the hypothesis is held, then L and L_R are very close. Under regularity we have

$$-2 \ln \lambda = -2 \left(\ln L_R - \ln L \right) \sim \chi^2[R] \tag{4.25}$$

where R is the number of restrictions imposed. We need the maximum likelihood estimators both with restrictions and without restrictions to evaluate the test statistic.

4.1.2 Wald Test

The Wald test is defined by

$$W = \left[c(\hat{\theta}) - q \right]^T \left\{ \text{var} \left[c(\hat{\theta}) - q \right] \right\}^{-1} \left[c(\hat{\theta}) - q \right] \sim \chi^2[R], \tag{4.26}$$

with $\hat{\theta}$ the maximum likelihood estimator without restrictions. The Wald test is evaluated at the maximum likelihood estimator without restrictions.

For any function $g(x)$ (linear or nonlinear), we have the Taylor expansion around the expectation value:

$$g(x) \approx g(\mu) + J(\mu) \cdot (x - \mu), \tag{4.27}$$

where $J(x) = \partial g(x)/\partial x$. Therefore we have

$$E[g(x)] \approx g(\mu) \tag{4.28}$$

and

$$\text{var}[g(x)] \approx J \Sigma J^T. \tag{4.29}$$

Using this result, we have

$$\text{var}\left[c(\hat{\theta}) - q\right] = C\,\text{var}[\hat{\theta}]\,C^T, \tag{4.30}$$

where $C(\hat{\theta}) = \partial c(\hat{\theta})/\partial \hat{\theta}$. So the Wald test can be written as

$$W = \left[c(\hat{\theta}) - q\right]^T \left\{C(\hat{\theta})\,\text{var}[\hat{\theta}]\,C^T(\hat{\theta})\right\}^{-1} \left[c(\hat{\theta}) - q\right] \sim \chi^2[R]. \tag{4.31}$$

For linear restrictions $L\theta = q$, $C = L$. The Wald test is

$$W = \left[L\hat{\theta} - q\right]^T \left\{L\text{var}[\hat{\theta}]L^T\right\}^{-1} \left[L\hat{\theta} - q\right] \sim \chi^2[R]. \tag{4.32}$$

For the simplest hypothesis test,

$$H_0 : \theta_i = 0, \tag{4.33}$$

the Wald test is

$$W = \hat{\theta}_i \left\{\text{var}[\hat{\theta}]_{i,i}\right\}^{-1} \hat{\theta}_i = \hat{\theta}_i^2/\sigma_i^2 \sim \chi^2[1]. \tag{4.34}$$

4.1.3 Lagrange Multiplier Statistic

The LM statistic (also called a score test) is defined by

$$LM = \left(\frac{\partial \ln L(\hat{\theta}_R)}{\partial \hat{\theta}_R}\right)^T \left\{I(\hat{\theta}_R)\right\}^{-1} \left(\frac{\partial \ln L(\hat{\theta}_R)}{\partial \hat{\theta}_R}\right) \sim \chi^2[R], \tag{4.35}$$

where

$$I(\hat{\theta}_R) = -E\left[\frac{\partial^2 \ln L(\hat{\theta}_R)}{\partial \hat{\theta}_R \partial \hat{\theta}_R}\right] \tag{4.36}$$

is the information matrix. All terms in the LM statistic are evaluated at the restricted estimator.

4.2 Linear Regression

Having first described various concepts around general parameter estimation and significance tests for variables, we now turn to the ordinary least squares (OLS) regression. In the next sections we will discuss further examples of linear regressions: principal component regression (PCR), partial least squares regression (PLS), and generalized linear model (GLM).

We can represent the data structure of a general modeling task as

X_1	X_2	$\cdots$	X_p	Y
x_{11}	x_{12}	$\cdots$	x_{1p}	y_1
x_{21}	x_{22}	$\cdots$	x_{2p}	y_2
$\cdots$	$\cdots$	$\cdots$	$\cdots$	$\cdots$
x_{n1}	x_{n2}	$\cdots$	x_{np}	y_n

We consider p independent variables x to predict one dependent variable y. In order to simplify the discussion in the following, we introduce the matrix notation $X : [n \times p], Y : [n \times 1], B : [p \times 1]$, where n is the number of observations (data records) and p is the number of independent variables.

4.2.1 Ordinary Least Squares (OLS) Regression

The basic assumption of linear regression is that the dependent variable y can be approximated by a linear combination of the independent variables x:

$$Y = X\beta + \varepsilon, \tag{4.37}$$

where β is a p-dimensional vector of to-be-determined constants,

$$E(\varepsilon|X) = 0 \tag{4.38}$$

and

$$E(\varepsilon\varepsilon^T|X) = \sigma^2 I. \tag{4.39}$$

The expected value of the error is zero and the standard deviation of the error is σ^2. Typically a stronger normality assumption is introduced when deriving test statistics, that the errors are normally distributed:

$$\varepsilon|X \sim N[0, \sigma^2 I]. \tag{4.40}$$

Let the estimation of the coefficients β be B. The linear regression is

$$\hat{y}(x) = B_0 + \sum_{j=1}^{p} B_j x_j = \sum_{j=0}^{p} B_j x_j. \tag{4.41}$$

For notational convenience we introduce a dummy variable $x_0 = 1$. In matrix form the linear regression requires the solving of the following matrix equation:

$$Y = XB + e. \tag{4.42}$$

The error sum of squares is $SSE = e^T e$,

$$SSE = (Y - XB)^T (Y - XB) = B^T \left(X^T X \right) B - 2(X^T Y)^T B + Y^T Y. \tag{4.43}$$

The goal is to find the set of parameters B that minimizes this error. To do so we differentiate the error with respect to the coefficients B:

$$\frac{\partial SSE}{\partial B} = 2\left[(X^T X)B - X^T Y\right] = 2X^T\left(\hat{Y} - Y\right), \tag{4.44}$$

where $\hat{Y} = XB$ is the approximation for Y.

We also calculate the second derivative,

$$\frac{\partial^2 SSE}{\partial B \partial B} = 2X^T X. \tag{4.45}$$

Minimizing the SSE (sum of squared errors) by setting the first derivative to zero leads to the normal equations

$$(X^T X)B = X^T Y. \tag{4.46}$$

The solution of the normal equations is

$$B = (X^T X)^{-1}(X^T Y). \tag{4.47}$$

The SSE is minimized at this choice of the parameters B. One of the reasons that linear regression with the mean square error minimization objective is such a popular technique is now apparent. The solution for the best fitting coefficients B is a closed form relation involving the inversion of a matrix and a matrix multiplication, and all the solution effort is in the dimensionality of p, which may be hundreds, instead of the dimensionality of n, which may be millions. Once $X^T X$ has been calculated, the linear regression solution requires just the inversion on this matrix. This all occurs because of (1) the linear form of the unknowns B and (2) the choice of the SSE as the objective to minimize: the SSE is quadratic in B, so the derivative is linear in B, which has a closed form solution.

We calculate the SSE at this minimum parameter set B and find

$$SSE = -(X^T Y)^T B + Y^T Y = -B^T(X^T X)B + Y^T Y. \tag{4.48}$$

Noting that $X^T\left(\hat{Y} - Y\right) = 0$, we have $\sum_{i=1}^n y_i = \sum_{i=1}^n \hat{y}_i$ and $\sum_{i=1}^n (y_i - \hat{y}_i)\,x_{ij} = 0$, $j = 1, 2, \cdots, p$. Therefore (1) the mean of the predicted values and the mean of the actual values are the same, and (2) the correlations between the xs and the residual of the y are zero.

Linear regression can be formulated as finding a linear combination of X such that the correlation between X and the residual of Y is zero. Noting that $SSE = -\hat{Y}^T \hat{Y} + Y^T Y$, we have

$$Y^T Y = (Y - \hat{Y})^T(Y - \hat{Y}) + \hat{Y}^T \hat{Y}. \tag{4.49}$$

Let $\bar{Y}$ be a column vector with all elements being the mean of Y. We have

$$(Y - \bar{Y})^T(Y - \bar{Y}) = Y^T Y - \bar{Y}^T \bar{Y} \tag{4.50}$$

and

$$(\hat{Y} - \bar{Y})^T(\hat{Y} - \bar{Y}) = \hat{Y}^T\hat{Y} - \bar{Y}^T\bar{Y}. \tag{4.51}$$

Therefore we have

$$(Y - \bar{Y})^T(Y - \bar{Y}) = (Y - \hat{Y})^T(Y - \hat{Y}) + (\hat{Y} - \bar{Y})^T(\hat{Y} - \bar{Y}). \tag{4.52}$$

Defining

$$R^2 = 1 - \frac{(Y - \hat{Y})^T(Y - \hat{Y})}{(Y - \bar{Y})^T(Y - \bar{Y})}, \tag{4.53}$$

we have

$$SSE = \left[(Y - \bar{Y})^T(Y - \bar{Y})\right](1 - R^2). \tag{4.54}$$

Defining $\sigma_y^2 = (Y - \bar{Y})^T(Y - \bar{Y})/n$, we have

$$SSE = n\,\sigma_y^2\,(1 - R^2). \tag{4.55}$$

Let's now consider two special cases, that of one-variable and two-variable linear regressions. First we transform each input variable and output variable in the following way (z-scaling) in order to work in a normalized space:

$$x \to (x - \mu_x)/\sigma_x, \quad y \to (y - \mu_y)/\sigma_y. \tag{4.56}$$

Since the input and output variables are now centered, the intercept is zero in this normalized space.

For a one-variable regression, note that $X^TX = Y^TY = n$ and $X^TY = n\rho_{xy}$, we have $B = \rho_{xy}$. Then $SSE = n\left(1 - \rho_{xy}^2\right)$ and $R^2 = \rho_{xy}^2$. Therefore for the single-variable regression, the larger the correlation is, the larger R^2 is.

For a two-variable regression, we have the following normal equations:

$$\begin{bmatrix} 1 & \rho_{x_1 x_2} \\ \rho_{x_1 x_2} & 1 \end{bmatrix} \cdot \begin{bmatrix} B_1 \\ B_2 \end{bmatrix} = \begin{bmatrix} \rho_{x_1 y} \\ \rho_{x_2 y} \end{bmatrix}. \tag{4.57}$$

We then find the coefficients

$$\begin{bmatrix} B_1 \\ B_2 \end{bmatrix} = \frac{1}{1 - \rho_{x_1 x_2}^2} \begin{bmatrix} \rho_{x_1 y} - \rho_{x_1 x_2}\rho_{x_2 y} \\ \rho_{x_2 y} - \rho_{x_1 x_2}\rho_{x_1 y} \end{bmatrix}, \tag{4.58}$$

and

$$SSE = n\left[1 - \frac{1}{1 - \rho_{x_1 x_2}^2}\left(\rho_{x_1 y}^2 + \rho_{x_2 y}^2 - 2\rho_{x_1 y}\rho_{x_2 y}\rho_{x_1 x_2}\right)\right]. \tag{4.59}$$

Finally we have

$$R^2 = \frac{1}{1 - \rho_{x_1 x_2}^2}\left(\rho_{x_1 y}^2 + \rho_{x_2 y}^2 - 2\rho_{x_1 y}\rho_{x_2 y}\rho_{x_1 x_2}\right). \tag{4.60}$$

In this two-variable case with several different correlation measurements, it is not easy to see when R^2 is maximum. Therefore a numerical approach is necessary to find the variables.

Returning to the general situation, the estimation of the coefficient vector can be written as

$$B = \beta + (X^T X)^{-1} X^T \varepsilon. \tag{4.61}$$

The expected value of the coefficient is:

$$E(B|X) = \beta \tag{4.62}$$

and its variance is

$$\text{var}[B] = E[(B - \beta)(B - \beta)^T | X]. \tag{4.63}$$

We have

$$\text{var}[B] = \sigma^2 (X^T X)^{-1}. \tag{4.64}$$

If we assume normality of the error term, $\varepsilon|X \sim N[0, \sigma^2 I]$, and note that

$$(X^T X)^{-1} X^T (\sigma^2 I) X (X^T X)^{-1} = \sigma^2 (X^T X)^{-1}, \tag{4.65}$$

we have

$$B|X \sim N[\beta, \sigma^2 (X^T X)^{-1}]. \tag{4.66}$$

For each coefficient we have

$$B_k|X \sim N[\beta_k, \sigma^2 (X^T X)_{kk}^{-1}]. \tag{4.67}$$

The least squares residual is

$$e = Y - XB = \left[1 - X(X^T X)^{-1} X^T \right] Y = MY = M\varepsilon, \tag{4.68}$$

where $M = 1 - X(X^T X)^{-1} X^T$. Note that M is idempotent and symmetric, i.e., $M^2 = M$ and $M^T = M$. Its trace is $\text{Tr}\, M = \text{Tr} \left[1 - X(X^T X)^{-1} X^T \right] = n - p$. The expected error sum of squares is

$$E(e^T e|X) = E(\varepsilon^T M \varepsilon|X) = \text{Tr}[E(\varepsilon\varepsilon^T)M] = (n - p)\sigma^2. \tag{4.69}$$

Therefore the unbiased estimation of σ^2 is

$$s^2 = \frac{e^T e}{n - p} = \frac{n\sigma_y^2 (1 - R^2)}{n - p}, \tag{4.70}$$

so we find $E(s^2|X) = \sigma^2$.

In a normalized space

$$\tilde{x} = \frac{x - \mu_x}{\sqrt{n}\,\sigma_x} \quad \text{and} \quad \tilde{y} = \frac{y - \mu_y}{\sqrt{n}\,\sigma_y}, \tag{4.71}$$

we have

$$\tilde{Y} = \tilde{X}\tilde{\beta} + \tilde{\varepsilon}, \tag{4.72}$$

$$\tilde{\varepsilon}|\tilde{X} \sim N[0, \tilde{\sigma}^2 I]. \tag{4.73}$$

In this space, $\tilde{Y}^T\tilde{Y} = 1$, $\tilde{X}^T\tilde{X}$ is a correlation matrix among X, and $\tilde{X}^T\tilde{Y}$ is a correlation vector between X and Y. The estimation of $\tilde{\sigma}^2$ is

$$\tilde{s}^2 = \frac{1}{n-p}(1 - R^2). \tag{4.74}$$

where p is the dimension of X plus one.

Under the normality assumption of the error term, as shown above, we can construct a statistic with standard normal distribution:

$$z_k = \frac{B_k - \beta_k}{\sqrt{\sigma^2 (X^T X)_{kk}^{-1}}} \sim N[0, 1]. \tag{4.75}$$

Note that

$$\frac{(n-p)s^2}{\sigma^2} = \frac{e^T e}{\sigma^2} = \left(\frac{\varepsilon}{\sigma}\right)^T M \left(\frac{\varepsilon}{\sigma}\right) \sim \chi^2[n-p]. \tag{4.76}$$

We can construct a statistic with the numerator from a standard normal distribution and denominator from a chi-square distribution with $(n-p)$ degrees of freedom:

$$t_k = \frac{\frac{B_k - \beta_k}{\sqrt{\sigma^2 (X^T X)_{kk}^{-1}}}}{\sqrt{\frac{(n-p)s^2}{\sigma^2} \cdot \frac{1}{n-p}}} = \frac{B_k - \beta_k}{\sqrt{s^2 (X^T X)_{kk}^{-1}}} \sim t[n-p]. \tag{4.77}$$

Since they are independent of each other, the constructed statistic has a t-distribution with $(n - p)$ degrees of freedom.

The confidence intervals for the parameters can be obtained from this distribution. Let

$$\hat{\sigma}_k = \sqrt{s^2 (X^T X)_{kk}^{-1}} \tag{4.78}$$

be the standard error of the estimator. Then the $100(1-\alpha)\%$ confidence interval of B_k is $\beta_k \pm t_{a/2}\hat{\sigma}_k$, where $t_{a/2}$ is the critical value from the t-distribution with $(n - p)$ degrees of freedom. The critical value of the t-distribution is defined as

$$\int_{t_\alpha}^{\infty} f(t)dt = \alpha. \tag{4.79}$$

For example, $t_{0.025}(8) = 2.306$. As an example, suppose $\beta_k = 0.9793$, $\hat{\sigma}_k = 0.0316$, and $n - p = 8$. Then the 95% confidence interval of the parameter is

$$\beta_k \pm t_{a/2}\hat{\sigma}_k = 0.9793 \pm 2.306 \times 0.0316 = (0.9064, 1.0522). \tag{4.80}$$

Under a translation transformation in the input and output spaces, namely

$x_j \to x_j - b_j$ $(j = 1, 2, ..., p)$ and $y \to y - b$. From $\hat{y} = B_0 + \sum_{j=1}^{p} B_j x_j = \sum_{j=0}^{p} B_j x_j$, we have:

$$\hat{y} - b = (B_0 + \sum_{j=1}^{p} B_j b_j - b) + \sum_{j=1}^{p} B_j(x_j - b_j). \tag{4.81}$$

Thus the coefficients do not change, but the intercept does. Let $X = [1, x]$, where $1 = [1, 1, ..., 1]^T$ is an $n \times 1$ matrix and x is an $n \times p$ matrix. We have

$$X^T X = \begin{bmatrix} n & n\mu \\ n\mu^T & x^T x \end{bmatrix} \tag{4.82}$$

where $\mu = [\mu_1, \mu_2, ..., \mu_p]$. By using the inversion of the partition matrix (3.16) we have

$$(X^T X)^{-1} = \begin{bmatrix} \frac{1}{n} + \mu\left[(x - 1\mu)^T(x - 1\mu)\right]^{-1}\mu^T & \cdots \\ \cdots & \left[(x - 1\mu)^T(x - 1\mu)\right]^{-1} \end{bmatrix}. \tag{4.83}$$

Here we only show the diagonal elements in the inverse matrix. Therefore the $(X^T X)_{kk}^{-1}$ ($k = 1, 2, ..., p$) terms do not depend on the origin of the input variables, but $(X^T X)_{00}^{-1}$ does depend on the origin of the other variables. Therefore t_k as constructed above is translation invariant.

The explicit form of $(X^T X)_{00}^{-1}$ is

$$(X^T X)_{00}^{-1} = \frac{1}{n} + \mu\left[(x - 1\mu)^T(x - 1\mu)\right]^{-1}\mu^T = \frac{1}{n} + \frac{1}{n}\tilde{\mu}\rho^{-1}\tilde{\mu}^T, \tag{4.84}$$

where $\tilde{\mu} = [\mu_1/\sigma_1, \mu_2/\sigma_2, ..., \mu_p/\sigma_p]$.

Under a scaling transformation in the input space, $x_j \to \alpha_j x_j$ ($j = 1, 2, ..., p$), note that $B_j x_j = (B_j/\alpha_j)(\alpha_j x_j)$, and we have

$$B_j \to \frac{1}{\alpha_j} B_j \ (j = 1, 2, ..., p) \tag{4.85}$$

and

$$X^T X \to \alpha X^T X \alpha, \tag{4.86}$$

where $\alpha = \text{diag}(\alpha_1, \alpha_2, ..., \alpha_p)$. Therefore

$$t_k = \frac{B_k - \beta_k}{\sqrt{s^2(X^T X)_{kk}^{-1}}} \tag{4.87}$$

does not change under a scaling transformation. It is scaling invariant.

The unbiased estimation of the variance of the coefficients is

$$\text{var}[B] = \sigma^2(X^T X)^{-1} = \frac{n(1 - R^2)\sigma_y^2}{n - p}(X^T X)^{-1}. \tag{4.88}$$

Thus the unbiased estimation of standard error is std error$_k = (\text{var}[B])_{kk}$. For $k \neq 0$,

$$\text{std error}_k = \sqrt{\frac{n(1-R^2)\sigma_y^2}{n-p}((x-1\mu)^T(x-1\mu))_{kk}^{-1}} = \frac{\sigma_y}{\sigma_k}\sqrt{\frac{1-R^2}{n-p}}\,\rho_{kk}^{-1}.$$

(4.89)

For the intercept, $k = 0$,

$$\text{std error}_0 = \sqrt{\frac{n(1-R^2)\sigma_y^2}{n-p}\left(\frac{1}{n} + \frac{1}{n}\tilde{\mu}\,\rho^{-1}\,\tilde{\mu}^T\right)}.$$

(4.90)

4.2.2 Interpretation of the Coefficients of Linear Regression

Suppose we have built a linear model based on p variables. Let us set the jth variable to the mean of that variable over all observations. The model then becomes

$$\hat{y}^0 = c_1 x_1 + c_2 x_2 + \cdots + c_j \bar{x}_j + \cdots + c_p x_p = \hat{y} + c_j(\bar{x}_j - x_j).$$

(4.91)

The sum of square error, $SSE^0 = \sum_{i=1}^n (y_i - \hat{y}_i^0)^2$, is $SSE^0 = SSE + n\,c_j^2\sigma_j^2$. Therefore the change of SSE is $\Delta SSE/n = c_j^2\sigma_j^2$. Note that the predicted variable, $\hat{y} = \sum_{j=0}^p c_j\,x_j$, can be rewritten as

$$\frac{\hat{y} - \bar{y}}{\sigma_y} = \sum_{j=1}^p \frac{c_j\sigma_j}{\sigma_y}\left(\frac{x_j - \bar{x}_j}{\sigma_j}\right).$$

(4.92)

Define $d_j = c_j\sigma_j/\sigma_y$, which is the coefficient in the normalized space. This means the change of SSE is

$$\frac{\Delta SSE}{n\,\sigma_y^2} = \left(\frac{c_j\sigma_j}{\sigma_y}\right)^2 = d_j^2.$$

(4.93)

Therefore the coefficient in the normalized space can be used to rank order the importance of variables. The larger this coefficient, the more important the variable is. It is generally a useful measure even for nonlinear models. From the above discussion by fixing one variable to be the mean, the change of SSE is

$$\frac{\Delta SSE}{n} = c_j^2\sigma_j^2 = \frac{c_j^2}{\left[\left(\frac{1}{n}(X-\mu)^T(X-\mu)\right)_{jj}\right]^{-1}}.$$

(4.94)

Alternatively, if we consider a model with p variables and another model with $p-1$ variables, the difference of SSE is:

$$\frac{\Delta SSE}{n} = \frac{c_j^2}{\left[\left(\frac{1}{n}X^T X\right)^{-1}\right]_{jj}}.$$

(4.95)

In general, these two approaches have different changes of SSE. If this variable is independent of other variables, i.e. the correlations between this variable and other variables are zero, and in the centered space, we have

$$\left[(X^T X)^{-1}\right]_{jj} = \left[\left((X - \mu)^T (X - \mu)\right)_{jj}\right]^{-1}. \tag{4.96}$$

In this case the two changes of SSE are the same.

Let's assign two variables to their means for all observations. The model then becomes

$$\hat{y}^0 = c_1 x_1 + \cdots + c_j \bar{x}_j + \cdots + c_k \bar{x}_k + \cdots + c_p x_p = \hat{y} + c_j(\bar{x}_j - x_j) + c_k(\bar{x}_k - x_k). \tag{4.97}$$

The sum of square errors, $SSE^0 = \sum_{i=1}^{n} (y_i - \hat{y}_i^0)^2$, is

$$SSE^0 = SSE + n\, c_j^2 \sigma_j^2 + n\, c_k^2 \sigma_k^2 + 2\, n\, c_j c_k \sigma_j \sigma_k \rho_{jk}. \tag{4.98}$$

Therefore the change of the SSE is

$$\begin{aligned}
\frac{\Delta SSE}{n} &= c_j^2 \sigma_j^2 + c_k^2 \sigma_k^2 + 2\, c_j c_k \sigma_j \sigma_k \rho_{jk} \\
&= \begin{bmatrix} c_j \sigma_j & c_k \sigma_k \end{bmatrix} \cdot \begin{bmatrix} 1 & \rho_{jk} \\ \rho_{jk} & 1 \end{bmatrix} \cdot \begin{bmatrix} c_j \sigma_j \\ c_k \sigma_k \end{bmatrix}.
\end{aligned} \tag{4.99}$$

This can be expressed in terms of the coefficients in the normalized space:

$$\frac{\Delta SSE}{n\sigma_y^2} = d_i^2 + d_j^2 + 2 d_i d_j \rho_{ij}. \tag{4.100}$$

Since there is no single coefficient associated with each variable in a nonlinear model, the generalization of testing the significance of variables for nonlinear models is not straightforward. But the concept discussed above can still be applied. The procedure for nonlinear models is to calculate the change of the SSE by fixing one variable to its average. This process can be used to measure the importance of variables in a nonlinear model. We set each variable to its mean for each data record and calculate the error of the model. Comparing with the original model error, if the error does not change then this variable is not important; if the error increases significantly then this variable is important.

X	Error
actual data	E_0
$x_1 = \bar{x}_1$	E_1
$x_2 = \bar{x}_2$	E_2
...	...
$x_p = \bar{x}_p$	E_p

We can expect that $E_i \geq E_0$ since if the error is less than the original model, then the original model should set the coefficient of the test variable to be zero and be retrained to achieve a better model. By ranking the error in the above table in descending order, the variables at the top are the most important ones.

4.2.3 Regression on Weighted Data

In many cases we wish to weight certain data points more than others. It is straightforward to extend linear regression to the case where different data points have different weights. Let the weight for the data point (x_i, y_i) be w_i. Define W as a diagonal matrix, $W = \text{diag}(w_1, w_2, \cdots, w_n)$ and w as sum of all weights, $w = \sum_{i=1}^{n} w_i$. The mean and standard deviation of variable x_i are

$$\mu_j = \sum_i w_i x_{ij} / \sum_i w_i \tag{4.101}$$

and

$$\sigma_j^2 = \sum_i w_i (x_{ij} - \mu_j)^2 / \sum_i w_i = \sum_i w_i x_{ij}^2 / \sum_i w_i - \mu_j^2. \tag{4.102}$$

The covariance matrix can be calculated as

$$\text{Cov}(x_j, x_k) = \frac{\sum_i w_i (x_{ij} - \mu_j)(x_{ik} - \mu_k)}{\sum_i w_i} = \frac{\sum_i w_i x_{ij} x_{ik}}{\sum_i w_i} - \mu_j \mu_k, \tag{4.103}$$

$$\text{Cov}(x_j, y) = \frac{\sum_i w_i (x_{ij} - \mu_j)(y_i - \mu_y)}{\sum_i w_i} = \frac{\sum_i w_i x_{ij} y_i}{\sum_i w_i} - \mu_j \mu_y \tag{4.104}$$

and the correlation matrix can be calculated as

$$\rho(x_j, x_k) = \text{Cov}(x_j, x_k) / (\sigma_j \sigma_k), \tag{4.105}$$

$$\rho(x_j, y) = \text{Cov}(x_j, y) / (\sigma_j \sigma_y), \tag{4.106}$$

$$\rho(y, y) = 1. \tag{4.107}$$

The SSE is

$$
\begin{aligned}
SSE &= \sum_i w_i [(XB)_i - Y_i]^2 = (XB - Y)^T W (XB - Y) \\
&= B^T (X^T W X) B - 2(X^T W Y)^T B + Y^T W Y.
\end{aligned}
\tag{4.108}
$$

Minimizing the SSE (least squares) leads to

$$\frac{\partial SSE}{\partial B} = 2(X^T W X)B - 2X^T W Y = 2X^T W \left(\hat{Y} - Y \right). \tag{4.109}$$

The normal equations are

$$(X^T W X)B = X^T W Y. \tag{4.110}$$

The solution of the normal equations is

$$B = (X^T W X)^{-1}(X^T W Y), \tag{4.111}$$

where we can see the simple modification from the previous unweighted least squares result. The SSE can be simplified as

$$SSE = -(X^T W Y)^T B + Y^T W Y. \tag{4.112}$$

In order to estimate the standard errors of the coefficients, we assume that

$$Y = X\beta + \frac{\sigma}{\sqrt{W}}\varepsilon, \tag{4.113}$$

where

$$E(\varepsilon|X) = 0 \quad \text{and} \quad E(\varepsilon\varepsilon^T|X) = I. \tag{4.114}$$

For each observation point the expected value of the error is zero and the standard deviation of the error is σ^2/w_i, which depends on the weight.

Typically a stronger normality assumption is introduced when deriving test statistics, that the errors are normally distributed

$$\varepsilon|X \sim N[0, I]. \tag{4.115}$$

Defining

$$R^2 = 1 - \frac{(Y - \hat{Y})^T W (Y - \hat{Y})}{(Y - \bar{Y})^T W (Y - \bar{Y})}, \tag{4.116}$$

we have

$$SSE = \left[(Y - \bar{Y})^T W (Y - \bar{Y})\right](1 - R^2) \tag{4.117}$$

and

$$SST = (Y - \bar{Y})^T W (Y - \bar{Y}). \tag{4.118}$$

Since $\sigma_y^2 = (Y - \bar{Y})^T(Y - \bar{Y})/w$, we have

$$SSE = w\,\sigma_y^2\,(1 - R^2). \tag{4.119}$$

The estimation of the coefficient can be written as

$$B = \beta + (X^T W X)^{-1} X^T W \frac{\sigma}{\sqrt{W}}\varepsilon. \tag{4.120}$$

The expected value of the coefficient is $E(B|X) = \beta$ and its variance is $\text{var}[B] = E[(B - \beta)(B - \beta)^T|X]$. We have

$$\text{var}[B] = \sigma^2(X^T W X)^{-1}. \tag{4.121}$$

If we assume normality of the error term, $\varepsilon|X \sim N[0, I]$, we have

$$B|X \sim N[\beta, \sigma^2(X^TWX)^{-1}]. \tag{4.122}$$

For each coefficient we have

$$B_k|X \sim N[\beta_k, \sigma^2(X^TWX)_{kk}^{-1}]. \tag{4.123}$$

The least squares residual is

$$e = Y - XB = \frac{1}{\sqrt{W}}\left[1 - \sqrt{W}X(X^TWX)^{-1}X^T\sqrt{W}\right]\sqrt{W}\,Y = \frac{1}{\sqrt{W}}M\sqrt{W}Y, \tag{4.124}$$

where $M = 1 - \sqrt{W}X(X^TWX)^{-1}X^T\sqrt{W}$. Note that M is idempotent and symmetric as it was in the unweighted case, i.e., $M^2 = M$ and $M^T = M$. Its trace is $\operatorname{Tr} M = \operatorname{Tr}\left[1 - \sqrt{W}X(X^TWX)^{-1}X^T\sqrt{W}\right] = n - p$ and $M\sqrt{W}X = 0$. The expected error sum of squares is

$$E(e^T W e|X) = \sigma^2 E(\varepsilon^T M\varepsilon|X) = \sigma^2 \operatorname{Tr}[E(\varepsilon\varepsilon^T)M] = (n-p)\sigma^2. \tag{4.125}$$

Therefore the unbiased estimation of σ^2 is

$$s^2 = \frac{e^T W e}{n - p}. \tag{4.126}$$

Namely $E(s^2|X) = \sigma^2$. Therefore the unbiased estimation of the variance of coefficients is

$$\operatorname{var}[B] = \sigma^2(X^TWX)^{-1} = \frac{w(1-R^2)\sigma_y^2}{n-p}(X^TWX)^{-1}. \tag{4.127}$$

Let $X = \begin{bmatrix} 1 & x \end{bmatrix}$, where $1 = [1, 1, ..., 1]^T$ is an $n \times 1$ matrix and x is an $n \times p$ matrix, we have

$$X^TWX = \begin{bmatrix} w & w\mu \\ w\mu^T & x^TWx \end{bmatrix} \tag{4.128}$$

where $\mu = [\mu_1, \mu_2, ..., \mu_p]$. By using the inversion of the partition matrix (3.16) we have

$$(X^TWX)^{-1} = \begin{bmatrix} D_0 & \cdots \\ \cdots & D \end{bmatrix}, \tag{4.129}$$

where

$$D_0 = \frac{1}{w} + \mu\left[(x - 1\mu)^TW(x - 1\mu)\right]^{-1}\mu^T, \tag{4.130}$$

and

$$D = \left[(x - 1\mu)^TW(x - 1\mu)\right]^{-1}. \tag{4.131}$$

The explicit form of $(X^T W X)_{00}^{-1}$ is

$$(X^T W X)_{00}^{-1} = D_0 = \frac{1}{w} + \frac{1}{w} \tilde{\mu} \rho^{-1} \tilde{\mu}^T, \tag{4.132}$$

where $\tilde{\mu} = [\mu_1/\sigma_1, \mu_2/\sigma_2, ..., \mu_p/\sigma_p]$. Thus the unbiased estimation of the standard error is std error$_k = (\text{var}[B])_{kk}$. For $k \neq 0$,

$$
\begin{aligned}
\text{std error}_k &= \sqrt{\frac{w(1-R^2)\sigma_y^2}{n-p} ((x-1\mu)^T W (x-1\mu))_{kk}^{-1}} \\
&= \frac{\sigma_y}{\sigma_k} \sqrt{\frac{1-R^2}{n-p} \rho_{kk}^{-1}}.
\end{aligned} \tag{4.133}
$$

For the intercept, $k = 0$,

$$\text{std error}_0 = \sqrt{\frac{w(1-R^2)\sigma_y^2}{n-p} \left(\frac{1}{w} + \frac{1}{w} \tilde{\mu} \rho^{-1} \tilde{\mu}^T. \right)} \tag{4.134}$$

4.2.4 Incrementally Updating a Regression Model with Additional Data

In many practical situations we have already found a best model using a regression over a large set of data points, and we wish to modify or update this fit with the introduction of a small number of additional data points without having to reconsider the entire, perhaps very large original data set. Recall the least squared regression model solves the normal equations

$$(X^T X)B = X^T Y. \tag{4.135}$$

The solution for the coefficients is

$$B = (X^T X)^{-1}(X^T Y). \tag{4.136}$$

Suppose that the above-mentioned solution is based on a training data set with n number of data points. Adding one more data point, (x, y), the matrices become

$$(X^T X)_{n+1} = (X^T X)_n + x^T x \tag{4.137}$$

and

$$(X^T Y)_{n+1} = (X^T Y)_n + x^T y. \tag{4.138}$$

From (3.10), we have

$$(X^T X)_{n+1}^{-1} = (X^T X)_n^{-1} - \frac{(X^T X)_n^{-1} (x^T x) (X^T X)_n^{-1}}{1 + x(X^T X)_n^{-1} x^T}. \tag{4.139}$$

Let's define $S_n = (X^T X)_n^{-1}$. Then we have

$$S_{n+1} = S_n - \frac{S_n (x^T x) S_n}{1 + x S_n x^T}. \tag{4.140}$$

The updated coefficients are

$$B_{n+1} = B_n + S_{n+1} \cdot x^T \cdot (y - xB_n). \tag{4.141}$$

It is clear that if the added point (x, y) is on the line (model) previously obtained, B does not change with the introduction of this new data point, whereas in general the model will be slightly adjusted. This procedure allows us to update linear regression models using new data points without calculations involving the previous, perhaps very large data set. One can also use the reverse of this process to remove particular data points, which allows, for example, a moving data window approach.

4.2.5 Partitioned Regression

If the independent variables are partitioned in terms of

$$X = \begin{bmatrix} X_1 & X_2 \end{bmatrix}, \tag{4.142}$$

then the partitioned regression can be formulated as

$$Y = X_1 B_1 + X_2 B_2 + \varepsilon. \tag{4.143}$$

The normal equations are

$$\begin{bmatrix} X_1^T X_1 & X_1^T X_2 \\ X_2^T X_1 & X_2^T X_2 \end{bmatrix} \cdot \begin{bmatrix} B_1 \\ B_2 \end{bmatrix} = \begin{bmatrix} X_1^T Y \\ X_2^T Y \end{bmatrix}. \tag{4.144}$$

The solution is

$$B_1 = \left(X_1^T X_1 \right)^{-1} X_1^T \left(Y - X_2 B_2 \right),$$

$$B_2 = \left(X_{2*}^T X_{2*} \right)^{-1} X_{2*}^T Y_*, \tag{4.145}$$

where $X_{2*} = M_1 X_2$, $Y_* = M_1 Y$. $M_1 = 1 - X_1 \left(X_1^T X_1 \right)^{-1} X_1^T$ with the property $M_1^2 = M_1$ and $M_1^T = M_1$.

4.2.6 How Does the Regression Change When Adding One More Variable?

Suppose we have the regression result from

$$Y = XB + e. \tag{4.146}$$

Now we add one additional variable z to the independent variables,

$$W = \begin{bmatrix} X & z \end{bmatrix}, \tag{4.147}$$

and the regression approximation becomes

$$Y = [\ X \quad z\ ] \cdot \begin{bmatrix} D \\ c \end{bmatrix} + u. \tag{4.148}$$

The covariance matrix is

$$W^T W = \begin{bmatrix} X^T X & X^T z \\ z^T X & z^T z \end{bmatrix}. \tag{4.149}$$

The coefficient estimate D is not necessarily equal to B. According to the result of the partitioned regression shown in last section, we have

$$D = \left(X^T X\right)^{-1} X^T \left(Y - z\,c\right), \tag{4.150}$$

$$c = z_*^T Y_* / (z_*^T z_*), \tag{4.151}$$

where $z_* = M\,z$, $Y_* = M\,Y$, and $M = 1 - X\left(X^T X\right)^{-1} X^T$. The new error term is

$$u = Y - X\,D - z\,c = e - z_*\,c. \tag{4.152}$$

Therefore the sum of square errors is

$$u^T u = e^T e - c^2 z_*^T z_* = e^T e \left(1 - r_{*yz}^2\right). \tag{4.153}$$

where r_{*yz} is the correlation between $Y*$ and $z*$:

$$r_{*yz}^2 = \frac{\left(Y_*^T z_*\right)^2}{\left(Y_*^T Y_*\right) \cdot \left(z_*^T z_*\right)}. \tag{4.154}$$

This correlation is called the partial correlation between Y and z with respect to X. The coefficient c can be expressed in terms of the partial correlation,

$$c = r_{*yz} \sqrt{Y_*^T Y_* / (z_*^T z_*)}. \tag{4.155}$$

We can see clearly that when adding one more variable the error can only decrease or remain unchanged.

The t-value for the t-test: $H_0 : c = 0$ is

$$t_z^2 = \frac{c^2}{\dfrac{u^T u}{n - (k+1)} \cdot (W^T W)_{k+1,k+1}^{-1}}, \tag{4.156}$$

where n is the number of observations and k is the parameters in the original model. From the inversion of the partition matrix, we have

$$(W^T W)_{k+1,k+1}^{-1} = \left[z^T z - z^T X (X^T X)^{-1} X^T z\right]^{-1} = 1/(z_*^T z_*). \tag{4.157}$$

Therefore the t-value is

$$t_z^2 = \left(\frac{r_{*yz}^2}{1 - r_{*yz}^2}\right) \cdot [n - (k+1)] \sim t[n - (k+1)]. \tag{4.158}$$

Another form of the t-value is

$$t_z^2 = \left(\frac{e^T e}{u^T u} - 1\right) \cdot [n - (k+1)]. \tag{4.159}$$

It is clear that the smaller the square error, the larger the t-value. Therefore when doing forward selection, the selection rules based on the square error and t-value are equivalent.

Note that

$$R_X^2 = 1 - e^T e/(Y^T Y) \tag{4.160}$$

and

$$R_{Xz}^2 = 1 - u^T u/(Y^T Y). \tag{4.161}$$

The change of R^2 when adding a new variable can be expressed as

$$R_{Xz}^2 = R_X^2 + \left(1 - R_X^2\right) \cdot r_{*yz}^2. \tag{4.162}$$

The R^2 always increases or remains the same when adding more variables in a regression. Two special cases are $R_0^2 = 0$ and $R_1^2 = r_{yz}^2$.

4.2.7 Linearly Restricted Least Squares Regression

Let's consider least squares regression with a linear restriction:

$$Y = XB_* + u \text{ subject to } LB_* = q. \tag{4.163}$$

This can be solved by using a Lagrangian function (see Section 9.1):

$$z = (Y - XB_*)^T (Y - XB_*) + 2\lambda^T (LB_* - q). \tag{4.164}$$

Note that

$$\frac{\partial z}{\partial B_*} = 2X^T (Y - XB_*) + 2L^T \lambda = 0, \tag{4.165}$$

and we have

$$\begin{bmatrix} X^T X & L^T \\ L & 0 \end{bmatrix} \cdot \begin{bmatrix} B_* \\ \lambda \end{bmatrix} = \begin{bmatrix} X^T Y \\ q \end{bmatrix}. \tag{4.166}$$

Using the properties of the inverse of a partitioned matrix we can express the coefficient $B*$ in terms of the coefficient of the regression without restriction $Y = XB + e$:

$$B_* = B - \left(X^T X\right)^{-1} L^T \left[L\left(X^T X\right)^{-1} L^T\right]^{-1} (LB - q). \tag{4.167}$$

The change of the sum of the square error,

$$\Delta SSE = SSE_* - SSE, \tag{4.168}$$

can be expressed as

$$\Delta SSE = (LB - q)^T \left[L(X^T X)^{-1} L^T \right]^{-1} (LB - q). \tag{4.169}$$

Noting the assumption of the linear regression, $Y = X\beta + \varepsilon$, and the hypothesis we will test, $L\beta = q$, we have

$$LB - q = L(X^T X)^{-1} X^T \varepsilon. \tag{4.170}$$

Substituting this term into ΔSSE, we have

$$\Delta SSE = \varepsilon^T R\varepsilon, \tag{4.171}$$

where

$$R = X(X^T X)^{-1} L^T \left[L(X^T X)^{-1} L^T \right]^{-1} L(X^T X)^{-1} X^T. \tag{4.172}$$

It is easy to see that the matrix R is idempotent and symmetric. We have the following properties of the matrix R: $RR = R$, $R^T = R$, and $\mathrm{Tr} R = l$, where l is the number of restrictions in L. Therefore we have

$$\Delta SSE = \varepsilon^T R\varepsilon \sim \chi^2[l]. \tag{4.173}$$

From the discussion in the previous OLS section, we have

$$SSE = \varepsilon^T M\varepsilon \sim \chi^2[n - p], \tag{4.174}$$

where $M = 1 - X(X^T X)^{-1} X^T$, n is the number of observations, and p is the number of parameters in the original model. We can now construct the following F-statistic:

$$F = \frac{\Delta SSE/l}{SSE/(n - p)} \sim F[l, \ n - p]. \tag{4.175}$$

Let's consider a special case for testing on single variable, $B_k = q_k$. We have

$$F = \frac{(B_k - q_k)^2}{s^2 (X^T X)_{kk}^{-1}} \sim F[1, \ n - p]. \tag{4.176}$$

This is the same result we have obtained before.

Let's consider another special case: $L = I_l$ ($l = p - 1$) and $q = 0$. This special case is to test all coefficients to be zero except the intercept term in regression. We have

$$F = \frac{R^2/(p - 1)}{(1 - R^2)/(n - p)} \sim F[p - 1, n - p]. \tag{4.177}$$

4.2.8 Significance of the Correlation Coefficient

Consider the n data points to be (x_i, y_i), $i = 1, 2, ..., n$ and ρ the correlation coefficient between x and y. Define:

$$t = \rho \cdot \sqrt{\frac{n-2}{1-\rho^2}}. \tag{4.178}$$

Under the null hypothesis: $\rho = 0$, t has a t-distribution:

$$t \sim t[n-2]. \tag{4.179}$$

Consider an example, $\rho = 0.5$ and $n = 10$. Is this significant at the $\alpha = 5\%$ significance level?

$$t = 0.5 \cdot \sqrt{\frac{10-2}{1-0.5^2}} = 1.63. \tag{4.180}$$

Note that $t_\alpha(8) = 1.86$. The parameter t is below the critical value t_α, therefore it is not significant at the 5% significance level.

4.2.9 Partial Correlation

Let us look at the correlation coefficients among three variables X, Y, and Z. Suppose X, Y, and Z are centered, and we have the regressions Y and Z against X:

$$Y = XB + e \text{ and } Z = XB + e. \tag{4.181}$$

The residuals of the regressions are $Y_* = M \cdot Y$ and $Z_* = M \cdot Z$, where $M = 1 - X(X^T X)^{-1} X^T$. Then the partial correlation between Y and Z is

$$\rho_{Y_* Z_*} = \frac{Y_*^T Z_*}{\sqrt{(Y_*^T Y_*) \cdot (Z_*^T Z_*)}} = \frac{Y^T M Z}{\sqrt{(Y^T M Y) \cdot (Z^T M Z)}}. \tag{4.182}$$

Note that

$$Y^T M Z = Y^T (1 - X(X^T X)^{-1} X^T) Z = n (\rho_{YZ} - \rho_{XY} \rho_{XZ}) \sigma_Y \sigma_Z \tag{4.183}$$

and similar results for $Z^T M Z$ and $Y^T M Y$. Therefore the partial correlation between Y and Z is

$$\rho_{Y_* Z_*} = \frac{\rho_{YZ} - \rho_{XY} \cdot \rho_{XZ}}{\sqrt{(1 - \rho_{XY}^2) \cdot (1 - \rho_{XZ}^2)}}. \tag{4.184}$$

4.2.10 Ridge Regression

When the independent variables are correlated, ordinary linear regression has difficulty because the $X^T X$ matrix approaches singularity. For example, if $x_1 = x_2$ in the training data, then $B_1 x_1 + B_2 x_2 = (B_1 + B_2) x_1$. We cannot determine B_1 and B_2 individually, but we can only determine $B_1 + B_2$. In this case we can add an extra term in the objective function to make the problem deterministic. In ridge regression, the extra term is $\lambda(B_1^2 + B_2^2)$. Note that $B_1^2 + B_2^2 \geq \frac{1}{2}(B_1 + B_2)^2$, the equality holding when $B_1 = B_2$. Therefore with this extra term in the objective function we have a unique solution.

In general, the objective function in ridge regression is

$$f(B) = \sum_{i=1}^{n} (y_i - \hat{y}_i)^2 + \sum_{j=1}^{p} \lambda_j B_j^2. \tag{4.185}$$

In matrix form it is

$$f(B) = (Y - XB)^T (Y - XB) + B^T \lambda B, \tag{4.186}$$

where $\lambda = \text{diag}(\lambda_1, \lambda_2, ..., \lambda_p)$. The first derivative is

$$\frac{\partial f(B)}{\partial B} = 2 \left[(X^T X)B - X^T Y \right] + 2\lambda B \tag{4.187}$$

and the second derivative is

$$\frac{\partial^2 f(B)}{\partial B \partial B} = 2(X^T X) + 2\lambda. \tag{4.188}$$

Setting the first derivative to zero leads to the normal equations

$$(X^T X + \lambda)B = X^T Y. \tag{4.189}$$

The solution of the normal equations is

$$B = (X^T X + \lambda)^{-1}(X^T Y). \tag{4.190}$$

If the original matrix $X^T X$ is singular, we can choose a diagonal matrix λ such that $X^T X + \lambda$ is not singular. Therefore we have a unique solution and we have avoided the difficulty of inverting the near-singular matrix $X^T X$.

4.3   Fisher's Linear Discriminant Analysis

For the case of two groups of populations, Fisher's linear discriminant analysis looks to find a direction in the input space to best separate the two populations. When all observations are projected to that direction, the means of the two groups have the maximum separation.

For an observation x, the projection in the direction of the vector w is $y = w^T x$. The objective function can be expressed as

$$J(w) = \frac{(m_{y1} - m_{y2})^2}{n_1 s_{y1}^2 + n_2 s_{y2}^2}, \tag{4.191}$$

where n_i is the number of observations, m_{yi} is the mean of y, and s^2_{yi} is the deviation of y in the group G_i ($i = 1, 2$). Our purpose is to find the vector w that maximizes $J(w)$.

Let $m_i = \frac{1}{n_i}\sum_{x \in G_i} x$. We have $m_{yi} = \frac{1}{n_i}\sum_{x \in G_i} y = w^T m_i$ and $s^2_{yi} = \frac{1}{n_i}\sum_{x \in G_i}(y - m_{yi})^2$. Noting that $(m_{y1} - m_{y2})^2 = \left[w^T(m_1 - m_2)\right]^2$ and $n_1 s^2_{y1} + n_2 s^2_{y2} = w^T B w$, where $B = \sum_{x \in G_1}(x - m_1)(x - m_1)^T + \sum_{x \in G_2}(x - m_2)(x - m_2)^T$, we can rewrite $J(w)$ as

$$J(w) = \frac{\left[w^T(m_1 - m_2)\right]^2}{w^T B w}. \tag{4.192}$$

Maximizing $J(w)$ leads to $w = c B^{-1}(m_1 - m_2)$, where c is any constant.

Alternatively, we can use a regression approach to find the direction. In the following we will show that a linear regression approach reaches the same result as in Fisher's discriminant analysis.

In a linear regression, we model y in terms of x:

$$y = w^T x + w_0 + e. \tag{4.193}$$

Let $y = a$ when $x \in G_1$ and $y = b$ when $x \in G_2$. In matrix form,

$$Y = XW + e, \tag{4.194}$$

where

$$X = \begin{bmatrix} u_1 & X_1 \\ u_2 & X_2 \end{bmatrix}, \quad Y = \begin{bmatrix} a\,u_1 \\ b\,u_2 \end{bmatrix}, \quad \text{and} \quad W = \begin{bmatrix} w_0 \\ w \end{bmatrix}. \tag{4.195}$$

Here u_1 and u_2 are column vectors with n_1 and n_2 elements 1, respectively. The normal equations are

$$(X^T X)\,W = X^T Y. \tag{4.196}$$

Working out the matrix multiplication, we have

$$\begin{bmatrix} n & (n_1 m_1 + n_2 m_2)^T \\ n_1 m_1 + n_2 m_2 & B + n_1 m_1 m_1^T + n_2 m_2 m_2^T \end{bmatrix} \cdot \begin{bmatrix} w_0 \\ w \end{bmatrix} = \begin{bmatrix} a n_1 + b n_2 \\ a n_1 m_1 + b n_2 m_2 \end{bmatrix}. \tag{4.197}$$

The solution of these equations is

$$\left[B + \frac{n_1 n_2}{n}(m_1 - m_2)(m_1 - m_2)^T \right] w = \frac{n_1 n_2}{n}(a - b)(m_1 - m_2). \tag{4.198}$$

Noting that $(m_1 - m_2)(m_1 - m_2)^T w$ is in the direction of $(m_1 - m_2)$, we then see that Bw is in the direction of $(m_1 - m_2)$, and finally w is in the direction of $B^{-1}(m_1 - m_2)$. Explicitly, we can work out the inverse of the matrix to obtain a closed formula of w:

$$
\begin{aligned}
w &= \left[B^{-1} - B^{-1} \frac{\frac{n_1 n_2}{n}(m_1 - m_2)(m_1 - m_2)^T}{1 + \frac{n_1 n_2}{n}(m_1 - m_2)^T B^{-1}(m_1 - m_2)} B^{-1} \right] \frac{n_1 n_2}{n}(a - b)(m_1 - m_2) \\
&= \left[\frac{n_1 n_2}{n}(a - b)\left(\frac{1}{1 + \frac{n_1 n_2}{n}(m_1 - m_2)^T B^{-1}(m_1 - m_2)} \right) \right] B^{-1}(m_1 - m_2).
\end{aligned}
$$

$$(4.199)$$

Therefore we have

$$
w = \alpha\, n\, B^{-1}(m_1 - m_2),
\tag{4.200}
$$

where

$$
\alpha = \left(\frac{n_1 n_2 (a - b)}{n^2} \right) \cdot \left(\frac{1}{1 + \frac{n_1 n_2}{n}(m_1 - m_2)^T B^{-1}(m_1 - m_2)} \right).
\tag{4.201}
$$

This is exactly the same as the one obtained from Fisher's linear discriminant analysis.

In a one-dimensional space, for two normal distribution functions $f_G(x) \sim N[\mu_G, \sigma_G^2]$ and $f_B(x) \sim N[\mu_B, \sigma_B^2]$, we have

$$
\begin{aligned}
\ln\left(\frac{f_G(x)}{f_B(x)} \right) = \; & -\frac{1}{2}\left(\frac{1}{\sigma_G^2} - \frac{1}{\sigma_B^2} \right) x^2 + \left(\frac{\mu_G}{\sigma_G^2} - \frac{\mu_B}{\sigma_B^2} \right) x \\
& -\frac{1}{2}\left(\frac{\mu_G^2}{\sigma_G^2} - \frac{\mu_B^2}{\sigma_B^2} \right) - \frac{1}{2}\ln\left(\frac{\det \sigma_G^2}{\det \sigma_B^2} \right).
\end{aligned}
\tag{4.202}
$$

If $\sigma_G = \sigma_B = \sigma$, then the expression can be simplified as

$$
\ln\left(\frac{f_G(x)}{f_B(x)} \right) = \frac{1}{\sigma^2}\left((\mu_G - \mu_B)x - \frac{1}{2}(\mu_G^2 - \mu_B^2) \right).
\tag{4.203}
$$

In a p-dimensional space, the multiple normal distribution function is

$$
f(x) = \frac{1}{(2\pi)^{p/2}(\det \Sigma)^{1/2}} e^{-\frac{1}{2}(x-\mu)^T \Sigma^{-1}(x-\mu)}.
\tag{4.204}
$$

For two distribution functions $f_G(x) \sim N[\mu_G, \Sigma_G]$ and $f_B(x) \sim N[\mu_B, \Sigma_B]$, we have

$$
\begin{aligned}
\ln\left(\frac{f_G(x)}{f_B(x)} \right) = \; & -\frac{1}{2}x^T \left(\Sigma_G^{-1} - \Sigma_B^{-1} \right) x + x^T \left(\Sigma_G^{-1}\mu_G - \Sigma_B^{-1}\mu_B \right) \\
& -\frac{1}{2}\left(\mu_G^T \Sigma_G^{-1}\mu_G - \mu_B^T \Sigma_B^{-1}\mu_B \right) - \frac{1}{2}\ln\left(\frac{\det \Sigma_G}{\det \Sigma_B} \right).
\end{aligned}
\tag{4.205}
$$

If $\Sigma_G = \Sigma_B = \Sigma$, then the expression can be simplified to

$$
\ln\left(\frac{f_G(x)}{f_B(x)} \right) = x^T \Sigma^{-1}(\mu_G - \mu_B) - \frac{1}{2}\left(\mu_G^T \Sigma^{-1}\mu_G - \mu_B^T \Sigma^{-1}\mu_B \right).
\tag{4.206}
$$

This is the basis of quadratic discriminant analysis.

4.4   Principal Component Regression (PCR)

The basic idea of principal component analysis (PCA) is to search for dominant directions in X-space and to use these dominant directions as a subspace to represent the whole space approximately. The principal components are only based on the data distribution in X-space. Even though it is a purely linear technique, it is an effective and widely used method to reduce the dimensionality of the X-space. The constructed principal components are the dominant directions in X-space. If one considers the data points to be unit mass points in the X-space, the principal components are the moments of inertia of the cloud of mass points. They are hierarchical (rank ordered by the eigenvalues, the first being the most important) and orthogonal. Mathematically, they are the directions that

$$\text{maximize } E = \sum_i (x_i \cdot p)^2$$
$$\text{subject to } \|p\| = 1. \tag{4.207}$$

In matrix form: $\sum_i (x_i \cdot p)^2 = p^T (X^T X) p$. The solution of this maximization can be obtained from the method of Lagrange multipliers:

$$z = p^T (X^T X) p - \lambda p^T p. \tag{4.208}$$

The solution is

$$(X^T X) p = \lambda p. \tag{4.209}$$

Define a matrix $U = [p_1, p_2, \cdots, p_n]$, whose columns are the vectors of the principal components, and a diagonal matrix composed of the eigenvalues, $\Lambda = \text{diag}(\lambda_1, \lambda_2, \cdots, \lambda_n)$. We have the following properties:

- $p_i^T p_j = \delta_{ij}$, (orthogonality)

- if $\lambda_i > \lambda_j$, then $E_i > E_j$.

The cross product can be expressed as

$$X^T X = U \Lambda U^T = \sum_{i=1}^{n} \lambda_i p_i p_i^T. \tag{4.210}$$

This is the spectral decomposition of a semi-definite positive matrix.

Principal component regression (PCR) is a regression method based on PCA. The basic idea is to find the directions in X-space that have the most variation (PCA), then do regression in this lower-dimensional space spanned by the most important of the principal components.

By reducing a high-dimensional space into two or three dimensions, we can better visualize what is going on in the high-dimensional space. This topic will be discussed in Section 10.1 on multi-dimensional scaling.

4.5   Factor Analysis

Consider a data matrix with n records and p variables:

	X_1	X_2	$\cdots$	X_p
1	x_{11}	x_{12}	$\cdots$	x_{1p}
2	x_{21}	x_{22}	$\cdots$	x_{2p}
$\cdots$	$\cdots$	$\cdots$	$\cdots$	$\cdots$
n	x_{n1}	x_{n2}	$\cdots$	x_{np}

In factor analysis, the basic assumption is that the p variables can be interpreted in terms of a linear combination of $m(m < p)$ variables (factors):

$$X_i - \mu_i = l_{i1}F_1 + l_{i2}F_2 + ... + l_{im}F_m + \varepsilon_i, \quad i = 1, 2, ..., p. \tag{4.211}$$

In matrix form we have

$$
\begin{array}{ccccccc}
X - \mu & = & L & F & + & \varepsilon & \\
\begin{bmatrix} x_1 - \mu_1 \\ x_2 - \mu_2 \\ \vdots \\ x_p - \mu_p \end{bmatrix} & = & L & \begin{bmatrix} F_1 \\ F_2 \\ \vdots \\ F_m \end{bmatrix} & + & \begin{bmatrix} \varepsilon_1 \\ \varepsilon_2 \\ \vdots \\ \varepsilon_p \end{bmatrix} & , \\
[p \times 1] & = & [p \times m] & [m \times 1] & & [p \times 1] &
\end{array}
\tag{4.212}
$$

where F, ε are independent with the following properties:

$$E[F] = 0, \ E[\varepsilon] = 0, \ E[\varepsilon F^T] = 0,$$
$$\mathrm{Cov}(F) = I, \ \mathrm{Cov}(\varepsilon) = \Psi. \tag{4.213}$$

We have

$$
\begin{aligned}
\mathrm{Cov}(X) &= E[(X - \mu)(X - \mu)^T] \\
&= E[(L \cdot F + \varepsilon)(L \cdot F + \varepsilon)^T] \\
&= LE[FF^T]L^T + E[LF\varepsilon^T + \varepsilon(LF)^T] + E[\varepsilon\varepsilon^T] \\
&= LL^T + \Psi.
\end{aligned}
\tag{4.214}
$$

Therefore we have the covariance matrix

$$\Sigma = LL^T + \Psi. \tag{4.215}$$

Its components are

$$\sigma_i^2 = \sum_{j=1}^m l_{ij}^2 + \Psi_i = h_i + \Psi_i. \tag{4.216}$$

The decomposition of the variance is

$$\sigma_i^2(\text{variance}) = h_i(\text{communality}) + \Psi_i(\text{specific variance}). \tag{4.217}$$

As an example, consider $p = 12, m = 2$. Then the degrees of freedom are

$$\begin{aligned} \Sigma: &\quad p(p+1)/2 = 78, \\ LL^T: &\quad p \times m = 24, \\ \Psi: &\quad p = 12. \end{aligned} \tag{4.218}$$

Thus the degrees of freedom are reduced from 78 to 36 by using a factor analysis framework. This is accomplished by forming the factors, which are then rigid new variables and the dimensionality is reduced. For further information see, for example, Johnson and Wichern (1992).

4.6 Partial Least Squares Regression (PLSR)

The idea of PLS regression is similar to PCA regression. Recall in PCA (PCR) we examined the X-space alone to find the directions that best explained the variance in the X data. These directions were presented in terms of a hierarchical series of orthogonal vectors called eigenvectors with their importance in explaining this variance measured by their eigenvalues. In PLS, we are trying to find the directions in X-space that most explain Y (with a linear relationship). So it is a dimension reduction technique that is based on the distribution in both X- and Y-spaces, and is thus a step beyond/better than PCR. The hierarchical series of orthogonal vectors in PLS are called the cardinal components (note there is also a less popular version of PLS in which the cardinal components are not orthogonal). There does not exist a closed-form noniterative process to find the cardinal components. We must use a recursive search algorithm to find the directions, which is described in detail in the book *Multivariate Calibration* by Martens and Naes (1989). Here is the algorithm, requiring an iteration over step 1 to step 5 to find A cardinal components:

PLS Algorithm

1. Find w to maximize covariance: $X \cdot w \sim Y (\|w\| = 1)$.

$$w = \frac{X^T Y}{\|X^T Y\|}$$

2. Find t, $X = t \cdot w^T + \varepsilon$.

$$t = X \cdot w$$

3. Find p, $X = t \cdot p^T + \varepsilon$.

$$p = \frac{X^T \cdot t}{\|t\|^2}$$

   Find q, $Y = t \cdot q + \varepsilon$.

$$q = \frac{Y^T \cdot t}{\|t\|^2}$$

4. new $X = X - t \cdot p^T$

   new $Y = Y - t \cdot q$.

5. Repeat step 1 to step 4 to find more cardinal components.

If X and Y are standard normalized, $X^T X$ is the correlation matrix and $X^T Y$ is the correlation between X and Y. After finding a number of cardinal components we can do a regression on the cardinal components:

$$\begin{aligned} X &= t_1 \cdot p_1^T + t_2 \cdot p_2^T + t_3 \cdot p_3^T + \cdots, \\ Y &= t_1 \cdot q_1 + t_2 \cdot q_2 + t_3 \cdot q_3 + \cdots. \end{aligned} \tag{4.219}$$

One substantial issue with the standard formulation of PLS is the iteration using the entire raw data set X and Y. For small to moderate numbers of records this is not an issue, but when one has hundreds of thousands to millions of records this process is very inefficient or intractable. In 1992, James Elliott at the Los Alamos National Laboratory reformulated the standard PLS algorithm entirely in terms of matrices $X^T X$ and $X^T Y$. He noticed that because the problem was completely linear, all the information required in the algorithm can be found in the $X^T X$ and $X^T Y$ matrix and vector. This allowed the algorithm to be applied to a problem using Citibank credit data with millions of records. The $X^T X$ and $X^T Y$ matrix/vectors needed to be calculated once, requiring a single pass through the perhaps millions of records, and the dimensionality is then reduced to the number of inputs instead of the number of records. Here is the reformulated PLS algorithm:

Reformulated PLS Algorithm

1. $w = \frac{X^T Y}{\|X^T Y\|}$

2. $p = \frac{(X^T X)w}{w^T (X^T X)w}$, $q = \frac{\|X^T Y\|}{w^T (X^T X)w}$

3. new $(X^T X) = X^T X - [w^T (X^T X)w]pp^T$

   new $(X^T Y) = X^T Y - \|X^T Y\| p$

4. Repeat step 1 through step 3 to find more cardinal components $1, 2, ..., A$.

5. $B = W(P^T W)^{-1}Q$, $W = [w_1, w_2, ..., w_A]$, $P = [p_1, p_2, ..., p_A]$, $Q = [q_1, q_2, ...q_A]^T$.

If the number of cardinal components is chosen the same as the dimension as the matrix $X^T X$, then PLSR is exactly the same as OLSR. Some advantages of PLSR are:

1. There is no problem when $X^T X$ is singular since it is an iterative technique.

2. The model is more robust than that of OLSR, especially when the data is very noisy.

3. It is helpful when OLSR model is overfitting (by selecting fewer cardinal components to reduce the performance of training and increase the performance of testing.)

4. It is a smarter algorithm than the more popular PCR since it takes Y into account in finding the best directions in X-space.

4.7 Generalized Linear Model (GLM)

In linear modeling the output or prediction is constructed as a linear combination of the inputs. The previous sections described a variety of ways to estimate the parameters in this linear combination. A straightforward extension of simple linear models is the formulation of generalized linear models (GLM), where the prediction uses a nonlinear transformation of a linear combination of the inputs. In this section, we follow the notation in the text by McCullagh and Nelder (1989).

For generalized linear regression, let the log-likelihood function from a single observation be written as

$$l = l(\theta, \varphi, y) = (y \cdot \theta - b(\theta)) / a(\varphi) + c(y, \varphi). \tag{4.220}$$

Here we assume $\theta = \theta(\mu)$, $\eta = \eta(\mu)$, $\eta = \sum_j \beta_j x_j$ and $\eta = \eta(\mu)$ is the link function to link the mean (μ) and the linear combination of predictors (η). Some examples of the link function are:

1. classical linear model: $\eta = \mu$

2. logit: $\eta = \ln(\mu/(1 - \mu))$

3. probit: $\eta = \Phi^{-1}(\mu)$

where $\Phi(\cdot)$ is the normal cumulative distribution function. The first and the second derivatives of the likelihood are

$$\partial l / \partial \theta = (y - b'(\theta)) / a(\varphi) \tag{4.221}$$

and

$$\partial^2 l / \partial \theta^2 = -b''(\theta) / a(\varphi). \tag{4.222}$$

From the relation $E(\partial l / \partial \theta) = 0$, we have the mean of Y

$$E(Y) = \mu = b'(\theta), \tag{4.223}$$

and from the relation

$$E(\partial^2 l / \partial \theta^2) + E(\partial l / \partial \theta)^2 = 0 \tag{4.224}$$

we have the variance of Y

$$\text{var}(Y) = E(Y - \mu)^2 = b''(\theta) \, a(\varphi). \tag{4.225}$$

Defining $V = b''(\theta)$, we have

$$\text{var}(Y) = V \, a(\varphi). \tag{4.226}$$

The first derivative of the likelihood with respect to the unknown parameters is

$$
\begin{aligned}
\frac{\partial l}{\partial \beta_j} &= \frac{\partial l}{\partial \theta} \frac{d\theta}{d\mu} \frac{d\mu}{d\eta} \frac{\partial \eta}{\partial \beta_j} \\
&= \frac{y - \mu}{a(\varphi)} \frac{1}{b''(\theta)} \frac{d\mu}{d\eta} x_j \\
&= \left[\frac{W}{a(\varphi)} \frac{d\eta}{d\mu} \right] (y - \mu) x_j \;.
\end{aligned}
\tag{4.227}
$$

where $W^{-1} = V (d\eta/d\mu)^2$. The second derivative is

$$\frac{\partial^2 l}{\partial \beta_j \partial \beta_k} = \left\{ \frac{\partial}{\partial \beta_k} \left[\frac{W}{a(\varphi)} \frac{d\eta}{d\mu} \right] \right\} (y - \mu) x_j - \frac{W}{a(\varphi)} x_j x_k. \tag{4.228}$$

Note that since $E(Y) = \mu$, the expectation value of the first term is zero. We have

$$E\left(\frac{\partial^2 l}{\partial \beta_j \partial \beta_k}\right) = -\frac{W}{a(\varphi)} x_j x_k. \tag{4.229}$$

Now applying the Newton–Raphson method, we have

$$E\left(\frac{\partial^2 l}{\partial \beta_0 \partial \beta_0}\right)(\beta - \beta_0) = -\frac{\partial l}{\partial \beta_0}. \tag{4.230}$$

Substituting the first and second derivatives, we have

$$\left[\sum_k \frac{W_0}{a(\varphi)} x_j x_k\right](\beta - \beta_0)_k = \sum \left[\frac{W_0}{a(\varphi)} \frac{d\eta_0}{d\mu_0}(y - \mu_0) x_j\right]. \tag{4.231}$$

This can be rewritten as

$$\left[\sum \frac{W_0}{a(\varphi)} x_j x_k\right]\beta_k = \sum \left[\frac{W_0}{a(\varphi)} x_j \left\{\eta_0 + \frac{d\eta_0}{d\mu_0} \cdot (y - \mu_0)\right\}\right]. \tag{4.232}$$

Let

$$z = \eta + \frac{d\eta}{d\mu} \cdot (y - \mu). \tag{4.233}$$

We have

$$\left[\sum \frac{W_0}{a(\varphi)} x_j x_k\right]\beta_k = \sum \frac{W_0}{a(\varphi)} x_j z_0. \tag{4.234}$$

In matrix form this is

$$\left[X^T W_0 X\right]\beta = X^T W_0 Z_0. \tag{4.235}$$

This is a linear regression with the weight W_0 and dependent variable Z_0. It is an iteratively reweighted least squares (IRLS) regression.

The link is called a canonical link if $\theta = \eta$. In this case

$$W = V = d\mu/d\eta. \tag{4.236}$$

Notice that in this case, $W d\eta/d\mu = 1$, and the expected value of the information matrix is the same as the observed one. Therefore the Fisher scoring is the same as the Newton–Raphson method for the canonical link.

Let us consider some special cases. In classical linear regression we assume the distribution is normal

$$f(y, \theta, \varphi) = \frac{1}{\sqrt{2\pi\sigma^2}} e^{-\frac{(y-\mu)^2}{2\sigma^2}} \tag{4.237}$$

and the link function is the identity relationship $\eta = \mu$. We have

$$l = \ln f(y, \theta, \varphi) = \frac{y \cdot \mu - \mu^2/2}{\sigma^2} - \frac{1}{2}\left(\frac{y^2}{\sigma^2} + \ln(2\pi\sigma^2)\right). \tag{4.238}$$

It is put into standard form by $\theta = \mu$, $\varphi = \sigma^2$, $a(\varphi) = \varphi$, $b(\theta) = \theta^2/2$ and $c(y, \varphi) = -\left(y^2/\sigma^2 + \ln(2\pi\sigma^2)\right)/2$. It is a canonical link and therefore $W = V = 1$ and $z = y$.

In the case of logistic regression the distribution function is binomial,

$$f(y, \theta, \varphi) = \mu^y(1 - \mu)^{1-y}, \tag{4.239}$$

and the link function is $\eta = \ln\left(\mu/(1 - \mu)\right)$. We have

$$l = \ln f(y, \theta, \varphi) = y \ln\left(\mu/(1 - \mu)\right) + \ln(1 - \mu). \tag{4.240}$$

It is put in standard form by $\theta = \ln\left(\mu/(1 - \mu)\right)$, $\varphi = 1$, $a(\varphi) = 1$, $b(\theta) = -\ln(1 - \mu) = \ln(1 + e^\theta)$, and $c(y, \varphi) = 0$. It is a canonical link and by noting that $d\mu/d\eta = \mu(1 - \mu)$, we have

$$W = V = \mu(1 - \mu) \tag{4.241}$$

and

$$z = \ln\left(\frac{\mu}{1 - \mu}\right) + \frac{y - \mu}{\mu(1 - \mu)}. \tag{4.242}$$

Refer to McCullagh and Nelder (1989) for more discussions of other distributions and applications.

4.8   Logistic Regression: Binary

For the case where the output is binary, the most common modeling method is logistic regression. One can use standard linear regression for binary output problems, but there are several reasons why this is not ideal. First, outliers have a much greater impact on linear regression, whereas they are naturally suppressed in logistic regression. Second, and more important, the assumptions of the distribution of errors in linear regression is that they are normally distributed, which is not true for binary outputs, in which case the errors follow a binomial distribution. Logistic regression is the natural choice for these types of modeling problems.

For a binary output variable (coded as 0 and 1), we can construct the maximum likelihood function as the objective function:

$$L = \prod_{i=1}^{n} \hat{y}_i^{y_i}(1 - \hat{y}_i)^{1-y_i}, \tag{4.243}$$

where n is the number of data points and y_i and $\hat{y}_i$ are actual output and predicted output for the data point i ($i = 1, 2, \cdots, n$), respectively. This form of likelihood function is very easy to understand. If y is 1, the larger the

$\hat{y}$ the better, while if y is 0, the smaller the $\hat{y}$ (or the larger the $1 - \hat{y}$) the better. This desire leads to the concise form $\hat{y}^y(1 - \hat{y})^{1-y}$.

Logistic regression uses the logistic function as a linking function to link the linear combination of input/exploratory variables and the output variable:

$$\hat{y}(x) = \frac{1}{1 + e^{-u(x)}}, \tag{4.244}$$

where $u(x)$ is a linear combination of the independent variables:

$$u(x) = \beta_0 + \sum_{j=1}^{p} \beta_j x_j = \sum_{j=0}^{p} \beta_j x_j. \tag{4.245}$$

As usual, we introduced $x_0 = 1$ for notional convenience. It is more convenient to working with the log-likelihood function

$$\ln L(\beta) = \sum_{i=1}^{n} [y_i \ln \hat{y}_i + (1 - y_i) \ln(1 - \hat{y}_i)]. \tag{4.246}$$

As described earlier, maximizing the log-likelihood function is equivalent to maximizing the likelihood because the log transform is monotonic.

In order to find the optimal fitting coefficients we need the first and second derivatives with respect to these coefficients. With the help of $\partial \hat{y}/\partial u = \hat{y}(1 - \hat{y})$ and $\partial u/\partial \beta_j = x_j$, we have the first derivative

$$\frac{\partial \ln L(\beta)}{\partial \beta_j} = \sum_{i=1}^{n} (y_i - \hat{y}_i) x_{ij}, \tag{4.247}$$

and the second derivative (the Hessian matrix)

$$\frac{\partial^2 \ln L(\beta)}{\partial \beta_j \partial \beta_k} = -\sum_{i=1}^{n} \hat{y}_i (1 - \hat{y}_i) x_{ij} x_{ik}. \tag{4.248}$$

Using the same matrix notation as in the preceding section, these can be expressed

$$\frac{\partial \ln L(\beta)}{\partial \beta} = X^T \left(Y - \hat{Y} \right) \tag{4.249}$$

and

$$\frac{\partial^2 \ln L(\beta)}{\partial \beta \partial \beta} = -X^T V X, \tag{4.250}$$

where $V = \text{diag}\,[\hat{y}_i(1 - \hat{y}_i)]$ is an $n \times n$ matrix. Comparing the first and second derivatives to those in the least square model, (4.44) and (4.45), we will find that the formulae are very similar. It is like a linear model with a weight. Because the weight depends on the unknown coefficients, there does not exist a closed form of the solution for the fitting parameters. The following Newton–Raphson iterative equation is used to search for the coefficients (see Section 9.3):

$$\beta = \beta_0 + (X^T V X)^{-1} \cdot \left[X^T (Y - \hat{Y}) \right].$$ (4.251)

At the point of the maximum likelihood function,

$$\partial \ln L(\beta) / \partial \beta = 0,$$ (4.252)

we have

$$\sum_{i=1}^{n} y_i = \sum_{i=1}^{n} \hat{y}_i$$ (4.253)

and

$$\sum_{i=1}^{n} (y_i - \hat{y}_i) x_{ij} = 0, \quad j = 1, 2, \cdots, p.$$ (4.254)

The averages of the predicted values and the actual values are the same, and the correlations between the residual and the xs are zero.

Consider a case where all the βs are zero except β_0. We then have

$$\hat{y}_i = \frac{n_1}{n_1 + n_0}, \quad \text{for all } i,$$ (4.255)

and the solution of the maximum likelihood estimation is

$$\beta_0 = \ln (n_1 / n_0),$$ (4.256)

where n_k is the number of data points with $y = k(k = 0, 1)$. This is the log-odds of the population. This is usually used as a starting point in searching for the coefficients of logistic regression. At this starting point the log-likelihood function is

$$\ln L(\beta_0) = n \left[\hat{y} \ln \hat{y} + (1 - \hat{y}) \ln(1 - \hat{y}) \right].$$ (4.257)

If the dependent variable has more than two choices, there are two possible generalizations depending on the characteristics of y. If y is ordinal, one possible regression is the ordinal regression. If y is nominal, it is a nominal regression. We will discuss these two forms of generalization in subsequent sections.

The Wald confidence intervals are sometimes called the normal confidence intervals. They are based on the asymptotic normality of the parameter estimators:

$$(B_j - \hat{\beta}_j) / \hat{\sigma}_j \sim N[0, 1],$$ (4.258)

where $\hat{\beta}_j$ is the maximum likelihood estimator of B_j and $\hat{\sigma}_j$ is the standard error estimator of $\hat{\beta}_j$. Then the $100(1 - \alpha)\%$ Wald confidence interval for B_j is given by

$$\hat{\beta}_j \pm z_{1-\alpha/2} \hat{\sigma}_j,$$ (4.259)

where z_p is the $100p$-th percentile of the standard normal distribution. Namely,

$$\int_{-\infty}^{z_p} \phi(x)dx = p. \tag{4.260}$$

For example, let $\alpha = 5\%$, then $z_{1-\alpha/2} = z_{0.975} = 1.96$. Therefore the 95% Wald confidence interval is $(\hat{\beta}_j - 1.96\,\hat{\sigma}_j, \ \hat{\beta}_j + 1.96\,\hat{\sigma}_j)$.

If each observation has a weight, the log-likelihood function becomes

$$\ln L(\beta) = \sum_{i=1}^{n} w_i \left[y_i \ln \hat{y}_i + (1 - y_i) \ln(1 - \hat{y}_i) \right]. \tag{4.261}$$

4.9 Logistic Regression: Multiple Nominal

The natural generalization of logistic regression is nominal regression, where the output takes three or more discrete values. This method is appropriate for both categorical and ordinal outputs. Ordinal outputs have a natural ordering while general categorical outputs may have no intrinsic ordering. In multiple nominal logistic regression there are K ($K \geq 3$) categories, coded as $0, 1, 2, \cdots, K-1$. The choice of y is in no specific order. The result is independent of the choice of base (which here is 0). We define $K-1$ equations

$$\ln(\hat{y}_k/\hat{y}_0) = u_k(x), \quad k = 1, 2 \ldots, K-1, \tag{4.262}$$

where $u_k(x)$ is a linear combination of the independent variables:

$$u_k(x) = \beta_{k0} + \sum_{j=1}^{p} \beta_{kj} x_j = \sum_{j=0}^{p} \beta_{kj} x_j, \quad k = 1, 2, \ldots, K-1. \tag{4.263}$$

For notational convenience we have introduced $u_0(x) = 0$. The probability of being in category k is

$$\hat{y}_k(x) = \frac{e^{u_k(x)}}{\sum_{k=0}^{K-1} e^{u_k(x)}}, \quad k = 0, 1, \ldots, K-1. \tag{4.264}$$

The result is independent of choice of base.

The likelihood function is defined by

$$\begin{aligned} L(\beta) &= \prod_{i=1}^{n} \left(\hat{y}_{i0}^{y_{i0}} \cdot \hat{y}_{i1}^{y_{i1}} \cdots \hat{y}_{i,K-1}^{y_{i,K-1}} \right) \\ &= \prod_{i=1}^{n} \prod_{k=0}^{K-1} \hat{y}_{ik}^{y_{ik}}, \end{aligned} \tag{4.265}$$

where

$$y_{ik} = \delta_{y_i,k} = \begin{cases} 1 & \text{if } y_i = k \\ 0 & \text{otherwise.} \end{cases} \tag{4.266}$$

For example, when $K = 3$ the dependent variable is coded as shown in the following table.

y	y_0	y_1	y_2
0	1	0	0
1	0	1	0
2	0	0	1

The logarithm of this likelihood function is

$$\ln L(\beta) = \sum_{i=1}^{n} \sum_{k=0}^{K-1} y_{ik} \ln \hat{y}_{ik}. \tag{4.267}$$

With the help of

$$\partial \hat{y}_{ik'} / \partial \beta_{kj} = \hat{y}_{ik'} \left(\delta_{kk'} - \hat{y}_{ik} \right) x_{ij}, \tag{4.268}$$

the first derivative is

$$\partial \ln L(\beta) / \partial \beta_{kj} = \sum_{i=1}^{n} \left(y_{ik} - \hat{y}_{ik} \right) x_{ij}, \tag{4.269}$$

where $k = 1, 2, \cdots, K - 1$ and $j = 0, 1, 2, \cdots, p$. In matrix form this becomes

$$\partial \ln L(\beta) / \partial \beta = X^T \left(Y - \hat{Y} \right). \tag{4.270}$$

At the point with the maximum likelihood we have

$$\partial \ln L(\beta) / \partial \beta_{kj} = 0, \tag{4.271}$$

where $k = 1, 2, \cdots, K - 1$ and $j = 0, 1, 2, \cdots, p$. So we have

$$\sum_{i=1}^{n} \hat{y}_{ik} = \sum_{i=1}^{n} y_{ik} \tag{4.272}$$

and

$$\sum_{i=1}^{n} \left(y_{ik} - \hat{y}_{ik} \right) x_{ij} = 0, \quad j = 1, 2, \cdots, p. \tag{4.273}$$

The averages of the predicted values and the actual values are the same, and the correlations between the residual and the xs are zero. The second derivative is

$$\frac{\partial^2 \ln L(\beta)}{\partial \beta_{kj} \partial \beta_{k'j'}} = -\sum_{i=1}^{n} \hat{y}_{ik} \left(\delta_{kk'} - \hat{y}_{ik'} \right) x_{ij} x_{ij'}, \tag{4.274}$$

where k, $k' = 1, 2, \cdots, K-1$ and j, $j' = 0, 1, 2, \cdots, p$. This is symmetric with respect to $k \leftrightarrow k'$ and $j \leftrightarrow j'$.

Let all the β_{kj}s be zero except β_{k0},

$$\hat{y}_{ik} = n_k / \sum_{k'=0}^{K-1} n_{k'} \tag{4.275}$$

for all i. Therefore the solution of the maximum likelihood estimation is $\beta_{k0} = \ln(n_k/n_0)$, where n_k is the number of ks. This is usually used as a starting point in searching for the coefficients of regression. Obviously if $k = 2$ then the formulation in this section is the same as the logistic regression shown in the last section.

4.10 Logistic Regression: Proportional Multiple Ordinal

There exist many possible ways to generalize logistic regression for multiple ordinal outputs. This differs from the previous multiple nominal in that we use multiple ordinals in situations where the output or dependent variable takes on multiple discrete values that can be logically ordered in some fashion. Here we only discuss proportional ordinal logistic regression. We code the categories in the order of $0, 1, 2, \cdots, K-1$, where K ($K \geq 3$) is the number of categories. The proportional ordinal logistic regression models the cumulative probabilities from the base category 0.

$$
\begin{aligned}
\hat{y}_0 &= \frac{1}{1+e^{-u_0(x)}} &&: p_0 \\
\hat{y}_1 &= \frac{1}{1+e^{-u_1(x)}} &&: p_0 + p_1 \\
&\quad \cdots \\
\hat{y}_{K-2} &= \frac{1}{1+e^{-u_{K-2}(x)}} &&: p_0 + p_1 + \cdots + p_{K-2} \\
\hat{y}_{K-1} &= 1 &&: p_0 + p_1 + \cdots + p_{K-2} + p_{K-1} = 1,
\end{aligned}
\tag{4.276}
$$

where p_k ($k = 0, 1, 2, \cdots, K-1$) is the probability of being the category k. $\hat{y}_k$ is the probability of $k' \leq k$. The underlining assumption in this model formulation is

$$\ln\left(\frac{\hat{y}_k}{1 - \hat{y}_k}\right) = u_k(x), \quad k = 0, 1, ..., K-2, \tag{4.277}$$

where $u_k(x)$ is expressed as a linear combination of the independent variables:

$$u_k(x) = \alpha_k + \sum_{j=1}^{p} \beta_j x_j, \quad k = 0, 1, ..., K-2. \tag{4.278}$$

The slopes, the vector β, are all the same for all k. Only the intercepts are different for the different classes k. If there are p variables then there are $p + (k - 1)$ parameters in the model. Note that $\hat{y}_k = \hat{p}_0 + \hat{p}_1 + \cdots + \hat{p}_k$, and we have $\hat{p}_k = \hat{y}_k - \hat{y}_{k-1}$. The likelihood function can be defined as

$$
\begin{aligned}
L(\beta) &= \prod_{i=1}^{n} \left(\hat{p}_{i0}^{y_{i0}} \cdot \hat{p}_{i1}^{y_{i1}} \cdots \hat{p}_{i,K-1}^{y_{i,K-1}} \right) \\
&= \prod_{i=1}^{n} \prod_{k=0}^{K-1} \hat{p}_{ik}^{y_{ik}} \\
&= \prod_{i=1}^{n} \prod_{k=0}^{K-1} (\hat{y}_{ik} - \hat{y}_{i,k-1})^{y_{ik}}.
\end{aligned} \tag{4.279}
$$

For notational convenience we define $\hat{y}_{i,-1} \equiv 0$ and $\hat{y}_{i,K-1} \equiv 1$. Because this is a multiple ordinal problem, $y_{ik} = \delta_{y_i, k}$. It is more convenient to work with the log likelihood,

$$
\ln L(\beta) = \sum_{i=1}^{n} \sum_{k=0}^{K-1} y_{ik} \ln (\hat{y}_{ik} - \hat{y}_{i,k-1}). \tag{4.280}
$$

As usual, in order to search for the coefficients we need the first and second derivatives with respect to the unknown coefficients. The first derivatives are

$$
\frac{\partial \ln L(\beta)}{\partial \beta_j} = \sum_{i=1}^{n} \sum_{k=0}^{K-1} y_{ik} \cdot (1 - \hat{y}_{ik} - \hat{y}_{i,k-1}) \, x_{ij}, \tag{4.281}
$$

$$
\frac{\partial \ln L(\beta)}{\partial \alpha_k} = \sum_{i=1}^{n} \left(\frac{y_{ik}}{\hat{p}_{ik}} - \frac{y_{i,k+1}}{\hat{p}_{i,k+1}} \right) \cdot \hat{y}_{ik} \cdot (1 - \hat{y}_{ik}), \tag{4.282}
$$

and the second derivatives are

$$
\frac{\partial^2 \ln L(\beta)}{\partial \beta_j \partial \beta_{j'}} = - \sum_{i=1}^{n} \sum_{k=0}^{K-1} y_{ik} \cdot [\hat{y}_{ik} (1 - \hat{y}_{ik}) + \hat{y}_{i,k-1} (1 - \hat{y}_{i,k-1})] \cdot x_{ij} x_{ij'}, \tag{4.283}
$$

$$
\begin{aligned}
\frac{\partial^2 \ln L(\beta)}{\partial \alpha_k \partial \alpha_{k'}} = - \sum_{i=1}^{n} &\left[\left(\frac{y_{ik}}{\hat{p}_{ik}^2} + \frac{y_{i,k+1}}{\hat{p}_{i,k+1}^2} \right) \cdot \delta_{kk'} - \left(\frac{y_{ik}}{\hat{p}_{ik}} - \frac{y_{i,k+1}}{\hat{p}_{i,k+1}} \right) \cdot \left(\frac{1 - 2\hat{y}_{ik}}{\hat{y}_{ik}(1 - \hat{y}_{ik})} \right) \cdot \delta_{kk'} \right. \\
&\left. - \frac{y_{ik}}{\hat{p}_{ik}^2} \delta_{k-1,k'} - \frac{y_{i,k+1}}{\hat{p}_{i,k+1}^2} \delta_{k+1,k'} \right] \cdot \hat{y}_{ik} (1 - \hat{y}_{ik}) \cdot \hat{y}_{ik'} (1 - \hat{y}_{ik'}),
\end{aligned} \tag{4.284}
$$

$$
\frac{\partial^2 \ln L(\beta)}{\partial \beta_j \partial \alpha_k} = - \sum_{i=1}^{n} (y_{ik} + y_{i,k+1}) \cdot \hat{y}_{ik} \cdot (1 - \hat{y}_{ik}) \cdot x_{ij}, \tag{4.285}
$$

where $j, j' = 1, 2, \cdots, p$ and $k, k' = 0, 1, \ldots, K - 2$.

If we let $\beta = 0$, then we have $\hat{p}_{ik} = n_k / \sum_{k'=0}^{K-1} n_{k'}$. Therefore the maximum likelihood estimation of intercepts are

$$
\alpha_k = \ln \left(\sum_{k'=0}^{k} n_{k'} \bigg/ \sum_{k'=k+1}^{K-1} n_{k'} \right), \tag{4.286}
$$

where n_k is the number of records with $y = k$. This is commonly used as a starting point for the iterative search for the coefficients.

4.11 Fisher Scoring Method for Logistic Regression

The general form of the likelihood function for both the multiple nominal logistic and proportional multiple ordinal logistic regressions is

$$L = \prod_{i=1}^{n} \prod_{k=0}^{K-1} \ln \hat{p}_{ik}^{y_{ik}}, \tag{4.287}$$

where n is the number of observations in the modeling data set and K is the number of categories for the dependent variable y. The dependent variable is coded into K target variables as $y_k = \delta_{y,k}$ ($k = 0, 1, ..., K - 1$) and $\hat{p}_k$ is the probability of y being in class k, ($y = k$). Note that $\sum_{k=0}^{K-1} y_k = 1$ and $\sum_{k=0}^{K-1} \hat{p}_k = 1$. The log likelihood from a single observation is

$$l = \sum_{k=0}^{K-1} y_k \ln \hat{p}_k. \tag{4.288}$$

In order to include the constraint $\sum_{k=0}^{K-1} \hat{p}_k = 1$, we introduce a Lagrange multiplier (see Section 9.1) in the likelihood function:

$$l = \sum_{k=0}^{K-1} y_k \ln \hat{p}_k - \lambda \left(\sum_{k=0}^{K-1} \hat{p}_k - 1 \right). \tag{4.289}$$

We calculate the first derivative of this likelihood function with respect to the free parameters:

$$\frac{\partial l}{\partial \beta_j} = \sum_{k=0}^{K-1} \frac{\partial \hat{p}_k}{\partial \beta_j} \frac{1}{\hat{p}_k} (y_k - \lambda \hat{p}_k). \tag{4.290}$$

Note that since $E\left(\partial l / \partial \beta_j\right) = 0$ and $E(y_k) = \hat{p}_k$, we find that $\lambda = 1$. Therefore we have

$$\frac{\partial l}{\partial \beta_j} = \sum_{k=0}^{K-1} \frac{\partial \hat{p}_k}{\partial \beta_j} \frac{1}{\hat{p}_k} (y_k - \hat{p}_k). \tag{4.291}$$

The second derivative with respect to the parameters is

$$\frac{\partial^2 l}{\partial \beta_j \partial \beta_{j'}} = \sum_{k=0}^{K-1} \left\{ \frac{\partial}{\partial \beta_{j'}} \left[\frac{\partial \hat{p}_k}{\partial \beta_j} \frac{1}{\hat{p}_k} \right] (y_k - \hat{p}_k) - \frac{\partial \hat{p}_k}{\partial \beta_j} \frac{1}{\hat{p}_k} \frac{\partial \hat{p}_k}{\partial \beta_{j'}} \right\}. \tag{4.292}$$

Noting that the expectation value of the first term is zero, we have

$$E\left(\frac{\partial^2 l}{\partial \beta_j \partial \beta_{j'}}\right) = -\sum_{k=0}^{K-1}\left\{\frac{\partial \hat{p}_k}{\partial \beta_j}\frac{1}{\hat{p}_k}\frac{\partial \hat{p}_k}{\partial \beta_{j'}}\right\}. \tag{4.293}$$

By introducing the matrix notation: $D_{kj} = \partial \hat{p}_k / \partial \beta_j$, a diagonal matrix $W_{kk} = 1/\hat{p}_k$, and column vectors $Y = (y_0, y_1, ..., y_{K-1})^T$ and $\hat{P} = (\hat{p}_0, \hat{p}_1, ..., \hat{p}_{K-1})^T$ we have

$$\frac{\partial \ln L}{\partial \beta} = \sum_{n=1}^{n} D_i^T W_i (Y_i - \hat{P}_i) \tag{4.294}$$

and

$$E\left(\frac{\partial^2 \ln L}{\partial \beta \partial \beta}\right) = -\sum_{i=1}^{n} D_i^T W_i D_i. \tag{4.295}$$

At the point where the likelihood function is maximum we have $\partial \ln L/\partial \beta = 0$. Therefore

$$\sum_{n=1}^{n} D_i^T W_i (Y_i - \hat{P}_i) = 0. \tag{4.296}$$

The Fisher scoring method for searching for the parameters is to iterate using

$$\beta = \beta_0 - \left\{E\left(\frac{\partial^2 \ln L}{\partial \beta_0 \partial \beta_0}\right)\right\}^{-1}\frac{\partial \ln L}{\partial \beta_0}. \tag{4.297}$$

Substituting the first derivative and expected second derivative into this equation, we have

$$\beta = \beta_0 + \left[\sum_{i=1}^{n} D_i^T W_i D_i\right]^{-1}\sum_{n=1}^{n} D_i^T W_i (Y_i - \hat{P}_i). \tag{4.298}$$

Given an initial parameter estimation β_0, this iterative equation finds a better estimation of β. The iteration continues until convergence. The covariance matrix of β at β_0 is estimated by

$$\text{cov}(\beta) = \left[\sum_{i=1}^{n} D_i^T W_i D_i\right]^{-1}. \tag{4.299}$$

It is evaluated at the estimated value β_0.

If $K = 2$ then the formulation is the binary logistic regression. In this case we have

$$D = \hat{p}_1(1 - \hat{p}_1)\begin{bmatrix} -1 \\ 1 \end{bmatrix} x, \tag{4.300}$$

$$W = \begin{bmatrix} 1/\hat{p}_0 & 0 \\ 0 & 1/\hat{p}_1 \end{bmatrix}, \tag{4.301}$$

and

$$Y - \hat{P} = (y_1 - \hat{p}_1) \begin{bmatrix} -1 \\ 1 \end{bmatrix}, \tag{4.302}$$

where $x = (x_1, x_2, ..., x_p)$. Therefore we have $D^T W D = \hat{p}_1(1 - \hat{p}_1)x^T x$ and $D^T W(Y - \hat{P}) = x^T(y_1 - \hat{p}_1)$. Then the iterative equation is

$$\beta = \beta_0 + \left[X^T W(\beta_0)X \right]^{-1} X^T (Y - \hat{P}_1(\beta_0)), \tag{4.303}$$

which can also be rewritten as

$$\left[X^T W(\beta_0)X \right] \beta = X^T W(\beta_0) \left[X\beta_0 + W^{-1}(\beta_0)(Y - \hat{P}_1(\beta_0)) \right]. \tag{4.304}$$

Namely

$$\left[X^T W(\beta_0)X \right] \beta = X^T W(\beta_0) Z(\beta_0), \tag{4.305}$$

where

$$z = x\beta_0 + \frac{y_1 - \hat{p}_1}{\hat{p}_1(1 - \hat{p}_1)} = \ln\left(\frac{\hat{p}_1}{1 - \hat{p}_1} \right) + \frac{y_1 - \hat{p}_1}{\hat{p}_1(1 - \hat{p}_1)}. \tag{4.306}$$

This is the iteratively reweighted least squares (IRLS) regression discussed in Section 4.7 on generalized linear regression.

4.12   Tobit Model: A Censored Regression Model

4.12.1   Some Properties of the Normal Distribution

We first show some properties of the normal distribution which are used in formulation of the Tobit model. Let φ and Φ be the pdf and cdf, respectively, of the standard normal distribution.

Lemma 4.1 *Let $x \sim N[\mu, \sigma^2]$ then*

$$E[x|x > a] = \mu + \sigma \frac{\varphi(\alpha)}{1 - \Phi(\alpha)}, \tag{4.307}$$

where $\alpha = (a - \mu)/\sigma$.

Proof 4.1 *Note that the conditional pdf is*

$$f(x|x > a) = \frac{f(x)}{\Pr(x > a)} \tag{4.308}$$

where $\Pr(x > a) = 1 - \Phi(\alpha)$. By performing the integral explicitly, we obtain this lemma.

Lemma 4.2 *Let* $x = \max(x^*, a)$ *and* $x^* \sim N[\mu, \sigma^2]$, *then*

$$E[x] = \Phi(\alpha) a + (1 - \Phi(\alpha)) \left(\mu + \sigma \frac{\varphi(\alpha)}{1 - \Phi(\alpha)} \right). \qquad (4.309)$$

Proof 4.2 *Note that* $E[x] - \Pr(x = a) a + \Pr(x > a) E[x|x > a]$ *where* $\Pr(x \le a) = \Phi(\alpha)$, $\Pr(x > a) = 1 - \Phi(\alpha)$. *Using Lemma 4.1, we have Lemma 4.2.*

As a special case when $a = 0$, we have

$$E[x] = \Phi(\mu/\sigma) \left(\mu + \sigma \frac{\varphi(\mu/\sigma)}{\Phi(\mu/\sigma)} \right). \qquad (4.310)$$

Lemma 4.3 $\frac{\varphi(x)}{\Phi(x)} \ge -x$ *for all* x.

Proof 4.3 *This lemma is a special case of the asymptotic expansion of* $\Phi(x)$, *(2.8) and (2.9), discussed in Section 2.1.2.*

4.12.2   Formulation of the Tobit Model

The Tobit model is a censored regression model where the observations on the dependent variable y_i are censored, meaning many are zero. For example, suppose we want to predict the charge-off amount for a bankcard account. For most accounts, the charge-off amounts are 0, while only a small number of accounts have a non-zero charge-off amount.

The Tobit model was first proposed by James Tobin in 1968. The model name of Tobit is from Tobin plus probit analysis. The underlying assumption is that there exists a latent variable y_i^* such that

$$y_i^* = \beta^T x_i + \varepsilon_i \qquad \varepsilon_i \sim N[0, \sigma^2]. \qquad (4.311)$$

The observed variable y_i is related to y_i^* by

$$y_i = \max(y_i^*, 0) = \begin{cases} y_i^* & y_i^* > 0 \\ 0 & y_i^* \le 0 \end{cases}. \qquad (4.312)$$

Here (β, σ) are the parameters we need to estimate from the data. Note that $y_i^* \sim N[\beta^T x_i, \sigma^2]$, from the above Lemma 4.2, and the predicted value is

$$\hat{y}_i = E[y_i|x_i] = \Phi(\beta^T x_i/\sigma) \left(\beta^T x_i + \sigma \frac{\varphi(\beta^T x_i/\sigma)}{\Phi(\beta^T x_i/\sigma)} \right). \qquad (4.313)$$

We will use the MLE method to estimate the parameters (β, σ). The likelihood function is

$$L(\beta, \sigma) = \prod_{y_i=0} \Pr(y_i^* \le 0) \cdot \prod_{y_i>0} \Pr(y_i^* > 0) f(y_i^*|y_i^* > 0). \qquad (4.314)$$

Note that $Pr(y_i^* \leq 0) = \Phi\left(-\beta^T x_i/\sigma\right)$, and

$$Pr(y_i^* > 0) f(y_i^* | y_i^* > 0) = \frac{1}{\sqrt{2\pi\sigma^2}} e^{-\frac{(y_i^* - \beta^T x_i)^2}{2\sigma^2}} = \frac{1}{\sigma}\varphi\left(\frac{y_i^* - \beta^T x_i}{\sigma}\right).$$

(4.315)

The likelihood function can be rewritten as

$$L(\beta, \sigma) = \prod_{y_i=0} \Phi\left(\frac{-\beta^T x_i}{\sigma}\right) \cdot \prod_{y_i>0} \frac{1}{\sigma}\varphi\left(\frac{y_i^* - \beta^T x_i}{\sigma}\right).$$

(4.316)

The log-likelihood function is

$$\ln L(\beta, \sigma) = \sum_{y_i=0} \ln \Phi\left(\frac{-\beta^T x_i}{\sigma}\right) - \frac{1}{2}\sum_{y_i>0}\left[\frac{(y_i^* - \beta^T x_i)^2}{\sigma^2} + \ln(2\pi\sigma^2)\right].$$

(4.317)

In MLE, it is more convenient to define new parameters $\gamma = \beta/\sigma$, $\theta = 1/\sigma$. Then the log-likelihood function in terms of (γ, θ) becomes

$$\ln L(\gamma, \theta) = \sum_{y_i=0} \ln \Phi\left(-\gamma^T x_i\right) - \frac{1}{2}\sum_{y_i>0}\left[(\theta\, y_i - \gamma^T x_i)^2 + \ln(2\pi) - \ln\theta^2\right].$$

(4.318)

The first derivatives are

$$\frac{\partial \ln L(\gamma, \theta)}{\partial \gamma} = \sum_{y_i=0} \frac{\varphi(-\gamma^T x_i)}{\Phi(-\gamma^T x_i)}(-x_i) + \sum_{y_i>0}(\theta\, y_i - \gamma^T x_i)\, x_i,$$

(4.319)

$$\frac{\partial \ln L(\gamma, \theta)}{\partial \theta} = \sum_{y_i>0}\left[-(\theta\, y_i - \gamma^T x_i)\, y_i + 1/\theta\right],$$

(4.320)

and the Hessian matrix (second derivative) is

$$H(\gamma, \theta) = \begin{bmatrix} \frac{\partial^2 \ln L(\gamma, \theta)}{\partial\gamma\partial\gamma} & \frac{\partial^2 \ln L(\gamma, \theta)}{\partial\gamma\partial\theta} \\ \frac{\partial^2 \ln L(\gamma, \theta)}{\partial\gamma\partial\theta} & \frac{\partial^2 \ln L(\gamma, \theta)}{\partial\theta^2} \end{bmatrix}$$

(4.321)

where

$$\frac{\partial^2 \ln L(\gamma, \theta)}{\partial\gamma\partial\gamma} = -\sum_{y_i=0} \frac{\varphi(-\gamma^T x_i)}{\Phi(-\gamma^T x_i)}\left(\frac{\varphi(-\gamma^T x_i)}{\Phi(-\gamma^T x_i)} - \gamma^T x_i\right) x_i x_i^T - \sum_{y_i>0} x_i x_i^T,$$

(4.322)

$$\frac{\partial^2 \ln L(\gamma, \theta)}{\partial\gamma\partial\theta} = \sum_{y_i>0} x_i y_i,$$

(4.323)

$$\frac{\partial^2 \ln L(\gamma, \theta)}{\partial\theta^2} = -\sum_{y_i>0}(y_i^2 + 1/\theta^2).$$

(4.324)

It can be shown that the Hessian matrix is always negative definite. Let (a, b) be any vector, we have

$$
(a^T, b) H \begin{pmatrix} a \\ b \end{pmatrix} = -\sum_{y_i=0} \frac{\varphi(-\gamma^T x_i)}{\Phi(-\gamma^T x_i)} \left(\frac{\varphi(-\gamma^T x_i)}{\Phi(-\gamma^T x_i)} - \gamma^T x_i \right) (a^T x_i)^2
$$
$$
-\sum_{y_i>0} \left[(a_i^T x - by)^2 + b^2/\theta^2 \right].
$$

(4.325)

From Lemma 4.3 of the normal distribution listed above, we have $\varphi(-\gamma^T x_i)/\Phi(-\gamma^T x_i) > \gamma^T x_i$. Thus

$$
(a^T, b) H \begin{pmatrix} a \\ b \end{pmatrix} < 0,
$$
(4.326)

and H is always negative definite. Therefore there is a global maximum solution of the log-likelihood function. We can use the Newton–Raphson method to get the MLE. Denoting the estimations of the parameters by $(\hat{\gamma}, \hat{\theta})$, the covariance of the estimation is

$$
\text{Cov}(\hat{\gamma}, \hat{\theta}) = -H^{-1}(\hat{\gamma}, \hat{\theta}).
$$
(4.327)

Finally, we have

$$
\text{Cov}(\hat{\beta}, \hat{\sigma}) = J \, \text{Cov}(\hat{\gamma}, \hat{\theta}) \, J^T,
$$
(4.328)

where J is the Jacobian:

$$
J = \frac{\partial(\beta, \sigma)}{\partial(\gamma, \theta)} = \begin{bmatrix} I/\theta & -\gamma/\theta^2 \\ 0 & -1/\theta^2 \end{bmatrix}.
$$
(4.329)

Chapter 5

Nonlinear Modeling

In Chapter 4, we discussed many of the important and popular linear modeling techniques. This chapter is devoted to the subject of nonlinear modeling techniques. We will cover neural networks, decision trees, additive models, support vector machine (SVM), and fuzzy logic systems.

We can logically divide the universe of machine learning algorithms into linear and nonlinear, where the linear techniques find the best-fit hyperplane in the space of the input variables that gives the closest fit to the distribution of the output variable. The next step toward nonlinearity can be classes of models that find local linear models in segmented regions of input space. One can look for local hyperplanes in boxes of carved-up input space. Tree methods achieve this by finding the best-carved-out hyperboxes (high-dimensional boxes) and then generally simply putting a flat plane (equal output values) in that box. More sophisticated tree methods can tilt these hyperplanes, building local linear regressions. We note in the latter cases the optimal cutpoints for the hyper boxes can be substantially different.

Fully nonlinear models, beyond local linear ones, include clustering, SVM, fuzzy systems, neural networks, and others. In general, the more nonlinear the modeling paradigm, the more powerful, and at the same time, the easier it is to overfit. The fundamental task of modeling is to find a best fit for an $n - 1$ dimensional hypersurface in an n-dimensional space, using sparse and noisy data points as the points to be fit, in conjunction with an objective function and a learning algorithm. The more free parameters available to describe the hypersurface, the better the fit can be but also the easier it is to overfit. The more nonlinear the technique, the more important it is to do separate testing, cross and out of time validation to avoid overfitting.

5.1 Naive Bayesian Classifier

Let y_k $(k = 1, 2, ..., K)$ be the possible classes of y and $P(y = y_k|x)$ be the probability of being in class y_k for a given x. In order to estimate $P(y = y_k|x)$, from Bayes' theorem, we have

$$P(y|x) = \frac{P(y)P(x|y)}{P(x)}. \tag{5.1}$$

We need to calculate the probability of $P(x|y) = P(x_1, x_2, ..., x_n|y)$. Note that

$$
\begin{aligned}
P(x_1, x_2, ..., x_n|y) &= P(x_1|y)P(x_2, ..., x_n|x_1, y) \\
&= P(x_1|y)P(x_2|x_1, y)P(x_3, ..., x_n|x_1, x_2, y) \\
&= P(x_1|y)P(x_2|x_1, y) \cdots P(x_n|x_1, x_2, \cdots, x_{n-1}, y).
\end{aligned} \tag{5.2}
$$

We see that $P(x|y)$ depends on many conditional probabilities.

The basic assumption in the Naive Bayesian classifier is that the distribution of x_i does not depend on the other independent variables within the class y:

$$P(x_i|x_1, x_2, \cdots, x_{i-1}, y) = P(x_i|y) \text{ for all } i = 1, 2, ... \tag{5.3}$$

Then under this assumption we have

$$P(x_1, x_2, ..., x_n|y) = \prod_{i=1}^{n} P(x_i|y). \tag{5.4}$$

We then have

$$P(y|x) = \frac{P(y)}{P(x)} \prod_{i=1}^{n} P(x_i|y). \tag{5.5}$$

Noting that

$$
\begin{aligned}
P(x) &= \sum_{k=1}^{K} P(x, y = y_k) \\
&= \sum_{k=1}^{K} P(y = y_k)P(x|y = y_k) \\
&= \sum_{k=1}^{K} \left[P(y = y_k) \prod_{i=1}^{n} P(x_i|y = y_k) \right],
\end{aligned} \tag{5.6}
$$

we have $\sum_{k=1}^{K} P(y = y_k|x) = 1$. Therefore this assumption is self-consistent.

For a given x, the maximum *a posteriori* (MAP) decision rule is to pick the class with the largest probability:

$$\text{Classifier}(x) = \arg\max_{y} P(y|x) = \arg\max_{y} \frac{P(y)}{P(x)} \prod_{i=1}^{n} P(x_i|y). \tag{5.7}$$

5.2 Neural Network

Neural networks is a very broad category that includes many network architectures, including multilayer perceptrons and normalized radial basis function networks. It includes unsupervised learning and supervised learning networks. Some authors loosely refer to any adaptive data-fitting method as a neural network because many classes of adaptive leaning algorithms can be mathematically mapped to a broad definition of neural networks. In popular writings a neural net architecture usually refers to a multilayer perceptron application, typically trained through back propagation. The books by Beale and Jackson (1990), Hertz et al. (1991), and Bishop (2006) are good references with many network architectures and many examples of applications.

5.2.1 Back Propagation Neural Network

Here we discuss the classic back propagation learning algorithm for a feed-forward neural network. As previously discussed, two commonly used objective functions are the mean square error (MSE) and maximum likelihood (ML). The problem is formulated so as to minimize the objective function.

The following picture shows the basic architecture of a multilayer perceptron. The first layer on the left is the input layer where the model inputs enter the mathematical formula. The final layer on the far right is the output layer. The middle layers are not exposed to the users and are called the hidden layers, with two hidden layers shown in the picture. Each layer consists of a set of nodes, each of which receives values from the previous node layers to the left, performs a mathematical operation on these values, and passes further values to then upstream nodes to the right. The typical operation of each node is to sum the values going into it from the previous nodes, and then "activate" if the sum exceeds a threshold. The values propagating to the right are then the node outputs (typically zero or 1) multiplied by a layer weight W. The weights are the free parameters to be obtained through data training.

The general rule for neural net/adaptive learning training is a gradient descent rule with a momentum term:

$$\Delta w_{ij}(t) = -\eta \cdot \frac{\partial E}{\partial w_{ij}} + \alpha \cdot \Delta w_{ij}(t-1), \qquad (5.8)$$

where E is the objective function, w_{ij} is the weight connecting the node j to i, η is the learning rate, and α is the momentum parameter. For multilayer perceptron architecture there does not exist a nice, closed form expression of the second derivative of the objective function with respect to weights; the learning rule using the second derivative, such as the Newton–Raphson method, is very lengthy. Therefore a back propagation rule is commonly used

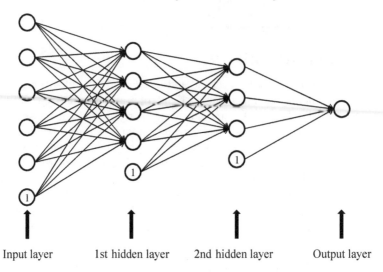

Input layer   1st hidden layer   2nd hidden layer   Output layer

FIGURE 5.1: The neural network architecture: The network shown has the architecture 5-4-3-1. It has five input nodes in the input layer, two hidden layers with four and three nodes, and one output node in the output layer. Each of the input layers and the hidden layers has one extra node with value 1 as an input for the intercept.

as the training rule. Note that at a node i the activation function is

$$V_i = g(h_i) = g\left(\sum_j w_{ij}V_j\right), \tag{5.9}$$

where V_i and V_j are the predicted values at nodes i and j, respectively. The weighted sum is over all nodes denoted by j in the previous layer connecting to the node i. We have:

$$\frac{\partial E}{\partial w_{ij}} = \frac{\partial E}{\partial V_i} \cdot \frac{\partial V_i}{\partial w_{ij}} = \frac{\partial E}{\partial V_i} g'(h_i)V_j = -\delta_i V_j, \tag{5.10}$$

where

$$\delta_i \equiv -\frac{\partial E}{\partial V_i} g'(h_i). \tag{5.11}$$

The gradient descent rule becomes

$$\Delta w_{ij}(t) = \eta\delta_i V_j + \alpha \cdot \Delta w_{ij}(t-1). \tag{5.12}$$

For a continuous target, we use the square error as the objective function:

$$E = \frac{1}{2}\sum_j (\zeta_j - V_j)^2, \tag{5.13}$$

where ζ_j is the actual value and V_j is the predicted value at the output node j. The sum is over all output nodes for a single training case. Its derivative with respect to V is

$$-\frac{\partial E}{\partial V_j} = \zeta_j - V_j. \tag{5.14}$$

For binary target $\zeta \in \{1, 0\}$, we choose the negative log-likelihood function as the objective function:

$$E = -\sum_j [\zeta_j \ln V_j + (1 - \zeta_j) \ln (1 - V_j)]. \tag{5.15}$$

Its derivative with respect to V is

$$-\frac{\partial E}{\partial V_j} = \frac{\zeta_j - V_j}{V_j(1 - V_j)}. \tag{5.16}$$

For a binary target labeled as $\zeta \in \{1, -1\}$, the negative log-likelihood function is

$$E = -\sum_j \left[\frac{1 + \zeta_j}{2} \ln \left(\frac{1 + V_j}{2} \right) V_j + \frac{1 - \zeta_j}{2} \ln \left(\frac{1 - V_j}{2} \right) \right]. \tag{5.17}$$

Its derivative with respect to V is

$$-\frac{\partial E}{\partial V_j} = \frac{\zeta_j - V_j}{(1 + V_j)(1 - V_j)}. \tag{5.18}$$

For the node j in the output layer, using the least square objective function, we have

$$\delta_j = (\zeta_j - V_j) \cdot g'(h_j). \tag{5.19}$$

Using the negative log-likelihood objective function, we have

$$\delta_j = \begin{cases} \left[\frac{\zeta_j - V_j}{V_j(1 - V_j)} \right] g'(h_j), & V_j \in \{1, 0\} \\ \left[\frac{\zeta_j - V_j}{(1 + V_j)(1 - V_j)} \right] g'(h_j), & V_j \in \{1, -1\}. \end{cases} \tag{5.20}$$

Note that the deltas are very similar with the differences as functions of V.

For the node j in the hidden layers,

$$\begin{aligned} \delta_j &= -g'(h_j) \cdot \frac{\partial E}{\partial V_j} \\ &= -g'(h_j) \cdot \sum_i \frac{\partial E}{\partial V_i} \cdot \frac{\partial V_i}{\partial V_j} \\ &= -g'(h_j) \cdot \sum_i \frac{\partial E}{\partial V_i} \cdot g'(h_i) w_{ij} \\ &= g'(h_j) \cdot \sum_i \delta_i \cdot w_{ij}. \end{aligned} \tag{5.21}$$

The sum is over all nodes denoted by i in the next layer.

Therefore V_j is calculated by forward propagation and δ_j is calculated by backward propagation through the network, respectively. The term back propagation neural network is based on this property.

The commonly used activation functions are:

Function	Activation function	First derivative
Logistic	$g(h) = \frac{1}{1+e^{-2\beta h}}$	$g'(h) = 2\beta \cdot g(1-g)$
Linear	$g(h) = 2\beta \cdot h$	$g'(h) = 2\beta$

This training algorithm is a very general model. Traditional linear regression and logistic regression are special cases for this algorithm. Linear regression is equivalent to the network without any hidden layers by using a linear activation function, and logistic regression is equivalent to the network without any hidden layers by using a logistic activation function (also equivalent to a single-node hidden layer).

We summarize the back propagation neural network algorithm with the gradient descent rule as follows:

Back Propagation Neural Network Algorithm

Initialize:

    1. Normalize all inputs x.

    2. Normalize target variable:

        if the target is a continous target, $y \rightarrow (y - \mu_y)/\sigma_y$

        else if the target is a binary target, transform to $y \in \{1, -1\}$.

    3. Initialize all weights in the network.

for $t = 1$ to Epochs do:

    1. Forward propagate: apply a training point x, calculate V_j,

        for all nodes j in network. Calculate the objective function.

    2. Backward propagate:

---

if node j is in the output layer, then

$$\delta_j = \begin{cases} (y_j - V_j) \cdot g'(h_j) & \text{square error function} \\ \frac{y_j - V_j}{(1+V_j)(1-V_j)} \cdot g'(h_j) & \text{negative log-likelihood function} \end{cases}$$

else if the node j is in the hidden layers

$$\delta_j = g'(h_j) \cdot \sum_i \delta_i \cdot w_{ij}$$

end if.

3. Update the weights:

$$\frac{\partial E}{\partial w_{ij}} = -\delta_i V_j$$

$$\Delta w_{ij}(t) = -\eta \cdot \frac{\partial E}{\partial w_{ij}} + \alpha \cdot \Delta w_{ij}(t-1)$$

end for.

If the target is continuous: $\hat{y}(x) = \mu_y + \sigma_y V_{out}$.

Else if target is binary: $\hat{p}_+(x) = (1 + V_{out})/2$.

The choice of the learning rate η plays a crucial role for the convergence speed, accuracy, and robustness of the algorithm. The first derivative of the objective function only tells the direction of searching, but it does not tell the step size for the searching. As a simple example, consider the goal to find the minimal point of the quadratic function $f(x) = ax^2$, starting from x_0. The gradient descent rule gives

$$x = x_0 - \eta \frac{df(x)}{dx} = x_0 - 2ax_0\eta. \tag{5.22}$$

The best choice of η is $\eta = 1/(2a)$, depending on a.

Here we introduce an adaptive gradient-based algorithm, the improved resilient backpropagation (iRprop) algorithm, with individual step sizes to overcome the inherent difficulty of the choice of the right learning rates. The details of the algorithm can be found in Riedmiller and Braun (1993) and Igel and Husken (2000). This learning algorithm only uses the sign of the first derivative, and the step size is adaptively learned from the previous move.

$$\Delta w_{ij}(t) = -sign\left(\frac{\partial E}{\partial w_{ij}}\right) \cdot \Delta$$

where Δ is the step size. The algorithm is summarized in the following:

iRprop Back Propagation Neural Network Algorithm

Initialize:

    1. Normalize all inputs x.

    2. Normalize the target

        if the target is a continous target, $y \rightarrow (y - \mu_y)/\sigma_y$

        else if the target is a binary target, transform to $y \in \{1, -1\}$.

    3. Initialize all weights in the network.

    4. $\eta^+ = 1.2$, $\eta^- = 0.5$, $\Delta_{\min} = 0$, $\Delta_{\max} = 50$, $\Delta^{(0)} = 0.1$, $\frac{\partial E}{\partial w}^{(0)} = 0$.

For $t = 1$ to Epochs do:

    1. Forward propagate: apply a training point x, calculate V_j,

        for all nodes j in network. Calculate the objective function.

    2. Backward propagate:

        if node j is in the output layer, then

$$\delta_j = \begin{cases} (y_j - V_j) \cdot g'(h_j) & \text{square error function} \\ \frac{y_j - V_j}{(1+V_j)(1-V_j)} \cdot g'(h_j) & \text{negative log-likelihood function} \end{cases}$$

        else if the node j is in the hidden layers

$$\delta_j = g'(h_j) \cdot \sum_i \delta_i \cdot w_{ij}$$

        end if.

    3. Update the weights:

$$\frac{\partial E}{\partial w_{ij}}^{(t)} = -\delta_i V_j$$

        if $\frac{\partial E}{\partial w_{ij}}^{(t-1)} \cdot \frac{\partial E}{\partial w_{ij}}^{(t)} \geq 0$ *then*

$$\Delta_{ij}^{(t)} = \min(\Delta_{ij}^{(t-1)} \cdot \eta^+, \Delta_{\max})$$

        else if $\frac{\partial E}{\partial w_{ij}}^{(t-1)} \cdot \frac{\partial E}{\partial w_{ij}}^{(t)} < 0$ *then*

$$\Delta_{ij}^{(t)} = \max(\Delta_{ij}^{(t-1)} \cdot \eta^-, \Delta_{\min})$$

$$\frac{\partial E}{\partial w_{ij}}^{(t)} = 0$$

        end if

$$w_{ij}^{(t+1)} = w_{ij}^{(t)} - sign\left(\frac{\partial E}{\partial w_{ij}}^{(t)}\right) \cdot \Delta_{ij}^{(t)}$$

end for.

If the target is continuous : $\hat{y}(x) = \mu_y + \sigma_y V_{out}$

Else if target is binary: $\hat{p}_+(x) = (1 + V_{out})/2$

5.3 Segmentation and Tree Models

Segmentation in general is the splitting of the data into separate, distinct groupings for ease of use. It is used in modeling to separate populations into distinct regions of input space, with the desire that the functional relationship between the input and output is as simple as possible. Here the process is done primarily for ease and optimal results by modelers. Segmentation is also a term used for such splitting in order to gain better qualitative understanding of entities, such as consumers. This second meaning may or may not be associated with a modeling task.

5.3.1 Segmentation

Segmentation in a modeling approach refers to the preseparation of data into two or several completely distinct sets, usually guided by expert knowledge, and distinct model building processes are done for each segment. One chooses this path when one has *a priori* belief that certain populations have fundamentally different input-output relationships, and this makes it easier for separate models to learn these different relationships, as opposed to hoping a global nonlinear model will discover these separate populations. Remember it is always best for the practitioner to help the model as much as possible by doing appropriate segmentation and building of good expert variables rather than relying on the model to figure this out. In this use of a segmented model the input record proceeds down a tree-based path to the particular segment model appropriate for that record.

This first use of segmentation is the process of dividing up input space into a number of separate partitions and a local model is built in each partition. The final global model is then simply the logical, piecewise combination of the different segment models. Typically there is a model splitting on one or only a few variables, and the model algorithm goes to separate submodels depending on the value of these segmentation input variables. In the final combined algorithm this splitting segmentation into submodels is usual invisible to the users of the model. The purpose of this segmentation is to try to separate input space into regions where local simple models do a better job of fitting the data, rather than force a complex model to fit all the data globally. A good model segmentation can result in a partitioning so that local linear models can do a fairly good fitting, and thus avoid the need for a global nonlinear model. In this mode the modeler uses his intuition along with iterative data discovery to identify such potential partitioning so that the resulting model complexity can be minimized.

The alternative use of segmentation in business applications is more familiar in marketing organizations. The goal here is to divide a population into groups so that similar "people" are in the same group and dissimilar people are in different groups. At a high level this is very similar to the modeler's use of the term, but for marketing segmentations it is less about local simple models for quantitative error reduction and more about qualitative groupings where people behave similarly in each group.

The fundamental concept of segmentation, specifically splitting input space into distinct subspaces for easier modeling or more homogeneous behavior, is the key aspect of all tree-based modeling algorithms. These fundamentals are the topics of the next sections.

5.3.2 Tree Models

Tree-based or tree-structured models are widely used in a variety of business problems. Their strength is in simplicity of presentation and understanding. The model presentation is usually intuitive and easy to deploy in practical operations. The reasoning logic is very clear for understanding explicitly and to develop insight around. There exist a group of well-known single tree-based algorithms and they are implemented in various packages, such as CART, CHAID, NCART, ID3, and C4.5. They differ in dealing with discrete and continuous outputs and using different criteria of information gain.

It is interesting to note that decision trees are popular algorithms to apply to the modeling segmentation tasks as well as the separations used for marketing, and they are frequently applied incorrectly both in the choice of algorithm and in the way it is used. For ease of distinctions we will refer to these different but similar modes as segmentations for modeling and for marketing.

Modeling segmentations are typically a partitioning of a space into a manageable number of boxes with the desired property that the input-output functional relationship in each separate box is as simple as possible, for example, linear. Because the result of a modeling segmentation looks very much like the result of a decision tree, a decision tree is frequently misapplied as the algorithmic process to create the desired segmentation. The crux is in the objective function used to decide where to make the partitions.

In most decision tree algorithms the objective is to maximize the within-group similarity of a target property, which simultaneously minimizes the between-group similarity (because the global total is a constant). Typically the target is a modeling output, or "y," and thus this technique finds partitions where the output value is different. This is the correct use of decision trees as a final modeling technique, but not as a modeling segmentation technique. The problem is that practitioners blindly use a decision tree to identify regions where the output is different when they should be searching for regions where local linear models are a good fit. This was described early on by others in the original algorithm descriptions, but has been successfully ignored in practice to the detriment of modeling.

In the marketing segmentation the goal should be to find regions where people are similar in some complex way other than a particular and single target variable relationship. Recent extensions of decision trees have been written by the authors of this book that generalize the segmentation objective function to complex combinations of multiple targets in an arbitrary combination of input and output spaces. This extension then allows both supervised (output space variables) and unsupervised (completely in input space), as well as an arbitrary mixture. Correct design of the objective function is critical in using decision trees in any mode other than as a pure modeling technique.

Summary for tree-based model applications:

1. Modeling Segmentation: When seeking to divide input space into a small number of distinct regions for which we will build a separate model in each region, the goal should be to make partitions where the resulting subregions have a simple relationship to the output. One should not look for partitions where the output value is similar. It is easy to choose a local linear model as an objective function, so we can look for partitions where a local linear model is a good fit.

2. Marketing Segmentation: Here we seek to divide entities into partitions where they are similar in some complex way. This frequently requires a combination of multiple targets (profitability, response, risk...), and could be an arbitrary combination of supervised and unsupervised.

3. Modeling by Itself: Here we seek to divide input space into many distinct boxes where in each box the model output will be a constant number. This is the mainline application of tree architectures to modeling. Here we seek boxes where the output values are as similar as possible.

Going forward we now describe some of the technical details of tree-based models in the context of using them for the final model (number 3 above) as opposed to for a segmentation (numbers 1 and 2).

In general, there are two classes of tree algorithms, the regression tree for a continuous target variable and the classification tree for a categorical target variable. For a more complete coverage of tree-based models, refer to the books *Classification and Regression Trees* by Breiman et al. (1984) and *The Elements of Statistical Learning: Data Mining, Inference, and Prediction* by Hastie et al. (2001).

In the construction of the subsets in tree-based modeling algorithms we desire to find cut points in any/all dimensions to divide the data so that the resulting "boxes" are homogeneous, that is, the data points in each box are similar. For supervised segmentation the similarity is typically that the output value is similar. A more sophisticated sense of similarity could be that the relation between the inputs and the outputs in that box are similar. This more sophisticated, rarely used similarity concept leads us naturally back to the previously discussed segmented model concept. For example, we could look for boxes where the data within the box all has a good fit using a simple linear model. This concept of similarity would lead to a model being a series of local linear models, as disjoint boxes in a high-dimensional space.

In tree-based models we seek to divide input space into many disjoint high-dimensional boxes that in union fill the entire input space. The boxes are chosen so that the data within the box is as similar as possible, and between the boxes the data is as different as possible. The concept of boxes rather than general clusters as used in clustering models means that we seek boundaries that are parallel to the dimensions in the space. Thus we seek a set of hierarchical cut points that will result in a good selection of these boxes.

We seek to divide space into these boxes with similar data in each box. We first consider all the data as a whole and find the best single cutpoint over all possible cutpoints in all possible dimensions. After this cut choice is made we divide the data into the resulting distinct boxes and continue with the same process in each leaf node in the tree. These methods are typically greedy in that we make the best next-cut choice based on where we are at any particular iteration.

5.3.3 Sweeping to Find the Best Cutpoint

Tree methods examine possible cutpoints in each candidate direction by moving test cutpoints systematically across a dimension with a controlled increment. Early sweeping methods used a constant increment as it swept across the input dimensions. More sophisticated methods allow the candidate cut point to move across each dimension optimally, by moving the test cutpoint one data point at a time, which is the best we can possibly do. To do this one needs an efficient method for evaluating the goodness of the resulting boxes, and this efficient methodology is described here.

Consider a trial cutpoint in an input dimension that divides the data into these two distinct groups. Let (N_1, μ_1, σ_1) and (N_2, μ_2, σ_2) be the number of observations, mean, and standard deviation for a single variable for populations 1 and 2, respectively. The total number of observations, mean, and standard deviation are

$$N = N_1 + N_2, \quad \mu = (N_1\mu_1 + N_2\mu_2)/N \tag{5.23}$$

and

$$\sigma_{tot}^2 = \sigma_{seg}^2 + N_1 N_2(\mu_1 - \mu_2)^2/N^2, \tag{5.24}$$

where $\sigma_{seg}^2 = \left(N_1\sigma_1^2 + N_2\sigma_2^2\right)/N$. Another form of the square of mean difference term is

$$N_1 N_2(\mu_1 - \mu_2)^2/N = N_1 N(\mu_1 - \mu)^2/N_2. \tag{5.25}$$

As an example, we can calculate the mean and standard deviation for a population when incrementally adding one data point or deleting one data point:

- Adding one data point

$$N' = N + 1, \quad \mu' = (N\mu + x)/(N + 1) \tag{5.26}$$

$$\sigma'^2 = N\sigma^2/(N + 1) + N(x - \mu)^2/(N + 1)^2. \tag{5.27}$$

- Deleting one data point

$$N' = N - 1, \quad \mu' = (N\mu - x)/(N - 1) \tag{5.28}$$

$$\sigma'^2 = N\sigma^2/(N-1) - N(x - \mu)^2/(N-1)^2. \tag{5.29}$$

In general, for multiple populations, the combined number of observations, mean, and standard deviation are

$$N = \sum_i N_i, \quad \mu = \sum_i N_i \mu_i / N \tag{5.30}$$

and

$$\sigma^2_{tot} = \sigma^2_{seg} + \sum_{ij} N_i N_j (\mu_i - \mu_j)^2 / \left(2N^2\right), \tag{5.31}$$

where $\sigma^2_{seg} = \sum_i N_i \sigma_i^2 / N$. Here it can be seen that minimizing the standard deviation within segments is equivalent to maximizing separation among segments. The second term in the equation can be expressed as the sum of square of the distance between the mean in each segment and the mean for overall population. Namely

$$\sum_i N_i (\mu_i - \mu)^2 / N = \sum_{ij} N_i N_j (\mu_i - \mu_j)^2 / \left(2N^2\right). \tag{5.32}$$

Therefore we have

$$N\sigma^2_{tot} = \sum_i N_i \sigma_i^2 + \sum_{ij} N_i N_j (\mu_i - \mu_j)^2 / (2N) \tag{5.33}$$

and

$$N\sigma^2_{tot} = \sum_i N_i \sigma_i^2 + \sum_i N_i (\mu_i - \mu)^2. \tag{5.34}$$

Since for each dimension we can write down the same equation, these equations are still valid in the n-dimensional space when the Euclidean distance measure has been used. This formula is commonly used in evaluating clustering results, similar to the R-squared measure in linear regression.

In a similar way we can calculate the covariance matrix from two populations, namely combining $\left(N_1, \mu_i^{(1)}, \sigma_{ij}^{(1)}\right)$ and $\left(N_1, \mu_i^{(2)}, \sigma_{ij}^{(2)}\right)$ into (N, μ_i, σ_{ij}), where $i, j = 1, 2, ..., p$:

$$N = N_1 + N_2, \quad \mu_i = \left(N_1 \mu_i^{(1)} + N_2 \mu_i^{(2)}\right)/N \tag{5.35}$$

and

$$\sigma_{ij} = \frac{N_1 \sigma_{ij}^{(1)} + N_2 \sigma_{ij}^{(2)}}{N_1 + N_2} + \frac{N_1 N_2 \left(\mu_i^{(1)} - \mu_i^{(2)}\right) \cdot \left(\mu_j^{(1)} - \mu_j^{(2)}\right)}{(N_1 + N_2)^2}. \tag{5.36}$$

The result of the variance shown above is a special case of this formula.

How do we evaluate a fuzzy clustering result? First we look at the case of the crisp clustering:

$$\sigma_{seg}^2 = \sum_k n_k \sigma_k^2 / \sum_k n_k = \left(\sum_i x_i^2 - \sum_k n_k \bar{x}_k^2 \right) / N. \tag{5.37}$$

For fuzzy clustering, the membership function, $\mu_i(k)$ (i index of data points and k index of clusters), has the properties: $\sum_k \mu_i(k) = 1$ and $\sum_i \mu_i(k) = n_k$. We have

$$\bar{x}_k = \sum_i \mu_i(k) x_i / \sum_i \mu_i(k) \tag{5.38}$$

and

$$\sigma_{seg}^2 = \sum_{i,k} \mu_i(k) (x_i - \bar{x}_k)^2 / N = \left(\sum_i x_i^2 - \sum_k n_k \bar{x}_k^2 \right) / N. \tag{5.39}$$

This form is exactly the same as the non-fuzzy version.

Let us consider the case when each observation has a weight. We have

$$N = N_1 + N_2, \quad W = W_1 + W_2, \quad \mu = (W_1 \mu_1 + W_2 \mu_2) / W \tag{5.40}$$

and

$$\sigma_{tot}^2 = \sigma_{seg}^2 + W_1 W_2 (\mu_1 - \mu_2)^2 / W^2, \tag{5.41}$$

where $\sigma_{seg}^2 = (W_1 \sigma_1^2 + W_2 \sigma_2^2) / W$. Another form of the square of the mean difference term is

$$W_1 W_2 (\mu_1 - \mu_2)^2 / W = W_1 W (\mu_1 - \mu)^2 / W_2. \tag{5.42}$$

In general, for multiple populations the combined number of observations, weights, mean, and standard deviation are

$$N = \sum_i N_i, \quad W = \sum_i W_i, \quad \mu = \sum_i W_i \mu_i / W \tag{5.43}$$

and

$$\sigma_{tot}^2 = \sigma_{seg}^2 + \sum_{ij} W_i W_j (\mu_i - \mu_j)^2 / (2 W^2), \tag{5.44}$$

where $\sigma_{seg}^2 = \sum_i W_i \sigma_i^2 / W$. Note the following three forms of the standard deviation:

$$\sigma^2 = \sum_i w_i (x_i - \mu)^2 / W = \sum_i w_i x_i^2 / W - \mu^2 = \sum_{i,j} w_i w_j (x_i - x_j)^2 / (2 W^2). \tag{5.45}$$

The second term in the equation can be expressed as the sum of square of the distance between the mean in each segment and the mean for overall population, namely

$$\sum_i W_i(\mu_i - \mu)^2/W = \sum_{ij} W_i\, W_j(\mu_i - \mu_j)^2/\left(2\,W^2\right). \qquad (5.46)$$

Therefore we have

$$W\,\sigma_{tot}^2 = \sum_i W_i\,\sigma_i^2 + \sum_{ij} W_i\, W_j(\mu_i - \mu_j)^2/(2\,W) \qquad (5.47)$$

and

$$W\,\sigma_{tot}^2 = \sum_i W_i\,\sigma_i^2 + \sum_i W_i\,(\mu_i - \mu)^2. \qquad (5.48)$$

5.3.4 Impurity Measure of a Population: Entropy and Gini Index

Let us consider a population with K different categories. We can introduce an impurity measure for the population in terms of population percentage for each category:

$$i(t) = \varphi(p_1, p_2, \cdots, p_K), \qquad (5.49)$$

where $p_i = n_i/n$ $(i = 1, 2, \cdots, K)$ is the population percentage of the category i within the population. The more impure the population is, the larger is the impurity measure. The impurity measure has the following properties:

1. $\varphi(p_1, p_2, \cdots, p_K)$ is a symmetric function of p_i.

2. $\varphi(p_1, p_2, \cdots, p_K)$ is maximum if and only if $p_i = 1/K$ for all i.

3. $\varphi(p_1, p_2, \cdots, p_K)$ is minimum if and only if the population contains only one category, i.e., $p_i = 1$ for one i and zero for all other categories.

4. $\varphi(rp_1 + sq_1, rp_2 + sq_2, \cdots, rp_K + sq_K) \geq r\varphi(p_1, p_2, \cdots, p_K) + s\varphi(q_1, q_2, \cdots, q_K)$ where $0 \leq r, s \leq 1$ and $r + s = 1$. The impurity never increases when splitting the population.

The total impurity of a tree T is the sum of the impurity over all the terminal nodes $(\tilde{T})$ weighted by the number percentage of observations:

$$I(T) = \sum_{t \in \tilde{T}} p(t) \cdot i(t). \qquad (5.50)$$

If the node t splits into t_L and t_R, then the change of impurity of the tree is

$$
\begin{aligned}
\Delta I(T) &= p(t) \cdot i(t) - p(t_L) \cdot i(t_L) - p(t_R) \cdot i(t_R) \\
&= [i(t) - p_L \cdot i(t_L) - p_R \cdot i(t_R)]\, p(t) \\
&= \Delta i(t) \cdot p(t)
\end{aligned}
\qquad (5.51)
$$

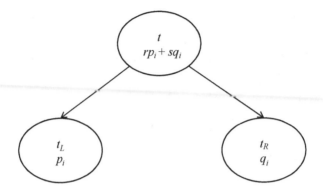

FIGURE 5.2: The information gain when splitting a node.

where $p_{L(R)} = p(t_{L(R)})/p(t)$.

There are many candidates satisfying these requirements, such as the entropy and the Gini index. We describe them in the following section.

Entropy and Information Gain

Entropy is an impurity measure that can be used to measure the randomness of a population. It is defined as

$$i(t) = -\sum_{i=1}^{K} p_i \ln p_i, \tag{5.52}$$

where $p_i = n_i/n$ $(i = 1, 2, \cdots, K)$ is the population percentage of the category i within the population. It is easy to see that the function is symmetric with respect to p_i. When one of p_i is one and all others are zero then $i(t)$ is zero. By constructing a Lagrange function, $L = -\sum_i p_i \ln p_i - \lambda(\sum_i p_i - 1)$ (see Section 9.1), we can verify that $i(t)$ goes to the maximum when p_i are all equal. Define a function

$$f(r) = -\sum_i (rp_i + sq_i) \ln(rp_i + sq_i) + r \sum_i p_i \ln p_i + s \sum_i q_i \ln q_i \tag{5.53}$$

where $0 \le r, s \le 1$ and $r + s = 1$. Note that $f(0) = f(1) = 0$ and

$$f''(r) = -\sum_i \frac{(p_i - q_i)^2}{rp_i + sq_i} \le 0. \tag{5.54}$$

According to Lemma A.3 in Appendix A we have $f(r) \ge 0$ for all r. Namely we have the following inequality:

$$-\sum_i (rp_i + sq_i) \ln(rp_i + sq_i) \ge -r \sum_i p_i \ln p_i - s \sum_i q_i \ln q_i. \tag{5.55}$$

If there exists an r_0 ($r_0 \neq 0, 1$) such that $f(r_0) = 0$, then $f(r) = 0$ for all $r \in [0, 1]$. Therefore the equality occurs if and only if $p_i = q_i$ for all i. The entropy measure therefore satisfies all requirements for an impurity measure.

As a special case when $K = 2$, let p and $(1 - p)$ be the population percentage within categories 1 and 2, respectively. Then the entropy is

$$i(p) = -p \ln p - (1 - p) \ln(1 - p). \tag{5.56}$$

It is 0 when p is either 0 or 1. When $p = 1/2$, it reaches the maximum value of $\ln 2$.

The entropy defined here is the same as the entropy defined in statistical mechanics. In statistical mechanics, the entropy is defined as

$$S = \ln W, \tag{5.57}$$

where W is the number of micro-states for a given macro-state. For the system described here, all particles are allocated into K states. Therefore

$$W = \frac{n!}{\prod\limits_{i=1}^{K} n_i!}. \tag{5.58}$$

Using Stirling's formula for large n, $\ln n! \approx n \ln n - n + \ln \sqrt{2\pi n}$, we then find

$$
\begin{aligned}
\ln W &\approx n \ln n - n + \ln \sqrt{2\pi n} - \sum_{i=1}^{K} (n_i \ln n_i - n_i + \ln \sqrt{2\pi n_i}) \\
&\approx n \ln n - \sum_{i=1}^{K} n_i \ln n_i \\
&= -n \sum_{i=1}^{K} p_i \ln p_i,
\end{aligned}
\tag{5.59}
$$

which establishes the desired relationship.

For any distribution function $f(x)$ of a continuous variable we can define the entropy as

$$H[f] = -\int f(x) \ln f(x) dx. \tag{5.60}$$

What is the form of the distribution such that the entropy is maximized? In the following we will show that the answer is the Gaussian distribution. Since the integral is invariant under shifting the whole curve of the distribution along the x-axis, without loss of generality we can assume the mean of the distribution is a constant and the variance is a constant. Therefore we can formulate the following optimization problem:

$$
\begin{aligned}
\text{maximize} \quad & H[f] = -\int f(x) \ln f(x) dx \\
\text{subject to} \quad & \int f(x) dx = 1 \\
& \int x f(x) dx = \mu \\
& \int x^2 f(x) dx = \mu^2 + \sigma^2.
\end{aligned}
\tag{5.61}
$$

Introducing three Lagrange multipliers for the constraints (see Section 9.1), we have the following Lagrangian

$$L[f] = -\int f(x) \ln f(x) dx - \lambda_0 \left[\int f(x) dx - 1 \right]$$
$$-\lambda_1 \left[\int x f(x) dx - \mu \right] - \lambda_2 \left[\int x^2 f(x) dx - \mu^2 - \sigma^2 \right]. \tag{5.62}$$

Setting the functional derivative to zero to find the extreme,

$$\frac{\delta L[f]}{\delta f} = -\int \left[\ln f(x) + 1 \right] \delta f(x) \, dx - \int \left[\lambda_0 + \lambda_1 x + \lambda_2 x^2 \right] \delta f(x) \, dx = 0, \tag{5.63}$$

we have

$$f(x) = e^{-(1+\lambda_0+\lambda_1 x+\lambda_2 x^2)}. \tag{5.64}$$

With these three constraints we can determine these three lambda parameters and finally we have

$$f(x) = \frac{1}{\sqrt{2\pi\sigma^2}} e^{-\frac{(x-\mu)^2}{2\sigma^2}}. \tag{5.65}$$

Therefore, among all distributions, when the distribution is Gaussian the entropy reaches the maximum value.

Gini Index

Another impurity measure of a population is the Gini index. It is defined as:

$$i(t) = \sum_{i \neq j} p_i p_j = 1 - \sum_i^K p_i^2 \tag{5.66}$$

where $p_i = n_i/n$ $(i = 1, 2, \cdots, K)$ is the population percentage of the category i within the population. It is easy to see that this function is symmetric with respect to p_i. When one of p_is is 1 and all others are zero then $i(t)$ is zero. By constructing the Lagrange function $L = 1 - \sum_i p_i^2 - \lambda \left(\sum_i p_i - 1 \right)$, (see Section 9.1), we can verify that $i(t)$ goes to the maximum when all p_is are all equal. Define a function

$$f(r) = 1 - \sum_i (rp_i + sq_i)^2 - r \left(1 - \sum_i p_i^2 \right) - s \left(1 - \sum_i q_i^2 \right) \tag{5.67}$$

where $0 \leq r, s \leq 1$ and $r + s = 1$. Note that $f(0) = f(1) = 0$ and

$$f''(r) = -\sum_i 2(p_i - q_i)^2. \tag{5.68}$$

According to Lemma A.3 in Appendix A we have $f(r) \geq 0$ for all r. Namely we have the following inequality:

$$1 - \sum_i (rp_i + sq_i)^2 \geq r \left(1 - \sum_i p_i^2 \right) + s \left(1 - \sum_i q_i^2 \right). \tag{5.69}$$

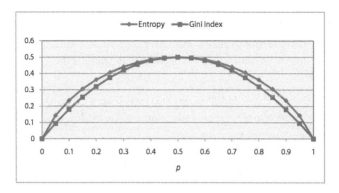

FIGURE 5.3: Entropy and Gini index for binary case: The entropy and Gini index are functions of p, a population percentage. The entropy shown is scaled as $[-p\ln p - (1-p)\ln(1-p)]/(2\ln 2)$ and the Gini index is $2p(1-p)$.

If there exists an r_0 ($r_0 \neq 0$, 1) such that $f(r_0) = 0$, then $f(r) = 0$ for all $r \in [0,1]$. Therefore the equality occurs if and only if $p_i = q_i$ for all i. The Gini index therefore satisfies all requirements for an impurity measure.

As a special case when $K = 2$, let p and $(1-p)$ be the population percentage within categories 1 and 2, respectively. Then the Gini index is

$$i(p) = 1 - \sum_{i=1}^{2} p_i^2 = 2p(1-p). \tag{5.70}$$

It is 0 when p is 0 or 1. When $p = 1/2$, it reaches the maximum value of $1/2$.

5.3.5 Chi-Square Splitting Rule

The chi-square criteria can be used as a splitting rule for a tree algorithm. For the case with K categories in a population, let n_k be the number of observations in the category k, and n_l and n_r be the number of observations of the left subtree and right subtree, respectively. We have the chi-square for measuring the difference between the left and right populations:

$$\chi_P^2 = n_l n_r \sum_{k=1}^{K} [p(k|l) - p(k|r)]^2 / n_k. \tag{5.71}$$

The larger χ_P^2 is, the better the splitting is. As a special case, if the population contains only two different categories, say, G for Good and B for Bad, we have

$$\chi_P^2 = \frac{n^2}{BG} \left\{ \frac{n_l n_r}{n} [p(G|l) - p(G|r)]^2 \right\}. \tag{5.72}$$

5.3.6 Implementation of Decision Trees

There are several possibilities for the types of the independent variables (X) and the target variable (Y) for building decision trees, as shown in the following table.

TABLE 5.1: The types of the independent variables (X) and the target variable (Y) for building decision trees.

X	Y
numerical	numerical
numerical	binary
numerical	categorical with the number of the possible values is larger than 2
categorical	numerical
categorical	binary
categorical	categorical with the number of the possible values is larger than 2

For illustration, in this section we only consider a special kind of tree, a binary split decision tree, by assuming that all independent variables (X) are numerical and each split in a node is binary (only two branches at each node).

For the binary split decision tree, each node can be labeled with an index starting with 1 from the root node. The nodes are at different levels of the tree starting with level 0 for the root node.

In the process of growing a tree we need to search all terminal nodes to find the best node to split. If we store the potential splitting information in each node, we don't need to recalculate the splitting again and again for each node. Therefore it is good idea to find all the information for potentially splitting a node when we create each node. We can design the structure of each node in a tree as shown in the following table

The algorithm for creating a decision tree is

1. Initialize the root node and find the best variable to split the node (but not actually splitting the node yet).

2. Find the best node to split from all current terminal nodes. Split the selected node into left and right nodes and insert into the tree.

3. Repeat Step 2 until you satisfy the stopping criteria.

4. Delete the auxiliary data in the terminal nodes.

5. Prune the tree if necessary.

6. Generate a report for the tree and output the scoring code.

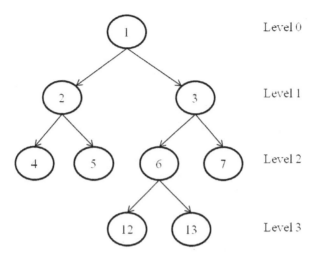

FIGURE 5.4: The structure of binary decision tree: each node is labeled with an index starting with 1 for the root node. If the index for a given node is i, then its left child's index is $2i$ and its right child's index is $2i+1$. The level of the node is (int) $\log_2$(index).

TABLE 5.2: The data structure of the node in a decision tree.

Variable	Comments
x	The data for all input variables of this node.
y	The data for the output variable of this node.
index	The index of this node. The root node has an index 1. If a node has an index i, its left child has an index $2i$ and its right child has an index $2i+1$.
level	Level of this node in a tree, level = (int)$\log_2$(index). The root node is at the level 0.
step	The number of steps to reach to split this node. The step for splitting the root node is 1.
variable	The variable to split this node to create its children.
cutpoint	The cutpoint of the variable to split this node ($\leq, >$) = (left node, right node).
gain	The gain of splitting this node using the splitting variable and the cutpoint.
n	The number of observations in this node.
n_1 or $\bar{y}$	The number of 1s for binary target variable or the mean of the target variable for the numerical target in this node.
terminal	The flag to indicate if it's a terminal node.

We use the information gain from the entropy or Gini index for binary target and the squared error for numerical target to find the best split. The stopping criteria are:

- No more splitting for a node when the node population is less than a threshold

- If the maximum level of the tree reaches a threshold (for example, if the maximum level is 6, then the tree has 6 levels)

- If the number of splittings reaches the maximum number (for example, we may decide that the tree should have no more than 10 splittings)

In order to print out the nodes in a tree, we need to walk through all the nodes in a certain order. For the tree with three levels shown above, we can construct a string with length 3 for each node. For each node, we can trace it from the root node to that node by left movement, right movement, or no movement (labeled by L = Left, R = Right, A = No move). The movements from the root node to each node are shown below:

```
1  = AAA
2  = LAA
3  = RAA
4  = LLA
5  = LRA
6  = RLA
7  = RRA
12 = RLL
13 = RLR
```

For example, in order to walk from the root to node 12, we need to move three steps: the 1st step is Right, the 2nd step is Left, and the 3rd step is Left. If we sort the list of strings, we get the correct order of nodes if we want to write a scoring code of a tree:

```
1  = AAA
2  = LAA
4  = LLA
5  = LRA
3  = RAA
6  = RLA
12 = RLL
13 = RLR
7  = RRA
```

Let x_i and c_i ($i = 1, 2, ..., 6$) be the decision variable and the cutpoint in the node i. Then the scoring code for the tree illustrated above is:

```
if (x1 <= c1) {
    if (x2 <= c2) {
        Node 4;
    } else {
        Node 5;
    }
} else {
    if (x3 <= c3) {
        if (x6 <= c6) {
            Node 12;
        } else {
            Node 13;
        }
    } else {
        Node 7;
    }
}
```

5.4 Additive Models

This section discusses the additive model in general and then covers the boosted model using trees as the base functions. The main references of this section are the two papers by Friedman (1999, 2001).

Let (x_i, y_i), $i = 1, 2, ..., n$ be n data points in the training sample, with each x being a p-dimensional vector (p independent variables). The purpose of building a model is to find a function $f(x)$ that fits the data y as well as possible. This fitting can be achieved by minimizing a loss function:

$$L(f) = \sum_{i=1}^{n} L(y_i, f(x_i)). \tag{5.73}$$

The model function $f(x)$ is a map: $R^p \to R$. Alternatively, we can interpret the function $f(x)$ as a point in an n-dimensional space:

$$f = (f(x_1), f(x_2), ..., f(x_n)). \tag{5.74}$$

The actual output of the n data points is also a point in the n-dimensional space:

$$y = (y_1, y_2, ..., y_n). \tag{5.75}$$

In this point of view, to build the best model is equivalent to find the best point in the n-dimensional space such that the loss function is minimized. Namely, we need to find a point f as close to y as possible. Of course, we must be careful to avoid overfitting.

As usual in an optimization problem, we can use a stepwise, iterative approach to find the best point:

$$f(x) = f_0(x) + h_1(x) + \dots + h_M(x), \tag{5.76}$$

where each additional function $h_i(x)$ helps f approach y better and better. For each individual problem, we can find the 0-order approximation, $f_0(x)$. Then at each step, the gradient descent method can be used to find next point:

$$f_m(x) = f_{m-1}(x) - \lambda_m g_m(x), \tag{5.77}$$

where the gradient of the loss function is

$$g_m(x) = \nabla L(f)|_{f_{m-1}(x)}. \tag{5.78}$$

Noting that the loss function is the sum of all n terms, we have

$$\frac{\partial L(f)}{\partial f(x_i)} = \frac{\partial L(y_i,\, f(x_i))}{\partial f(x_i)}. \tag{5.79}$$

Therefore we have

$$g_{mi} = \left[\frac{\partial L(y_i,\, f(x_i))}{\partial f(x_i)}\right]_{f(x_i)=f_{m-1}(x_i)}. \tag{5.80}$$

A line search can be used to find the step size:

$$\begin{aligned}
\lambda_m &= \arg\min_\lambda L(f_{m-1}(x) - \lambda\, g_m(x)) \\
&= \arg\min_\lambda \sum_{i=1}^{n} L(y_i,\, f_{m-1}(x_i) - \lambda\, g_m(x_i)).
\end{aligned} \tag{5.81}$$

After M steps, we have the desired approximation function as

$$f_M(x) = f_0(x) - \sum_{m=1}^{M} \lambda_m g_m(x). \tag{5.82}$$

If each observation has a weight, the loss function becomes

$$L(f) = \sum_{i=1}^{n} w_i L(y_i,\, f(x_i)), \tag{5.83}$$

where w_i is the weight for the ith observation. A line search to find the step size becomes

$$\lambda_m = \arg\min_\lambda \sum_{i=1}^{n} w_i L(y_i,\, f_{m-1}(x_i) - \lambda\, g_m(x_i)). \tag{5.84}$$

5.4.1 Boosted Tree

Let's consider a special case of an additive model when the base learner is a tree. The function is approximately expressed as the sum of a series of trees,

$$f_M(x) = T_0(x) + T_1(x) + \dots + T_M(x). \tag{5.85}$$

At each step we build a tree:

$$f_m(x) = f_{m-1}(x) + T_m(x). \tag{5.86}$$

Comparing to the gradient descent method discussed above, we can find what the target of each tree is:

$$T_m(x) \leftrightarrow -\lambda_m \, g_m(x). \tag{5.87}$$

Thus, we can use the negative gradient of a loss function as a target to build a tree. We call it a pseudo-residual since it is not necessarily a typical residual. The form of this pseudo-residual depends on the form of loss function.

$$\tilde{y}_m(x_i) = -g_{mi} = -\left[\frac{\partial L(y_i, f(x_i))}{\partial f(x_i)} \right]_{f(x_i)=f_{m-1}(x_i)}. \tag{5.88}$$

We use the data points, $(x_i, \tilde{y}_m(x_i))$, $i = 1, 2, \dots, n$ to build a tree with J_m nodes and the region of the jth ($j = 1, 2, \dots, J_m$) node is specified by R_{mj}. In this step a regression tree is built using a least-squares splitting criterion. It is represented as

$$t_m(x) = \sum_{j=1}^{J_m} \tilde{y}_{mj} \, I(x \in R_{mj}). \tag{5.89}$$

Here $\tilde{y}_{mj} = \text{mean}_{x \in R_{mj}}(\tilde{y}_{mi})$. We used the notation $I(e)$ such that $I(e) = 1$ if e is true, while $I(e) = 0$ if e is false. Now we need to figure out what the step size is. Note that

$$\min_{\lambda} \sum_{j=1}^{J_m} \sum_{x \in R_{mj}} L(y_i, f_{m-1}(x_i) + \lambda \, t_m(x_i))$$
$$\geq \sum_{j=1}^{J_m} \min_{\lambda} \sum_{x \in R_{mj}} L(y_i, f_{m-1}(x_i) + \lambda \, t_m(x_i)). \tag{5.90}$$

Since there is only one parameter to optimize in the LHS, while there are J_m parameters to optimize in the RHS, this inequality is obviously held. Therefore if we search across λ in each node, the loss function is more optimal. We have

$$\lambda_{mj} = \arg\min_{\lambda} \sum_{x \in R_{mj}} L(y_i, f_{m-1}(x_i) + \lambda \, t_m(x_i)). \tag{5.91}$$

Since $t_m(x_i)$ is a constant in the region R_{mj}, and by defining $\gamma = \lambda \, t_m(x_i)$, we have

$$\gamma_{mj} = \arg\min_{\gamma} \sum_{x \in R_{mj}} L(y_i, f_{m-1}(x_i) + \gamma). \tag{5.92}$$

Finally, the function approximation in the mth step is

$$f_m(x) = f_{m-1}(x) + \sum_{j=1}^{J_m} \gamma_{mj} I(x \in R_{mj}). \tag{5.93}$$

The boosted tree algorithm with weights can be summarized as follows:

Boosted Tree Algorithm

$f_0(x)$: find a 0th order approximation.

for $m = 1$ to M do :

$$\tilde{y}(x_i) = - \left[\frac{\partial L(y_i, f(x_i))}{\partial f(x_i)} \right]_{f(x_i)=f_{m-1}(x_i)}, \quad i = 1, 2, ..., n$$

build a tree with J_m nodes, R_{mj}, based on $(x_i, \tilde{y}_i)$

$$\gamma_{mj} = \arg\min_{\gamma} \sum_{x_i \in R_{mj}} w_i L(y_i, f_{m-1}(x_i) + \gamma)$$

$$f_m(x) = f_{m-1}(x) + \sum_{j=1}^{J_m} \gamma_{mj} I(x \in R_{mj})$$

end for

5.4.2   Least Squares Regression Boosting Tree

The simplest boosting tree is the least squares regression boosting tree. For a continuous target variable y, we use the squared error loss function

$$L(y, f(x)) = \frac{1}{2}(y - f(x))^2. \tag{5.94}$$

The residual is

$$\tilde{y}(x_i) = - \left[\frac{\partial L(y_i, f(x_i))}{\partial f(x_i)} \right] = y_i - f(x_i). \tag{5.95}$$

This is the residual of the current model on the ith observation. We can build a tree model based on the residual of the model so far. We then calculate a new residual based on a new tree. This process continues until a certain accuracy of model performance has been reached. We use the data points, $(x_i, \tilde{y}_m(x_i))$, $i = 1, 2, ..., n$ to build a tree with J_m nodes and the jth node is specified by R_{mj}. γ_{mj} ($j = 1, 2, ..., J_m$) can be found by solving the following optimization problem:

$$\gamma_{mj} = \arg\min_{\gamma} \sum_{x_i \in R_{mj}} (y_i - f_{m-1}(x_i) - \gamma)^2. \tag{5.96}$$

It is easy to see the best solution of γ is the mean of the residual in each node, namely

$$\gamma_{mj} = \sum_{x_i \in R_{mj}} (y_i - f_{m-1}(x_i))/n_{mj}, \qquad (5.97)$$

where n_{mj} is the number of observation in the node R_{mj}.

The least squares regression boosting tree with weights can be summarized as follows:

Least Squares Regression Boosting Tree Algorithm

Assumption: y continuous target

Calculate population mean of $y : \bar{y}$

$f_0(x) = \bar{y}$

for $m = 1$ to M do:

$\tilde{y}(x_i) = y_i - f_{m-1}(x_i), \; i = 1, 2, ..., n$

build a tree with J_m nodes, R_{mj}, based on $(x_i, \tilde{y}_i)$

$$\gamma_{mj} = \frac{\sum\limits_{x_i \in R_{mj}} w_i \tilde{y}(x_i)}{\sum\limits_{x_i \in R_{mj}} w_i}$$

$$f_m(x) = f_{m-1}(x) + \sum_{j=1}^{J_m} \gamma_{mj} I(x \in R_{mj})$$

end for

5.4.3 Binary Logistic Regression Boosting Tree

As a special case consider a binary logistic regression in terms of a boosted tree. For $y \in \{1, 0\}$, if we let p be the probability of y to be 1, the binomial log-likelihood function is

$$l(y, p) = \ln \left(p^y (1 - p)^{1-y} \right) = y \ln p + (1 - y) \ln(1 - p). \qquad (5.98)$$

For notational convenience we use $y \in \{1, -1\}$ in the rest of this section. Also we use the symmetric logistic regression form

$$p(x) = \frac{e^{f(x)}}{e^{f(x)} + e^{-f(x)}} = \frac{1}{1 + e^{-2f(x)}}. \qquad (5.99)$$

The inverse relationship is

$$f(x) = \frac{1}{2} \ln \left(\frac{p(x)}{1 - p(x)} \right). \qquad (5.100)$$

Then the log-likelihood function is

$$l(y, p) = \left(\tfrac{1+y}{2}\right) \ln p + \left(\tfrac{1-y}{2}\right) \ln(1 - p). \tag{5.101}$$

The 0-order approximation of $f(x)$ is

$$f_0(x) = \tfrac{1}{2} \ln\left(\tfrac{n_1}{n_{-1}}\right) = \tfrac{1}{2} \ln\left(\tfrac{1+\bar{y}}{1-\bar{y}}\right). \tag{5.102}$$

The binomial log-likelihood function can be expressed as

$$l(y, f(x)) = \ln\left(\frac{1}{1 + e^{-2y f(x)}}\right). \tag{5.103}$$

Define the loss function as the negative of the binomial log-likelihood function:

$$L(y, f(x)) = -l(y, f(x)) = \ln\left(1 + e^{-2y f(x)}\right). \tag{5.104}$$

The pseudo-residual is

$$\tilde{y}(x_i) = -\left[\frac{\partial L(y_i, f(x_i))}{\partial f(x_i)}\right] = \frac{2y_i}{1 + e^{2y_i f(x_i)}}. \tag{5.105}$$

We can use the data points, $(x_i, \tilde{y}_m(x_i))$, $i = 1, 2, ..., n$ to build a tree with J_m nodes and the jth node is specified by R_{mj}. γ_{mj} $(j = 1, 2, ..., J_m)$ can be found by solving the following optimization problem:

$$\gamma_{mj} = \arg\min_{\gamma} \sum_{x_i \in R_{mj}} \ln\left[1 + e^{-2y_i(f_{m-1}(x_i) + \gamma)}\right]. \tag{5.106}$$

There is no closed-form solution for this optimization problem, but we can use the Newton–Raphson method,

$$x = x_0 - f'(x_0)/f''(x_0). \tag{5.107}$$

Define an objective function

$$g(\gamma) = \sum_{x_i \in R_{mj}} \ln\left[1 + e^{-2y_i(f_{m-1}(x_i) + \gamma)}\right]. \tag{5.108}$$

The first and the second derivatives, respectively, are

$$g'(\gamma) = -\sum_{x_i \in R_{mj}} \frac{2y_i}{1 + e^{2y_i(f_{m-1}(x_i) + \gamma)}}, \tag{5.109}$$

$$g''(\gamma) = \sum_{x_i \in R_{mj}} (2y_i)^2 \left[\frac{1}{1 + e^{2y_i(f_{m-1}(x_i) + \gamma)}} - \frac{1}{\left(1 + e^{2y_i(f_{m-1}(x_i) + \gamma)}\right)^2}\right]. \tag{5.110}$$

Setting $\gamma = 0$, we have

$$g'(0) = - \sum_{x_i \in R_{mj}} \tilde{y}_i, \qquad (5.111)$$

$$g''(0) = \sum_{x_i \in R_{mj}} \tilde{y}_i \, (2y_i - \tilde{y}_i). \qquad (5.112)$$

From the Newton–Raphson method, we have

$$\gamma_{mj} = -\frac{g'(0)}{g''(0)} = \frac{\sum_{x_i \in R_{mj}} \tilde{y}_i}{\sum_{x_i \in R_{mj}} \tilde{y}_i \, (2y_i - \tilde{y}_i)}. \qquad (5.113)$$

Finally, these two ideas can be incorporated into the algorithm. First, a shrinkage parameter $0 < \nu \leq 1$ can be introduced to control the learning rate of the procedure. The study by Friedman showed that small values ($\nu \leq 0.1$) lead to much better generalization error:

$$f_m(x) = f_{m-1}(x) + \nu \sum_{j=1}^{J_m} \gamma_{mj} \, I(x \in R_{mj}). \qquad (5.114)$$

Second, at each step, instead of training the full data set, a subsample of the training data is drawn at random (without replacement) from the full training data set. These two features can be easily implemented in the algorithm.

The boosting tree algorithm for binary logistic regression with weights can be summarized as follows:

Logistic Regression Boosting Tree Algorithm

Assumption : $y \in \{1, -1\}$

Calculate population mean of $y : \bar{y}$

$f_0(x) = \frac{1}{2} \ln \left(\frac{1+\bar{y}}{1-\bar{y}} \right)$

for $m = 1$ to M do :

$\quad \tilde{y}(x_i) = \frac{2y_i}{1+e^{2y_i f(x_i)}} \big|_{f(x_i)=f_{m-1}(x_i)}$, $i = 1, 2, \ldots, n$

$\quad$ build a tree with J_m nodes, R_{mj}, based on $(x_i, \tilde{y}_i)$

$$\gamma_{mj} = \frac{\sum_{x_i \in R_{mj}} w_i \tilde{y}_i}{\sum_{x_i \in R_{mj}} w_i \tilde{y}_i \, (2y_i - \tilde{y}_i)}$$

$$f_m(x) = f_{m-1}(x) + \sum_{j=1}^{J_m} \gamma_{mj} \, I(x \in R_{mj})$$

end for

$p_+(x) = \frac{1}{1+e^{-2f_M(x)}}$

$p_-(x) = \frac{1}{1+e^{2f_M(x)}}$

5.5 Support Vector Machine (SVM)

The SVM approach is straightforward conceptually and begins with the ideas of simple linear classifiers. Consider a two-class classification problem where we wish to identify a hyperplane that best separates the two types of data points in the multidimensional input space, similar to our use of the Fisher discriminant algorithm. In the SVM approach we try to find the best linear hyperplane that provides the largest error tolerance on both sides of this separation plane.

The most important way SVM differs from the straightforward linear classifiers is the use of an extension of the input space to a higher dimension. One can always find a hyperplane that provides perfect classification in a sufficiently high and properly chosen hyperspace. What SVM does is to create an extended hyperspace beyond the original input space using a nonlinear kernel mapping. The best separation hyperplane is then found in this extended hyperspace, and the resulting classifier is then, in general, nonlinear in the original input space.

5.5.1 Wolfe Dual

Let's consider a general nonlinear optimization problem:

$$\underset{x}{\text{minimize}} \quad f(x) \qquad x = [n \times 1]$$

$$\text{subject to} \quad h_i(x) = 0, \quad i = 1, 2, ..., m \tag{5.115}$$

$$g_i(x) \geq 0, \quad i = 1, 2, ..., p.$$

We are searching for the minimum value of $f(x)$ in an n-dimensional space with m equality constraints and p inequality constraints. The Wolfe dual of this optimization problem is

$$\underset{x, \lambda, \mu}{\text{maximize}} \quad f(x) - \sum_{i=1}^{m} \lambda_i h_i(x) - \sum_{i=1}^{p} \mu_i g_i(x)$$

$$\text{subject to} \quad \nabla f(x) - \sum_{i=1}^{m} \lambda_i \nabla h_i(x) - \sum_{i=1}^{p} \mu_i \nabla g_i(x) = 0 \tag{5.116}$$

$$\mu_i \geq 0, \quad i = 1, 2, ..., p.$$

Now we are searching in $(n + m + p)$-dimensional space, (x, λ, μ), with $p + 1$ constraints.

The Wolfe dual can be understood by the Lagrange dual discussed in Section 9.9.2 and the following lemma.

Lemma 5.1 *Let $f(x, \lambda)$ be a linear function in λ. Define $L(\lambda) = \min_x f(x, \lambda)$ without any constraint in x, then $L(\lambda)$ is a concave function in λ.*

Proof 5.1 *Let* $\lambda_2 = \alpha \lambda_1 + (1 - \alpha)\lambda_3$, $\alpha \in [0, 1]$. *Since* $f(x, \lambda)$ *is a linear function in* λ, *we have for any* x

$$f(x, \lambda_2) = \alpha f(x, \lambda_1) + (1 - \alpha)f(x, \lambda_3). \tag{5.117}$$

Let $x_i = \arg\min_x f(x, \lambda_i)$, *for* $i = 1, 2, 3$, *we have*

$$
\begin{aligned}
f(x_2, \lambda_2) &= \alpha f(x_2, \lambda_1) + (1 - \alpha)f(x_2, \lambda_3) \\
&\geq \alpha \min_x(f(x, \lambda_1)) + (1 - \alpha)\min_x(f(x, \lambda_3)) \\
&= \alpha f(x_1, \lambda_1) + (1 - \alpha)f(x_3, \lambda_3).
\end{aligned}
\tag{5.118}
$$

Therefore $L(\lambda_2) \geq \alpha L(\lambda_1) + (1 - \alpha)L(\lambda_3)$. $L(\lambda)$ *is a concave function of* λ.

For example, consider the simple optimization problem:

$$
\begin{aligned}
&\underset{x}{\text{minimize}} \quad x^2 \\
&\text{subject to} \quad x \geq 1.
\end{aligned}
\tag{5.119}
$$

Its Wolfe dual is

$$
\begin{aligned}
&\underset{x, \lambda}{\text{maximize}} \quad f(x, \lambda) = x^2 - 2\lambda(x - 1) \\
&\text{subject to} \quad 2x - 2\lambda = 0 \\
&\qquad\qquad\quad \lambda \geq 0.
\end{aligned}
\tag{5.120}
$$

The Wolfe dual can be simplified to

$$
\begin{aligned}
&\underset{\lambda}{\text{maximize}} \quad L(\lambda) = -\lambda^2 + 2\lambda \\
&\text{subject to} \quad \lambda \geq 0.
\end{aligned}
\tag{5.121}
$$

The solution is $x = 1$, $\lambda = 1$. This provides the solution of the original simple optimization problem.

5.5.2 Linearly Separable Problem

Let's discuss how to describe a plane in an n-dimensional space. First consider a linear equation

$$w^T x + b = 0, \tag{5.122}$$

where $x = [n \times 1]$, $w = [n \times 1]$ are vectors. For any two points satisfying this equation we have

$$w^T(x_1 - x_2) = 0. \tag{5.123}$$

This means that w and $(x_1 - x_2)$ are perpendicular to each other. Therefore all points satisfying this equation form a plane, and the vector w is perpendicular to this plane. Note that $w^T x = \|w\| \, \|x\| \, \cos(\theta) = \|w\| \, d$. The shortest distance from the origin to the plane is $d = |b| / \|w\|$. This is a perpendicular line from the origin to the plane in the direction of w.

Let $x = x_0 + \alpha \, w$ and x_0 be a point on the plane. Then $w^T x + b = \alpha \|w\|^2$. Therefore we find that

- $w^T x + b \geq 0$ defines a half space in the direction of w separated by the plane, and

- $w^T x + b \leq 0$ defines a half space in the direction of $-w$ separated by the plane.

For the linearly separable case we can construct a plane such that all data points with $y = 1$ are on one side of the plane, and all data points with $y = -1$ are on the other side of the plane. There are many possible planes to separate two classes. We need to introduce a criterion to find the "best" plane.

Suppose we have a plane $w^T x + b = 0$. We move the plane as much as possible along the direction of w such that the new plane still separates the classes. We have a new plane:

$$w^T x + b = k. \tag{5.124}$$

In the same way, we move the plane as much as possible along the direction of $-w$ such that the new plane still separates the classes. We have another plane:

$$w^T x + b = -k'. \tag{5.125}$$

It is always possible to adjust the original plane such that the k and k' are the same. Also, we can rescale the parameters (w, b) such that $k = 1$. So we have two extreme planes:

$$w^T x + b = 1 \tag{5.126}$$

and

$$w^T x + b = -1. \tag{5.127}$$

We can argue that for many possible pairs of planes, the best choice is that these two planes have the largest separation. Note that the distance between these two planes is $d = 2 / \|w\|$. The optimization problem to search w and b is given by

$$
\begin{aligned}
\underset{w,\, b}{\text{minimize}} \quad & \tfrac{1}{2} \|w\|^2 \\
\text{subject to} \quad & y_i(w^T x_i + b) \geq 1, \quad i = 1, 2, \ldots, m,
\end{aligned}
\tag{5.128}
$$

where (x_i, y_i) is the ith training point, and m is the number of the total training points. The Wolfe dual of this problem is

$$\underset{w,\,b,\,\alpha}{\text{maximize}} \quad \tfrac{1}{2}\|w\|^2 - \sum_{i=1}^{m} \alpha_i \left[y_i(w^T x_i + b) - 1 \right]$$

$$\text{subject to} \quad w - \sum_{i=1}^{m} \alpha_i y_i x_i = 0$$

$$\sum_{i=1}^{m} \alpha_i y_i = 0 \tag{5.129}$$

$$\alpha_i \geq 0, \ i = 1, 2, ..., m.$$

This simplifies to

$$\underset{\alpha}{\text{minimize}} \quad \tfrac{1}{2} \sum_{i,j=1}^{m} \alpha_i \alpha_j y_i y_j \, x_i^T x_j - \sum_{i=1}^{m} \alpha_i$$

$$\text{subject to} \quad \sum_{i=1}^{m} \alpha_i y_i = 0 \tag{5.130}$$

$$\alpha_i \geq 0, \ i = 1, 2, ..., m.$$

This is a quadratic programming problem.

5.5.3 Linearly Inseparable Problem

More realistically the data points are probably linearly inseparable in the original input space. We can introduce a penalty parameter C to move a misclassified data point into the right class. Then the problem becomes

$$\underset{w,\,b,\,z}{\text{minimize}} \quad \tfrac{1}{2}\|w\|^2 + C \sum_{i=1}^{m} z_i$$

$$\text{subject to} \quad y_i(w^T x_i + b) + z_i \geq 1 \tag{5.131}$$

$$z_i \geq 0, \ i = 1, 2, ..., m.$$

For an almost linearly separable problem, most zs should be 0. In the similar way, we can construct the Wolfe dual problem as

$$\underset{w,\,b,\,z,\,\alpha,\,\mu}{\text{maximize}} \quad \tfrac{1}{2}\|w\|^2 + C \sum_{i=1}^{m} z_i - \sum_{i=1}^{m} \alpha_i \left[y_i(w^T x_i + b) + z_i - 1 \right] - \sum_{i=1}^{m} \mu_i z_i$$

$$\text{subject to} \quad w - \sum_{i=1}^{m} \alpha_i y_i x_i = 0$$

$$\sum_{i=1}^{m} \alpha_i y_i = 0$$

$$C - \alpha_i - \mu_i = 0$$

$$\alpha_i \geq 0$$

$$\mu_i \geq 0 \tag{5.132}$$

$$i = 1, 2, ..., m.$$

After simplifying, this becomes

$$
\begin{aligned}
\underset{\alpha}{\text{minimize}} \quad & \frac{1}{2} \sum_{i,j=1}^{m} \alpha_i \alpha_j y_i y_j \, x_i^T x_j - \sum_{i=1}^{m} \alpha_i \\
\text{subject to} \quad & \sum_{i=1}^{m} \alpha_i y_i = 0 \\
& 0 \leq \alpha_i \leq C, \ i = 1, 2, ..., m.
\end{aligned}
\tag{5.133}
$$

This is a quadratic programming problem. It is clear that this problem becomes the problem in the previous section as $C \to \infty$.

This is one of the support vector classification algorithms C-SVC [Boser et al. (1992) and Cortes and Vapnik (1995)]. The relationship between C-SVC and regressions with specific loss functions is discussed in Section 5.5.6.

5.5.4   Constructing Higher-Dimensional Space and Kernel

Sometimes, the data is linearly inseparable in a low-dimensional space, but it is fairly straightforward to separate in a higher-dimensional space. A simple example in a two-dimensional space is that all data points within a circle belong to one class and outside of the circle belong to the other class. It is impossible to construct a straight line to separate two classes, but it is easy to do so if we add two more dimensions (x^2, y^2).

In general we can construct a higher-dimensional space,

$$x \to \varphi(x). \tag{5.134}$$

Then we can construct an optimization problem in this new space just by making the following substitution:

$$x_i^T x_j \to \varphi^T(x_i)\,\varphi(x_j). \tag{5.135}$$

In order to avoid constructing a higher-dimensional space explicitly, the kernel method has been introduced:

$$\varphi^T(x_i)\,\varphi(x_j) \to K(x_i, x_j). \tag{5.136}$$

The most common kernels used are:

- Linear: $K(x_i, x_j) = x_i^T x_j$

- Polynomial: $K(x_i, x_j) = (\gamma\, x_i^T x_j + c_0)^d$

- Radial basis function (RBF): $K(x_i, x_j) = e^{-\gamma |x_i - x_j|^2}$

- Sigmoid: $K(x_i, x_j) = \tanh(\gamma\, x_i^T x_j + c_0)$.

In these different expressions γ, c_0, d are kernel parameters.

Here are two examples of the polynomial kernels and their connection to the constructed higher-dimensional space:

Let $x^T = (x_1, x_2)$, $y^T = (y_1, y_2)$. We have:

$$
\begin{aligned}
(x^T y + 1)^2 &= (1 + x_1 y_1 + x_2 y_2)^2 \\
&= (1, \sqrt{2}\,x_1, \sqrt{2}\,x_2, x_1^2, x_2^2, \sqrt{2}\,x_1 x_2)\,(1, \sqrt{2}\,y_1, \sqrt{2}\,y_2, y_1^2, y_2^2, \sqrt{2}\,y_1 y_2)^T \\
&= \varphi^T(x)\,\varphi(y),
\end{aligned}
$$

(5.137)

where $\varphi^T(x) = (1, \sqrt{2}\,x_1, \sqrt{2}\,x_2, x_1^2, x_2^2, \sqrt{2}\,x_1 x_2)$.

As a second example we have

$$
\begin{aligned}
(x^T y)^2 &= (x_1 y_1 + x_2 y_2)^2 \\
&= (x_1^2, x_2^2, \sqrt{2}\,x_1 x_2)\,(y_1^2, y_2^2, \sqrt{2}\,y_1 y_2)^T \\
&= \varphi^T(x)\,\varphi(y),
\end{aligned}
$$

(5.138)

where $\varphi^T(x) = (x_1^2, x_2^2, \sqrt{2}\,x_1 x_2)$.

5.5.5 Model Output

The predicted value from the constructed model is

$$
\begin{aligned}
\hat{f}(x) &= w^T x + b \\
&= \sum_{i=1}^{m} \alpha_i y_i x_i^T x + b \\
&\rightarrow \sum_{i=1}^{m} \alpha_i y_i \varphi^T(x_i) \cdot \varphi(x) + b \quad \text{extend into a higher-dimensional space} \\
&\rightarrow \sum_{i=1}^{m} \alpha_i y_i\, K(x_i, x) + b \quad\quad \text{use a kernel.}
\end{aligned}
$$

(5.139)

In general the predicted value is expressed in terms of a kernel:

$$
\hat{f}(x) = \sum_{i=1}^{m} \alpha_i y_i\, K(x_i, x) + b.
$$

(5.140)

5.5.6 C-Support Vector Classification (C-SVC) for Classification

In Section 5.5.3, we have discussed one of the support vector classification algorithms C-SVC. In this section we show that C-SVC can be classified as a regression problem with a different loss function. As in Section 5.5.3, let's consider the binary case with the target variable labeled as $y_i \in \{1, -1\}$. If $y_i = 1$, the best solution is $\hat{y}_i \geq 1$. Thus the loss function is

$$L(y_i, \hat{y}_i) = \begin{cases} 0 & \text{if } \hat{y}_i \geq 1 \\ 1 - \hat{y}_i & \text{if } \hat{y}_i < 1. \end{cases} \tag{5.141}$$

If $y_i = -1$ the best solution is $\hat{y}_i \leq -1$. Thus the loss function is

$$L(y_i, \hat{y}_i) = \begin{cases} 0 & \text{if } \hat{y}_i \leq -1 \\ 1 + \hat{y}_i & \text{if } \hat{y}_i \geq -1. \end{cases} \tag{5.142}$$

In general, the loss function can be expressed as $L(y_i, \hat{y}_i) = (1 - y_i\hat{y}_i)^+$. The objective function for the optimization problem to find w, b is

$$f(w, b) = \sum_{i=1}^{m} (1 - y_i\hat{y}_i)^+ + \frac{\beta}{2}\|w\|^2. \tag{5.143}$$

The squared error loss function which is used in linear regression is

$$L(y_i, \hat{y}_i) = (y_i - \hat{y}_i)^2 = y_i^2 \left(1 - y_i\hat{y}_i/y_i^2\right)^2 = (1 - y_i\hat{y}_i)^2. \tag{5.144}$$

The negative log-likelihood function which is used in logistic regression is

$$L(y_i, \hat{y}_i) = -\ln\left[(1 + y_i\,\hat{y}_i)/2\right]. \tag{5.145}$$

Therefore C-SVC can be classified as a regression problem with a different loss function. In SVM, if we add a point to training data set and if this point is far away from the support plane and is on the correct side, it is not useful and does not change the surface location. The only useful points are the support vectors. On the other hand, in linear and logistic regression, adding a point far away from the plane will change the model coefficients.

5.5.7 ε-Support Vector Regression (ε-SVR) for Regression

In this section we present ε-SVR, one of the support vector regression algorithms [Vapnik (1998)]. The ε-SVR support vector regression problem can be formulated as

$$\begin{aligned} \underset{w,b,\xi,\xi^*}{\text{minimize}} \quad & \tfrac{1}{2}\|w\|^2 + C\sum_{i=1}^{m}(\xi_i + \xi_i^*) \\ \text{subject to} \quad & -(\varepsilon + \xi_i) \leq y_i - (w^T x_i + b) \leq \varepsilon + \xi_i^* \\ & \xi_i \geq 0,\ \xi_i^* \geq 0,\ i = 1, 2, ..., m. \end{aligned} \tag{5.146}$$

Here C and ε are given constants. Its Wolfe dual is

$$\underset{w,b,\xi,\xi^*,\alpha,\alpha^*,\eta,\eta^*}{\text{maximize}} \quad L(w,b,\xi,\xi^*,\alpha,\alpha^*,\eta,\eta^*) = \tfrac{1}{2}\|w\|^2 + C\sum_{i=1}^m (\xi_i + \xi_i^*)$$

$$-\sum_{i-1}^m \alpha_i \left(y_i - w^T x_i - b + \varepsilon + \xi_i\right)$$

$$-\sum_{i=1}^m \alpha_i^* \left(-y_i + w^T x_i + b + \varepsilon + \xi_i^*\right)$$

$$-\sum_{i=1}^m \eta_i \xi_i - \sum_{i=1}^n \eta^* \xi_i^*$$

subject to $\quad \alpha_i \geq 0, \alpha_i^* \geq 0, \eta_i \geq 0, \eta_i^* \geq 0, \ i = 1, 2, ..., n.$

(5.147)

The derivatives of $L = L(w,b,\xi,\xi^*,\alpha,\alpha^*,\eta,\eta^*)$ with respect to (w,b,ξ,ξ^*) are

$$\begin{aligned}
\frac{\partial L}{\partial w_k} &= w_k + \sum_{i=1}^m \alpha_i x_{ik} - \sum_{i=1}^m \alpha_i^* x_{ik}, \\
\frac{\partial L}{\partial b} &= \sum_{i=1}^m \alpha_i - \sum_{i=1}^m \alpha_i^*, \\
\frac{\partial L}{\partial \xi_i} &= C - \alpha_i - \eta_i, \\
\frac{\partial L}{\partial \xi_i^*} &= C - \alpha_i^* - \eta_i^*.
\end{aligned}$$

(5.148)

Setting all the derivatives to zero we have

$$\begin{aligned}
w_k &= \sum_{i=1}^m \left(\alpha_i^* - \alpha_i\right) x_{ik}, \\
\sum_{i=1}^m \left(\alpha_i - \alpha_i^*\right) &= 0, \\
\eta_i &= C - \alpha_i, \\
\eta_i^* &= C - \alpha_i^*.
\end{aligned}$$

(5.149)

Using these equations to simplify the objective function leads to

$$\underset{\alpha,\alpha^*}{\text{maximize}} \quad L(\alpha,\alpha^*) = -\tfrac{1}{2}\sum_{i,j=1}^m \left(\alpha_i^* - \alpha_i\right) K\left(x_i, x_j\right) \left(\alpha_j^* - \alpha_j\right)$$

$$+\sum_{i=1}^m \left(\alpha_i^* - \alpha_i\right) y_i - \varepsilon \sum_{i=1}^m \left(\alpha_i^* + \alpha_i\right)$$

(5.150)

subject to $\quad \sum_{i=1}^m \left(\alpha_i^* - \alpha_i\right) = 0$

$$0 \leq \alpha_i, \alpha_i^* \leq C, \ i = 1, 2, ..., n,$$

where $K(x_i, x_j) = x_i^T x_j = \sum_k x_{ik} x_{jk}$. Given the solution of α^*, α we have

$$w = \sum_{i=1}^m \left(\alpha_i^* - \alpha_i\right) x_i.$$

(5.151)

For a given data point the predicted value is

$$\hat{y}(x) = w^T x + b = \sum_{i=1}^{m} (\alpha_i^* - \alpha_i) K(x_i, x) + b. \tag{5.152}$$

In matrix notation, $X = [m \times p], \alpha = [m \times 1], \alpha^* = [m \times 1], Q = XX^T$,

$$w = X^T(\alpha^T - \alpha), \tag{5.153}$$

$$\hat{y}(x) = (\alpha^* - \alpha)^T X x + b. \tag{5.154}$$

The ε-SVR can be formulated in terms of a regression problem with constraints. The objective function is

$$L = V(y - \hat{y}) + \frac{\beta}{2}\|w\|^2. \tag{5.155}$$

Therefore the regression problem is to find w, b through the following minimization problem:

$$\underset{w,b}{\text{minimize}} \left\{ V(y - \hat{y}) + \frac{\beta}{2}\|w\|^2 \right\}, \tag{5.156}$$

where the loss is a function of the residual $r = y - \hat{y}$:

$$V(r) = \begin{cases} 0 & \text{if } |r| \leq \varepsilon \\ |r| - \varepsilon & \text{if } |r| > \varepsilon. \end{cases} \tag{5.157}$$

For a given ith point there are three possible values of the residual and they can be represented by the pair (ξ_i, ξ_i^*):

$$\begin{aligned} |r_i| \leq \varepsilon & \quad (\xi_i, \xi_i^*) = (0, 0), \\ r_i \leq -\varepsilon & \quad (\xi_i, \xi_i^*) = (-\varepsilon - r_i, 0), \\ r_i \geq \varepsilon & \quad (\xi_i, \xi_i^*) = (0, r_i - \varepsilon). \end{aligned} \tag{5.158}$$

The loss function becomes

$$\begin{aligned} L &= \sum_{i=1}^{m} (\xi_i + \xi_i^*) + \frac{\beta}{2}\|w\|^2 \\ &= \beta \left\{ \frac{1}{2}\|w\|^2 + \frac{1}{\beta} \sum_{i=1}^{m} (\xi_i + \xi_i^*) \right\} \end{aligned} \tag{5.159}$$

It can be seen that the regression with constraints is equivalent to ε-SVR with $C = 1/\beta$.

5.5.8 The Probability Estimate

From SVM for classification, like C-SVC, the output is a label for each data point from the decision value. In this section, we discuss the probability estimation from the decision values [Chang and Lin (2011)]. From SVM we have the estimation of the decision value $\hat{f}(x)$ for each data point x as described in Section 5.5.5:

#	$\hat{f}(x)$	Target Label
1	...	...
...	...	...
m	...	...

For a binary classification problem ($K = 2$) we can build a logistic regression model to estimate the probability

$$\hat{p}(x) = \frac{1}{1 + e^{-A\,\hat{f}(x) - B}}. \tag{5.160}$$

For a multi-class classification problem ($K > 2$), we can build pair-wise $K(K-1)/2$ logistic models,

$$\hat{p}_{ij}(x) = \frac{1}{1 + e^{-A_{ij}\,\hat{f}_{ij}(x) - B_{ij}}}, \tag{5.161}$$

where p_{ij} is the pair-wise probability $p_{ij}(x) = P(y = i|y = i \text{ or } j, x)$. Ultimately we want to estimate $p_i(x) = P(y = i|x)$. Noting that

$$p_i(x) = P(y = i|y = i \text{ or } j, x) P(y = i \text{ or } j|x), \tag{5.162}$$

we have $p_{ji}(x)p_i(x) = p_{ij}(x)p_j(x)$. A natural selection for estimating p_i is

$$\begin{aligned}
\underset{p_i, i = 1, 2, \ldots, K}{\text{minimize}} \quad & \tfrac{1}{2} \sum_{i,j=1}^{K} (p_{ji}(x)p_i(x) - p_{ij}(x)p_j(x))^2 \\
\text{subject to} \quad & \sum_{i=1}^{K} p_i(x) = 1, p_i(x) \geq 0, \ i = 1, 2, \ldots, K.
\end{aligned} \tag{5.163}$$

The objective function can be simplified to

$$\begin{aligned}
\tfrac{1}{2} \sum_{i,j=1}^{K} (p_{ji}p_i - p_{ij}p_j)^2 &= \sum_{i,j=1}^{K} (p_{ji}^2 p_i^2 - p_{ij}p_{ji}p_i p_j) \\
&= \sum_{i,j=1}^{K} p_i \left(\sum_{k=1}^{K} p_{ki}^2 \delta_{ij} - p_{ij}p_{ji} \right) p_j \\
&= \sum_{i,j=1}^{K} p_i Q_{ij} p_j,
\end{aligned} \tag{5.164}$$

where $Q_{ij} = \sum_{k=1}^{K} p_{ki}^2 \delta_{ij} - p_{ij}p_{ji}$. Therefore the problem becomes a quadratic programming problem:

$$\underset{p}{\text{minimize}} \quad \tfrac{1}{2}p^T Q p$$

$$\text{subject to} \quad \sum_{i=1}^{K} p_i = 1, p_i \geq 0, i = 1, 2, ..., K. \tag{5.165}$$

5.6 Fuzzy Logic System

A fuzzy logic system is a very broad topic. It includes fuzzy classification, fuzzy binning, fuzzy neural networks, and fuzzy decision trees. Here we discuss a simple fuzzy logic system combining some fuzzy rules into a single more complicated rule. For an excellent tutorial, refer to "Fuzzy Logic Systems for Engineering: A Tutorial" by Mendel (1995).

5.6.1 A Simple Fuzzy Logic System

Let's consider a fuzzy system with P inputs, K outputs, and R rules, as shown in the following table:

	rule 1	$\cdots$	rule R	rule 1	$\cdots$	rule R	
x_1	(μ_{11}, σ_{11})	$\cdots$	(μ_{R1}, σ_{R1})	C_{11}	$\cdots$	C_{R1}	y_1
x_2	(μ_{12}, σ_{12})	$\cdots$	(μ_{R2}, σ_{R2})	C_{12}	$\cdots$	C_{R2}	y_2
		$\cdots$			$\cdots$		
x_P	(μ_{1P}, σ_{1P})	$\cdots$	(μ_{RP}, σ_{RP})	C_{1K}	$\cdots$	C_{RK}	y_K
	w_1	$\cdots$	w_R	w_1	$\cdots$	w_R	

The model is constructed by the weighted average from R rules,

$$\hat{y}_k(x) = \frac{\sum_{r=1}^{R} w_r(x) \cdot C_{rk}}{\sum_{r=1}^{R} w_r(x)}, \quad k = 1, 2, \cdots, K, \tag{5.166}$$

where the weights are in Gaussian form

$$w_r(x) = \prod_{j=1}^{P} \exp\left(-\frac{(x_j - \mu_{rj})^2}{2\sigma_{rj}^2}\right). \tag{5.167}$$

The squared error from a single data point is

$$E(x) = \frac{1}{2} \sum_{k=1}^{K} (\hat{y}_k(x) - y_k(x))^2. \tag{5.168}$$

Note that

$$\frac{\partial \hat{y}_k}{\partial w_r} = \frac{C_{rk} - \hat{y}_k}{\sum\limits_{r=1}^{R} w_r}, \tag{5.169}$$

$$\frac{\partial \ln w_r}{\partial \mu_{rj}} = \frac{x_j - \mu_{rj}}{\sigma_{rj}^2}, \tag{5.170}$$

and

$$\frac{\partial \ln w_r}{\partial \sigma_{rj}} = \frac{(x_j - \mu_{rj})^2}{\sigma_{rj}^3}. \tag{5.171}$$

The first derivatives of E with respect to μ_{rj}, σ_{rj}, and C_{rk} are

$$\frac{\partial E}{\partial \mu_{rj}} = \left[\sum_{k=1}^{K} (\hat{y}_k - y_k)(C_{rk} - \hat{y}_k) \right] \cdot \left[\frac{\mu_r (x_j - \mu_{rj})}{\sigma_{rj}^2} \right], \tag{5.172}$$

$$\frac{\partial E}{\partial \sigma_{rj}} = \left[\sum_{k=1}^{K} (\hat{y}_k - y_k)(C_{rk} - \hat{y}_k) \right] \cdot \left[\frac{\mu_r (x_j - \mu_{rj})^2}{\sigma_{rj}^3} \right], \tag{5.173}$$

$$\frac{\partial E}{\partial C_{rk}} = \mu_r \cdot (\hat{y}_k - y_k), \tag{5.174}$$

where $\mu_r = w_r / \sum_{r=1}^{R} w_r$. With these first derivatives, the unknown parameters μ_{rj}, σ_{rj}, and C_{rk} can be found by using an iterative search such as the gradient descent method described previously.

5.7 Clustering

Clustering algorithms comprise a popular family of nonlinear modeling techniques. The concept of clustering entails examing the given data records as points in an N-dimensional space, and to find natural groupings of these points that help us understand the structure of the data. These natural groupings then aid in interpolation/extrapolation between the given data, which of course is the essence of predictive modeling. Clustering methods can be either unsupervised, where we look for natural groupings in the input space only, or supervised, where we look for such groupings with respect to a known output, typically categorical.

Some of the early clustering methods were the Kohonen self-organizing map (SOM) and the related supervised version learning vector quantization (LVQ). Closely related to clustering is the nearest neighbor technique, which simply returns the output value of the closest data point to the test data point.

A fundamental need in clustering is a quantitative distance metric to assess how close any two points are to each other. A general distance metric is the Minkowski distance,

$$D(x_1, x_2) = \left[\sum_j |x_{1j} - x_{2j}|^p \right]^{1/p}. \tag{5.175}$$

The selected value of p gives different shapes to the "nearness neighborhood" around any point. The value $p = 2$ gives the familiar Euclidean distance, and the nearness neighborhood is a sphere around a point. The choice $p = 1$ gives the Manhattan (city block) distance and the nearness neighborhood is an N-dimensional diamond. The value $p = \infty$ is the Chebyshev distance, and the nearness neighborhood is an N-dimensional cube around the point. One can thus imagine the shape of the nearness neighborhood for other choices of p.

A simple extension of the Minkowski distance is the Mahalanobis distance,

$$D(x_1, x_2) = \left[(\mathbf{x}_1 - \mathbf{x}_2)^T \Sigma^{-1} (\mathbf{x}_1 - \mathbf{x}_2) \right], \tag{5.176}$$

where the covariance matrix is used to rotate and z-scale all the dimensions. This can naturally be extended to nonspherical nearness neighborhoods similar to the generalized Minkowski distance.

As one can imagine, clustering depends completely on these measures of nearness, which in turn depend on the scaling of the space. Typically one does the z-scaling in all dimensions before clustering is used. It is very dangerous and virtually useless to attempt clustering in a space where all the dimensions do not have the same meaning of nearness.

5.7.1 K Means, Fuzzy C Means

The most popular unsupervised clustering algorithms are the K means and the continuously smoothed version fuzzy C means. In both of these algorithms one needs to predecide how many clusters to divide the data into. The cluster centers are at first set randomly and then iteratively moved until the cluster centers settle into the natural groupings of the data points. Here is the algorithm for K means clustering:

1. Decide how many clusters you want (K). Initialize these cluster center locations randomly.

2. Use the selected distance measure to assign all the data points to their nearest cluster center.

3. Incrementally move the new location for each cluster center toward the centroid (center of mass) of all the data points in that cluster.

4. Continue to iterate until the cluster center locations have converged sufficiently.

The fuzzy C means algorithm is very similar, except now each data point has a fractional membership to each of the C clusters, with the fraction related to the distance to that cluster center.

Both of these methods are somewhat sensitive to the initialization of the cluster centers, so multiple trials with different initializations should be performed to understand this sensitivity.

Once one has the location of the cluster centers we assign an output value to each of the cluster centers in any fuzzy weighted way we desire (e.g., majority voting for categorical, weighted average for continuous). Then when presented with a test vector we assign the output as a weighted or voted value from the nearest cluster center.

5.7.2   Nearest Neighbor, K Nearest Neighbor (KNN)

Recall that our general goal in predictive modeling is to assign an output value to any new data point whose output we do not know, using as a guide a set of previously assembled data with known outputs. A straightforward geometric way to achieve this goal is via the concepts of clustering, and to simply find the nearest data points. Consider a set of data points each with given values of the independent variables x and a given value of the single dependent variable y. Place these known points into the N-dimensional space of the independent variables, recognizing that each point has a known value of y.

Our modeling task is to assign a prediction to any test data point with independent variable values given but no dependent variable value known. Place this test data point in the N-dimension space and find the nearest data point whose output y we know, and use that nearest neighbor's y-value as the predicted output for this test point. K nearest neighbor extends this concept by considering the K nearest data points instead of the single nearest, and one can use a distance weighting of these K values as desired.

These nearest neighbor techniques are straightforward to use and are in a sense a trivial model. The downside is that one needs to calculate the distance of the test point to all known-output data points, so nearest neighbor models are trivial to train but CPU intensive to use. This is why people tend to use K means or fuzzy C means, which have some CPU-intensive training time but are very fast for prediction once trained. Once trained, these clustering methods have all the training data information encoded in the cluster values (locations, output/class), and the evaluation of a test vector is then very fast.

5.7.3   Comments on Clustering Methods

One can easily design many variations of clustering using these basic concepts. Ideas include:

Gravitational Clustering: Consider each data point as a mass point stationary in space. Scatter into this space a set of K cluster centers with mass that are allowed to move until they settle down, similar to K means. Use gravitational attraction to move these cluster centers until they find their equilibrium points. One can use a variable mass to weight each point as desired.

Electrostatic Clustering: Similar to gravitational clustering, but here each point has an electrostatic charge and is attracted to all other points. With one charge type on the fixed data points and a single different charge type on the moving cluster centers this is identical to gravitation, but analogous to electrostatics one can consider different charge types on the fixed data points, positive or negative, and let the cluster centers be both attracted to and repelled by their respective fixed data charge points. This is then a supervised clustering method and can be used with as many output categories as desired.

Local Density-Based Clustering: Move cluster centers to where there is a high density of point distribution that is not already covered/shielded by other cluster centers.

Finally, we note some general issues with clustering techniques.

Scaling: As described above, clustering methods depend strongly on the choice of the distance metric and the scaling of the different dimensions. If one does not do a good job in scaling the data the concept of nearness is not the same in each direction, and clustering breaks down.

The curse of dimensionality: Nonintuitive things happen in data spaces as dimensionality increases. Data points quickly become sparse, and most points become closer to edges than interior points as dimensionality increases. Clustering algorithms tend to scale poorly with the number of dimensions. Be wary of blindly applying clustering algorithms in anything but low to moderate dimensionality.

Noise: The addition of any dimension with substantial noise can quickly defeat a clustering algorithm. Because the method seeks nearness, any new dimension added with random locations can quickly overwhelm dimensions with information.

In summary, clustering algorithms are popular, intuitive, and widely used. They are also highly susceptible to bad choices in scaling and dimensionality. It is usually a mistake to attempt clustering in any dimensionality higher than a few, and clustering in high dimensions can be very problematic, with the problems being mostly hidden.

Chapter 6

Time Series Analysis

6.1 Fundamentals of Forecasting

Modeling for time series is conceptually similar to other modeling problems, but one major distinction is that usually the next value of the series is highly related to the most recent values, with a time-decaying importance in this relationship to previous values. Because of this property a different set of machinery has evolved for the special case of time series modeling, sometimes loosely called forecasting or even prediction.

We note that a different path to time series modeling has emerged from the machine learning community as opposed to the more traditional methods coming from statistical approaches—the ones covered here. This alternative approach from machine learning considers a time series as a (possibly complex) dynamic system, where the series of values have some to-be-discovered (possibly nonlinear) relationship. This alternative is motivated by the study of complex dynamic systems, including chaotic systems, and the essence of the approach is through embedding the series into a multidimensional phase space, similar to a Poincaré map. The most common approach here is to consider the next value in a time series to be an unknown (to-be-modeled) nonlinear combination of the past few values. This dynamical systems, machine learning approach is generally not the mainstream approach to forecasting, but one should be aware of this alternative approach in the event the following-described mainstream path yields unsatisfactory results. A simple example of such a class of problems is the logistic (quadratic) map, which is itself a chaotic dynamic system for certain parameters and can not be solved via ARIMA, but which is trivially solved using the embedding approach in conjunction with any nonlinear modeling technique.

When we model a time series we first wish to simplify it as much as possible. If the series has properties that change substantially over time (like the average or average variation), we preprocess the series to remove these complications, doing our best to make it stationary (statistical properties constant in time). First we note that often there are both trends and seasonality in many data sets. Linear trends are removed by doing a first difference on the time series, where one models the *differences* between the values at each time step instead of the value at each time step. This is the "I" for Integrated in the ARIMA nomenclature.

Seasonality can be identified and removed as follows. First one identifies the natural periodicity of the data. This can be done in a variety of ways, such as (1) through expert understanding of the dynamics, (2) through statistical analysis using different window lengths, or (3) through frequency analysis looking for the fundamental frequency(ies). Once one identifies the natural repetitive season one can align all the data to this seasonal behavior, e.g., plotting all the different yearly data on top of each other showing the natural seasonal trends. An average of these curves can be computed and subtracted (or divided) out from all the data.

Most time series modeling incorporates many of these processes via the ARIMA methodology. The use of the partial autocorrelation function explicitly accounts for the relationships of future data points—simple statistical linear correlation to the past values, reducing the task of the remainder of the ARIMA model training to be required to learn the nonobvious relationships. The moving average process helps mitigate noise.

The ARIMA methodology is inherently linear. It is interesting to note that most mainline forecasting limits itself to linear modeling, similar to the widespread use of simple regressions in practical business applications. The GARCH methodology is essentially built around autocorrelation and a return to a moving average. Other nonlinear methodologies certainly exist, such as nonlinear models based on embedding, and have primarily arisen out of the machine learning community as opposed to the statistics community.

Often one encounters multiple time series prediction problems where one desires to simultaneously predict the output of multiple time series using all the time series as inputs. This category of problems is a straightforward extention of the single time series prediction methodology, only that multiple time series should be inputs to each of the single prediction models for each separate time series.

The main references of this section are the books by Wei (1990) and Chatfield (1996).

6.1.1 Box–Cox Transformation

In many practical problems the variables to be predicted are not normally distributed, yet much of the modeling machinery is designed for normal distributions of outputs and errors. This also occurs in many time series problems, and a simple and often-used process is to transform the data into a set that more closely resembles a normal distribution. For example, stock prices are not normally distributed, but a reasonable model is that the log of the stock returns is normally distributed.

The Box–Cox power transformation was introduced for this purpose. Noting that $\int x^n dx = x^{n+1}/(n+1)$ and $\int x^{-1} dx = \ln x$, it seems that $\ln x$ in some ways behaves similar to x^0. Define a function of λ as $f(\lambda) = (x^\lambda - 1)/\lambda$. Note that $\lim_{\lambda \to 0} (x^\lambda - 1)/\lambda = \ln x$, we can define the following function, which (based on the noted limit property) is a continuous function of λ:

$$f(x, \lambda) = \begin{cases} (x^\lambda - 1)/\lambda & \lambda \neq 0 \\ \ln x & \lambda = 0. \end{cases} \tag{6.1}$$

This is the Box–Cox transformation. One explores various values of the transforming parameter λ that make the transformed data closest to normally distributed. There have been many variations and extensions of the Box–Cox transformation.

6.1.2 Smoothing Algorithms

Smoothing algorithms remove high-frequency noise in a time series by using information around the surrounding data points. A simple smoothing algorithm is a moving window, which slides a window width $2q$ across the data points, replacing points with an average across this window. The simplest moving average smoothing algorithm is to use uniform weights, $w(k) = 1/(2q+1)$. Therefore the smoothing equation is

$$\tilde{x}_t = \frac{1}{2q+1} \sum_{k=-q}^{q} x_{t+k}. \tag{6.2}$$

The weights do not have to be constant in this window—they may fall off as one gets further from the center point. Let's look at some examples in the expansion of $\left(\frac{1}{2} + \frac{1}{2}\right)^{2q}$:

$$
\begin{aligned}
q = \tfrac{1}{2}: \quad & \left(\tfrac{1}{2} + \tfrac{1}{2}\right) = \tfrac{1}{2} + \tfrac{1}{2} \\
q = 1: \quad & \left(\tfrac{1}{2} + \tfrac{1}{2}\right)^2 = \tfrac{1}{4} + \tfrac{2}{4} + \tfrac{1}{4} \\
q = \tfrac{3}{2}: \quad & \left(\tfrac{1}{2} + \tfrac{1}{2}\right)^3 = \tfrac{1}{8} + \tfrac{3}{8} + \tfrac{3}{8} + \tfrac{1}{8}.
\end{aligned}
\tag{6.3}
$$

In general,

$$\left(\tfrac{1}{2} + \tfrac{1}{2}\right)^{2q} = \sum_{k=-q}^{q} \frac{1}{2^{2q}} C_{2q}^{q+k} = \sum_{k=-q}^{q} w(k), \tag{6.4}$$

where $w(k) = C_{2q}^{q+k}/2^{2q}$. A smoothing algorithm with growing/decaying weights is

$$\tilde{x}_t = \sum_{k=-q}^{q} w(k)\, x_{t+k}. \tag{6.5}$$

It can be shown that $w(k)$ approaches a normal distribution when q is large. Note that

$$w(k) = \frac{1}{2^{2q}} \frac{(2q)!}{(q+k)!(q-k)!}. \tag{6.6}$$

When q is large and k is small, we can use the following Stirling approximation of the factorial, $x! \approx (x/e)^x \sqrt{2\pi x}$:

$$w(k) \approx \frac{\sqrt{2}}{\sqrt{2\pi q}} \frac{1}{(1+k/q)^{q+k+1/2}(1-k/q)^{q-k+1/2}}. \tag{6.7}$$

Further making the approximation of $(1+1/x)^x \approx e$ when x is large, we have

$$w(k) \approx \frac{1}{\sqrt{2}} \frac{1}{\sqrt{2\pi(q/4)}} e^{-\frac{k^2}{2(q/4)}}. \tag{6.8}$$

We conclude that when k is small, this approximates to the normal distribution with the variance $q/4$.

If the smoothing algorithm can only use the data up to the current time, then

$$\tilde{x}_t = \sum_{k=0}^{\infty} w(k) x_{t-k}. \tag{6.9}$$

Let's consider the case of exponential smoothing, $w(k) = \alpha (1-\alpha)^k$, $0 < \alpha < 1$ $(k = 0, 1, 2, ...)$,

$$\tilde{x}_t = \sum_{k=0}^{\infty} \alpha(1-\alpha)^k x_{t-k}. \tag{6.10}$$

This is called an exponential weighted moving average (EWMA). It can be rewritten as

$$\tilde{x}_t = \alpha x_t + (1-\alpha)\tilde{x}_{t-1}, \tag{6.11}$$

with α being the smoothing decay parameter. This is a very easy and useful method to provide smoothing to any time series. The choice of the parameter α determines the degree of past memory and smoothing.

Other more complicated and useful exponential smoothing methods extend to trends (double) and seasonality (triple). See Holt (1957) and Winters (1960).

6.1.3 Convolution of Linear Filters

Let's consider two linear filters a and b: $x_t \xrightarrow{a} y_t \xrightarrow{b} z_t$ and their combination denoted by $x_t \xrightarrow{c} z_t$. Let $y_t = \sum_r a_r x_{t+r}$ and $z_t = \sum_s b_s y_{t+s}$. We have:

$$z_t = \sum_s b_s \sum_r a_r x_{t+s+r} = \sum_s \left[\sum_r a_r b_{s-r} \right] x_{t+s} = \sum_s c_s x_{t+s}. \tag{6.12}$$

Therefore $c_s = \sum_r a_r b_{s-r}$. This is the convolution of a and b, denoted as $\{c\} = \{a\} * \{b\}$. As an example: $\{\frac{1}{2}, \frac{1}{2}\} * \{\frac{1}{2}, \frac{1}{2}\} = \{\frac{1}{4}, \frac{1}{2}, \frac{1}{4}\}$.

6.1.4 Linear Difference Equation

The most general linear difference equation is

$$X_t + c_1 X_{t-1} + \ldots + c_n X_{t-n} = e_t. \tag{6.13}$$

This is a non-homogeneous equation. The homogeneous equation is

$$X_t + c_1 X_{t-1} + \ldots + c_n X_{t-n} = 0. \tag{6.14}$$

As we learned in the solution of linear (differential) equations, if $X_t^{(h)}$ is a solution to the homogeneous equation and $X_t^{(p)}$ is a particular solution of the non-homogeneous equation, then $X_t^{(h)} + X_t^{(p)}$ is the general solution of the non-homogeneous equation. Therefore it is more useful to look for the general solution of the homogeneous equation.

Introducing a backshift operator B, $BX_t = X_{t-1}$, the homogenous equation can be expressed as

$$C(B)X_t = 0, \tag{6.15}$$

where $C(B) = 1 + c_1 B + \ldots + c_n B^n$. This is called an auxiliary equation associated with the linear difference equation. Let $X_t = R^t$ be a solution of the homogeneous equation, that is,

$$R^t + c_1 R^{t-1} + \ldots + c_n R^{t-n} = 0. \tag{6.16}$$

It is equivalent to

$$R^n + c_1 R^{n-1} + \ldots + c_n = 0. \tag{6.17}$$

If all n roots are distinct, then the general solution is

$$X_t = \sum_{i=1}^{n} b_i R_i^t. \tag{6.18}$$

If R_i is the root of multiplicity m_i of the equation, then it can be rewritten as

$$R^n + c_1 R^{n-1} + \ldots + c_n = \prod_{i=1}^{N} (R - R_i)^{m_i} \tag{6.19}$$

where $\sum_{i=1}^{N} m_i = n$. Then we have

$$C(B) = 1 + c_1 B + \ldots + c_n B^n = \prod_{i=1}^{N} (1 - R_i B)^{m_i}. \tag{6.20}$$

Note that

$$(1 - RB)R^t f(t) = R^t f(t) - RR^{t-1} f(t-1) = R^t (1 - B) f(t). \tag{6.21}$$

Using a repeated application of this equation we have

$$(1 - RB)^m R^t f(t) = R^t (1 - B)^m f(t). \tag{6.22}$$

Therefore

$$(1 - RB)^m R^t t^j = 0 \tag{6.23}$$

for $j = 0, 1, ..., m - 1$.

Therefore the general solution is

$$X_t = \sum_{i=1}^{N} \sum_{j=0}^{m_i-1} b_{ij} R_i^t t^j. \tag{6.24}$$

If R_i is a complex root of multiplicity m_i, then R_i^* is also a root of the same multiplicity, since the coefficients of the equation are real. Let $R_i = r\,e^{i\theta}$, then $R_i^t = r^t\,e^{i\theta t}$. Therefore $t^j r^t \cos\theta\, t$ and $t^j r^t \sin\theta\, t$, $(0 \le j < m_i)$, are both solutions.

For example, consider a process $X_t = X_{t-1} + X_{t-2}$, with initial condition $X_1 = 1$ and $X_2 = 1$. Its auxiliary equation is $R^2 = R + 1$ and its solutions are $R_1 = (1 + \sqrt{5})/2$ and $R_2 = (1 - \sqrt{5})/2$ (note this also surfaces as the "golden ratio" constant). The general solution is $X_t = b_1 R_1^t + b_2 R_2^t$. By imposing the initial condition, $X_1 = 1$ and $X_2 = 1$, we have:

$$X_t = \frac{1}{\sqrt{5}}\left[\left((1 + \sqrt{5})/2\right)^t - \left((1 - \sqrt{5})/2\right)^t\right], \quad t = 1, 2, ... \tag{6.25}$$

6.1.5　The Autocovariance Function and Autocorrelation Function

For a stationary process $\{X_t\}$, the (constant) mean and variance are

$$E[X_t] = \mu, \quad \mathrm{Var}[X_t] = E[(X_t - \mu)^2] = \sigma^2. \tag{6.26}$$

The covariance between X_t and X_{t+k} is a function of k:

$$\gamma_k = \mathrm{Cov}(X_t, X_{t+k}) = E[(X_t - \mu)(X_{t+k} - \mu)]. \tag{6.27}$$

The correlation between X_t and X_{t+k} is

$$\rho_k = \frac{\mathrm{Cov}(X_t, X_{t+k})}{\sqrt{\mathrm{Var}(X_t)}\sqrt{\mathrm{Var}(X_{t+k})}} = \frac{\gamma_k}{\gamma_0}. \tag{6.28}$$

This is called the autocorrelation function (ACF). It is the correlation of the values in a series with their lagged values.

Given a time series with n observations, $X_1, X_2, ..., X_n$. The sample mean is

$$\bar{X} = \frac{1}{n}\sum_{t=1}^{n} X_t. \tag{6.29}$$

The sample autocovariance is

$$\gamma_k = \frac{1}{n} \sum_{t=1}^{n-k} (X_t - \bar{X})(X_{t+k} - \bar{X}), \quad k = 0, 1, 2, \dots . \tag{6.30}$$

The sample autocorrelation is

$$\rho_k = \frac{\gamma_k}{\gamma_0} = \frac{\sum_{t=1}^{n-k} (X_t - \bar{X})(X_{t+k} - \bar{X})}{\sum_{t=1}^{n} (X_t - \bar{X})^2}, \quad k = 0, 1, 2, \dots . \tag{6.31}$$

6.1.6 The Partial Autocorrelation Function

For a given time series, X_t, X_{t+1}, ..., X_{t+k-1}, X_{t+k}, the partial autocorrelation function (PACF) is the correlation between the residuals of X_t and X_{t+k} after the regressions on X_{t+1}, ..., X_{t+k-1}.

Note that the partial correlation between Y and z after regression on X is related to the coefficient of z of the regression of Y on X and z, i.e.,

$$c = r_{*Yz} \sqrt{Y_*^T Y_* / (z_*^T z)}. \tag{6.32}$$

See (4.155). In the following we will show that $Y_*^T Y_* = z_*^T z$ in this case. Therefore the coefficient is the partial correlation function.

Let's consider a regression of X_{t+k} on X_{t+1}, ..., X_{t+k-1}:

$$\begin{aligned}
\hat{X}_{t+k} &= \alpha_1 X_{t+k-1} + \alpha_2 X_{t+k-2} + \dots + \alpha_{k-1} X_{t+1} + e_{t+k} \\
&= \sum_{i=1}^{k-1} \alpha_i X_{t+k-i} + e_{t+k} .
\end{aligned} \tag{6.33}$$

Note that

$$(X^T X)_{ij} = E[X_{t+k-i} X_{t+k-j}] = \gamma(i - j) \tag{6.34}$$

and

$$(X^T Y)_i = E[X_{t+k-i} X_{t+k}] = \gamma(i). \tag{6.35}$$

Therefore the normal equations are

$$\sum_{j=1}^{k-1} \gamma(i - j)\alpha_j = \gamma(i). \tag{6.36}$$

Likewise, for the regression of X_t on X_{t+1}, ..., X_{t+k-1}:

$$\begin{aligned}
\hat{X}_t &= \beta_1 X_{t+1} + \beta_2 X_{t+2} + \dots + \beta_{k-1} X_{t+k-1} + e_t \\
&= \sum_{i=1}^{k-1} \beta_i X_{t+i} + e_t.
\end{aligned} \tag{6.37}$$

Note that

$$(X^T X)_{ij} = E[X_{t+i} X_{t+j}] = \gamma(i - j) \tag{6.38}$$

and

$$(X^T Y)_i = E[X_{t+i} X_t] = \gamma(i). \tag{6.39}$$

Therefore the normal equations are

$$\sum_{j=1}^{k-1} \gamma(i - j)\beta_j = \gamma(i). \tag{6.40}$$

Therefore we have $\alpha_i = \beta_i$. Note that $E[(Y - \hat{Y})^T (Y - \hat{Y})] = E[Y^T Y - (X^T Y)^T B]$, so we have

$$
\begin{aligned}
E[(X_t - \hat{X}_t)(X_t - \hat{X}_t)] &= E[(X_{t+k} - \hat{X}_{t+k})(X_{t+k} - \hat{X}_{t+k})] \\
&= \gamma(0) - \sum_{i=1}^{k-1} \alpha_i \gamma(i).
\end{aligned}
\tag{6.41}
$$

We are now ready to consider a regression of X_{t+k} on $X_t, X_{t+1}, ..., X_{t+k-1}$:

$$
\begin{aligned}
\hat{X}_{t+k} &= \varphi_{k1} X_{t+k-1} + \varphi_{k2} X_{t+k-2} + ... + \varphi_{kk} X_t + e_{t+k} \\
&= \sum_{i=1}^{k} \varphi_{ki} X_{t+k-i} + e_{t+k}.
\end{aligned}
\tag{6.42}
$$

Note that

$$(X^T X)_{ij} = E[X_{t+k-i} X_{t+k-j}] = \gamma(i - j), \tag{6.43}$$

and

$$(X^T Y)_i = E[X_{t+k-i} X_{t+k}] = \gamma(i). \tag{6.44}$$

The normal equations are

$$\sum_{j=1}^{k} \gamma(i - j)\varphi_{kj} = \gamma(i), \tag{6.45}$$

or using ACF functions:

$$\sum_{j=1}^{k} \rho(i - j)\varphi_{kj} = \rho(i). \tag{6.46}$$

Therefore the coefficient of X_t is

$$\varphi_{kk} = |\rho(i - j), \rho(i)| / |\rho(i - j)|. \tag{6.47}$$

This notation means that the numerator is the same as the denominator except for its last column being replaced by $\rho(i)$. The explicit form is

$$\varphi_{11} = \rho(1) \tag{6.48}$$

$$\varphi_{22} = \frac{\begin{vmatrix} 1 & \rho(1) \\ \rho(1) & \rho(2) \end{vmatrix}}{\begin{vmatrix} 1 & \rho(1) \\ \rho(1) & 1 \end{vmatrix}} \tag{6.49}$$

$$\varphi_{33} = \frac{\begin{vmatrix} 1 & \rho(1) & \rho(1) \\ \rho(1) & 1 & \rho(2) \\ \rho(2) & \rho(1) & \rho(3) \end{vmatrix}}{\begin{vmatrix} 1 & \rho(1) & \rho(2) \\ \rho(1) & 1 & \rho(1) \\ \rho(2) & \rho(1) & 1 \end{vmatrix}} \tag{6.50}$$

$$\dots \tag{6.51}$$

$$\varphi_{kk} = \frac{\begin{vmatrix} 1 & \rho(1) & \rho(2) & \dots & \rho(k-2) & \rho(1) \\ \rho(1) & 1 & \rho(1) & \dots & \rho(k-3) & \rho(2) \\ \dots & \dots & \dots & \dots & \dots & \dots \\ \rho(k-1) & \rho(k-2) & \rho(k-3) & \dots & \rho(1) & \rho(k) \end{vmatrix}}{\begin{vmatrix} 1 & \rho(1) & \rho(2) & \dots & \rho(k-2) & \rho(k-1) \\ \rho(1) & 1 & \rho(1) & \dots & \rho(k-3) & \rho(k-2) \\ \dots & \dots & \dots & \dots & \dots & \dots \\ \rho(k-1) & \rho(k-2) & \rho(k-3) & \dots & \rho(1) & 1 \end{vmatrix}}. \tag{6.52}$$

The Durbin–Levinson algorithm can be used to recursively calculate φ_{kk}, $k = 1, 2, \dots$ without calculating the determinant directly. See Brockwell and Davis (1991).

6.2 ARIMA Models

The autoregressive integrated moving average (ARIMA) approximation is a very popular linear methodology for time series modeling. In its most general form, ARIMA(p, d, q), we write

$$\varphi_p(B)(1 - B)^d X_t = \theta_q(B) a_t, \tag{6.53}$$

where the autoregressive part is

$$\varphi_p(B) = 1 - \varphi_1 B - \varphi_2 B^2 - \dots - \varphi_p B^p, \tag{6.54}$$

and the moving average part is

$$\theta_q(B) = 1 + \theta_1 B + \theta_2 B^2 + ... + \theta_q B^q. \tag{6.55}$$

The integrated part is formed from the lag operator B in $(1 - B)$ which forms differences. When $d = 1$ this forms the difference between two adjacent values in the time series. When $d = 0$, the ARIMA(p, d, q) process becomes an ARMA(p, q), autoregressive moving average process.

$$\varphi_p(B)X_t = \theta_q(B)a_t, \tag{6.56}$$

or explicitly

$$X_t = \varphi_1 X_{t-1} + \varphi_2 X_{t-2} + ... + \varphi_p X_{t-p} + a_t + \theta_1 a_{t-1} + ... + \theta_q a_{t-q}. \tag{6.57}$$

Any stationary ARMA(p, q) process can be transformed into a pure AR or a pure MA:

$$(\varphi_p(B)/\theta_q(B)) X_t = a_t \tag{6.58}$$

or

$$\pi(B)X_t = a_t, \tag{6.59}$$

and

$$X_t = (\theta_q(B)/\varphi_p(B)) a_t \tag{6.60}$$

or

$$X_t = \psi(B)a_t \tag{6.61}$$

where $\pi(B)\psi(B) = 1$.

The meaning of AR is easy to understand, but the MA is less obvious. For the MA part we can assume the model depends on the unknown variables, which are the random noise items in MA.

6.2.1   MA(q) Process

Let's consider a more general MA process

$$X_t = \psi(B)a_t, \tag{6.62}$$

where a_t is a white noise, with $E[a_t] = 0$ and $\text{Var}[a_t] = \sigma_a^2$.

$$\gamma(k) = E[X_t X_{t+k}] = \sum_{i=0}^{\infty} \sum_{j=0}^{\infty} \psi_i \psi_j E[a_{t-i} a_{t+k-j}]. \tag{6.63}$$

Note that $E[a_i a_j] = \sigma_a^2 \delta_{ij}$. We have

$$\gamma(k) = E[X_t X_{t+k}] = \sigma_a^2 \sum_{i=0}^{\infty} \psi_i \psi_{i+k}, \quad k \geq 0. \tag{6.64}$$

Define an autocovariance generating function as

$$\gamma(B) = \sum_{k=-\infty}^{\infty} \gamma(k)B^k. \tag{6.65}$$

We have

$$\gamma(B) = \sigma_a^2 \sum_{k=-\infty}^{\infty} \sum_{i=0}^{\infty} \psi_i B^{-i} \psi_{i+k} B^{k+i} = \sigma_a^2 \psi(B)\psi(B^{-1}). \tag{6.66}$$

This form is very useful to calculate $\gamma(k)$.

Let $\psi_i = \theta_i$ for $i = 0, 1, ..., q$ and otherwise are all zero. We have an MA(q) process:

$$X_t = \theta_q(B)a_t. \tag{6.67}$$

We have the ACF:

$$\gamma(k) = \begin{cases} \sigma_a^2 \sum\limits_{i=0}^{q-k} \theta_i \theta_{i+k} & q \geq k \geq 0 \\ 0 & k > q \end{cases} \tag{6.68}$$

and

$$\rho(k) = \begin{cases} \sum\limits_{i=0}^{q-k} \theta_i \theta_{i+k} \Big/ \sum\limits_{i=0}^{q} \theta_i^2 & q \geq k \geq 0 \\ 0 & k > q. \end{cases} \tag{6.69}$$

MA(1) Process

When $p = 0$, $q = 1$, the process is MA(1):

$$X_t = a_t + \theta_1 a_{t-1}. \tag{6.70}$$

The ACF is

$$\gamma(k) = \begin{cases} \sigma_a^2(1 + \theta_1^2) & k = 0 \\ \sigma_a^2 \theta_1 & k = 1 \\ 0 & k > 1 \end{cases} \tag{6.71}$$

and

$$\rho(k) = \begin{cases} \frac{\theta_1}{1+\theta_1^2} & k = 1 \\ 0 & k > 1. \end{cases} \tag{6.72}$$

MA(2) Process

When $p = 0$, $q = 2$, the process becomes MA(2):

$$X_t = a_t + \theta_1 a_{t-1} + \theta_2 a_{t-2}. \tag{6.73}$$

The ACF is

$$\gamma(k) = \begin{cases} \sigma_a^2(1 + \theta_1^2 + \theta_2^2) & k = 0 \\ \sigma_a^2\theta_1(1 + \theta_2) & k = 1 \\ \sigma_a^2\theta_2 & k = 2 \\ 0 & k > 2, \end{cases} \qquad (6.74)$$

and

$$\rho(k) = \begin{cases} \frac{\theta_1(1+\theta_2)}{1+\theta_1^2+\theta_2^2} & k = 1 \\ \frac{\theta_2}{1+\theta_1^2+\theta_2^2} & k = 2 \\ 0 & k > 2. \end{cases} \qquad (6.75)$$

6.2.2   AR(p) Process

When $q = 0$, the ARMA(p, q) becomes AR(p):

$$X_t = \varphi_p(B)a_t = \varphi_1 X_{t-1} + \varphi_2 X_{t-2} + \dots + \varphi_p X_{t-p} + a_t. \qquad (6.76)$$

We have

$$E[X_t X_{t-k}] = E[X_{t-k}(\varphi_1 X_{t-1} + \varphi_2 X_{t-2} + \dots + \varphi_p X_{t-p})] + E[X_{t-k}a_t]. \quad (6.77)$$

Noting that $E[X_{t-k}a_t] = 0$ for $k > 0$, we have

$$\gamma(k) = \varphi_1\gamma(k-1) + \varphi_2\gamma(k-2) + \dots + \varphi_p\gamma(k-p), \quad k > 0. \qquad (6.78)$$

This is the Yule–Walker equation.

If $\varphi_p(B) = \prod_{i=1}^{N}(1 - R_i B)^{m_i}$, then the solution of the Yule–Walker equation is

$$\rho(k) = \sum_{i=1}^{N}\sum_{j=0}^{m_i-1} b_{ij}R_i^t t^j, \quad k > 0. \qquad (6.79)$$

The coefficients can be determined by the initial conditions.

For a stationary process, $|R_i| < 1$, and the ACF exponentially decays in terms of k.

AR(1) Process

When $p = 1$, $q = 0$, the process becomes AR(1). This is also called a first-order Markov process, where the value at the next step depends only on the previous step:

$$X_t = \varphi_1 X_{t-1} + a_t. \qquad (6.80)$$

The Yule–Walker equation is

$$\gamma(k) = \varphi_1\gamma(k-1), \quad k > 0. \qquad (6.81)$$

Noting that $\gamma(0) = \varphi_1\gamma(1) + E[a_t X_t]$ and $E[a_t X_t] = E[a_t a_t] = \sigma_a^2$, we have

$$\gamma(k) = \begin{cases} \frac{\sigma_a^2}{1-\varphi_1^2} & k = 0 \\ \varphi_1^k \gamma(0) & k > 0 \end{cases} \tag{6.82}$$

and

$$\rho(k) = \varphi_1^k, \quad k > 0. \tag{6.83}$$

AR(2) Process

When $p = 2$, $q = 0$, the process becomes AR(2):

$$X_t = \varphi_1 X_{t-1} + \varphi_2 X_{t-2} + a_t. \tag{6.84}$$

The Yule–Walker equation is

$$\gamma(k) = \varphi_1\gamma(k-1) + \varphi_2\gamma(k-2), \quad k > 0. \tag{6.85}$$

Note that

$$\gamma(1) = \varphi_1\gamma(0) + \varphi_2\gamma(1) \tag{6.86}$$

$$\gamma(2) = \varphi_1\gamma(1) + \varphi_2\gamma(0) \tag{6.87}$$

and

$$\gamma(0) = \varphi_1\gamma(1) + \varphi_2\gamma(2) + \sigma_a^2. \tag{6.88}$$

We have

$$\gamma(0) = \sigma_a^2 \frac{1 - \varphi_2}{1 - \varphi_2 - \varphi_1^2 - \varphi_2^2 - \varphi_1^2\varphi_2 + \varphi_2^3}, \tag{6.89}$$

$$\rho(1) = \frac{\varphi_1}{1 - \varphi_2} \tag{6.90}$$

and

$$\rho(2) = \frac{\varphi_1^2 + \varphi_2 - \varphi_2^2}{1 - \varphi_2}, \tag{6.91}$$

and $\rho(k), k > 2$, can be obtained from the recursive function.

Alternatively, we can have the explicit expression for the ACF. The roots of the auxiliary equation, $R^2 = \varphi_1 R + \varphi_2$, are

$$R_1 = \left(\varphi_1 + \sqrt{\varphi_1^2 + 4\varphi_2}\right)/2, \quad \text{and} \quad R_2 = \left(\varphi_1 - \sqrt{\varphi_1^2 + 4\varphi_2}\right)/2. \tag{6.92}$$

We have the ACF expression

$$\rho(k) = \left(\frac{\rho(1) - R_2}{R_1 - R_2}\right) R_1^k + \left(\frac{R_1 - \rho(1)}{R_1 - R_2}\right) R_2^k, \quad k > 0. \tag{6.93}$$

6.2.3   ARMA(p, q) Process

The ARMA(p, q) process is

$$\varphi_p(B)X_t = \theta_q(B)a_t. \tag{6.94}$$

Explicitly, we have

$$X_t = \varphi_1 X_{t-1} + \varphi_2 X_{t-2} + \ldots + \varphi_p X_{t-p} + a_t + \theta_1 a_{t-1} + \ldots + \theta_q a_{t-q}. \tag{6.95}$$

We have

$$\begin{aligned} \gamma(k) &= \varphi_1 \gamma(k-1) + \varphi_2 \gamma(k-2) + \ldots + \varphi_p \gamma(k-p) \\ &\quad + E[X_{t-k}(a_t + \theta_1 a_{t-1} + \ldots + \theta_q a_{t-q})]. \end{aligned} \tag{6.96}$$

Noting that $E[a_i X_j] = 0$ for $i > j$ and $E[a_i X_i] = \sigma_a^2$, we have the Yule–Walker equation:

$$\begin{aligned} \gamma(k) &= \varphi_1 \gamma(k-1) + \cdots + \varphi_p \gamma(k-p) + \sigma_a^2 \sum_{j=k}^{q} \psi_{j-k}\theta_j, \quad k \le q, \\ \gamma(k) &= \varphi_1 \gamma(k-1) + \cdots + \varphi_p \gamma(k-p), \quad k > q, \end{aligned} \tag{6.97}$$

where the ψ's are the coefficients of the equivalent MA process. The Yule–Walker equation in ARMA(p, q) is the same as that in AR(p) for $k > q$.

ARMA(1, 1) Process

When $p = q = 1$, it is an ARMA$(1, 1)$ process:

$$X_t = \varphi_1 X_{t-1} + a_t + \theta_1 a_{t-1}. \tag{6.98}$$

The Yule–Walker equation is

$$\gamma(k) = \varphi_1 \gamma(k-1), \quad k > 1. \tag{6.99}$$

Noting that

$$X_t = \frac{1 + \theta_1 B}{1 - \varphi_1 B} a_t = [1 + (\varphi_1 + \theta_1)B + \ldots]a_t, \tag{6.100}$$

we have $E[a_t X_t] = \sigma_a^2$ and $E[a_{t-1} X_t] = \sigma_a^2(\varphi_1 + \theta_1)$. Therefore we have

$$\gamma(0) = \varphi_1 \gamma(1) + \sigma_a^2 + \sigma_a^2 \theta_1(\theta_1 + \varphi_1) \tag{6.101}$$

and

$$\gamma(1) = \varphi_1 \gamma(0) + \sigma_a^2 \theta_1. \tag{6.102}$$

Therefore we have

$$\gamma(k) = \begin{cases} \frac{1 + \theta_1(\theta_1 + 2\varphi_1)}{1 - \varphi_1^2} \sigma_a^2 & k = 0 \\[2mm] \frac{(\theta_1 + \varphi_1)(1 + \theta_1 \varphi_1)}{1 - \varphi_1^2} \sigma_a^2 & k = 1 \\[2mm] \varphi_1^{k-1} \gamma(1) & k > 1 \end{cases} \tag{6.103}$$

and

$$\rho(k) = \begin{cases} \frac{(\theta_1+\varphi_1)(1+\theta_1\varphi_1)}{1+\theta_1(\theta_1+2\varphi_1)} & k = 1 \\ \varphi_1^{k-1}\rho(1) & k > 1. \end{cases}$$

(6.104)

Estimation and forecasts using ARMA models are complicated topics and we will not discuss them here. See Brockwell and Davis (1991) and Wei (1990).

6.3   Survival Data Analysis

Survival data analysis can be applied to a variety of business problems when a future discrete event has a possibility of occurring (which we would like to predict), and we are not interested in what happens beyond that particular discrete event (we say that this new state then stays frozen). Examples include account attrition and risk modeling. Let us look at the performance window from the month 0 to the month t_{max}. During the $(t_{max} + 1)$ months window each account can stay in the original state or move to one of the K states and keep the same state afterward. Let $f(t, k)$ be the instantaneous probability that an account is in the state k at time t, and $F(t, k)$ be the cumulative probability of $f(t, k)$. Let $f(t) = \sum_{k=1}^{K} f(t, k)$ be the instantaneous probability that an account is in any one of the K states at time t and its cumulative probability be $F(t) = \sum_{k=1}^{K} F(t, k)$. The survival function is defined as $S(t) = 1 - F(t)$. The hazard function $h(t, k)$ is the probability of being in the state k given in the state 0 in the previous month:

$$h(t, k) = f(t, k)/S(t - 1)$$

(6.105)

and the total hazard function is the sum over all K states,

$$h(t) = \sum_{k=1}^{K} h(t, k).$$

(6.106)

The following figure shows the time windows and definitions of the functions.

With the help of this figure, it is straightforward to find the relationship among the functions f, F, and h. Note that $F(-1) = 0, S(-1) = 1$ for notional convenience.

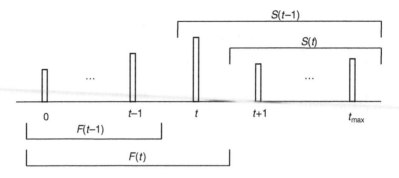

FIGURE 6.1: The probability, cumulative probability, and survival function.

	In terms of f and F	In terms of h
$f(t)$	$= F(t) - F(t-1)$	$= h(t) \cdot \prod_{j=0}^{t-1} (1 - h(j))$
$F(t)$	$= \sum_{j=0}^{t} f(j)$	$= 1 - \prod_{j=0}^{t} (1 - h(j))$
$S(t)$	$= 1 - F(t)$	$= \prod_{j=0}^{t} (1 - h(j))$
$h(t)$	$= \frac{f(t)}{S(t-1)} = \frac{f(t)}{1-F(t-1)}$	

and

	In terms of f and F	In terms of h
$f(t,k)$	$= F(t,k) - F(t-1,k)$	$= h(t,k) \cdot \prod_{j=0}^{t-1} (1 - h(j))$
$F(t,k)$	$= \sum_{j=0}^{t} f(j,k)$	
$S(t,k)$	$= F(\infty,k) - F(t,k)$	
$h(t,k)$	$= \frac{f(t,k)}{S(t-1)} = \frac{f(t,k)}{1-F(t-1)}$	

For the observation i there are two possibilities in the performance window:

1. At time y_i the event v_i happened: $0 \le y_i \le t_{\max}$, $1 \le v_i \le K$. In this case the contribution to the likelihood function is $f(y_i, v_i)$:

$$f(y_i, v_i) = h(y_i, v_i) \cdot \prod_{t=0}^{y_i-1} (1 - h(t)). \tag{6.107}$$

2. Nothing happened and the observation is in the original state: $y_i =$

$t_{\max}$, $v_i = 0$. In this case the contribution to the likelihood function is $S(t_{\max})$:

$$S(y_i) = \prod_{t=0}^{y_i} (1 - h(t)).$$ (6.108)

For n accounts, the likelihood function can be written as

$$L = \prod_{i=1}^{n} \left[f(y_i, v_i)^{1-\delta_{v_i,0}} \cdot S(y_i)^{\delta_{v_i,0}} \right].$$ (6.109)

By using the equations of f and S in terms of the hazard function we have

$$L = \prod_{i=1}^{n} \left\{ h(y_i, v_i)^{1-\delta_{v_i,0}} (1 - h(y_i))^{\delta_{v_i,0}} \cdot \prod_{t=0}^{y_i-1} (1 - h(t)) \right\}.$$ (6.110)

Finally, by defining $h(t, 0) = 1 - h(t)$, we have the likelihood function in terms of the hazard function:

$$L = \prod_{i=1}^{n} \left[h(y_i, v_i) \cdot \prod_{t=0}^{y_i-1} h(t, 0) \right].$$ (6.111)

This is the same likelihood function as for the multi-nominal logistic regression by stacking the monthly data into each observation. If the independent variables are not time dependent, we can construct the data file by using weights.

Let's now consider survival analysis in the continuous time framework. The hazard function is defined in the continuous time as

$$h(t) = f(t)/S(t),$$ (6.112)

or

$$dS(t)/S(t) = -h(t)dt, \quad S(0) = 1.$$ (6.113)

The solution of this simple differential equation is

$$S(t) = e^{-\int_0^t h(\tau)d\tau}.$$ (6.114)

Then the distribution density function is

$$f(t) = h(t)S(t) = h(t) e^{-\int_0^t h(\tau)d\tau}.$$ (6.115)

Note that $F(0) = 0$, $S(0) = 1$. The relationship among the functions, $f, F,$ and h are listed in the following table:

	In term of f and F	In terms of h
$f(t)$	$= F'(t)$	$= h(t) \cdot e^{-\int_0^t h(\tau)d\tau}$
$F(t)$	$= \int_0^t f(\tau)d\tau$	$= 1 - e^{-\int_0^t h(\tau)d\tau}$
$S(t)$	$= 1 - F(t)$	$= e^{-\int_0^t h(\tau)d\tau}$
$h(t)$	$= \frac{f(t)}{S(t)} = \frac{f(t)}{1-F(t)}$	

6.3.1   Sampling Method

Let n_k be the number of records with the outcome k $(k = 0, 1, 2, \cdots, K)$ in the full-expanded data. The proportion of event records is

$$\pi = \frac{\sum\limits_{k=1}^{K} n_k}{n_0 + \sum\limits_{k=1}^{K} n_k} \quad \text{or} \quad \frac{\pi}{1 - \pi} = \frac{\sum\limits_{k=1}^{K} n_k}{n_0}. \tag{6.116}$$

If there are too many records with $k = 0$ in the data set or if π is too small, we can keep all the event records and randomly sample the non-event records with selection probability r. Specify a larger proportion of event records $\rho > \pi$:

$$\rho = \frac{\sum\limits_{k=1}^{K} n_k}{r \cdot n_0 + \sum\limits_{k=1}^{K} n_k} \quad \text{or} \quad \frac{\rho}{1 - \rho} = \frac{\sum\limits_{k=1}^{K} n_k}{r \cdot n_0}. \tag{6.117}$$

We have the selection probability for the non-event records:

$$r = (1 - \rho)\pi / (\rho(1 - \pi)). \tag{6.118}$$

The sampled data set can be constructed in two ways. The first way is to fit the model based on the sample and then correct the bias caused by the sampling. Note that

$$\ln(n_k/n_0) = \ln(n_k/(r \cdot n_0)) + \ln r. \tag{6.119}$$

So we have

$$\ln(p_k/p_0) = \ln(p_k/(r \cdot p_0)) + \ln r. \tag{6.120}$$

Therefore the regression result for the non-sampling data set can be obtained from the regression based on the sampling data set by adding a constant term. For the case of a binary outcome $(K = 1)$, let $\hat{q}(x)$ be the modeling probability with sampled data and $\hat{p}(x)$ be the modeling probability from the original unsampled data. We assume the relationship holds for the observation level, and we have

$$\ln(\hat{p}(x)/(1 - \hat{p}(x))) = \ln(\hat{q}(x)/(1 - \hat{q}(x))) + \ln r. \tag{6.121}$$

Defining $\ln(\hat{q}(x)/(1 - \hat{q}(x))) = \hat{s}(x)$, we have

$$\hat{p}(x) = \frac{\hat{q}(x)}{\hat{q}(x) + r^{-1}(1 - \hat{q}(x))} = \frac{1}{1 + r^{-1}e^{-\hat{s}(x)}}. \tag{6.122}$$

Note that $\sum_i \hat{q}(x) = n_1$ in logistic regression modeling, but in general $\sum_i \hat{p}(x) \neq n_1$.

Alternatively, we can add a weight, $1/r$, in the sampling records. The regression from the sample data with weights is the final result and no adjustment is necessary.

6.4 Exponentially Weighted Moving Average (EWMA) and GARCH(1, 1)

Many important time series do not have the nice property of stationarity, where the mean and standard deviation are constant, even after the above-described transformations. Perhaps the most important of these time series with changing standard deviation is financial data, e.g., stock market data.

When the variance (square of the standard deviation) of the time series changes in time, the series is called heteroscedastic, as opposed to homoscedastic when the variance is constant. In a heteroscedastic time series frequently the most important property to forecast is the variance, which is the goal of the ARCH and GARCH models. For example, the variance is the fundamental property required for options pricing. Indeed, the Black–Scholes model (assumptions: random walk of log normal returns) reduces all standard options prices to be measured in volatility, which is then the essential characteristic to be forecast.

The beginning of the ARCH/GARCH models is the concept of an exponentially weighted moving average for the variance.

6.4.1 Exponentially Weighted Moving Average (EWMA)

We will describe this methodology using time series data, which we can think of as a time series of a stock price $S(t)$. The return is defined as

$$u_i = \ln\left(S_i/S_{i-1}\right), \tag{6.123}$$

where S_i is the value at the end of day i. Note that if x is small, $\ln(1+x) = x - \frac{1}{2}x^2 + \frac{1}{3}x^3 + ...$, when $S_i/S_{i-1} \sim 1$ we have

$$u_i = \ln\left(1 + (S_i - S_{i-1})/S_{i-1}\right) \approx (S_i - S_{i-1})/S_{i-1}. \tag{6.124}$$

We assume that the variance is a weighted average from the returns in the last m days:

$$\sigma_n^2 = \sum_{i=1}^{m} \alpha_i u_{n-i}^2, \tag{6.125}$$

with the weights normalized as $\sum_{i=1}^{m} \alpha_i = 1$. Let $\alpha_{i+1} = \lambda\alpha_i$, $\lambda \in [0, 1]$, then

$$1 = \sum_{i=1}^{m} \alpha_i = \alpha_1(1 + \lambda + ... + \lambda^{m-1}) = \alpha_1 \left(1 - \lambda^m\right)/(1 - \lambda), \tag{6.126}$$

and we have $\alpha_1 = (1 - \lambda)/(1 - \lambda^m)$. Note that

$$
\begin{aligned}
\sigma_n^2 &= \alpha_1 u_{n-1}^2 + \alpha_2 u_{n-2}^2 + ... + \alpha_m u_{n-m}^2 \\
&= \alpha_1 u_{n-1}^2 + \lambda(\alpha_1 u_{n-1-1}^2 + ... + \alpha_m u_{n-1-m}^2) - \lambda\alpha_m u_{n-m-1}^2 \\
&= \alpha_1 u_{n-1}^2 + \lambda\sigma_{n-1}^2 - \lambda\alpha_m u_{n-m-1}^2
\end{aligned}
$$

$$(6.127)$$

Making an approximation on $\alpha_1 \approx 1 - \lambda$ and neglecting the third term, we have the following recursive equation:

$$
\sigma_n^2 = (1 - \lambda)\, u_{n-1}^2 + \lambda\, \sigma_{n-1}^2. \tag{6.128}
$$

This is the exponentially weighted moving average (EWMA) model for the variance.

6.4.2 ARCH and GARCH Models

The idea of the ARCH/GARCH volatility forecasting models is that the volatility is a moving average with adjustable weights that are fit by some optimization process, typically maximizing the likelihood. Let V_L be a long-run average variance.

ARCH(m) model (AutoRegressive Conditional Heteroscedacity):

$$
\sigma_n^2 = \gamma V_L + \sum_{i=1}^m \alpha_i u_{n-i}^2, \quad \gamma + \sum_{i=1}^m \alpha_i = 1. \tag{6.129}
$$

GARCH (p, q) model (Generalized AutoRegressive Conditional Heteroscedacity):

$$
\sigma_n^2 = \gamma V_L + \sum_{i=1}^p \alpha_i u_{n-i}^2 + \sum_{i=1}^q \beta_i \sigma_{n-i}^2. \tag{6.130}
$$

The most common GARCH model is with $p = q = 1$.

GARCH(1, 1) model:

$$
\sigma_n^2 = \gamma V_L + \alpha\, u_{n-1}^2 + \beta\, \sigma_{n-1}^2, \quad \gamma + \alpha + \beta = 1. \tag{6.131}
$$

How do we estimate the parameters γ, α, β, and V_L? Here we make an assumption: in day i, if we know σ_i^2 (which will be predicted), then u_i is normally distributed with variance σ_i^2. Then the maximum likelihood function is

$$
L = \prod_{i=1}^m \left(\frac{1}{\sqrt{2\pi\sigma_i^2}} e^{-u_i^2/(2\sigma_i^2)} \right). \tag{6.132}
$$

If we let $v_i = \sigma_i^2$, we have

$$
\begin{aligned}
\ln L &= \sum_{i=1}^{m} \left(-\tfrac{1}{2}\ln(2\pi) - \tfrac{1}{2}\ln(v_i) - u_i^2/(2v_i) \right) \\
&\sim \sum_{i=1}^{m} \left(-\ln(v_i) - u_i^2/v_i \right) .
\end{aligned}
\tag{6.133}
$$

Here u_i are observed and the v_i are generated according to the model, so γ, α, β, and V_L can be estimated by a maximum likelihood estimation. Let $\omega = \gamma V_L$. The following table is the problem set-up.

i	S_i	$u_i = (S_i - S_{i-1})/S_{i-1}$	$v_i = \sigma_i^2$	$-\ln(v_i) - u_i^2/v_i$
1	$\checkmark$	—	—	—
2	$\checkmark$	$\checkmark$	—	—
3	$\checkmark$	$\checkmark$	u_2^2	$\checkmark$
4	$\checkmark$	$\checkmark$	$\omega + \alpha\, u_3^2 + \beta\, \sigma_3^2$	$\checkmark$
...	...	...	...	...
m	$\checkmark$	$\checkmark$	$\checkmark$	$\checkmark$

After estimating ω, α, β, we have $\gamma = 1 - \alpha - \beta$ and $V_L = \omega/\gamma$.

We have implemented "*garch()*" for the GARCH(1, 1) model in DataMinerXL (see Appendix B) using the Nelder–Mead algorithm. The Nelder–Mead algorithm is a powerful method to find the minimum values of multivariate functions using only function values, without any derivative information. The detailed description of the algorithm can be found in Lagarias et al. (1998).

Chapter 7

Data Preparation and Variable Selection

An important philosophy in machine learning is that one should not expect the model to do all the difficult work, not even a powerful nonlinear model. In practical situations with finite and noisy data, it is useful to encode the inputs as best as possible using expert knowlege and good statistical practices. Yes, this generally reduces potential information to the model, but in practice it allows the model to focus its efforts in the right areas. Good thought to encoding variables is fundamental to successful modeling. Do not expect your model to do the heavy lifting. Help the model as much as possible with thoughtful data encoding and expert variable creation.

In practical problems it always helps to (1) fully understand the nature of the problem and the data and (2) engage domain experts as much as is possible. Understanding the nature of the problem and the data include clarity about the task at hand: exactly what are you trying to predict, what can be used in this prediction. This will help in the design of the target variable, the model framework, and the objective function. Domain experts can help with understanding the nature of the data, definitions of the various fields, where they come from, the population and timeframes of the data sample, likely sources of data noise and error, and the underlying dynamics that helps guide the level of complexity to structure in the model. Further, discussions with the domain experts can help in the creation of expert variables, typically nonlinear combinations of raw data fields that have powerful predictive potential. Common examples include ratios of fields, maximum/minimums on fields or field combinations, if/and combinations of fields. Even in moderate dimensions and with large data sets, data poorly fills the space. Precomputing expert variables is much better than hoping your favorite powerful nonlinear modeling technique will sort out possibly complex combinations of raw fields in a sparsely filled space.

An important characteristic to consider in how to transform variables is whether or not there is a metric in that dimension. For example, most continuous variables have a metric—a concept of nearness. Two field values that are closer to each other have meaning implied in that closeness. Fifty dollars is closer to 60 dollars than it is to 10 dollars. Most categorical fields do not have this metric. Blue, green, and red are different colors with (generally) no concept of nearness. In the encoding of variables we need to be aware of these concepts of metrics, with or without continuity, and whether or not they are preserved in transformations. For example, z-scaling, log scaling, and quantile binning preserve metrics but WOE transformations do not.

7.1 Data Quality and Exploration

Generally the first task to perform with a data set is to do simple data quality examination and exploration of univariate distributions. These first exploration exercises help us get an understanding of the variation and quality of the data set. We examine each field in the data separately and calculate simple statistics, and then examine the distribution as best as possible. For continuous fields we can bin the data and visually examine the distribution. This may take multiple passes through the data to get reasonable binning for examination. For categorical variables we can visually inspect the number of occurrences of the most common and uncommon values of the field. We may find that the field has only one value in the data, in which case it is a useless field (it is then really a label for the entire data set). We may find some rare outliers that may need special care. In these preliminary data explorations we begin to get the feel for the quality of the data as we visually inspect some of the unusual aspects of the field values. We may find special characters or values that were unexpected, which could be the result of noise, data errors, or mistakes in the data extract process.

It is useful to have a standard data quality process that one runs first on any new data set and to visually examine the field values and distributions. This should be done even with hundreds of fields, and it is therefore important to have a well-defined set of summary statistics to examine. We typically separate fields into continuous and categorical and look at different aspects of these separately. For the continuous fields we calculate the mean, standard deviation, min, max, and do our best to visually inspect the shape of the univariate distribution, looking for outliers and hints on how to scale and transform the field as described below.

For the categorical variables we enumerate the number of occurrences of all possible values and print out the most and least common dozens of these values to get an idea of the completeness, coverage, and quality of the data. In these tables it is not unusual to discover fields with data errors, unexpected or "impossible" values, as well as fields with most or all the values identical.

7.2 Variable Scaling and Transformation

Some techniques are robust to large variations in scale among the potential input variables, but most techniques are very sensitive to this scaling. In general, many methods involve explicit or implicit measuring of nearness of data points in a multidimensional space, and if this space has different scalings in different dimensions these measurements are distorted.

The most common and basic scaling technique is z-scaling, where one computes a mean μ_i and standard deviation σ_i for each continuous input dimension separately, and then computes the z-scaled transformed variables as

$$x_i' = (x_i - \mu_i)/\sigma_i. \tag{7.1}$$

This most common scaling ensures that variables with "reasonable" distributions are all scaled to be centered and to have the same spread.

Frequently in practical problems variables may be closer to a lognormal distribution rather than a normal distribution. This commonly occurs with fields measuring money, time, distance, or quantities that have physical units in their scales (dollars, minutes, miles...). This is a consequence of natural exponential relations in physically meaningful quantities, which gives rise to the fascinating Benford law. Examples are that consumer purchasing power is proportional to wealth, and income is related to wealth, so there are natural lognormal distributions in money fields in financial data. For such variables a simple log transform, $x_i' = \log x_i$, puts these variables into a more natural scale for modeling.

Another common scaling/transformation methodology is to transform a variable to quantiles, such as deciles or percentiles. Here we simply sort all the data records in descending order for a variable x_i, and then replace the value x_i by its quantile. We do this separately for each independent variable. This robust transformation works well for most highly skewed distributions. This is equivalent to the equal population binning described below.

These three variable scaling techniques do not surrender the possibility of variable interactions, which can happen when one uses the weight of evidence transformation described later.

7.3 How to Bin Variables

In order to do nonlinear transformation it is often convenient to discretize or bin the variables. There are many possible ways to bin variables, some of which are described here. We consider binning in a univariate manner, where the binning in each dimension/feature is done independently, but all these methodologies can be extended as needed to two or higher dimensions being considered simultaneously.

Binning is a practical methodology to encode continuous variables into robust forms for machine learning algorithms. At first it may not seem obvious why one would bin an already continuous variable since one generally loses information in this process. Machine learning algorithms can easily handle continuous variables, so why do binning? There are two primary reasons for binning input variables: (1) a pre-translation of the input variable directly into a simple representation of the output variable can help the model better learn the relationship between the input and the output, and (2) binning can provide statistical smoothing and therefore robustness in the modeling process.

7.3.1 Equal Interval

First, the simplest way to bin is to use an equal interval. Let x_{min} and x_{max} be the minimum and maximum values for variable x, respectively. We cut the whole range into k groups with equal interval, $d = (x_{max} - x_{min})/k$. The ith bin corresponds to the range $(x_{min} + (i - 1)d, x_{min} + i\,d)$. This binning method is very sensitive to the selection of x_{min} and x_{max}, and so the careful treatment of outliers is critical in this method. Usually we use the natural limits or the mean and standard deviation to decide x_{min} and x_{max}, for example $\mu \pm 5\sigma$ can be reasonable choices for the outer bounds. Because outliers can frequently affect the mean and standard deviation, a more robust methodology is to iteratively calculate μ and σ, "push" the data to be inside the range $\mu \pm 5\sigma$, and then recalculate μ and σ, continuing this process until reasonable convergence. A variant of this simple binning approach is to bin fields in the normalized z-scaled space discussed above. Common sense judgment is needed.

7.3.2 Equal Population

A second method is to use an equal population in each bin. Basically, we first sort n observations in terms of x and assign each observation a rank from 1, 2, ..., to n. Then the *bin* number for observation i is:

$$bin = 1 + \text{int}\left((i - 1)\,g/n\right) \tag{7.2}$$

where int(.) is the integer part of a given number. Special attention is needed for the tier/boundary observations so that observations with the exact same values should be in the same bin, otherwise confusion exists across bin boundaries.

The same idea is applied to the histogram transformation. Any variable can be transformed into between 0 and 1 by using $x \to n(x)/n$, where $n(x)$ is the number of observations with the values less than or equal to x.

7.3.3 Tree Algorithms

A third method is to use a tree algorithm in one-dimensional space. The Gini index, entropy, chi-squared, or KS criteria can be used to determine the cutpoint of the variable. Recursive splitting and merging methods are used to decide the multiple cutpoints for a variable. Sometimes a combination of the above-mentioned methods is used to get the optimal binning. For example, we may use the chi-square test or t-test to see if the neighboring bins are significantly different. If they are not, merge the pair of neighboring bins. This procedure could be recursive and until all neighboring bins are significantly different.

The main purpose for grouping values of variables is to enhance the stability of transformation and to build more robust models.

7.4 Interpolation in One and Two Dimensions

Consider two separate points in a two-dimensional space. The line connecting these two points is

$$y = y_1 + \frac{y_2 - y_1}{x_2 - x_1} \cdot (x - x_1). \tag{7.3}$$

It can be rewritten as

$$y = \frac{l_1 y_1 + l_2 y_2}{l_1 + l_2}, \tag{7.4}$$

where $l_1 = x_2 - x$ and $l_2 = x - x_1$. Graphically, it is a linear interpolation.

Now consider four distinct points in three-dimensional space. There are many possible ways to do the interpolation. Let's first do the one-dimensional interpolation twice in the x-direction:

$$z_{12} = \frac{l_1 z_1 + l_2 z_2}{l_1 + l_2} \tag{7.5}$$

and

$$z_{34} = \frac{l_2 z_3 + l_1 z_4}{l_1 + l_2}, \tag{7.6}$$

then do the one-dimensional interpolation once in the y-direction:

$$z = \frac{l_3 z_{12} + l_4 z_{34}}{l_3 + l_4} = \frac{\sum_{i=1}^{4} A_i z_i}{\sum_{i=1}^{4} A_i}, \tag{7.7}$$

where $l_3 = y_2 - y$ and $l_4 = y - y_1$.

This is the weighted average with weights being the areas opposite to that point. While the choice of doing x or y first is arbitrary, the results are the same.

7.5   Weight of Evidence (WOE) Transformation

It is very common that the relationship between the independent variable and dependent variable is not linear. In order to easily capture the nonlinear relationship between the input and output variables and to use the variable effectively, it is frequently helpful to do special, somewhat trivial nonlinear transformation. The term "nonlinear" relationship here could be misleading for categorical variables, since there is no "linear" relationship for categorical variables.

We are frequently asked why should we do a nonlinear transformation since the model, if it is a nonlinear technique, can find these needed nonlinearities. The answer is both philosophical and practical. The practical reason is that many complex modeling projects face very large data sets in moderate to high dimensions. Under these conditions several effects occur, many of which are nonintuitive, such as all points being closer to boundaries than the interior. First, it is problematic to use substantially nonlinear methods in high dimensional space, regardless of the amount of data. With sparse data we are in severe danger of overfitting. With a surplus of data we can find our methods to be computationally limited, as well as still having the overfitting issue. We frequently find that for such large data sets the search for nonlinearity is difficult and the linear models perform fairly well and tend to be more robust. The general philosophical answer is that you should always encode your data as best as possible to reduce the work of the model as much as possible.

Let's consider a problem with a binary output. In order to apply the WOE method we first need to discretize the input variables. For each input variable x, it could be categorical (here this means nominal) or continuous (here this means numerical or ordinal). A categorical variable is already discretized and its categories are predefined. While we can only group values that are nearby for continuous variables, we can do any grouping for categorical variables. First we bin each input variable. For each continuous variable we use the above-described binning methods to bin into a certain number of bins. We can use the recursive splitting method or the recursive merging method to get the appropriated number of bins.

Let b and g be the numbers of bads and goods in a given bin, respectively. Note the following identity:

$$\frac{1}{1 + e^{-\ln(b/g)}} = \frac{b}{g + b}. \tag{7.8}$$

We will use the log-odds as the transformation in the logistic regression model:

$$x \rightarrow x' = \ln(b/g) \tag{7.9}$$

and use the bad rate in a linear regression model:

$$x \rightarrow x' = b/(g+b). \tag{7.10}$$

The log-odds transformation and the bad rate transformation are called weight of evidence (WOE) transformations. WOE is one of the simplest and most economic ways to find a nonlinear transformation of the variables. When applied to a categorical variable, WOE can be interpreted as a translation of a categorical variable to a continuous variable. Usually, for the log-odds transformation the WOE is normalized as

$$WOE = \ln(b/g) - \ln(B/G) \tag{7.11}$$

and for the bad rate transformation the WOE is normalized as

$$WOE = b/(g+b) - B/(G+B) \tag{7.12}$$

or

$$WOE = \frac{b/(g+b)}{B/(G+B)}, \tag{7.13}$$

where B and G are the numbers of the total bads and total goods, respectively, in the modeling population.

Similarly for the continuous output, we can define the normalized WOE as

$$WOE = \bar{y} - \bar{Y}, \tag{7.14}$$

where $\bar{y}$ is the mean of the output variable in a given bin and $\bar{Y}$ is the mean of the output variable for the modeling population.

It is straightforward to generalize the one-dimensional binning algorithm into two-dimensional or higher dimensions. We first find the most important pairs of variables: x_1 and x_2. Bin x_1 and x_2 independently and then work on the grid in terms of the cross product of x_1 and x_2. We can do recursive merging of cells to have a smaller number of combinations. Generalization to higher dimensions is rarely used in practice because of the number of combinations of variable cross products.

Transforming the input variable into some form of the output, such as using the bad rate or log odds, has both benefits and penalties. The benefits are that we encode potential nonlinearities into relationships that are much easier for the model to discover. The penalty is that we have lost the original information about the value of the original variable x, and any possible interaction (multidimensional) effects are lost. In practice the described transformations are generally sound since nonlinearities tend to occur more frequently than multidimensional effects.

Consider a situation with a single categorical variable input x and a single output binary variable y, with the possible categories of the single input variable being A, B, and C. Construct a data count table:

x	y	Count	$\hat{y}$
A	1	n_{A1}	a
A	0	n_{A0}	a
B	1	n_{B1}	b
B	0	n_{B0}	b
C	1	n_{C1}	c
C	0	n_{C0}	c

Since there is only one input x and it can take only one of three possible values (A, B, or C), there are only three possible model outputs $\hat{y}$, and we denote them as a, b, and c. We examine ways to find best estimates for the model output, specifically we look at using either the log-likelihood or mean squared error (MSE) objective.

The likelihood function is

$$L = [a^{n_{A1}}(1-a)^{n_{A0}}] \cdot [b^{n_{B1}}(1-b)^{n_{B0}}] \cdot [c^{n_{C1}}(1-c)^{n_{C0}}], \tag{7.15}$$

and the log-likelihood function is

$$\begin{aligned} \ln L \quad = \quad & [n_{A1}\ln a + n_{A0}\ln(1-a)] + [n_{B1}\ln b + n_{B0}\ln(1-b)] \\ & + [n_{C1}\ln c + n_{C0}\ln(1-c)]. \end{aligned} \tag{7.16}$$

Taking the derivative with respect to a, b, and c, which are essentially the model parameters, we have

$$\frac{\partial \ln L}{\partial a} = \frac{n_{A1}}{a} - \frac{n_{A0}}{1-a} \tag{7.17}$$

and the similar equations for b and c. Setting the derivative to zero gives the best estimators, and we have

$$a = \frac{n_{A1}}{n_{A1}+n_{A0}}, \quad b = \frac{n_{B1}}{n_{B1}+n_{B0}}, \quad \text{and} \quad c = \frac{n_{C1}}{n_{C1}+n_{C0}}. \tag{7.18}$$

Now consider a sum of squared errors (MSE) as our objective function:

$$E = n_{A1}(1-a)^2 + n_{A0}a^2 + n_{B1}(1-b)^2 + n_{B0}b^2 + n_{C1}(1-c)^2 + n_{C0}c^2. \tag{7.19}$$

Taking the derivative with respect to a, b, and c, we have

$$\frac{\partial E}{\partial a} = -2(1-a)\,n_{A1} + 2a\,n_{A0} \tag{7.20}$$

and similar equations for b and c. Setting these to zero yields the same results as using the MLE objective function.

In summary, when we are encoding categorical variables to be used in linear models, we should choose different encodings depending on the model type. One somewhat common methodology which is easy to use but usually not very good is to transform a single categorical variable that takes N discrete possible outputs into an N-dimensional binary-valued vector. This is not recommended because this method will substantially increase dimensionality, which is always the opposite direction of where we want to go. We would rather choose methods that replace the single categorical variable with an appropriate encoded single value, and the dimensionality is not changed.

Let u be the transformed encoded variable for the original variable x. For a linear regression model,

$$\hat{y} = c_0 + c_1 u(x) \tag{7.21}$$

and we choose the ideal encoding to be

$$u(x) = \begin{cases} a & x = A, \\ b & x = B, \\ c & x = C. \end{cases} \tag{7.22}$$

For logistic regression,

$$\hat{y} = \frac{1}{1 + e^{-u(x)}}, \tag{7.23}$$

we should set

$$u(x) = \begin{cases} \ln\left(\frac{a}{1-a}\right) & x = A, \\ \ln\left(\frac{b}{1-b}\right) & x = B, \\ \ln\left(\frac{c}{1-c}\right) & x = C. \end{cases} \tag{7.24}$$

If the variable is used in linear regression, $u = a$, then use the average for the encoding. If the variable is used in logistic regression, then we should use the log odds

$$u = \ln\left(\frac{a}{1-a}\right) = \ln\left(\frac{n_{A1}}{n_{A0}}\right). \tag{7.25}$$

This is called weight of evidence encoding for the variables.

For a categorical variable or a numerical variable with binning, the numbers of goods (output is 0) and bads (output is 1) in each category and overall are listed as following:

Category	Good	Bad
A	g	b
B	...	...
C	...	...
Total	G	B

The bad rate in a category is

$$r = \frac{b}{b+g}.$$ (7.26)

The overall bad rate is:

$$r_0 = \frac{B}{B+G}.$$ (7.27)

Then the risk index in a category is defined as the normalized bad rate:

$$\text{Risk index} = \frac{r}{r_0} = \frac{\frac{b}{b+g}}{\frac{B}{B+G}}.$$ (7.28)

If b or g is small, a smoothing factor can be introduced into this risk index, for example with a small number $n = 50$,

$$\text{Risk index} = \frac{\frac{b+n\cdot r_0}{b+g+n}}{r_0} = \frac{\frac{r + \frac{n}{b+g}\cdot r_0}{1 + \frac{n}{b+g}}}{r_0} = \frac{\frac{r}{r_0} + \frac{n}{b+g}}{1 + \frac{n}{b+g}}.$$ (7.29)

We can interpret this as the bad rate with a smoothing factor in a category. It is the weighted average of r and r_0 with weights 1 and $n/(b+g)$, respectively. Alternatively, the risk index with a smoothing factor can be interpreted as the weighted average of risk index r/r_0 and 1 with weights 1 and $n/(b+g)$, respectively. It can be seen that the risk index is not sampling invariant, while the WOE or log odds is sampling invariant. In the same way, if b or g is small, we can add a smoothing factor into WOE:

$$WOE = \ln\left(\frac{b + n\cdot \frac{B}{B+G}}{g + n\cdot \frac{G}{B+G}}\right) - \ln\left(\frac{B}{G}\right).$$ (7.30)

7.6 Variable Selection Overview

The process of variable selection and creation is fundamental to building statistical models. Some of the most powerful variables can be those created specifically for the modeling task at hand with particular thought to the specific target and objective function. Domain knowledge and expert information can help substantially in designing special variables.

Once a large pool of candidate variables has been created the next task is to select from this pool a subset that provides the best balance between predictive power and stability. Some may wonder why not just use all possible variables with the goal of providing the most powerful predictive model. There are several reasons why this is not a good strategy for practical reasons. The primary reason is future stability. Frequently many variables may have some relation to the target that is either spurious or otherwise is not expected to continue into the future. Many of these potential variables can be excluded by *a priori* thought and examination, that is, one should explicitly remove from the pool variables that are expected to undergo changes or modifications in the future. Others should be considered for exclusion if for any reason they have been modified in the data. Examples in this category include revised econometric data, in which case one should try to obtain the original, unrevised data.

In general, one should always be thinking of how the model is to be applied, what data with what quality will be known at the time of model use, and to use exactly and only the data that will be seen by the model in use going forward. The goal of model building should be to build the most useful model for going forward use as opposed to the best performing model on paper. One can always build models that look very good on paper but will not perform well in the future, which should be the bane of all good modelers.

The best tool we have for building robust, stable models is out of sample validation. Certainly one divides the data into separate training and testing, but one should also have a holdout sample that best represents what the model will be working on in its go-forward environment. Typically this is an out-of-time sample of the most recent data. A good general process is to use one time sample to train/test, using the out-of-time sample as little as possible, identify the model structure and variables, generate training/testing and out-of-time sample statistics of model performance. Finally, after this has all been done it is frequently wise to retrain the model using the most relevant data set which usually includes the holdout, out-of-time sample. Once this has been done there are no testing model performance statistics to be reported on this final model, since all the data is used in the building. This may seem a bit unnatural, but the reasoning is to use the careful training/testing/out-of-time process to ensure no overfitting. Once the variables have been chosen and the model structure/complexity has been selected, these are kept the same and all the most relevant data (including the most recent) is then used in a final retrain.

The principle of parsimony is appropriate for model building and usually results in the most stable and robust model. The fundamental step is to do careful variable selection and elimination, where our goal again is to build the best performing model for future and ongoing use.

Most variable selection methods are univariate and work very well at identifying the most predictive variables in most practical applications. There are times when strong interactions occur which are nonlinear mixing of two or more variables, and univariate methods can sometimes fail to find these. Higher-order variable selection processes exist, such as two-stage fuzzy curves and surfaces [Lin et al. (1996)]. While these are indeed practical and powerful they can sometimes be computationally expensive.

Variable selection, also called feature selection methods, can be roughly divided into filter methods and wrapper methods. The filter methods identify the important modeling inputs generally without regard to the model that will later be used, and the wrapper methods for variable reduction work in close combination with the algorithm that will be used in the later modeling process.

7.7 Missing Data Imputation

Invariably the data sets we have at our disposal are less than perfect. There is certainly noise in all real data sets, as well as outliers (real and spurious), and missing data values. By this we mean records that contain blanks or other missing value indicators in the places for particular fields. If these fields are missing for too many records we consider not using these fields. If there are not too many records with these missing fields and they are unbiased (the missing fields occur randomly on the records) we can consider leaving these records out of the model building. Sometimes we can do neither, so we need a method to impute/approximate these missing field values.

The following four methods are commonly used to impute missing values.

1. Mean, median, or mode: Simply calculate the mean, median, or mode of the values present and use that for the missing data.

2. Meaning: e.g., 0, min, or max, based on the meaning of the data fields. This could be very tricky. For example, what is the MOB (month-on-book) of a mortgage account if one does not have a mortgage trade.

3. In terms of y: Use the same odds method described previously. That is, if a field value is missing, assemble all other records that have the field value present and examine the subset at that particular value of the output for the missing record. One can then use an average of the inputs on the records that have the same output. This is sketched in Figure 7.1.

4. Model-based imputation method: For instance, the expectation-maximization (EM) algorithm discussed in Section 9.11. Section 8.2 of Zangari et al. (1996) gives an example of imputing a missing data point in a time series using the EM algorithm.

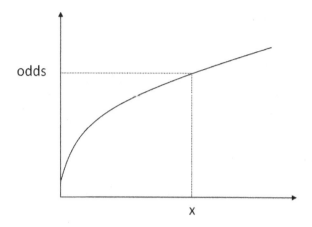

FIGURE 7.1: Imputation of missing values using the same odds method: For a given variable, the odds for all data points with missing values is the same as that for all data points with a certain range of values.

7.8   Stepwise Selection Methods

Among the variable selection methods, forward selection is the easiest method and the most common in practice. The stepwise and backward selection methods are variations of forward selection, but a little bit more complicated. Here we only discuss the forward selection method in detail. Backward selection is similar to forward selection but in the "opposite direction." Forward and backward are special cases of stepwise selection. All stepwise selection methods are similar in that at any point in the selection process there is a pool of selected variables out of a universe of possible variables, and then one examines all possible individual variables to either increase or decrease the selected set by exactly one, hence the moniker "stepwise." Stepwise selection processes are greedy in that we make the best next choice based on where we are now.

In forward selection we start with no selected variables out of the pool of n possible model variables. We then build n separate models, each using exactly one of the possible variables. We select the single variable that alone provides the best model. We then progress by building $n-1$ models each using the previously selected variable along with all the other $n-1$ possible variables. We then select the two variables that provide the best model and proceed to build $n-2$ models using the already selected two variables and all the other possible variables individually, and so on. Thus we progress in a stepwise fashion forward building up a set of best variables, and at each step in the process we evaluate which remaining variable adds the most incremental value.

In backward selection we start with all possible n variables and stepwise remove all possible single variables to find the best $n-1$ variable model, and then continue monotonically removing variables one at a time until we reach a desired set of variables.

General stepwise selection progresses by adding or subtracting exactly one variable at each step, but the step could be either adding or removing a variable.

Since this variable selection is inherently tied to a model building process for evaluation, it is of the wrapper class of feature selection algorithms. Stepwise selections can be done with either linear or nonlinear models, and below we describe it for simple linear regressions.

7.8.1   Forward Selection in Linear Regression

Using a matrix sweep operation, we can easily formulate the forward selection procedure.

1. First construct a cross-product matrix. Note that the X and Y data must be centered (mean zero), but not necessarily normalized.

XX	XY
XY	YY

2. Pick up the most significant variable in terms of t-test and its p-value less than the threshold. Sweep the matrix in terms of the selected variable.

$$
t_x^2 = \left(\frac{r_{*yx}^2}{1 - r_{*yx}^2} \right) \cdot [n - (k+1)]
$$

$$
= \left(\frac{\frac{(Y_*^T x_*)^2}{(Y_*^T Y_*) \cdot (x_*^T x_*)}}{1 - \frac{(Y_*^T x_*)^2}{(Y_*^T Y_*) \cdot (x_*^T x_*)}} \right) \cdot [n - (k+1)] \tag{7.31}
$$

   where k is the number of parameters in the original model.

3. Repeat Step 2 until you reach the specified number of variables or no more variables are found to be significant.

7.8.2   Forward Selection in Logistic Regression

There are many selection logic formulations based on a variety of tests, such as the likelihood ratio test and the score test. Since the score test is the most efficient for variable selection computationally, we will discuss those details in this section. It is called the residual χ^2 test based on the score test, using the Lagrange multipliers (LM) method.

Suppose we have a model that already uses variables x_1, x_2, ..., x_t, and we want to test the significance of the $(s - t)$ other variables: x_{t+1}, x_{t+2}, ..., x_s. The residual χ^2 test is a score test for $H_0 : \beta_{t+1} = \beta_{t+2} = ... = \beta_s = 0$. The test statistic is

$$LM = \left(\frac{\partial \ln L}{\partial \hat{\beta}_R}\right)^T \left\{I(\hat{\beta}_R)\right\}^{-1} \left(\frac{\partial \ln L}{\partial \hat{\beta}_R}\right) \sim \chi^2[s - t], \qquad (7.32)$$

where $\hat{\beta}_R = (\hat{\beta}_1, \hat{\beta}_2, ..., \hat{\beta}_t, 0, 0, ..., 0)$ and $I(\hat{\beta}_R) = -E\left[\frac{\partial^2 \ln L}{\partial \hat{\beta}_R \partial \hat{\beta}_R}\right]$ is the information matrix . The t coefficients are estimated for the model with t variables.

If $s = t + 1$, we can use the residual χ^2 test to test the significance of the variable x_{t+1}. Since the t coefficients are estimated from the model with t variables, we have

$$\frac{\partial \ln L}{\partial \hat{\beta}_1} = \frac{\partial \ln L}{\partial \hat{\beta}_2} = ... = \frac{\partial \ln L}{\partial \hat{\beta}_t} = 0. \qquad (7.33)$$

Therefore the score test statistic is

$$\begin{aligned} LM &= \left(\frac{\partial \ln L}{\partial \hat{\beta}_R}\right)^T \left\{I(\hat{\beta}_R)\right\}^{-1} \left(\frac{\partial \ln L}{\partial \hat{\beta}_R}\right) \\ &= \left(\frac{\partial \ln L}{\partial \hat{\beta}_{t+1}}\right)^T \{I\}^{-1}_{t+1,\,t+1} \left(\frac{\partial \ln L}{\partial \hat{\beta}_{t+1}}\right) \sim \chi^2[1]. \end{aligned} \qquad (7.34)$$

The larger LM is, the more significant x_{t+1} is. Since it only needs to fit the model with t variables and computes the first derivative and Hessian matrix with the given estimator, the computation is not expensive. This process can be used for forward selection in logistic regression.

7.9 Mutual Information, KL Distance

Perhaps the best univariate, model-independent metric to measure the information value in a variable is built from concepts around mutual information. The mutual information between two random variables x and y is given by

$$I(X, Y) = \sum_{x,y} p(x, y) \ln \frac{p(x, y)}{p(x)p(y)}, \qquad (7.35)$$

where $p(x)$ and $p(y)$ are the probability distributions over x and y, and $p(x, y)$ is the joint probability distribution. This is related to the entropy

$$H(X) = - \sum_{all\ states} p(x) \ln p(x) \qquad (7.36)$$

and the conditional entropy

$$H(X|Y) = -\sum_{x,y} p(x,y) \ln p(x|y) \tag{7.37}$$

through

$$I(X,Y) = H(X) - H(X|Y). \tag{7.38}$$

Another related quantity is the relative entropy, also called the Kullback–Leibler distance (KL distance, KL divergence), which measures the differences between two probability distributions and is given by

$$D(p||q) = \sum_{x} p(x) \ln \frac{p(x)}{q(x)}. \tag{7.39}$$

This in itself is asymmetric, but in practical uses a symmetric version can be made through

$$D_S(p||q) = \sum_{x} p(x) \ln \frac{p(x)}{q(x)} + \sum_{x} q(x) \ln \frac{q(x)}{p(x)} = \sum_{x} [p(x) - q(x)] \ln \frac{p(x)}{q(x)}. \tag{7.40}$$

The Kullback–Leibler distance is a very good way to measure the differences between two distributions. It is also sometimes known as the information divergence and is related to the cross entropy.

7.10 Detection of Multicollinearity

Identifying and removing highly correlated variables is one of the most important tasks in model building. In this section we will discuss two approaches based on pair-wise correlation and variance decomposition, respectively.

The first approach is only based on pair-wise correlation and tries to select and delete some variables with high correlations to one another, giving a threshold of correlation. In theory this approach cannot resolve the problem of multicollinearity completely, but in practice it is a very effective method. After deleting some variables, the correlations among remaining variables are all less than the given threshold. The second approach has been suggested by Belsley et al. (1980) through variance decomposition. It can tell which variables might be the source of multicollinearity.

The first step in the first approach is to identify all pairs of variables with high correlation. We can construct a graph with the variables represented by vertices and correlations represented by edges. In general, the graph consists of a cluster of connected graphs. In each connected graph, all variables are connected to at least one variable. Then we will select and delete variables based on the correlation with a target variable. The procedure can be summarized as follows:

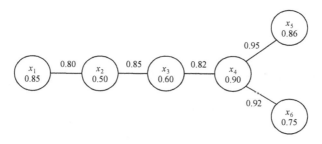

FIGURE 7.2: Selection of variables with multicollinearity: The number inside each circle is the correlation between the variable and the target variable and the number in the edge is the correlation between the two adjacent variables.

1. Set a threshold of the correlation for removing the correlated variables, e.g., 0.80 or 0.95, etc.

2. Construct graphs only showing the correlations with the absolute values larger than the threshold. The graph is a disconnected cluster of subgraphs.

3. Do the same selection in each connected graph.

    (a) Select the variable with the largest absolute value of correlation with the target variable.

    (b) Delete all variables directly connected to the selected variable.

    (c) Repeat (a) and (b), until all variables either are selected or deleted.

Here we give an example. We choose a threshold of correlation of 0.80. Then we have a connected graph only showing the variables with correlations larger than 0.80. The number inside each circle is the correlation between the variable and the target variable and the number in the edge is the correlation between the two adjacent variables. According to the above procedure we have the following iterations:

1. Iteration 1: select x_4, delete x_3, x_5, and x_6.

2. Iteration 2: select x_1 and delete x_2.

Finally, the variables x_1 and x_4 are selected and the variables x_2, x_3, x_5, and x_6 are deleted.

Belsley's approach is based on the covariance matrix of the least squares coefficient vector, $X^T X$, where all diagonal elements are normalized to 1. The spectral decomposition of the symmetric positive definite matrix is

$$X^T X = U\Lambda U^T \tag{7.41}$$

and its matrix inversion is

$$\left(X^T X\right)^{-1} = U \Lambda^{-1} U^T. \tag{7.42}$$

The diagonal element of the inverse matrix is

$$\left(X^T X\right)^{-1}_{kk} = \sum_l U^2_{kl} / \lambda_l. \tag{7.43}$$

By defining a matrix

$$\pi_{kl} = \frac{U^2_{kl} / \lambda_l}{\left(X^T X\right)^{-1}_{kk}}, \tag{7.44}$$

we have $\sum_l \pi_{kl} = 1$. This matrix can be listed in the following table where λ_l is ordered from the largest to the smallest:

Eigenvalue	Condition Index	X_1	X_2	...	X_p
λ_1	1	π_{11}	π_{21}	...	π_{p1}
λ_2	$\sqrt{\lambda_1/\lambda_2}$	π_{12}	π_{22}	...	π_{p2}
...	...	...	...	...	...
λ_p	$\sqrt{\lambda_1/\lambda_p}$	π_{1p}	π_{2p}	...	π_{pp}

This table allows us to closely examine the linear interdependence of the variables. We can see the decaying importance of the variables as ordered by the eigenvalues, and also the linear correlation between the variables after scaling by the eigenvalues. For more discussions on how to use this collinearity diagnostics see Belsley et al. (1980).

Chapter 8

Model Goodness Measures

In the construction of models one attempts to find the best fit of a mathematical expression (formula, rules, ...) to a set of given data by adjusting free parameters in the model. This can be thought of as fitting an $(n-1)$–dimensional hypersurface to points existing in an n-dimensional space. In this fitting process one tries to find this set of best parameters according to some definition of "best." Included in this concept of best are (1) some quantitative measure of goodness of fit to an objective function and (2) the need for the model to generalize beyond the particular given data set. Generally these are competing and somewhat conflicting goals. Specifically, one can fit the model exactly to the given data, but when new data comes sometimes the fit is not as good for this new data. Thus the standard practice of separating data into training, testing, and validation sets has become routine in machine learning. In this chapter we discuss a variety of topics around the concept of model fitting/generalization and the ways to measure the goodness of a model fit. If a model fits the training data well but not the testing data we say that the model is overfit, which is a cardinal sin in modeling.

8.1 Training, Testing, Validation

Consider a simple one-dimensional modeling task where we have a single input only. We have been given a data set to build our model, and the data is a set of records each with a single independent (input) variable and a single dependent (output) variable. Our desire in model building is to fit a curve to this data in a way that is useful for some purpose, typically to estimate the output value for some input value that we may have never seen before. So our goal is to fit a curve through these data points so that when we get new data points, the fitted curve will be a close fit also for these new, previously unseen data points. That is, we want the model to generalize well to new data that we have not seen before.

In this simple problem we could introduce a polynomial fit that would exactly go through each of the given data points with a zero fitting error, but this high-degree polynomial would probably not be a good fit for any new data that we may collect. This is because most data has noise and/or is produced by a very complex process involving some random nature, such as consumer behavior. Recognizing this fundamental nature of data we back off on trying to fit the given data exactly and allow some tolerance in the model fit with the hope that the model will generalize better to previously unseen data. We are guided by Occam's razor principle and choose the simplest model that will "adequately" explain the data, and this process gives us a better chance at good generalization. Thus there is a tradeoff between the goodness of fit in the given data for building the model and the fit for new data that we have not seen before.

The traditional methodology to achieve this ability to generalize is to separate the data into distinct sets, one for training and another for testing. One builds the best candidate model on the training data and then evaluates on the test data, which was not used in the model building process. One iterates through this process, doing variable selection and model structure choices (e.g., degree of nonlinearity or level of complexity), using the testing data to periodically see how well the model generalizes. If the uses of the testing data are too frequent one can have another set of data called a holdout/validation sample that is only used close to the end of this iterative process. Of course if one then goes back to the model building process this holdout data is no longer a pure holdout sample since it has been used in evaluating the goodness of the model. The art of modeling includes good judgment in balancing model complexity with training and testing performance.

Figure 8.1 shows the qualitative behavior of the model errors on the training and testing data sets. As one increases complexity (more parameters, higher nonlinearity, more inputs, more training iterations...) the error on the training data continues to move lower but at some point in complexity the corresponding model error on the testing data (not used for model training) stops getting lower and actually starts to increase. This is due to overfitting in some part of the modeling process. We use this principle to decide the level of complexity for our model.

Model building is the process of finding a functional relationship between inputs and an output. Sometimes time is an important consideration in that this functional relationship drifts in time; models decay in their predictive performance. This is always true for consumer behavior models, for example, because consumer attitudes, needs, and desires change along with the socioeconomic environment. Because of this nonstationarity drift in functional relationships we seek to build models that are not only robust to unseen data during the model building timeframe, but perhaps more importantly to unseen data from a time future to the model building timeframe. Thus we frequently have set aside data sets that are not only testing (not used in model building), but also future to the model build data. This is referred to as out-of-time testing.

In all of these data sets we need a quantitative methodology to evaluate how well the model has fit the data for any of the data sets (training, test-

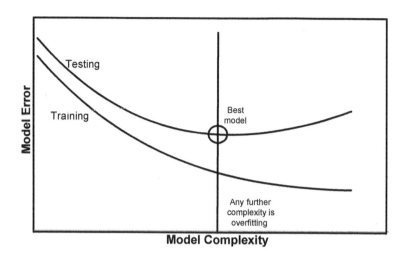

Model Complexity

FIGURE 8.1: The model error decreases monotonically as the model complexity increases, but at some point the testing data shows that the model is overfitting. The best model generally is at the point where the testing error is lowest.

ing, holdout, out-of-time). The variety of quantitative objective functions to measure model goodness is the subject of the rest of this chapter.

8.2 Continuous Dependent Variable

To evaluate the effectiveness of a model, or the model performance, it is always useful to construct the following table. First sort the score (model output) from high to low and then bin the observations into g groups (for example, population percentiles). Finally compute the entries in the following table:

Bin	#Obs	Score Min	Score Max	Score Mean	Actual Mean	Actual Cum. Mean	Lift	Cum. Lift
1								
2								
...								
g								
Total								

Let μ_i be the mean of the actual (as opposed to model output) performance in the bin i, μ_0 be the overall mean of actual performance, and cum_μ_i be the cumulative mean of actual performance from bin 1 to the bin i. Then the lift and cumulative lift are

$$\text{Lift}_i = \mu_i/\mu_0 \qquad (8.1)$$

and

$$\text{cum\_Lift}_i = \text{cum\_}\mu_i/\mu_0 \qquad (8.2)$$

From linear regression we have

$$
\begin{array}{ccccc}
\sum\limits_i (y_i - \bar{y})^2 & = & \sum\limits_i (\hat{y}_i - \bar{y})^2 & + & \sum\limits_i (y_i - \hat{y}_i)^2 \\
SST & = & SSR & + & SSE,
\end{array} \qquad (8.3)
$$

where y_i is the actual value, $\hat{y}_i$ is the predicted value, and $\bar{y}$ is the average of all actual values; SST is the corrected total sum of squares, SSR is the sum of squares for regression, and SSE is the sum of squares for the error.

Similar to a KS measure for a binary output situation, we can define a "pseudo-KS" measure for continuous output:

$$KS(i) = \left| \frac{\sum\limits_{j=1}^{i} y_j}{\sum\limits_{j=1}^{n} y_j} - \frac{i}{n} \right| = \left| \frac{\sum\limits_{j=1}^{i} (y_j - \bar{y})}{\sum\limits_{j=1}^{n} y_j} \right|. \qquad (8.4)$$

The KS can be defined by the maximum: $KS = \max_i KS(i)$. For the binary case, it is proportional to the standard KS measure.

It is clear to see that this measure does not depend on the scale of y but it does depend on the origin of y. That is, it is not translational invariant. In most cases this measure can be used to rank order the importance of variables for continuous output model problems.

Note that the R^2 goodness measure is defined by

$$R^2 = SSR/SST = 1 - SSE/SST. \qquad (8.5)$$

When the number of variables increases, R^2 increases or keeps the same, but never decreases. Thus we need to be cautious of using this measure to compare across models with different numbers of variables.

We can define an adjusted R^2, adjusted by the degree of freedom:

$$R_a^2 = 1 - \frac{SSE/(n-p)}{SST/(n-i)} = 1 - \frac{n-i}{n-p}(1 - R^2), \qquad (8.6)$$

where n is the number of observations, p is the number of free parameters in the current model, and $i = 1$ if there is an intercept, otherwise $i = 0$. When the number of variables increases, R_a^2 may increase or decrease, depending on the magnitude of the changes of R^2 and $n - p$.

Another model performance measure adjusted by number of parameters is the Mallows' C_p

$$
\begin{aligned}
C_p &= (n - p_0)\frac{SSE}{SSE_0} - (n - 2p) \\
&= (n - p_0)\frac{1-R^2}{1-R_0^2} - (n - 2p),
\end{aligned} \qquad (8.7)
$$

where n is the number of observations, p is the number of free parameters in the current model, and p_0 is the number of all possible parameters. When the number of variables increases, C_p may increase or decrease, depending on the magnitude of the changes of R^2 and $n - 2p$.

8.2.1 Example: Linear Regression

In this section, we give an example of linear regression using the functions in DataMinerXL package. For a complete description of DataMinerXL, please refer to Appendix B.

The data set is generated by calling the function

$$matrix\_random(10, 5, , , 100)$$

which generates 10 observations with five random variables, x_1, x_2, x_3, x_4, x_5, from the uniform distribution. The target variable y is defined by

$$y = x_1 + 2\,x_2 + 3\,x_3 + x_5.$$

The function

$$linear\_reg(x, y, weight, lambda)$$

performs the linear regression with three independent variables, x_1, x_2, x_3. The output from the linear regression is as follows.

TABLE 8.1: Analysis of variance for linear regression.

Number of Records	10
Number of Parameters	4
R-Square	0.96567
Adj R-Square	0.94850

	DF	Sum	Mean	F Value	P Value
SSR	3	14.13736	4.71245	56.25034	0.00009
SSE	6	0.50266	0.08378		
SST	9	14.64002	1.62667		

RMSE	0.28944
Y Mean	3.40431
Coeff Var	8.502%

The function

$$linear\_reg\_forward\_select(x, y, pvalue, steps, startsWith, weight)$$

performs forward selection in linear regression. Here x is x_1, x_2, x_3, x_4 and the p-value is 0.2. Below is the summary of linear regression forward selection.

TABLE 8.2: Model parameter estimates of the linear regression.

#	Variable	Estimate	Standard Error	t Value	P Value
0	Intercept	0.60756	0.27740	2.19021	0.07105
1	x_1	0.53779	0.31837	1.68921	0.14214
2	x_2	2.00931	0.31003	6.48107	0.00064
3	x_3	3.12629	0.28982	10.78703	0.00004

TABLE 8.3: Summary of linear regression forward selection.

Step	Variable Selected	Partial R-Square	R-Square	F Value	P Value
1	x_3	0.67638	0.67638	16.72051	0.00349
2	x_2	0.27295	0.94934	37.71355	0.00047
3	x_1	0.01633	0.96567	2.85342	0.14214

TABLE 8.4: Analysis of variance for linear regression.

Number of Records	10
Number of Parameters	4
R-Square	0.96567
Adj R-Square	0.94850

	DF	Sum	Mean	F Value	P Value
SSR	3	14.13736	4.71245	56.25034	0.00009
SSE	6	0.50266	0.08378		
SST	9	14.64002	1.62667		

RMSE	0.28944
Y Mean	3.40431
Coeff Var	8.502%

TABLE 8.5: Model parameter estimates of the linear regression.

#	Variable	Estimate	Standard Error	t Value	P Value
0	Intercept	0.60756	0.27740	2.19021	0.07105
1	x_3	3.12629	0.28982	10.78703	0.00004
2	x_2	2.00931	0.31003	6.48107	0.00064
3	x_1	0.53779	0.31837	1.68921	0.14214

8.3　Binary Dependent Variable (Two-Group Classification)

8.3.1　Kolmogorov–Smirnov (KS) Statistic

One of the most frequent problems the practitioner faces is a classification problem into one of two groups. Here the output records have labels such as 0 and 1, and the predicted output (output of the model) is a continuous number generally from 0 to 1. This model output (score) could be thought of as the likelihood or probability that the record belongs to the class with real output 1. This binary classification problem is so frequent that we sometimes loosely call the two categories "goods" and "bads," such as in credit risk or fraud risk classification.

Let s be the score in consideration, and $f_g(s)$ and $f_b(s)$ are the score distributions of the actual good and bad populations. Then the Kolmogorov–Smirnov (KS) statistic is defined as the maximum separation of these cumulative distributions:

$$KS = \max_s |F_g(s) - F_b(s)| = \max_s \left| \int^s (f_g(s') - f_b(s')) \, ds' \right|. \qquad (8.8)$$

Sometimes the KS is defined as $KS(s) = \int^s (f_g(s') - f_b(s')) \, ds'$ and the above-defined KS as the maximum KS.

Suppose the total number of good observations and bad observations are G and B, respectively. At any score cutpoint s, let g and b be the number of good observations and number of bad observations for scores less than s. Then the numbers of good observations and bad observations are $(G - g)$ and $(B - b)$, respectively, for the score larger than s. Then

$$d_1 = \frac{g}{G} - \frac{g+b}{G+B} = KS \cdot \frac{B}{G+B} \qquad (8.9)$$

and

$$d_2 = \frac{g+b}{G+B} - \frac{b}{B} = KS \cdot \frac{G}{G+B} \qquad (8.10)$$

where

$$KS = \frac{g}{G} - \frac{b}{B}. \qquad (8.11)$$

Note that at any score cutpoint, d_1 and d_2 are proportional to KS and $d_1 + d_2 = KS$.

Let $\Delta KS = \frac{\Delta g}{G} - \frac{\Delta b}{B} = 0$. We have $\frac{\Delta b}{\Delta g + \Delta b} = \frac{B}{G+B}$. That is, in the gains-chart, the location in score bins where the bad rate is the same as overall bad rate, the KS reaches the maximum.

The following table is useful to evaluate the performance of a binary model:

Bin	Score min	Score max	Score mean	#Total	#Goods	#Bads	%Cum Goods	%Cum Bads
1								
2								
...								
g								
Total								

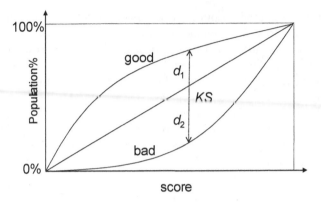

FIGURE 8.2: Kolmogorov–Smirnov (KS) statistic.

Odds	Lift	%Goods	%Bads	KS

8.3.2 Confusion Matrix

The confusion matrix is constructed by looking at the cross-table of the actual and predicted categories. First examine the score distribution and make a score cut, $\hat{p}_0$. If $\hat{p} \geq \hat{p}_0$, then $\hat{y} = 1$, otherwise $\hat{y} = 0$. This is considered a score cutoff where all the records above the cutoff are predicted to be category 1 and all the records below category 0. Then the following table is the confusion matrix:

		Actual	
		1	0
Predicted	1	n_{11}	n_{10}
	0	n_{01}	n_{00}

		Actual	
		1	0
Predicted	1	true positive	false positive
	0	false negative	true negative

In this table the diagonals are the number of records correctly predicted and the off diagonals are the incorrect predictions, showing both the false positives and false negatives. Frequently these two different types of errors have different penalties, or different business values for the misclassifications. This confusion matrix representation can help identify the effects of various candidate score cutoffs.

Let $N_1 = n_{11} + n_{01}$ and $N_0 = n_{10} + n_{00}$ be the number of records with $y = 1$ and $y = 0$, respectively. The sensitivity is the true positive rate and the specificity is the true negative rate,

$$\text{sensitivity} = n_{11}/N_1$$
$$\text{specificity} = n_{00}/N_0. \tag{8.12}$$

8.3.3 Concordant and Discordant

Let N_1 and N_0 be the numbers of records with $y = 1$ and $y = 0$, respectively. In order to look at model performance we need to rank order observations by the score in descending order. A good model will have most of observations with $y = 1$ at the top of the list and observations with $y = 0$ at the bottom of the list. We will examine all possible pairs of observations with $y = 1$ and $y = 0$. There are $N_1 N_0$ pairs of 1 and 0 and they belong to one of the following three categories:

- concordant: n_C is the number of pairs of $(i, j) = (1, 0)$

- discordant : n_D is the number of pairs of $(i, j) = (0, 1)$

- tie: n_T is the number of pairs of $(i, j) = (0, 1)$, or $(1, 0)$ with the same score

where $i < j$ and $n_C + n_D + n_T = N_1 N_0$. Somers' D concordance statistic, Tau-a, and Gamma are defined by

$$\text{Somers' D} = \frac{n_C - n_D}{N_1 N_0},$$
$$\text{Tau-a} = \frac{n_C - n_D}{N(N-1)/2}, \tag{8.13}$$
$$\text{Gamma} = \frac{n_C - n_D}{n_C + n_D}.$$

Let's look at an example. Let $N_1 = 9$ and $N_0 = 18$. Then $N = N_1 + N_0 = 27$, $N(N - 1)/2 = 351$ (the number of all possible 1-1, 1-0, 0-1, 0-0 pairs), and $N_1 N_0 = 162$ (the number of all 1-0 or 0-1 pairs). Suppose $n_C = 136$, $n_D = 21$, and $n_T = 5$. Then we have the following statistic:

$$\text{Somers' D} = 71.0\%,$$
$$\text{Tau-a} = 0.328, \tag{8.14}$$
$$\text{Gamma} = 0.732.$$

We show a method for how to count n_C, n_D, and n_T in the following. First sort the data by score in descending order. Considering the possible tie of scores, we need to aggregate the data into records with unique scores.

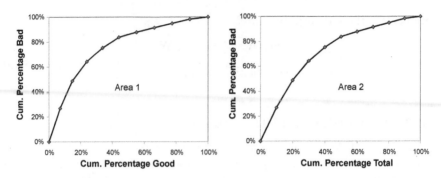

FIGURE 8.3: Receiver operating characteristic (ROC) curve.

Then we can count n_C, n_D, and n_T from this table. Mathematically, they can be written as

$$\left.\begin{aligned}
n_C &= \sum_{i=1}^{K} \left(n_0(i) \sum_{j<i} n_1(j) \right), \\
n_D &= \sum_{i=1}^{K} \left(n_1(i) \sum_{j<i} n_0(j) \right), \\
n_T &= \sum_{i=1}^{K} n_1(i)\, n_0(i),
\end{aligned}\right\} \tag{8.15}$$

where K is the number of distinct scores. If all scores are different, then $K = n$. By reading record by record we can find n_C, n_D, and n_T from the following iteration:

$$\begin{aligned}
n_C &\leftarrow n_C + n_0\, cum\_n_1 \\
n_D &\leftarrow n_D + n_1\, cum\_n_0 \\
n_T &\leftarrow n_T + n_1\, n_0 \\
cum\_n_1 &\leftarrow cum\_n_1 + n_1 \\
cum\_n_0 &\leftarrow cum\_n_0 + n_0
\end{aligned} \tag{8.16}$$

Let's look at the area under the receiver operating characteristic (ROC) curve and see the relationship with concordant and discordant. The area under cumulative percentage good vs. cumulative percentage bad chart is given by

$$\begin{aligned}
\text{Area}_1 &= \frac{1}{N_1 N_0} \sum_{i=1}^{K} n_0(i) \tfrac{1}{2} \left(\sum_{j<i} n_1(j) + \sum_{j\le i} n_1(j) \right) \\
&= \frac{1}{N_1 N_0} \sum_{i=1}^{K} n_0(i) \left(\sum_{j<i} n_1(j) + \tfrac{1}{2} n_1(i) \right) \\
&= \frac{1}{N_1 N_0} \left(n_C + \tfrac{1}{2} n_T \right).
\end{aligned} \tag{8.17}$$

The area under cumulative percentage total vs. cumulative percentage bad chart is

$$
\begin{aligned}
\text{Area}_2 &= \frac{1}{N N_1} \sum_{i=1}^{K} (n_1(i) + n_0(i)) \frac{1}{2} \left(\sum_{j<i} n_1(j) + \sum_{j \leq i} n_1(j) \right) \\
&= \frac{1}{N N_1} \sum_{i=1}^{K} (n_1(i) + n_0(i)) \left(\sum_{j<i} n_1(j) + \tfrac{1}{2} n_1(i) \right) \\
&= \frac{1}{N N_1} \left(n_C + \tfrac{1}{2} n_T + \tfrac{1}{2} N_1^2 \right).
\end{aligned}
\tag{8.18}
$$

The relationship between these two areas is

$$
\text{Area}_2 = \frac{N_0}{N} \text{Area}_1 + \frac{N_1}{2N}.
\tag{8.19}
$$

As a special case, suppose the model is perfect, then all records with $y = 1$ are at the top of the list and all records with $y = 0$ are at the bottom of the list. It is easy to see that the area under cumulative percentage good vs. cumulative percentage bad chart, Area_1, and the area under cumulative percentage total vs. cumulative percentage bad chart, Area_2, are:

$$
\text{Area}_1 = 1 \quad \text{and} \quad \text{Area}_2 = 1 - N_1/(2N).
\tag{8.20}
$$

It is clear that this special case satisfies the above equation.

8.3.4 R^2 for Logistic Regression

The generalization of R^2 to a more general linear model is

$$
R^2 = 1 - (L(0)/L(\beta))^{2/n} = 1 - e^{2[\ln L(0) - \ln L(\beta)]/n},
\tag{8.21}
$$

where $L(0)$ is the likelihood function when only including the intercept and $L(\beta)$ is the likelihood function including the intercept and all independent variables in discussion. Note that when including more variables $L(\beta)$ increases and therefore R^2 increases.

The best possible model is that $\hat{y} = y$, that is, $\hat{y} = 1$ when $y = 1$ and $\hat{y} = 0$ when $y = 0$ for all data records. In this case the likelihood function is the maximum, $L(\beta) = \prod_{i=1}^{n} \hat{y}_i^{y_i} (1 - \hat{y}_i)^{1-y_i} = 1$, and it reaches the maximum R^2,

$$
R^2_{\max} = 1 - [L(0)]^{2/n} = 1 - e^{2[\ln L(0)]/n}.
\tag{8.22}
$$

We can define $\tilde{R}^2$ scaled by $R^2_{\max}$, called the max-rescaled R^2:

$$
\tilde{R}^2 = \frac{R^2}{R^2_{\max}} = \frac{1 - e^{2[\ln L(0) - \ln L(\beta)]/n}}{1 - e^{2[\ln L(0)]/n}}.
\tag{8.23}
$$

This scaled R^2 measure is good for comparing performance across models that have different numbers of inputs, and is a more fair comparison in these cases.

8.3.5 AIC and SBC

Another measure of model performance adjusted by the number of parameters is Akaike's information criterion (AIC):

$$\text{AIC} = -2\ln L + 2k, \tag{8.24}$$

where L is the likelihood function and k is the number of parameters. Note that the more free parameters, the larger is L, but it is not obvious how AIC changes depending on the magnitudes of changes $2\ln L$ and $2k$.

Another performance measure is Schwartz's criterion (SC), Schwartz's Bayesian criterion (SBC), or Bayesian information criterion (BIC):

$$\text{SC} = \text{SBC} = \text{BIC} = -2\ln L + k\ln n, \tag{8.25}$$

where L is the likelihood function, k is the number of parameters, and n is the number of observations. Note that the more free parameters, the larger is L, but the change of SBC depends on the magnitudes of changes $2\ln L$ and $k\ln n$.

8.3.6 Hosmer–Lemeshow Goodness-of-Fit Test

Pearson's chi-square statistic χ_p^2 is

$$\chi_p^2 = \sum_i (O_i - E_i)^2 / E_i, \tag{8.26}$$

and the deviance χ_D^2 is

$$\chi_D^2 = 2\sum_i O_i \ln(O_i/E_i), \tag{8.27}$$

where O_i is the observed frequency and E_i is the expected frequency in the cell i. The relationship between the chi-square statistic and the deviance can be seen as follows. When $O_i \sim E_i$, by noting that $(1+x)\ln(1+x) \approx x + x^2/2$ for $x \sim 0$, we have

$$
\begin{aligned}
\chi_D^2 &= 2\sum_i O_i \ln(O_i/E_i)\\
&= 2\sum_i E_i \left(1 + \tfrac{O_i - E_i}{E_i}\right) \ln\left(1 + \tfrac{O_i - E_i}{E_i}\right)\\
&\approx 2\sum_i E_i \left(\tfrac{O_i - E_i}{E_i} + \tfrac{1}{2}\left(\tfrac{O_i - E_i}{E_i}\right)^2\right)\\
&= \sum_i \tfrac{(O_i - E_i)^2}{E_i}.
\end{aligned}
\tag{8.28}
$$

The Hosmer–Lemeshow chi-square statistic proposed by Hosmer and Lemeshow (1989) is constructed as follows. First sort the records in descending order of the score, then bin the observations into g groups. In each group

TABLE 8.6: The numbers of the observed and predicted in each group for the Hosmer and Lemeshow test.

Group	n_i	O_i	$n_i \bar{p}_i$	$n_i - O_i$	$n_i(1 - \bar{p}_i)$
1	200	48	56.25	152	143.75
2	200	43	40.61	157	159.39
3	200	44	35.07	156	164.93
4	200	38	30.98	162	169.02
5	200	18	27.47	182	172.53
6	200	26	24.45	174	175.55
7	200	22	21.39	178	178.61
8	200	17	18.27	183	181.73
9	200	19	15.19	181	184.81
10	200	5	10.32	195	189.68

count how many total observations, denoted by n_i, how many observations with $y = 1$, denoted by O_i, and the average score, denoted by $\bar{p}_i$. Then we have the following table.

Finally the Hosmer–Lemeshow chi-square statistic is defined by the Pearson's chi-square statistic from this table:

$$
\begin{aligned}
\chi^2_{HL} &= \sum_{i=1}^{g} \frac{(O_i - n_i \bar{p}_i)^2}{n_i \bar{p}_i} + \sum_{i=1}^{g} \frac{(n_i - O_i - n_i(1 - \bar{p}_i))^2}{n_i(1 - \bar{p}_i)} \\
&= \sum_{i=1}^{g} \frac{(O_i - n_i \bar{p}_i)^2}{n_i \bar{p}_i (1 - \bar{p}_i)} \sim \chi^2(g - 2).
\end{aligned}
\tag{8.29}
$$

For the example given in the table, $\chi^2_{HL} = 14.4382$ and the p-value is $\mathrm{Prob}(\chi^2 > \chi^2_{HL}, 8) = 0.0710$.

8.3.7 Example: Logistic Regression

In this section, we give an example of the logistic regression using the functions in DataMinerXL package. For a complete description of DataMinerXL, refer to Appendix B. The data set is generated by calling the function

$$matrix\_random(100, 5, , , 100),$$

which generates 100 observations, 5 random variables, x_1, x_2, x_3, x_4, x_5, from the uniform distribution. The binary target variable y is defined by

$$y = x_1 + 2x_2 + 3x_3 + 4x_5$$

$$\text{if } (y > 5) \text{ then } y = 1$$

$$\text{else } y = 0.$$

The function

$$logistic\_reg(x, y, weight)$$

performs the logistic regression. The model performance is shown in the following table.

TABLE 8.7: Model performance of the logistic regression.

y	Freq	Percent
ALL	100	100.0%
1	51	51.0%
0	49	49.0%
Probability Modeled is for y	1	
Number of Parameters	5	

	Intercept Only	Full Model		
AIC	140.58943	107.37392		
SC	143.19460	120.39977		
-2LogL	138.58943	97.37392		
R-Square		0.33778		
Max-rescaled R-Square		0.45043		
%Concordant	84.4%	Somers' D	0.68788	
%Discordant	15.6%	Gamma	0.68788	
%Tied	0.0%	Tau-a	0.34727	
#Pairs	2499	c	0.84394	

TABLE 8.8: Model parameter estimates of the logistic regression.

#	Variable	Estimate	Standard Error	Wald Chi-Square	p-Value
0	Intercept	-4.50869	1.11809	16.26095	0.00006
1	x1	0.14764	0.86437	0.02918	0.86437
2	x2	4.46650	1.05086	18.06532	0.00002
3	x3	4.61041	1.11625	17.05905	0.00004
4	x4	-0.11318	0.93611	0.01462	0.90377

The function

$$logistic\_reg\_forward\_select(x, y, pvalue, steps, startsWith, weight)$$

performs forward selection in logistic regression. Here x is x_1, x_2, x_3, x_4 and the p-value is 0.25. The same data set is used in this forward selection procedure. Below is the summary of the logistic regression forward selection.

TABLE 8.9: Summary of logistic regression forward selection.

Step	Variable Selected	Score Chi-Square	p-Value
1	x2	16.74265	0.00004
2	x3	20.98851	0.00000

Model Performance

y	Total Frequency
ALL	100
1	51
0	49
Probability Modeled is for y	1
Number of Parameters	3

	Intercept Only	Full Model	
AIC	140.58943	103.41328	
SC	143.19460	111.22879	
-2LogL	138.58943	97.41328	
R-Square		0.33752	
Max-rescaled R-Square		0.45008	
%Concordant	84.4%	Somers' D	0.68788
%Discordant	15.6%	Gamma	0.68788
%Tied	0.0%	Tau-a	0.34727
#Pairs	2499	c	0.84394

TABLE 8.10: Model parameter estimates from logistic regression forward selection.

#	Variable	Estimate	Standard Error	Wald Chi-Square	p-Value
0	Intercept	−4.52642	0.97695	21.46645	0.00000
1	x2	4.50774	1.03499	18.96893	0.00001
2	x3	4.63034	1.11333	17.29724	0.00003

8.4 Population Stability Index Using Relative Entropy

The relative entropy is widely used as a measure of population stability index (PSI) in the score stability tracking as illustrated in the following table.

The PSI for comparing the baseline distribution p and scoring month dis-

TABLE 8.11: Population stability index (PSI) calculation.

Bin	Score Interval	Development Baseline Percent (p)	Scoring Request Percent (q)	PSI
1	0–10	10.2%	11.0%	0.0006
2	11–20	10.5%	8.0%	0.0068
3	21–30	9.6%	12.9%	0.0098
4	31–40	7.1%	10.1%	0.0106
5	41–50	8.2%	9.3%	0.0014
6	51–60	11.4%	12.2%	0.0005
7	61–70	11.9%	9.2%	0.0069
8	71–80	9.1%	8.2%	0.0009
9	81 -90	9.9%	8.0%	0.0040
10	91–100	12.1%	11.1%	0.0009
Total	0–100	100.0%	100.0%	0.0424

tribution q is defined as

$$PSI = \sum_{i=1}^{g} (p_i - q_i) \ln (p_i/q_i). \tag{8.30}$$

One can see that this is the symmetric version of the Kullback–Leibler distance between the two distributions. Lewis (1992) has the following recommendation for score stability: the PSI should remain less than 0.1. If it is between 0.1 and 0.25, it needs careful monitoring. If it is greater than 0.25, the population stability (i.e., variable stability) is suspect.

The PSI is also used in attribute stability tracking for a model (see Lewis (1992)). One frequently generates a characteristic analysis report for monitoring the attributes. For a model with a categorical variable with fixed score points for each category, we can list the score points attributed to individual attribute, as illustrated for the attribute "Home Ownership" in the following table.

TABLE 8.12: Characteristic analysis for monitoring the stability of attributes.

Home Ownership	Baseline (p_i)	Current (q_i)	Shift ($q_i - p_i$)	Score Contribution $c\bar{x}$	Score Difference ($q_i - p_i$)$c\bar{x}$
Own	45%	39%	−6%	60	−3.6
Rent	52%	55%	3%	40	1.2
Unknown	3%	6%	3%	50	1.5
Total	100%	100%	–	–	−0.9

For a model with a linear relationship between the score and numerical variables, we assume that the $\bar{x}$s are the same for the baseline and current populations in each bin, but in reality they are not necessarily the same with small differences. Under this assumption, we can generate the same characteristic analysis for numerical variables. The total score difference shown in this example is the score shift, -0.9 points, from the development population to the current population based on the change in this characteristic alone.

Chapter 9

Optimization Methods

The search for optimality can be thought of as a search through the space formed by the union of all free parameters and some objective function. This can be easily envisioned in three dimensions, and easily extended conceptually to higher dimensions. Consider a situation where we have only two free parameters and an objective function, which of course will vary depending on the value of the free parameters. Typically, we are trying to fit a model by adjusting these free parameters in such a way as to optimize an objective function: minimize an error or maximize some other modeled performance (profit, revenue). The model designer has complete freedom in selecting both the model structure as well as formulating an appropriate objective function that best suits the goals of the problem.

Think of the objective function as the z-direction rising above an x-y plane spanned by the two free parameters. Without loss of generality one can consider that the task is to minimize this objective function over the set of all possible values of these free parameters. The objective function is then a surface that rides above this x-y plane, and our goal is to find the minimum. If the objective function is the model error, we are then seeking the location in parameter space (the x-y plane) whose parameter choice results in the model having the lowest error. This error surface above the space of model parameters is sometimes called the fitness landscape.

Conceptually there are many ways to locate this set of parameter values that minimizes this fitness landscape, that is to locate the point in the (hyper)plane that has the minimum height above it in the z-direction. Generally, in order to evaluate a point in the parameter space hyperplane we need to numerically compute the objective function. This requires a model evaluation at that set of parameter values.

With this knowledge we can think of ways to find the minimum in the fitness landscape. If (1) the hyperspace has small enough dimensions (not too many free parameters), (2) the fitness landscape is not too complex, and (3) the numerical evaluation of the objective function is not too costly in machine time, we might naively try an exhaustive search. Here we might divide up parameter space using a grid and simply compute the objective function at every grid point, then select the best point. This approach cannot work in practice since the dimensionality of the parameter space is almost always too high. Directed search methodologies are required.

Searches can be separated into the two categories of local and global.

Local searches examine the topology of a local region of the fitness landscape and decide where in parameter space to move next. Global methodologies do not limit themselves to the local properties of the fitness surface, and thus are more powerful but also more costly. The gradient descent methodologies are local while genetic algorithms and simulated annealing are global search methodologies.

The topology of the fitness landscape is primarily determined by the complexity of both the data to be fit and the complexity of the model. If the underlying process that produced the data is fairly simple, one could hope to approximate it with a relatively simple model architecture, perhaps even a linear regression model. In the case of linear regression, if one uses a least-squares measure of model error, the fitness landscape (error surface) is a hyperparaboloid rising above the parameter hyperplane. In this case there is a single minimum location of this fitness landscape, and it is both a global and a local minimum. One cannot find subregions of the hyperplane that have a local minimum of the objective function inside it and not on the boundary. In this case one can analytically find the location of this minimum set of parameters, hence we have a closed-form solution for the optimal set of parameters in linear regression. Even with this closed-form solution the numerical calculations often involve the inversion of a close-to-singular matrix, so approximate methods are used, discussed in Sections 9.2 through 9.5. Some of these methods use only the first derivative and some also require the second derivative. The previously mentioned Nelder–Mead algorithm, a version of the simplex method, doesn't require any differentiation.

However, many modeling techniques are nonlinear, and the resulting fitness landscape becomes much more complex. Frequently there exist multiple local minima in this surface, that is, there are regions in parameter space that have an interior minimum point. The existence of these local minima points causes difficulty for many optimization algorithms, particularly the broad class of local gradient descent searches which can easily fall into these local minima. One then needs a search methodology that is robust to possible existence of these local minima. Two of these are discussed in Sections 9.6 and 9.7.

9.1 Lagrange Multiplier

The method of Lagrange multipliers is a solution approach to optimization problems that are subject to constraints. We have encountered various applications of this method earlier, for example, in matrix inversion, principal component analysis, Fisher scoring for logistic regression, and the Gini index. It is a very handy way to formulate many constrained optimization problems. Here we describe the foundation for this useful method.

Let's first consider a simple minimization problem that has a constraint:

$$\text{minimize} \quad z = f(x_1, x_2)$$
$$\text{subject to} \quad g(x_1, x_2) = 0. \tag{9.1}$$

We can rewrite the constraint to express x_1 as a function of x_2, i.e., $x_1 = x_1(x_2)$. Then the objective function becomes a single variable function without constraints: $z = f(x_1(x_2), x_2)$. Taking a derivative with respect to x_2, we have

$$\frac{\partial f}{\partial x_1} \cdot \frac{\partial x_1}{\partial x_2} + \frac{\partial f}{\partial x_2} = 0 \tag{9.2}$$

$$\frac{\partial g}{\partial x_1} \cdot \frac{\partial x_1}{\partial x_2} + \frac{\partial g}{\partial x_2} = 0. \tag{9.3}$$

Eliminating $\partial x_1 / \partial x_2$, we have

$$\frac{\partial f / \partial x_1}{\partial g / \partial x_1} = \frac{\partial f / \partial x_2}{\partial g / \partial x_2} = \lambda. \tag{9.4}$$

Finally we have three simultaneous equations

$$\frac{\partial f}{\partial x_1} - \lambda \frac{\partial g}{\partial x_1} = 0 \tag{9.5}$$

$$\frac{\partial f}{\partial x_2} - \lambda \frac{\partial g}{\partial x_2} = 0 \tag{9.6}$$

$$g(x_1, x_2) = 0. \tag{9.7}$$

There are only three variables in these three equations. In general there is a unique solution. It is equivalent to construct a three-variable Lagrange by adding a multiplier of the constraint,

$$L(x_1, x_2, \lambda) = f(x_1, x_2) - \lambda g(x_1, x_2), \tag{9.8}$$

and then minimizing the function L, with λ being a free, unrestricted parameter. Therefore the variable elimination leads to the method of the Lagrange multiplier. This conclusion holds for general cases involving more variables.

In general we have a minimization problem with n variables and m constraints of equalities, where $m < n$:

$$\text{minimize} \quad z = f(x_1, x_2, \cdots, x_n)$$
$$\text{subject to} \quad g_i(x_1, x_2, \cdots, x_n) = 0, \ i = 1, 2, \cdots, m. \tag{9.9}$$

From these m constraints we can express the first m variables in terms of remaining $n-m$ variables $x_i = x_i(x_{m+1}, \cdots, x_n)$, $i = 1, 2, \cdots, m$. Therefore we have

$$\frac{\partial f}{\partial x_1} \cdot \frac{\partial x_1}{\partial x_j} + \cdots + \frac{\partial f}{\partial x_m} \cdot \frac{\partial x_m}{\partial x_j} + \frac{\partial f}{\partial x_j} = 0 \tag{9.10}$$

$$\frac{\partial g_i}{\partial x_1} \cdot \frac{\partial x_1}{\partial x_j} + \cdots + \frac{\partial g_i}{\partial x_m} \cdot \frac{\partial x_m}{\partial x_j} + \frac{\partial g_i}{\partial x_j} = 0 \qquad (9.11)$$

where $i = 1, 2, \cdots, m$ and $j = m+1, \cdots, n$. It is much easier to work in matrix form:

$$
\begin{bmatrix}
\frac{\partial f}{\partial x_1} & \cdots & \frac{\partial f}{\partial x_m} \\
\frac{\partial g_1}{\partial x_1} & \cdots & \frac{\partial g_1}{\partial x_m} \\
\cdots & \cdots & \cdots \\
\frac{\partial g_m}{\partial x_1} & \cdots & \frac{\partial g_m}{\partial x_m}
\end{bmatrix}
\cdot
\begin{bmatrix}
\frac{\partial x_1}{\partial x_{m+1}} & \cdots & \frac{\partial x_1}{\partial x_n} \\
\cdots & \cdots & \cdots \\
\frac{\partial x_m}{\partial x_{m+1}} & \cdots & \frac{\partial x_m}{\partial x_n}
\end{bmatrix}
= -
\begin{bmatrix}
\frac{\partial f}{\partial x_{m+1}} & \cdots & \frac{\partial f}{\partial x_n} \\
\frac{\partial g_1}{\partial x_{m+1}} & \cdots & \frac{\partial g_1}{\partial x_n} \\
\cdots & \cdots & \cdots \\
\frac{\partial g_m}{\partial x_{m+1}} & \cdots & \frac{\partial g_m}{\partial x_n}
\end{bmatrix}.
$$

$$(m+1) \times m \qquad\qquad m \times (n-m) \qquad\qquad (m+1) \times (n-m)$$

The dimensions of these matrices are shown below them. Suppose the rank of the first matrix is m. Then the first row can be written as a linear combination of the other rows, namely,

$$\frac{\partial f}{\partial x_i} - \lambda_1 \cdot \frac{\partial g_1}{\partial x_i} - \lambda_2 \cdot \frac{\partial g_2}{\partial x_i} - \cdots - \lambda_m \cdot \frac{\partial g_m}{\partial x_i} = 0, \quad i = 1, 2, \cdots, m. \quad (9.12)$$

With the matrix equation, it is also true for the matrix on the right side, i.e.,

$$\frac{\partial f}{\partial x_i} - \lambda_1 \cdot \frac{\partial g_1}{\partial x_i} - \lambda_2 \cdot \frac{\partial g_2}{\partial x_i} - \cdots - \lambda_m \cdot \frac{\partial g_m}{\partial x_i} = 0, \quad i = m+1, m+2, \cdots, n, \quad (9.13)$$

and we have

$$\frac{\partial f}{\partial x_i} - \lambda_1 \cdot \frac{\partial g_1}{\partial x_i} - \lambda_2 \cdot \frac{\partial g_2}{\partial x_i} - \cdots - \lambda_m \cdot \frac{\partial g_m}{\partial x_i} = 0, \quad i = 1, 2, \cdots, n \quad (9.14)$$

$$g_i(x_1, x_2, \cdots, x_n) = 0, \ i = 1, 2, \cdots, m. \qquad (9.15)$$

There are $(n+m)$ variables and equations. There it is equivalent to constructing the following Lagrange function

$$L(x_1, x_2, \cdots, x_n, \lambda_1, \lambda_2, \cdots, \lambda_m) = f(x_1, x_2, \cdots, x_n)$$
$$- \sum_{j=1}^{m} \lambda_j \cdot g_j(x_1, x_2, \cdots, x_n). \qquad (9.16)$$

Therefore the method of variable elimination leads to the method of the Lagrange multiplier.

9.2 Gradient Descent Method

The simplest search algorithm is the gradient descent method. It is an iterative search algorithm and requires the first derivative as the search direction. It has the problem of only examining the local properties of the fitness landscape via the first derivative and thus is susceptible to finding only a local minimum. Modifications of these local methods including adding momentum terms or shrinking step sizes can help in these local directed search methods.

The Taylor expansion of the objective function $f(x)$ is

$$f(x) = f(x_0) + (x - x_0) \cdot \nabla f(x_0) + \frac{1}{2}(x - x_0) \cdot H(x_0) \cdot (x - x_0) + \cdots \quad (9.17)$$

and its derivative

$$\nabla f(x) = \nabla f(x_0) + H(x_0) \cdot (x - x_0) + \cdots \quad (9.18)$$

where $\nabla f(x) = \frac{\partial f(x)}{\partial x}$ is the first derivative and $H(x) = \frac{\partial^2 f(x)}{\partial x \partial x}$ is the second derivative, i.e., the Hessian matrix. The gradient descent method uses the first derivative as the searching direction.

Let's first consider searching for the minimum. The iteration equation for searching for the minimum value is

$$x = x_0 - \lambda \cdot \nabla f(x_0), \quad (9.19)$$

where λ is a step size and should be positive. The first-order optimal step size is determined by

$$\frac{d}{d\lambda} f[x_0 - \lambda \cdot \nabla f(x_0)] = 0. \quad (9.20)$$

We have

$$\nabla f(x) \cdot \nabla f(x_0) = 0. \quad (9.21)$$

So the gradients at the starting point and the ending point are perpendicular. Neglecting the higher terms in the Taylor expansion of the first derivative, we have

$$\nabla f(x) = \nabla f(x_0) + H(x_0) \cdot (x - x_0). \quad (9.22)$$

Therefore we find the optimal step size

$$\lambda = \frac{\nabla f(x_0) \cdot \nabla f(x_0)}{\nabla f(x_0) \cdot H(x_0) \cdot \nabla f(x_0)} \quad (9.23)$$

for searching for the minimum.

It is clear from this expression that if the Hessian matrix is positive definite the step size is positive. The iterative searching equation only requires the first derivative. But the step size is determined by the first and second derivatives. If the second derivative is difficult to obtain then we can use the first derivative to approximate the second derivative. Then the step size can be determined in terms of the first derivative. Each step should guarantee the objective function goes to a smaller value. If the step is too big so that the resulting value of the objective function does not decrease, redo the step with half the step size: $\lambda/2 \to \lambda$, until the ending point has a smaller value of the objective function.

If we search for the maximum value of the objective function, we can obtain the corresponding formulation from that for searching the minimum by substituting $f(x) \rightarrow -f(x)$. Therefore the gradient descent method for searching the maximum is

$$x = x_0 + \lambda \cdot \nabla f(x_0) \tag{9.24}$$

and the step size is

$$\lambda = - \left(\frac{\nabla f(x_0) \cdot \nabla f(x_0)}{\nabla f(x_0) \cdot H(x_0) \cdot \nabla f(x_0)} \right). \tag{9.25}$$

For searching the minimum and maximum value we have the same iterative equation:

$$x = x_0 - \left(\frac{\nabla f(x_0) \cdot \nabla f(x_0)}{\nabla f(x_0) \cdot H(x_0) \cdot \nabla f(x_0)} \right) \cdot \nabla f(x_0). \tag{9.26}$$

For a one-dimensional problem, we have the following familiar formula:

$$x = x_0 - f'(x_0)/f''(x_0), \tag{9.27}$$

which is Newton's method for finding the zero of the first derivative of the function f.

9.3 Newton–Raphson Method

In order to find the minimum or maximum point of the objective function $f(x)$, we start with the Taylor expansion of the object function,

$$f(x) = f(x_0) + (x - x_0) \cdot \nabla f(x_0) + \frac{1}{2} (x - x_0) \cdot H(x_0) \cdot (x - x_0) + \cdots \tag{9.28}$$

and its derivative,

$$\nabla f(x) = \nabla f(x_0) + H(x_0) \cdot (x - x_0) + \cdots \tag{9.29}$$

where $H(x) = \frac{\partial^2 E(x)}{\partial x \partial x}$ is the Hessian matrix. At the extremum of f we have $\nabla f(x) = 0$, which leads to

$$x = x_0 - H^{-1}(x_0) \cdot \nabla f(x_0). \tag{9.30}$$

This is suitable for searching for a minimum or maximum. It is the Newton–Raphson method, for which we need both the first and second derivatives of the objective function. If the objective function does not decrease after this step, make the step half, until the ending point has a smaller value for minimum problem and the larger value for maximum problem. This is a generalization of the Newton–Raphson method in one-dimensional space to search the minimum or maximum value:

$$x = x_0 - f'(x_0)/f''(x_0). \tag{9.31}$$

To search for roots of $f(x)$, we expand the function in terms of the Taylor series:

$$f(x) = f(x_0) + f'(x_0)(x - x_0) + \cdots . \tag{9.32}$$

Neglecting the higher order, we have

$$x = x_0 - f(x_0)/f'(x_0). \tag{9.33}$$

For an x^2 objective function, one step is enough to find the solution since the higher-order derivatives are zero and the Taylor expansion is exact at second order.

From the Taylor expansion of the objective function, we can see that if H is positive definite then the objective function has a minimum value, and if H is negative definite then the objective function has the maximum value.

Let's look at some properties of the Hessian matrix. Consider the objective function in two spaces α and β, when α and β are both n-dimensional spaces. We have

$$\frac{\partial f}{\partial \beta} = \frac{\partial f}{\partial \alpha}\frac{\partial \alpha}{\partial \beta} \tag{9.34}$$

$$H(\beta) = \left(\frac{\partial \alpha}{\partial \beta}\right)^T H(\alpha) \left(\frac{\partial \alpha}{\partial \beta}\right) + \frac{\partial f}{\partial \alpha}\frac{\partial^2 \alpha}{\partial \beta \partial \beta}. \tag{9.35}$$

When we search the optimal value in α-space we have $\partial f/\partial \alpha = 0$. Therefore we have

$$\frac{\partial f}{\partial \beta} = 0 \tag{9.36}$$

$$H(\beta) = \left(\frac{\partial \alpha}{\partial \beta}\right)^T H(\alpha) \left(\frac{\partial \alpha}{\partial \beta}\right). \tag{9.37}$$

It is also an optimal point in β-space. Note that these equations only hold at the optimal point. Note that at the optimal point

$$x^T H(\beta)x = \left(\frac{\partial \alpha}{\partial \beta}x\right)^T H(\alpha) \left(\frac{\partial \alpha}{\partial \beta}x\right). \tag{9.38}$$

$H(\alpha)$ and $H(\beta)$ are both positive definite or both negative definite. At the optimal point, we have

$$H^{-1}(\beta) = \left[\frac{\partial \alpha}{\partial \beta}\right]^{-1} H^{-1}(\alpha) \left[\left(\frac{\partial \alpha}{\partial \beta}\right)^T\right]^{-1}$$
$$= \left(\frac{\partial \beta}{\partial \alpha}\right) H^{-1}(\alpha) \left(\frac{\partial \beta}{\partial \alpha}\right)^T. \tag{9.39}$$

9.4   Conjugate Gradient Method

The conjugate gradient method is an iterative method for numerical solutions or optimization which finds the search direction in terms of conjugate directions with respect to the Hessian matrix. Each step in the search space is in a new direction orthogonal to the previous step, which helps maximize convergence in as few steps as possible.

Let's first consider the minimization problem. Let $g(x) = -\nabla f(x)$, and the search direction is constructed as

$$d_i = g_i + \gamma_{i-1} \cdot d_{i-1} \tag{9.40}$$

and the iterative equation is

$$x_{i+1} = x_i + \lambda_i \cdot d_i \tag{9.41}$$

where d_i is the direction of line search and λ_i is the step size in the ith iteration. The gradient descent method only uses the gradient as the direction for searching. The conjugate gradient method uses the linear combination of the gradient at the point and the search direction in the previous step. The search direction in the first step is the same as gradient, i.e., $\gamma_0 = 0$ and $d_1 = g_1$. There are two parameters, γ_{i-1} and λ_i, in each iteration. γ_{i-1} is determined by forcing the search directions d_i and d_{i-1} to be conjugate with respect to the Hessian matrix:

$$d_{i-1} \cdot H \cdot d_i = 0. \tag{9.42}$$

We have

$$\gamma_{i-1} = - \left(\frac{g_i \cdot H \cdot d_{i-1}}{d_{i-1} \cdot H \cdot d_{i-1}} \right). \tag{9.43}$$

The step size λ_i is determined by

$$\frac{d}{d\lambda_i} f\left(x_i + \lambda_i \cdot d_i\right) = 0. \tag{9.44}$$

We have

$$g_{i+1} \cdot d_i = 0. \tag{9.45}$$

The step size is determined from this equation, but it may be a nonlinear equation and it may be difficult to solve.

Up to this point, all equations are exact and we have not made any approximations. Now we make an approximation of the gradient. Neglecting the higher-order terms we have

$$\nabla f(x) = \nabla f(x_0) + H(x_0) \cdot (x - x_0). \tag{9.46}$$

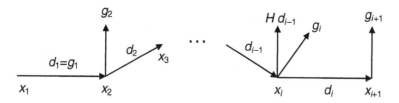

FIGURE 9.1: The search direction in each iteration in the conjugate gradient method.

We have

$$g_{i+1} = g_i - \lambda_i H_i d_i. \tag{9.47}$$

From $g_{i+1} \cdot d_i = 0$, and noting that $g_i \cdot d_i = g_i \cdot (g_i + \gamma_{i-1} d_{i-1}) = g_i \cdot g_i$ we have

$$\lambda_i = \frac{g_i \cdot g_i}{d_i \cdot H_i \cdot d_i}. \tag{9.48}$$

The equation for γ_i can be simplified to

$$\gamma_i = \frac{g_{i+1} \cdot (g_{i+1} - g_i)}{g_i \cdot g_i}. \tag{9.49}$$

The diagram shows the search paths from the initial point through each iteration. It should be emphasized that d_i is perpendicular to $H\, d_{i-1}$ and g_{i+1}. The first property is from the requirement that two searching directions are conjugate with respect to the Hessian matrix and it decides γ_{i-1} and the second property decides the step size of each search.

In summary, for a minimization problem, we have the following iterative equation in the conjugate gradient method:

$$d_i = g_i + \left(\frac{g_i \cdot (g_i - g_{i-1})}{g_{i-1} \cdot g_{i-1}} \right) d_{i-1} \tag{9.50}$$

$$x_{i+1} = x_i + \left(\frac{g_i \cdot g_i}{d_i \cdot H_i \cdot d_i} \right) d_i. \tag{9.51}$$

For a maximization problem $g(x) = \nabla f(x)$, the search direction is constructed as

$$d_i = g_i + \gamma_{i-1} \cdot d_{i-1} \tag{9.52}$$

and the iterative equation is

$$x_{i+1} = x_i + \lambda_i \cdot d_i \tag{9.53}$$

where γ_{i-1} and λ_i are

$$\gamma_i = \frac{g_{i+1} \cdot (g_{i+1} - g_i)}{g_i \cdot g_i} \tag{9.54}$$

and

$$\lambda_i = -\left(\frac{g_i \cdot g_i}{d_i \cdot H_i \cdot d_i}\right). \tag{9.55}$$

In summary, for a maximization problem, we have the following iterative equation in the conjugate gradient method:

$$d_i = g_i + \left(\frac{g_i \cdot (g_i - g_{i-1})}{g_{i-1} \cdot g_{i-1}}\right) d_{i-1} \tag{9.56}$$

$$x_{i+1} = x_i - \left(\frac{g_i \cdot g_i}{d_i \cdot H_i \cdot d_i}\right) d_i. \tag{9.57}$$

Actually the formulation of the maximization problem can be easily obtained from that of the minimization problem by substituting $f(x) \to -f(x)$.

For the simple objective function, x^2, this method needs only two iterations to find the optimal point.

9.5 Quasi-Newton Method

In the quasi-Newton method, only the first derivative is needed; the second derivative is approximated based on the first derivative.

The Newton–Raphson method is based on the following Taylor expansion:

$$\nabla f(x) \approx \nabla f(x_i) + \nabla^2 f(x_i) \cdot (x - x_i). \tag{9.58}$$

It requires the first derivative and inverse of the Hessian matrix of the objective function. The quasi-Newton method finds the inverse of the Hessian matrix iteratively based on the first derivative, so we do not need to explicitly compute the second derivative. We are searching for the matrix H iteratively and it plays the same role as the inverse of the Hessian matrix in the Newton method:

$$x_{i+1} - x_i = H_{i+1} \cdot [\nabla f(x_{i+1}) - \nabla f(x_i)]. \tag{9.59}$$

We initialize at a starting point $H_1 = I$ and expect that $\lim_{i \to \infty} H_i = [\nabla^2 f(x)]^{-1}$. Let $p_i = x_{i+1} - x_i$ and $q_i = g_{i+1} - g_i$ where $g_i = \nabla f(x_i)$, then the quasi-Newton condition is

$$p_i = H_{i+1} \cdot q_i. \tag{9.60}$$

We expect that there is a correction term for H in each iteration and it can be written as

$$H_{i+1} = H_i + \Delta H_i. \tag{9.61}$$

H_{i+1} can be constructed in terms of p_i, q_i, and H_i to satisfy the quasi-Newton condition and follows the expected limiting process. Two updating formulas are well known. The first is the DFP (Davidon–Fletcher–Powell) updating formula,

$$H_{i+1} = H_i + \left(\frac{p_i\, p_i^T}{p_i^T\, q_i} - \frac{H_i\, q_i\, q_i^T\, H_i}{q_i^T\, H_i\, q_i} \right). \tag{9.62}$$

It is obvious that this satisfies the quasi-Newton condition. The second is the BFGS (Broyden–Fletcher–Goldfarb–Shanno) updating formula,

$$
\begin{aligned}
H_{i+1} \;=\;& H_i + \left(\frac{p_i\, p_i^T}{p_i^T\, q_i} - \frac{H_i\, q_i\, q_i^T\, H_i}{q_i^T\, H_i\, q_i} \right) \\
&+ q_i^T\, H_i\, q_i \left(\frac{p_i}{p_i^T\, q_i} - \frac{H_i\, q_i}{q_i^T\, H_i\, q_i} \right) \cdot \left(\frac{p_i^T}{p_i^T\, q_i} - \frac{q_i^T\, H_i}{q_i^T\, H_i\, q_i} \right).
\end{aligned}
\tag{9.63}
$$

The first correction term in BFGS is the same as the correction term in DFP and the second correction term in BFGS is the extra term. Again, it is easy to see that this satisfies the quasi-Newton condition.

In summary, the quasi-Newton method takes the following steps:

1. Select an initial point x_1, calculate $g_1 = \nabla f(x_1)$, and let $H_1 = I$ be the identity matrix.

2. Search direction and updating rule:

$$
\begin{aligned}
d_i &= -H_i \cdot g_i \\
x_{i+1} &= x_i + \lambda\, d_i
\end{aligned}
\tag{9.64}
$$

where λ is the step size. If the step is too big such that the objective function does not move to a favorable point, make the step size half. For a minimization problem, we can pick an appropriate step size and move to the new point with a smaller objective function, while for a maximization problem, move to the new point with a larger objective function.

3. The updating formula are:

$$
\begin{aligned}
g_{i+1} &= \nabla f(x_{i+1}), \\
p_i &= x_{i+1} - x_i, \\
q_i &= g_{i+1} - g_i, \\
H_{i+1} &= H_i + \Delta H_i.
\end{aligned}
\tag{9.65}
$$

ΔH_i can be found using either the BFG or BFGS updating formula.

4. Check stopping criteria and go to step 2 or stop.

9.6 Genetic Algorithms (GA)

A genetic algorithm (GA) is an evolutionary-based iterative search process, where at each iteration step many candidate solutions are created and evaluated. After evaluation, a new generation of candidates is created from the previous generation through biologically inspired breeding, with genetic material mixed from the previous best performing solutions, along with random evolutionary forces including mutation and crossover.

A GA is a powerful global search methodology but is intrinsically inefficient, primarily due to the necessity to evaluate an objective function on many candidates at each generation, and then allow the "evolutionary forces" to eventually drive toward increasingly good solutions. It works well if one has very large resources and millions of years.

9.7 Simulated Annealing

Consider again the concept of the fitness landscape as a complex surface riding above a hyperplane spanned by the possible values of the model parameters. Our desire is to find the minimum of this fitness landscape, and the values of the parameters at this minimum. This will then be our desired best model.

Simulated annealing is a search methodology explicitly designed to avoid and to escape from local minima. It is inspired by the physical metallugical process of hardening through annealing, a process whereby metals are guided into their hardest state through repeated heating and rapid cooling. One heats the metal to get a random orientation of molecules, then quickly cools to freeze in that configuration. One then heats to a lower temperature than before, with a less-than-random resulting orientation, and the molecules begin to align into lower-energy states. This process continues with the temperature lower at each heating step until a close-to-minimum energy state is achieved, with tightly organized molecules creating optimal metal strength.

In simulated annealing we begin with a trial point on the fitness landscape, evaluate the objective function, then move in a random direction to another point with a jump size proportional to an artificial temperature. If the new point is lower in the landscape, we continue from there in the same manner, otherwise we return to our lower previous position and continue from there. As this iterative process continues we lower the temperature/step size.

One can conceptualize this as a planar surface with the complex objective function over it. We put a ping pong ball into this surface and want it to settle to the lowest point. If we let the ball roll to a stop we have found what is likely a local minimum, and have performed a gradient descent. If we pick up the surface and shake it, the ball rattles around and samples many other locations on the surface. In simulated annealing we shake the surface and slowly reduce the intensity of shaking (the temperature). The ball then has a good chance of finding the lowest point on the fitness landscape.

9.8   Linear Programming

Linear programming is the name given to the mathematical problem of optimizing (finding the maximum or minimum) a linear function of variables (the objective function) subject to a set of linear constraints. The constraints can take the form of either equalities or inequalities. Many practical problems of science and industry can be expressed in this form, and consequently linear programming is an important field of applied mathematics. The major reference of this section is the book by Press et al. (1992).

The most general form of linear programming with n primary constraints and $m\,(=m_1 + m_2 + m_3)$ additional constraints is

$$\text{maximize} \quad z = a_0 \cdot x$$

$$\text{subject to} \quad x_j \geq 0, \qquad j = 1, \ldots, n$$

$$a_i \cdot x \leq b_i \quad i = 1, \ldots, m_1 \tag{9.66}$$

$$a_i \cdot x \geq b_i \quad i = m_1 + 1, \ldots, m_1 + m_2$$

$$a_i \cdot x = b_i \quad i = m_1 + m_2 + 1, \ldots, m_1 + m_2 + m_3$$

where $b_i \geq 0\,(i = 1, \ldots, m), x = (x_1, \ldots x_n)$ and $a_i = (a_{i1}, \ldots a_{in})\,(i = 0, 1, \ldots, m)$ are n-dimensional vectors. Here the n primary constraints are $x_j \geq 0, j = 1, \ldots, n$.

Let us introduce three kinds of vectors. A feasible vector is a vector that satisfies the $m + n$ constraints, which means it is feasible as a potential maximal solution. A feasible basic vector is a feasible vector that satisfies n of the original constraints (n primary constraints and m additional constraints) as equalities. An optimal feasible vector is a feasible vector that maximizes the objective function, which is what we are searching for. The fundamental theorem of linear optimization establishes the relationship between the optimal feasible vector and the feasible basic vectors. It is stated as: if an optimal feasible vector exists, then it must be one of the feasible basic vectors. With this theorem in order to find the optimal feasible vector, we only need to search among the feasible basic vectors and find the optimal one. The best feasible basic vector is the optimal feasible vector. The problem now is to find n equalities from $m + n$ constraints. There are $C_{n+m}^m = \frac{(m+n)!}{m!n!}$ possible systems of equations. It is not practical to try out all possibilities to find the optimal one. The simplex method is an effective method to find the optimal feasible vector and it is described below.

The simplex algorithm begins with the realization that the linear constraints each cut the search space by hyperplanes. Each constraint is simply a hyperplane. The combination of all these constraints form a convex polygon in the x-space, bounded by all these linear constraint surfaces. Further, since the objective function to be optimized is linear, the objective function is a hyperplane across this polygon, and the maximum value of the objective function therefore must occur at the boundary of the polygon. Finally, since the polygon faces are flat and the objective function is a hyperplane, the maximal value of the objective function must occur at one of the vertices of the convex polygon formed by the intersection of all the constraints. The simplex algorithm is an efficient method to traverse all the edges of this polygon, evaluating the objective function at each vertex until one finds the maximal value and thus the solution to the optimization problem.

First, any linear programming program can be translated into the following normal form:

$$\text{maximize} \quad z = a_0 \cdot x$$

$$\text{subject to} \quad x_j \geq 0, \quad j = 1, ..., n \tag{9.67}$$

$$a_i \cdot x = b_i \quad i = 1, ..., m.$$

By introducing a slack variable in each inequality constraint, the inequality constraint can be translated into an equality constraint:

$$a_i \cdot x \leq b_i \quad \Rightarrow \quad a_i \cdot x + y_i = b_i, \ y_i \geq 0$$

$$a_i \cdot x \geq b_i \quad \Rightarrow \quad a_i \cdot x - y_i = b_i, \ y_i \geq 0. \tag{9.68}$$

Let's consider a special case of the normal form, called the restricted normal form. In that form the m constraints can be written in terms of m equations with m-variables on the left (left-hand or basic variables) and $n - m$ variables on the right (right-hand or non-basic variables). For example, let x_1, ..., x_m be left-hand variables and x_{m+1}, x_{m+2}, ..., x_n be right-hand variables, then the constraints in the restricted form are:

$$x_i = b_i + \sum_{j=m+1}^{n} a_{ij} x_j, \quad i = 1, ..., m \tag{9.69}$$

where $b_i \geq 0 \, (i = 1, ..., m)$. Also the objective function can be expressed in terms of the right-hand variables x_{m+1}, x_{m+2}, ..., x_n as:

$$z = c_0 + \sum_{j=m+1}^{n} c_j x_j. \tag{9.70}$$

From this restricted form, we have a feasible basic vector:

$$x_i = \begin{cases} b_i & i = 1, 2, ..., m \\ 0 & i = m+1, .m+2, ... n \end{cases} \tag{9.71}$$

with the objective function $z = c_0$.

From this feasible basic vector, we can find a new feasible basic vector with the larger objective function. Suppose $c_j > 0 \, (j \in \{m+1, m+2, ..., n\})$, we can increase x_j from 0 until one of the left-hand variables, say x_i, becomes 0. That is a feasible basic function with a larger objective function. Try all possible ways to increase one of the variables from $x_{m+1}, x_{m+2}, ..., x_n$ and find a variable with the largest objective function. We then exchange variables $x_i \Leftrightarrow x_j$ and form a new restricted normal form. The procedure is repeated until we find the optimal feasible solution or verify that there is no optimal solution.

By introducing the artificial variables, any normal form can be translated into a restricted normal form with an auxiliary objective function:

$$\begin{aligned} \text{maximize} \quad & z' = -\sum_{i=1}^{m} z_i \\ \text{subject to} \quad & x_j \geq 0, \quad j = 1, ..., n \\ & z_i \geq 0, \quad i = 1, ..., m \\ & z_i = b_i - a_i \cdot x \quad i = 1, ..., m. \end{aligned} \tag{9.72}$$

After some exchanges of variables, all z-variables are moved to the right-hand side. From this exchanged restricted form, we can find a feasible basic vector. Then we discard all z-variables and switch to the original objective function and continue to exchange variables until the optimal vector has been reached.

In summary, the following matrix set-up can be used for the general linear programming problem:

			x_1 ... x_n	y_1 ... y_{m_1}	y_{m_1+1}	...	$y_{m_1+m_2}$
z			a_0	0 ... 0	0		0
z_1	b_1			-1			
...	...			...			
z_{m_1}	b_{m_1}			-1			
z_{m_1+1}	b_{m_1+1}				1		
...			$-a_i$			...	
$z_{m_1+m_2}$	$b_{m_1+m_2}$						1
$z_{m_1+m_2+1}$	$b_{m_1+m_2+1}$						
...							
$z_{m_1+m_2+m_3}$	$b_{m_1+m_2+m_3}$						
z'							

The constraints have been arranged in the order of $\leq, \geq, =$. The computer program can be readily written in terms of the matrix manipulation based on this matrix representation.

We have developed a function, $linear\_prog(c, constraints)$, in DataMin-erXL, Refer to Appendix B for a complete list of functions in DataMinerXL. Two inputs of the linear programming function are

- "c" is the coefficients in the objective function

- "constraints" is constraints

Here we give some examples of linear programming problems.

Problem 9.1: *This problem has a solution:*

$$\begin{aligned} \text{maximize} \quad & z = x_1 + 8x_2 + 2x_3 \\ \text{subject to} \quad & x_j \geq 0, \quad j = 1, 2, 3 \\ & x_1 + 2x_2 + 5x_3 \leq 10 \\ & 7x_1 + 2x_2 + 2x_3 \leq 12. \end{aligned} \quad (9.73)$$

The input "c" is

1	8	2

and the input "constraints" is

1	2	5	<=	10
7	2	2	<=	12

There exists a solution and it is $x = (0, 5, 0), z = 40$.

Problem 9.2: *This problem does not have a solution because the objective function is unbounded:*

$$\begin{aligned} \text{maximize} \quad & z = 2x_1 + 7x_2 \\ \text{subject to} \quad & x_j \geq 0, \quad j = 1, 2 \\ & 6x_1 + x_2 \geq 8 \\ & 5x_1 + 3x_2 \geq 13 \\ & 3x_1 + 2x_2 \geq 7. \end{aligned} \quad (9.74)$$

Clearly, the objective function is unbounded.

Problem 9.3: *This problem has contradicting constraints:*

$$\text{maximize} \quad z = 4x_1 + 3x_2$$

$$\text{subject to} \quad x_j \geq 0, \quad j = 1, 2$$

$$x_1 + 3x_2 \leq 4 \tag{9.75}$$

$$3x_1 + 4x_2 \geq 14.$$

There is no feasible area and therefore there is no solution.

Problem 9.4: *This problem has a solution:*

$$\text{maximize} \quad z = -3x_1 - 4x_2$$

$$\text{subject to} \quad x_j \geq 0, \quad j = 1, 2$$

$$3x_1 + x_2 \leq 9 \tag{9.76}$$

$$x_1 + 2x_2 \leq 8$$

$$x_1 + x_2 \geq 2.$$

By graphing we can find the optimal vector is $x = (2, 0), z = -6$.

Problem 9.5: *This problem has a solution:*

$$\text{maximize} \quad z = 10x_1 + 2x_2 + 3x_3 + 4x_4$$

$$\text{subject to} \quad x_j \geq 0, \quad j = 1, ..., 4$$

$$x_1 + 3x_3 + x_4 \leq 20$$

$$2x_2 - 9x_4 \leq 2 \tag{9.77}$$

$$x_2 - x_3 + 2x_4 \geq 5$$

$$x_1 + x_2 + x_3 + x_4 = 10.$$

There exists a solution and it is $x = (7.5, 0, 0, 2.5)$, $z = 85$.

9.9 Nonlinear Programming (NLP)

In this section, we will present the general nonlinear programming (GNLP) problem. Then we discuss the simplest nonlinear programming, the quadratic programming (QP), and related linear complementarity programming (LCP).

Finally, we present the sequential quadratic programming (SQP) to solve general nonlinear problem. For a more complete discussion on nonlinear programming, refer to the books *Numerical Optimization* by Nocedal and Wright (1999) and *Convex Optimization* by Boyd and Vandenberghe (2004).

9.9.1   General Nonlinear Programming (GNLP)

Let's consider a general nonlinear optimization problem:

$$
\begin{aligned}
\text{minimize} \quad & f(x) \qquad x = [n \times 1] \\
\text{subject to} \quad & h_i(x) = 0, \quad i = 1, 2, ..., m \\
& g_i(x) \geq 0, \quad i = 1, 2, ..., p.
\end{aligned}
\tag{9.78}
$$

Introducing slack variables (s_i) allows us to transform the inequality constraints to equality constraints: $g_i(x) - s_i^2 = 0$. Now we are working on the space (x, s). Introducing Lagrange multipliers $\lambda_i \, (i = 1, ..., m)$ and $\mu_i \, (i = 1, ..., p)$, we have

$$
L(x, s, \lambda, \mu) = f(x) - \sum_{i=1}^{m} \lambda_i h_i(x) - \sum_{i=1}^{p} \mu_i(g_i(x) - s_i^2).
\tag{9.79}
$$

Taking the first derivative with respect to x, s_i, λ_i, μ_i, respectively, we have the following equations:

$$
\begin{aligned}
& \nabla f(x) - \sum_{i=1}^{m} \lambda_i \nabla h_i(x) - \sum_{i=1}^{p} \mu_i \nabla g_i(x) = 0 \\
& \mu_i s_i = 0 \\
& h_i(x) = 0 \\
& g_i(x) - s_i^2 = 0.
\end{aligned}
\tag{9.80}
$$

Note that $\mu_i s_i = 0$ and $g_i(x) - s_i^2 = 0$ imply that $\mu_i g_i = 0$ and $g_i(x) \geq 0$. Let x_0 be the solution of the above equations and x be a neighboring point satisfying the constraints, and $l = x - x_0$. Then we have

$$
\frac{\partial f(x_0)}{\partial l} - \sum_{i=1}^{m} \lambda_i \frac{\partial h_i(x_0)}{\partial l} - \sum_{i=1}^{p} \mu_i \frac{\partial g_i(x_0)}{\partial l} = 0.
\tag{9.81}
$$

We have $\partial f(x_0)/\partial l \geq 0$ and $\partial h_i(x_0)/\partial l = 0$. Note that if $\mu_i \neq 0$, then $g_i(x_0) = 0$, and by the constraints we have $\partial g_i(x_0)/\partial l > 0$. Thus $\mu_i \geq 0$. The Lagrange multipliers for the equality constraints have no restriction, but for the inequality constraints the multipliers must be nonnegative. Therefore, we have the following equations:

$$\nabla f(x) - \sum_{i=1}^{m} \lambda_i \nabla h_i(x) - \sum_{i=1}^{p} \mu_i \nabla g_i(x) = 0$$

$$h_i(x) = 0$$

$$\mu_i g_i = 0 \qquad (9.82)$$

$$g_i(x) \geq 0$$

$$\mu_i \geq 0.$$

This is called the Karush–Kuhn–Tucker (KKT) necessary optimality condition.

9.9.2 Lagrange Dual Problem

The general nonlinear optimization problem can be written

$$\text{minimize} \quad f(x) \qquad x = [n \times 1]$$

$$\text{subject to} \quad h_i(x) = 0, \quad i = 1, 2, ..., m \qquad (9.83)$$

$$g_i(x) \geq 0, \quad i = 1, 2, ..., p.$$

Let $D = \text{dom}(f) \cap \text{dom}(h) \cap \text{dom}(g)$ be the problem domain and p^* be the optimal value. Note that the domain does not impose the constraints and it contains the feasible region. Introducing Lagrange multipliers (called dual variables), λ_i $(i = 1, ..., m)$ and μ_i $(i = 1, ..., p)$, we define a Lagrangian:

$$L(x, \lambda, \mu) = f(x) - \sum_{i=1}^{m} \lambda_i h_i(x) - \sum_{i=1}^{p} \mu_i g_i(x). \qquad (9.84)$$

The Lagrange dual function for any dual variables (λ, μ) is defined by:

$$L(\lambda, \mu) = \min_{x \in D} L(x, \lambda, \mu) = \min_{x \in D} \left\{ f(x) - \sum_{i=1}^{m} \lambda_i h_i(x) - \sum_{i=1}^{p} \mu_i g_i(x) \right\}. \qquad (9.85)$$

For any λ and $\mu \geq 0$, we have $L(\lambda, \mu) \leq p^*$. We can establish this relationship as follows. Let $\tilde{x}$ be a feasible point, namely, $h_i(\tilde{x}) = 0$, $g_i(\tilde{x}) \geq 0$. We have

$$L(\tilde{x}, \lambda, \mu) = f(\tilde{x}) - \sum_{i=1}^{m} \lambda_i h_i(\tilde{x}) - \sum_{i=1}^{p} \mu_i g_i(\tilde{x}) \leq f(\tilde{x}). \qquad (9.86)$$

Thus $L(\lambda, \mu) \leq L(\tilde{x}, \lambda, \mu) \leq f(\tilde{x})$ for all feasible points. Therefore we have

$$L(\lambda, \mu) \leq p^*. \qquad (9.87)$$

The dual function gives lower bounds on the optimal value p^* of the original problem. A natural question is, for all possible (λ, μ), what is the maximum value of $L(\lambda, \mu)$? Can it reach to p^*?

Now we define a problem called the Lagrange dual problem (the original problem is called the primal problem):

$$
\begin{aligned}
&\underset{\lambda, \mu}{\text{maximize}} \quad L(\lambda, \mu) \\
&\text{subject to} \quad \mu_i \geq 0, \; i = 1, 2, ..., p.
\end{aligned} \tag{9.88}
$$

This is the same as the original problem except now we are working in the space of the Lagrangian multipliers as variables. Let d^* be the optimal value. Then we have

$$
d^* \leq p^* \qquad \text{weak duality.} \tag{9.89}
$$

In the case of strong duality, the following equality holds:

$$
d^* = p^* \qquad \text{strong duality.} \tag{9.90}
$$

The difference $(p^* - d^*)$ is called the optimal duality gap.

Here we give a simple example to illustrate the concept of the Lagrange dual problem.

$$
\begin{aligned}
&\underset{x,y}{\text{minimize}} \quad x^2 + y^2 \\
&\text{subject to} \quad x + y \geq 2.
\end{aligned} \tag{9.91}
$$

It is clear that the optimal solution of this primal problem is $(x, y) = (1, 1)$ and $p^* = 2$. Let

$$
L(\lambda) = \underset{x,y}{\text{minimize}} \, L(x, y, \lambda) = \underset{x,y}{\text{minimize}} \left(x^2 + y^2 - 2\lambda(x + y - 2) \right), \tag{9.92}
$$

for any given $\lambda \geq 0$. The solution is $x = y = \lambda$, and $L(\lambda) = -2\lambda^2 + 4\lambda$. Then we have the solution for the dual problem $\lambda = 1, d^* = 2$. For this problem, $p^* = d^* = 2$, the optimal duality gap is 0.

9.9.3   Quadratic Programming (QP)

As a special case of nonlinear programming, the quadratic programming problem is

$$
\begin{aligned}
&\text{minimize} \quad f(x) = c^T x + \tfrac{1}{2} x^T H x \\
&\text{subject to} \quad Ax \geq b, \quad i = 1, 2, ..., m \\
&\qquad\qquad\quad x \geq 0, \quad i = 1, 2, ..., p,
\end{aligned} \tag{9.93}
$$

where the dimensions of the variables are $x = [n \times 1]$, $A = [m \times n]$, $b = [m \times 1]$. Any quadratic objective function with linear constraints can be transformed into this standard form. Any equality constraint can be written as an inequality constraint. If a variable is a free variable without a constraint, then it can be written as $x = u - v$, $u \geq 0$ and $v \geq 0$. After a linear variable transformation, the matrix is still positive semi-definite in the transformed space, if the original one is positive semi-definite.

By introducing Lagrange multipliers λ and μ, we have

$$c + Hx - A^T\lambda - \mu = 0$$

$$\lambda^T(Ax - b) = 0$$

$$\mu^T x = 0 \tag{9.94}$$

$$Ax - b \geq 0$$

$$x, \lambda, \mu \geq 0.$$

Introducing slack variables $s = Ax - b$, we have the following equations:

$$\mu = Hx - A^T\lambda + c$$

$$s = Ax - b$$

$$\lambda^T s = 0 \tag{9.95}$$

$$\mu^T x = 0$$

$$x, \lambda, \mu, s \geq 0.$$

In the matrix form we have

$$\begin{bmatrix} \mu \\ s \end{bmatrix} = \begin{bmatrix} H & -A^T \\ A & 0 \end{bmatrix} \begin{bmatrix} x \\ \lambda \end{bmatrix} + \begin{bmatrix} c \\ -b \end{bmatrix}$$

$$\begin{bmatrix} \mu^T & s^T \end{bmatrix} \begin{bmatrix} x \\ \lambda \end{bmatrix} = 0 \tag{9.96}$$

$$x, \lambda, \mu, s \geq 0.$$

This is in the form of a linear complementarity problem (LCP) discussed in Section 9.9.4:

$$w = mz + q$$

$$w^T z = 0 \tag{9.97}$$

$$w, z \geq 0$$

where

$$m = \begin{bmatrix} H & -A^T \\ A & 0 \end{bmatrix}, \quad q = \begin{bmatrix} c \\ -b \end{bmatrix}$$

$$z = \begin{bmatrix} x \\ \lambda \end{bmatrix}, \quad w = \begin{bmatrix} \mu \\ s \end{bmatrix}. \tag{9.98}$$

Note that $z^T m z = x^T H x$; if H is positive definite, then so is m.

The General Form of Quadratic Programming

The most general form of quadratic programming is

$$\text{minimize} \quad f(x) = c^T x + \tfrac{1}{2} x^T H x$$

$$\text{subject to} \quad Ex = d, \tag{9.99}$$

$$Ax \geq b.$$

If we let $x = u - v$, $u \geq 0$ and $v \geq 0$, we have the following canonical form in terms of u and v:

$$\text{minimize} \quad f(x) = \begin{bmatrix} c^T & -c^T \end{bmatrix} \begin{bmatrix} u \\ v \end{bmatrix} + \tfrac{1}{2} \begin{bmatrix} u^T & v^T \end{bmatrix} \begin{bmatrix} H & -H \\ -H & H \end{bmatrix} \begin{bmatrix} u \\ v \end{bmatrix}$$

$$\text{subject to} \quad \begin{bmatrix} E & -E \\ -E & E \\ A & -A \end{bmatrix} \begin{bmatrix} u \\ v \end{bmatrix} \geq \begin{bmatrix} d \\ -d \\ b \end{bmatrix}.$$

$$u, v \geq 0$$

$$\tag{9.100}$$

We have developed a function, $quadratic\_prog(c, H, constraints)$, in DataMinerXL. Refer to Appendix B for a complete list of functions in DataMinerXL. The three inputs of the quadratic programming function are:

- "c" is the coefficients of the linear terms of x in the objective function,

- "H" is the coefficients of the quadratic terms of x in the objective function,

- "constraints" is the constraints.

Problem 9.6: *Here we give an example of a quadratic programming with three variables and four linear inequality constraints.*

$$\text{minimize} \quad z = 2x_1^2 + 6x_2^2 + 10x_3^2 - 6x_1x_2 + 3x_1x_3 - 4x_2x_3$$

$$- 2x_1 + 5x_2 + 8x_3$$

$$\text{subject to} \quad x_1 + 3x_2 + x_3 \geq 6 \tag{9.101}$$

$$\text{all variables nonnegative.}$$

For this problem, the input "c" is

$$\overline{\begin{array}{ccc} -2 & 5 & 8 \end{array}},$$

the input "H" is

$$
\begin{array}{rrr}
4 & -6 & 3 \\
-6 & 12 & -4 \\
3 & -4 & 20
\end{array} ,
$$

and the input "constraints" is

$$
\begin{array}{ccccc}
1 & 3 & 1 & >= & 6 \\
1 & 0 & 0 & >= & 0 \\
0 & 1 & 0 & >= & 0 \\
0 & 0 & 1 & >= & 0
\end{array} .
$$

The solution is $x = (2.5357, 1.1548, 0.0000)$, $z = 3.9940$.

Efficient Frontier

We discuss an application of the quadratic programming in portfolio optimization. In portfolio optimization we need to minimize the variance given a return from a linear combination of returns. The location in return/variance space of this minimization is called the efficient frontier. It defines a set of points where one can achieve the best return with a given risk (using variance as the measure of risk), or equivalently the least risk with a given return. The problem can be represented by

$$
\begin{aligned}
\text{minimize} \quad & \sigma_p^2 = \sum_{i=1}^{n} \sum_{j=1}^{n} w_i w_j \sigma_{ij} \\
\text{subject to} \quad & \sum_{i=1}^{n} w_i = 1 \\
& \sum_{i=1}^{n} w_i r_i = r_p
\end{aligned}
\tag{9.102}
$$

where r_i is the ith return and σ_{ij} is the covariance between the ith return and the jth return, $i, j = 1, 2, ..., n$. r_p is a given return of a portfolio and σ_p^2 is the variance of portfolio return. If we ignore the sign of weights, then by introducing Lagrange multipliers (see Section 9.1) we have the Lagrangian:

$$
f = \sum_{i=1}^{n} \sum_{j=1}^{n} w_i w_j \sigma_{ij} + 2\lambda_1 \left(\sum_{i=1}^{n} w_i - 1 \right) + 2\lambda_2 \left(\sum_{i=1}^{n} w_i r_i - r_p \right).
\tag{9.103}
$$

We have

$$
\begin{aligned}
& \sum_{j=1}^{n} \sigma_{ij} w_j + \lambda_1 + \lambda_2 r_i = 0 \\
& \sum_{i=1}^{n} w_i = 1 \\
& \sum_{i=1}^{n} w_i r_i = r_p.
\end{aligned}
\tag{9.104}
$$

In matrix form the equation becomes

$$
\begin{bmatrix}
\sigma_{11} & \cdots & \sigma_{1n} & 1 & r_1 \\
\vdots & \cdots & \vdots & \vdots & \vdots \\
\sigma_{n1} & \cdots & \sigma_{nn} & 1 & r_n \\
1 & \cdots & 1 & 0 & 0 \\
r_1 & \cdots & r_n & 0 & 0
\end{bmatrix}
\begin{bmatrix}
w_1 \\
\vdots \\
w_n \\
\lambda_1 \\
\lambda_2
\end{bmatrix}
-
\begin{bmatrix}
0 \\
\vdots \\
0 \\
1 \\
r_p
\end{bmatrix}
\tag{9.105}
$$

Solving this equation, we have the weights and minimum variance. Since the weights are linear in terms of r_p, the minimum variance is a quadratic function of r_p. So the efficient frontier is a parabolic curve, $\sigma_{\min}^2 = a\,r_p^2 + br_p + c$.

If we must impose constraints on the weights then this problem becomes one of quadratic programming problems.

9.9.4 Linear Complementarity Programming (LCP)

The class of problems called LCP can be written

$$
w = mz + q
$$

$$
w^T z = 0 \tag{9.106}
$$

$$
w, z \geq 0
$$

where m is an $n \times n$ matrix and w, z, q are $n \times 1$ vectors. Note that if all components of q are nonnegative then $z = 0$ and $w = q$ is a trivial solution.

Let's discuss Lemke's algorithm published in Lemke (1965) to solve the LCP. The reference of this section is the book *Linear Complementarity, Linear and Nonlinear Programming* by Murty (1988).

We introduce an artificial variable z_0, and construct the following problem:

$$
w = mz + ez_0 + q
$$

$$
w^T z = 0 \tag{9.107}
$$

$$
w, z, z_0 \geq 0
$$

where e is a vector with all components 1. If there is a solution of the problem and $z_0 = 0$, then it is also a solution of the original LCP problem.

In Lemke's algorithm, a series of solutions of the new problem are constructed until we find a solution with $z_0 = 0$ or confirm that there is no solution. It is very easy to find a solution for the new problem. We are trying to exchange the variables between the variables on the left-hand side and that on the right-hand side.

1. Find i such that q_i is the minimum; then we have:

$$z_0 = l(z_1, ..., z_n, w_i) + (-q_i)$$

$$w_j = l(z_1, ..., z_n, w_i) + (q_j - q_i), \quad j \neq i \tag{9.108}$$

where $l(...)$ is a general symbolic notation of linear combination. From here, we can read a solution by setting all variables on the right-hand side to be 0 and all variables on the left-hand side to be the constant terms (all nonnegative):

$$z_0 = -q_i$$

$$w_j = q_j - q_i, \quad j \neq i \tag{9.109}$$

$$z_1, ..., z_n, w_i = 0.$$

The net result is to pick z_0 and drop w_i among the variables on the left-hand side, called the basic vector.

2. Note that z_i and w_i are all on the right-hand side and we need to find an equation to move z_i to the left-hand side. It is clear to pick the equation with a negative coefficient and minimize the ratio of the constant term and absolute coefficient. It ensures that the constant terms are all nonnegative for all equations after exchanging variables.

3. Repeat Step 2 until the stopping criteria reaches one of the following stages:

   • At some stage of the algorithm, z_0 may exchange to the right-hand side, or become equal to zero for the constant term. Then a solution has been found.

   • At some stage of the algorithm, the coefficients for the pivot variable are all positive, and the algorithm terminates.

The procedure discussed above can be manipulated in terms of matrix operations. Constructing the following matrix, we can formulate the procedure as follows:

	w_1	$\cdots$	w_n	z_1	$\cdots$	z_n	z_0	q
w_1								
$\cdots$		I			$-M$		$-e$	q
w_n								

1. Find a row i such that q_i is the minimum, then pivot the matrix in terms of the element (i, z_0). Then the index has been changed: pick z_0 and drop w_i in the basic vector.

2. Pick up the complement variable of the variable dropped in the last step. In that column find a row among the rows with positive coefficients and the minimum ratio of the constant term and the coefficient. Pivot the matrix in terms of that element.

3. Repeat Step 2 until the stopping criteria.

- At some stage of the algorithm, z_0 may drop out of the basic vector, or become equal to zero for the constant term. Then a solution has been found.

- At some stage of the algorithm, the coefficients for the pivot variable are all non-positive, the algorithm terminates.

It can be shown that if m is a positive semi-definite matrix and the algorithm terminates, then there is no solution of the LCP. Let $w_1 = mz_1 + q$ and $w_2 = mz_2 + q$, we have $w_1 - w_2 = m(z_1 - z_2)$. Thus

$$(z_1 - z_2)^T (w_1 - w_2) = (z_1 - z_2)^T m(z_1 - z_2). \tag{9.110}$$

Since the LHS is non-positive and the RHS is non-negative, then $z_1 = z_2$ if m is a positive definite matrix. Therefore for the positive definite matrix the solution is unique. For the positive semi-definite matrix Lemke's algorithm gives a definite answer: it either gives a solution or tells there is no solution.

9.9.5 Sequential Quadratic Programming (SQP)

Sequential quadratic programming (SQP) is a methodology to solve general nonlinear programs by sequentially solving a series of simpler quadratic programs. The following is the SQP method proposed by Schittkowski. Refer to Schittkowski (1981a), (1981b), and (1983) for detailed analysis of the algorithms.

Quadratic Approximation of the NLP

The general NLP is

$$\text{minimize} \quad f(x)$$

$$\text{subject to} \quad g_j(x) = 0, \quad j = 1, 2, ..., me \tag{9.111}$$

$$g_j(x) \geq 0, \quad j = me + 1, ..., m.$$

Its quadratic approximation is

minimize $\quad \frac{1}{2}d^T H_k d + (\nabla f(x_k))^T d + \frac{1}{2}\rho_k \delta^2$

subject to $\quad (\nabla g(x_k))^T d + (1-\delta)g_j(x_k) \left\{ \begin{array}{c} = \\ \geq \end{array} \right\} 0, \, j \in J_k^*$

$\qquad\qquad (\nabla g(x_k))^T d + g_j(x_k) \geq 0, \, j \in K_k^*$ $\qquad\qquad\qquad$ (9.112)

$\qquad\qquad 0 \leq \delta \leq 1.$

Initialization

Let n be the number of variables and m be the number of constraints. The variables are initialized as follows:

$$x[n \times 1] = 0, \; v[m \times 1] = 0, \; B[n \times n] = I_n, \; \rho = 1, \; r[m \times 1] = 1. \quad (9.113)$$

Lagrange Multipliers in QP

The KKT optimality condition for QP is

$$\nabla_d \left[\tfrac{1}{2}d^T H d + (\nabla f(x))^T d \right] - \sum_{j=1}^{m} u_j \nabla_d \left[(\nabla g_j(x))^T d + g_j(x) \right] = 0. \quad (9.114)$$

Then we have $Au = Hd + \nabla f(x)$, where A is a $[n \times m]$ matrix with the elements

$$A_{ij} = \partial g_j(x)/\partial x_i. \quad (9.115)$$

We only need the columns of matrix A with the indices in J^*. These are the active constraints. Therefore, we have

$$u = (A_{J^*}^T A_{J^*})^{-1} A_{J^*}^T (H d + \nabla f(x)). \quad (9.116)$$

Active Set

$$J_k^* = \{1, ..., me\} \cup \left\{ j \,|\, me < j \leq m, \, g_j(x_k) \leq \varepsilon \text{ or } v_j^{(k)} > 0 \right\}, \quad (9.117)$$

$$J = \{1, ..., me\} \cup \{j \,|\, me < j \leq m, \, g_j(x_k) \leq v_j/r_j\}. \quad (9.118)$$

Update Penalty Parameter ρ

The penalty parameter ρ is updated according to the following relation with $k = 0, 1, 2, \ldots$ being the iteration index.

$$\rho_{k+1} = \max\left(\rho_0, \frac{\rho^*(d_k^T A_k u_k)^2}{(1 - \delta_k)^2 d_k^T H_k d_k}\right) \tag{9.119}$$

where $\rho^* > 1$ is a constant. For example, $\rho^* = 2$.

Update Penalty Parameter r

The penalty parameter r is updated through the following, where again $k = 0, 1, 2, \ldots$ is the iteration index.

$$r_j^{(k+1)} = \max\left(\sigma_j^{(k)} r_j^{(k)}, \frac{2m(u_j^{(k)} - v_j^{(k)})^2}{(1 - \delta_k) d_k^T H_k d_k}\right), j = 1, 2, \ldots, m, \tag{9.120}$$

$$\sigma_j^{(k)} = \min\left(1, k/\sqrt{r_j^{(k)}}\right), \tag{9.121}$$

and $\sigma_j^{(0)} = 1$.

Update d and u

If QP fails then we use the following update rule for d and u:

$$d_k = -B_k^{-1} \nabla_x \Phi_{r_k}(x_k, v_k),$$
$$u_k = v_k - \nabla_v \Phi_{r_k}(x_k, v_k). \tag{9.122}$$

After straightforward calculations we have

$$\nabla_x \Phi_r(x, v) = \nabla f(x) - \sum_{j \in J}(v_j \nabla g_j(x) - r_j g_j(x) \nabla g_j(x)), \tag{9.123}$$

$$(\nabla_v \Phi_r(x, v))_i = \begin{cases} -g_i(x) & \text{if } i \in J, \\ -v_j/r_j & \text{if } i \in K. \end{cases} \tag{9.124}$$

Stopping Criterion

When the following four conditions are satisfied the program terminates.

1. $d_k^T H_k d_k \le \varepsilon^2$,

2. $\sum_{j=1}^{m} \left| u_j^{(k)} g_j(x_k) \right| \le \varepsilon$,

3. $\|\nabla_x L(x_k, u_k)\|^2 \leq \varepsilon$,

4. $\sum\limits_{j=1}^{me} |g_j(x_k)| + \sum\limits_{j=me+1}^{m} |\min(0, g_j(x_k)| \leq \sqrt{\varepsilon}$,

where the Lagrange function is defined as

$$L(x_k, u_k) = f(x_k) - \sum_{j=1}^{m} u_j g_j(x), \qquad (9.125)$$

and

$$\nabla_x L(x_k, u_k) = \nabla_x f(x_k) - \sum_{j=1}^{m} u_j \nabla g_j(x) = \nabla_x f(x_k) - \nabla g(x) \cdot u. \quad (9.126)$$

Line Search

Given $f(0)$ and $f'(0)$ we want to search α to find the minimum of $f(\alpha)$ in the interval $[0, 1]$:

1. $\alpha = 1$

2. If $f(\alpha) \leq f(0) + \mu \alpha f'(0)$ then stop

3. Else $\alpha = \max(\beta \alpha, \bar{\alpha})$ Go to 2

where $\bar{\alpha}$ is the value with the minimum function under the quadratic approximation using $f(0)$, $f'(0)$, and $f(\alpha)$:

$$\bar{\alpha} = \frac{-\alpha^2 f'(0)}{2 (f(\alpha) - f(0) - f'(0)\alpha)}. \qquad (9.127)$$

Note that $\bar{\alpha}$ is not necessarily in the range $[0, \alpha]$. If $\bar{\alpha}$ is too close to $\bar{\alpha}$, we can reset it to a smaller number. For example: if $\bar{\alpha} > 0.95\alpha$ then $\bar{\alpha} > 0.5\alpha$. Here the searching function is defined in terms of the augmented Lagrange function:

$$\phi_k(\alpha) = \Phi_{r_{k+1}} \left(\begin{pmatrix} x_k \\ v_k \end{pmatrix} + \alpha \begin{pmatrix} d_k \\ u_k - v_k \end{pmatrix} \right) \qquad (9.128)$$

$$\phi_k'(0) = \nabla \Phi_{r_{k+1}} \begin{pmatrix} x_k \\ v_k \end{pmatrix} \cdot \begin{pmatrix} d_k \\ u_k - v_k \end{pmatrix}. \qquad (9.129)$$

The augmented Lagrange function is

$$\Phi_r(x, v) = f(x) - \sum_{j \in J} \left(v_j g_j(x) - \tfrac{1}{2} r_j g_j(x)^2 \right) - \tfrac{1}{2} \sum_{j \in K} v_j^2 / r_j. \qquad (9.130)$$

Damped BFGS Formula

Computing the Hessian of the objective function is a typical need of many optimization tasks, and it is not always easy or even possible to directly compute it if it is ill conditioned. We therefore seek alternative ways to compute this Hessian. One such alternative is the BFGS approach. In this section we discuss an extension of the BFGS approach to the more difficult case where the Hessian contains some negative eigenvalues in the region around the solution we are seeking.

Note that from the Taylor expansion

$$\nabla f(x) \approx \nabla f(x_i) + \nabla^2 f(x_i) \cdot (x - x_i), \tag{9.131}$$

we have

$$\nabla f(x_{i+1}) - \nabla f(x_i) = H_{i+1} \cdot (x_{i+1} - x_i). \tag{9.132}$$

From this relation we wish to estimate/compute the Hessian iteratively. We initialize the starting point at $H_1 = I$ and expect that $\lim_{i \to \infty} H_i = \nabla^2 f(x)$. Let $p_i = x_{i+1} - x_i$ and $q_i = g_{i+1} - g_i$ where $g_i = \nabla f(x_i)$. Then the quasi-Newton condition is

$$q_i = H_{i+1} \cdot p_i. \tag{9.133}$$

We expect that there is a correction term for H in each successive iteration, which can be written as

$$H_{i+1} = H_i + \Delta H_i. \tag{9.134}$$

H_{i+1} can be constructed in terms of p_i, q_i, and H_i so as to satisfy the quasi-Newton condition and the desired limiting property. The DFP (Davidon–Fletcher–Powell) updating formula is

$$H_{i+1} = H_i + \left(\frac{q_i q_i^T}{p_i^T q_i} - \frac{H_i p_i p_i^T H_i}{p_i^T H_i p_i} \right). \tag{9.135}$$

It is obvious that this satisfies the quasi-Newton condition.

At this point we introduce the modification to the BFGS formula that obviates the problem of the ill-conditioned nature of the Hessian. Let $r_i = cq_i + (1 - c)H_i p_i$, where c is defined as

$$c = \begin{cases} 1 & \text{if } p_i^T q_i \geq 0.2 p_i^T H_i p_i \\ \frac{0.8 p_i^T H_i p_i}{p_i^T H_i p_i - p_i^T q_i} & \text{if } p_i^T q_i < 0.2 p_i^T H_i p_i. \end{cases} \tag{9.136}$$

Replacing $q_i \to r_i$ in the standard formula we have

$$H_{i+1} = H_i + \left(\frac{r_i r_i^T}{p_i^T r_i} - \frac{H_i p_i p_i^T H_i}{p_i^T H_i p_i} \right). \tag{9.137}$$

This formula guaranties that if H_i is positive definite then H_{i+1} is also positive definite. Since we begin the iterations with the well-conditioned identity matrix, this damping guarantees that each successive iterative step keeps the approximate Hessian positive definite.

Some Test Cases of SQP

Here we show some test cases of the SQP process. We note that the initial value for searching is often very critical. Sometimes the iteration diverges, and trying different initial values may allow the algorithm to get to the correct answer.

Problem 9.7: *This test case is the linearly constrained Betts function from Hock and Schittkowski (1981):*

$$\text{minimize} \quad f(x_1, x_2) = 0.01x_1^2 + x_2^2 - 100$$

$$\text{subject to} \quad 2 \le x_1 \le 50$$

$$-50 \le x_2 \le 50 \tag{9.138}$$

$$10x_1 - x_2 \ge 10.$$

There exists a solution: $x = (2, 0)$, $f = -99.96$.

Problem 9.8: *This test case is the Rosen–Suzuki problem which is a function of four variables with three nonlinear constraints on the variables. It is Problem 43 of Hock and Schittkowski (1981).*

$$\text{minimize} \quad f(x_1, x_2) = x_1^2 + x_2^2 + 2x_3^2 + x_4^2 - 5x_1 - 5x_2 - 21x_3 + 7x_4$$

$$\text{subject to} \quad -x_1^2 - x_2^2 - x_3^2 - x_4^2 - x_1 + x_2 - x_3 + x_4 + 8 \ge 0$$

$$-x_1^2 - 2x_2^2 - x_3^2 - 2x_4^2 + x_1 + x_4 + 10 \ge 0$$

$$-2x_1^2 - x_2^2 - x_3^2 - 2x_1 + x_2 + x_4 + 5 \ge 0.$$

$$\tag{9.139}$$

The solution is $x = (0, 1, 2, -1)$, $f = -44$.

Problem 9.9: *A simple test case with a linear constraint:*

$$\text{minimize} \quad f(x_1, x_2) = x_1^2 + x_2^2$$

$$\text{subject to} \quad x_1 + x_2 \ge 1. \tag{9.140}$$

The solution is $x = (0.5, 0.5)$, $f = 0.5$.

Problem 9.10: *This test case is from Schittowski (2002):*

$$\text{minimize} \quad f = -x_1 x_2 x_3$$

$$\text{subject to} \quad x_1 + 2x_2 + 2x_3 \geq 0$$

$$-x_1 - 2x_2 - 2x_3 + 72 \geq 0 \tag{9.141}$$

$$0 \leq x_1 \leq 100$$

$$0 \leq x_2 \leq 100.$$

The solution is $x = (24, 12, 12)$, $f = -3456$.

Problem 9.11: *This test case is the problem 12.7 in Bronson and Naadimuthu (1997):*

$$\text{minimize} \quad f = (x_1 - x_2)^2 + (x_3 - 1)^2 + 1$$

$$\text{subject to} \quad x_1^5 + x_2^5 + x_3^5 = 16. \tag{9.142}$$

The solution is $x = ((15/2)^{1/5}, (15/2)^{1/5}, 1) = (1.49628, 1.49628, 1)$, $f = 1$.

Problem 9.12: *A simple test case without constraints:*

$$\text{minimize} \quad f = (x_1 - 10)^2 + (x_2 - 20)^2$$

$$\text{subject to} \quad \text{no constraints.} \tag{9.143}$$

The solution is $x = (10, 20)$, $f = 0$.

Problem 9.13: *This test case is the problem 3.10 in Bronson and Naadimuthu (1997). This is a linear programming problem.*

$$\text{minimize} \quad f = 2x_1 + 3x_2$$

$$\text{subject to} \quad x_1 + x_2 \geq 2$$

$$2x_1 + x_2 \leq 10 \tag{9.144}$$

$$x_1 + x_2 \leq 8$$

$$x_1, x_2 \text{ nonnegative.}$$

The solution is $x = (2, 0)$, $f = 4$.

9.10 Nonlinear Equations

The general form of a set of nonlinear equations is

$$F_i(x_1, x_2, ..., x_N) = 0, \quad i = 1, 2, ..., N. \tag{9.145}$$

Taking a Taylor series around x_0, we have

$$F_i(x) = F_i(x_0) + \sum_{j=1}^{N} \partial F_i / \partial x_j (x - x_0)_j + O((x - x_0)^2). \tag{9.146}$$

By defining the Jacobian matrix as $J_{ij} = \partial F_i / \partial x_j$, in matrix notation, $x = (x_1, x_2, ..., x_N)^T$ and $F = (F_1, F_2, ..., F_N)^T$, we have

$$F(x) = F(x_0) + J(x_0) \cdot (x - x_0) + O((x - x_0)^2). \tag{9.147}$$

Let $F(x) = 0$ and neglecting terms of second and higher order, we have

$$x = x_0 - J^{-1}(x_0) \cdot F(x_0). \tag{9.148}$$

This is the Newton–Raphson method.

If the nonlinear equations are derived from the MLE we might be able to simplify the Jacobian matrix. The Fisher scoring method is to use the expected value of the Jacobian matrix instead of the observed value in the Newton–Raphson method:

$$x = x_0 - [E(J(x_0))]^{-1} \cdot F(x_0) \tag{9.149}$$

In some circumstances the choice of $E(J(x_0))$ is much simpler than $J(x_0)$ and the iterative equation is much more efficient to search for the solution of the nonlinear equations.

Alternatively, we can formulate the problem in terms of an optimization problem. Construct a function

$$f(x_1, x_2, ..., x_N) = \frac{1}{2} \sum_{i=1}^{N} F_i^2((x_1, x_2, ..., x_N). \tag{9.150}$$

Then the solution is

$$x = \arg \min_x f(x_1, x_2, ..., x_N). \tag{9.151}$$

Using the Newton–Raphson method, we have

$$x = x_0 - H^{-1}(x_0) \nabla f(x_0), \tag{9.152}$$

where

$$\nabla f(x) = J^T F, \tag{9.153}$$

$$H(f) = J^T J + \sum_{k=1}^{N} F_k H(F_k). \tag{9.154}$$

When the search point is approaching the optimal solution, $H(f) \approx J^T J$, and we have

$$x = x_0 - (J^T J)^{-1} J^T F = x_0 - J^{-1} F. \tag{9.155}$$

Therefore we have the same iteration equation.

9.11 Expectation-Maximization (EM) Algorithm

The expectation-maximization (EM) algorithm is a framework to deal with optimization problems when there are missing variables or latent variables. Recall that in model fitting we have a set of free parameters that we want to adjust so that they optimize some measure of goodness, typically either a measure of error (such as the MSE) or alternatively the likelihood function. The EM process allows us to approach the best set of model parameters that will maximize the likelihood function through an iterative process. To illustrate the concept of the EM algorithm, we first discuss the two-component mixture model.

For a single normal distribution, the log-likelihood function is

$$l(\mu, \sigma^2; x) = \sum_{i=1}^{n} \ln \varphi_{\mu,\sigma^2}(x_i) = -\sum_{i=1}^{n} \left[\frac{(x_i - \mu)^2}{2\sigma^2} + \frac{1}{2} \ln(2\pi\sigma^2) \right]. \tag{9.156}$$

The first derivatives with respect to μ and σ^2 are

$$\frac{\partial l(\mu, \sigma^2; x)}{\partial \mu} = \sum_{i=1}^{n} \left(\frac{x_i - \mu}{\sigma^2} \right), \tag{9.157}$$

$$\frac{\partial l(\mu, \sigma^2; x)}{\partial \sigma^2} = \sum_{i=1}^{n} \left[\frac{(x_i - \mu)^2}{2\sigma^4} - \frac{1}{2\sigma^2} \right]. \tag{9.158}$$

Therefore the maximum likelihood estimator is

$$\mu = \frac{1}{n} \sum_{i=1}^{n} x_i, \quad \sigma^2 = \frac{1}{n} \sum_{i=1}^{n} (x_i - \mu)^2. \tag{9.159}$$

We discussed the use of the maximum likelihood estimation approach earlier in Chapter 4. For the two-component mixture model, we have a set of numbers that come from two different normal distributions. Let the mixture rate be $p(1) = 1 - \pi$ and $p(2) = \pi$. We have

$$
\begin{aligned}
p(x) &= p(x,1) + p(x,2) = p(x|1)p(1) + p(x|2)p(2) \\
&= (1 - \pi)\varphi_{\mu_1,\sigma_1^2}(x) + \pi\varphi_{\mu_2,\sigma_2^2}(x)
\end{aligned}
\tag{9.160}
$$

The log-likelihood function is

$$
l(\theta; x) = \sum_{i=1}^{n} \ln\left[(1 - \pi)\varphi_{\mu_1,\sigma_1^2}(x) + \pi\varphi_{\mu_2,\sigma_2^2}(x)\right],
\tag{9.161}
$$

where $\theta = (\pi, \mu_1, \sigma_1^2, \mu_2, \sigma_2^2)$ are the parameters to be best fit to the data. Since there is a summation within the log function, maximizing this log-likelihood function is relatively difficult. It is generally necessary to use a numerical procedure like the Newton–Raphson method to estimate the parameters. The problem becomes much simpler if we know a latent variable, γ, such that if $\gamma = 0$ then the sampled point is from the distribution 1 and if $\gamma = 1$ then the sampled point is from the distribution 2, namely

$$
p(x, \gamma = 0) = (1 - \pi)\varphi_{\mu_1,\sigma_1^2}(x)
\tag{9.162}
$$

and

$$
p(x, \gamma = 1) = \pi\varphi_{\mu_2,\sigma_2^2}(x).
\tag{9.163}
$$

In this case we can write down the log-likelihood function as

$$
\begin{aligned}
l_0(\theta; x, \gamma) &= \sum_{i=1}^{n} \left[(1 - \gamma_i)\ln[(1 - \pi)\varphi_{\mu_1,\sigma_1^2}(x_i)] + \gamma_i \ln[\pi\varphi_{\mu_2,\sigma_2^2}(x_i)]\right] \\
&= \sum_{i=1}^{n} \left[(1 - \gamma_i)\ln\varphi_{\mu_1,\sigma_1^2}(x_i)\right] + \sum_{i=1}^{n} \left[\gamma_i \ln\varphi_{\mu_2,\sigma_2^2}(x_i)\right] \\
&\quad + \sum_{i=1}^{n} [(1 - \gamma_i)\ln(1 - \pi) + \gamma_i \ln\pi].
\end{aligned}
\tag{9.164}
$$

Note that the five unknown parameters are now separated into three distinct terms, and we can optimize each term separately to achieve the maximum point for the total. Note that

$$
\frac{\partial l_0(\theta; x, \gamma)}{\partial\pi} = \sum_{i=1}^{n} \left(-\frac{1 - \gamma_i}{1 - \pi} + \frac{\gamma_i}{\pi}\right).
\tag{9.165}
$$

We have the estimation in terms of a weighted mean and variance:

$$
\pi = \sum_{i=1}^{n} \gamma_i/n
\tag{9.166}
$$

$$
\mu_1 = \frac{\sum_{i=1}^{n}(1 - \gamma_i)x_i}{\sum_{i=1}^{n}(1 - \gamma_i)}, \quad \sigma_1^2 = \frac{\sum_{i=1}^{n}(1 - \gamma_i)(x_i - \mu_1)^2}{\sum_{i=1}^{n}(1 - \gamma_i)}
\tag{9.167}
$$

$$\mu_2 = \frac{\sum\limits_{i=1}^{n} \gamma_i x_i}{\sum\limits_{i=1}^{n} \gamma_i}, \quad \sigma_2^2 = \frac{\sum\limits_{i=1}^{n} \gamma_i (x_i - \mu_2)^2}{\sum\limits_{i=1}^{n} \gamma_i}. \tag{9.168}$$

The above results are based on the assumption that we know γ. Actually, we do not know γ, but we can use the calculation of an expectation value to estimate γ. The expectation value of γ is

$$\hat{\gamma}_i = E[\gamma_i] = \frac{\pi \varphi_{\mu_2, \sigma_2^2}(x_i)}{(1 - \pi)\varphi_{\mu_1, \sigma_1^2}(x_i) + \pi \varphi_{\mu_2, \sigma_2^2}(x_i)}. \tag{9.169}$$

Given an estimate of γ we can then maximize the unknown parameters θ. This process iterates through the expectation (E) of γ and the maximization (M) of γ until sufficient convergence is reached.

In summary, the EM algorithm for a two-component mixture model is

1. Initialize $\hat{\theta}^0 = (\pi, \mu_1, \sigma_1^2, \mu_2, \sigma_2^2)$.

2. *E*-step: Estimate the latent variable at the jth iteration $\hat{\gamma}_i^j = \frac{\pi \varphi_{\mu_2, \sigma_2^2}(x_i)}{(1-\pi)\varphi_{\mu_1, \sigma_1^2}(x_i) + \pi \varphi_{\mu_2, \sigma_2^2}(x_i)}$.

3. *M*-step: Update $\hat{\theta}^{j+1} = \hat{\theta}^{j+1}(\hat{\theta}^j, x, \hat{\gamma}^j)$.

4. Repeat 2 and 3 until convergence.

This procedure can be generalized into the general EM algorithm beyond the two-component mixture model. Given a dataset of x, we want to build a model using a framework with unknown parameters θ to be determined so that they provide a best fit to the data. Here x and θ may be represented by a matrix and a vector. The log-likelihood function is

$$l(\theta; x) = \sum_{i=1}^{n} \ln p(x_i | \theta). \tag{9.170}$$

If the optimization problem is too difficult we can introduce latent variables with the attempt to simplify the problem. If we let the latent or missing variables be x^m, then the log-likelihood function including these new variables becomes

$$l_0(\theta; x, x^m) = \sum_{i=1}^{n} \ln p(x_i, x_i^m | \theta). \tag{9.171}$$

At the jth iteration, given x and $\hat{\theta}^j$, we have the distribution of x^m, denoted by $p(x^m | x, \hat{\theta}^j)$. Now we need to establish a relationship between $l(\theta; x)$ and $l_0(\theta; x, x^m)$. Note that

$$p(x, x^m | \theta) = p(x^m | x, \theta) p(x | \theta). \tag{9.172}$$

Taking the log of both sides we have

$$l(\theta; x) = l_0(\theta; x, x^m | x, \hat{\theta}^j) - \sum_{i=1}^{n} \ln p(x_i^m | x_i, \theta). \qquad (9.173)$$

This equality is held for every possible value of x^m. Taking the expectation on the RHS as an estimate, we have

$$l(\theta; x) = \underset{x^m}{E}[l_0(\theta; x, x^m | x, \hat{\theta}^j)] - \sum_{i=1}^{n} \int dx^m p(x_i^m | x_i, \hat{\theta}^j) \ln p(x_i^m | x_i, \theta). \quad (9.174)$$

Letting $Q(\theta, \hat{\theta}^j) = E_{x^m}[l_0(\theta; x, x^m | x, \hat{\theta}^j)]$, we have

$$l(\theta; x) - l(\hat{\theta}^j; x) = Q(\theta, \hat{\theta}^j) - Q(\hat{\theta}^j, \hat{\theta}^j) + \sum_{i=1}^{n} \int dx^m p(x_i^m | x_i, \hat{\theta}^j) \ln \frac{p(x_i^m | x_i, \hat{\theta}^j)}{p(x_i^m | x_i, \theta)}$$

$$\geq Q(\theta, \hat{\theta}^j) - Q(\hat{\theta}^j, \hat{\theta}^j).$$

$$(9.175)$$

If we can maximize $Q(\theta, \hat{\theta}^j)$, we can push the value of $l(\theta; x)$ higher. So the rule for updating θ is

$$\hat{\theta}^{j+1} = \arg \max_{\theta} Q(\theta, \hat{\theta}^j). \qquad (9.176)$$

But it is not necessary to exactly solve this secondary optimization if this optimization problem is too hard, since as long as $Q(\theta, \hat{\theta}^j) > Q(\hat{\theta}^j, \hat{\theta}^j)$, we can push the value of $l(\theta; x)$ higher.

In summary, the EM algorithm is:

1. Initialize $\hat{\theta}^0$.

2. *E*-step: Estimate the latent variables x^m to evaluate the expectation value $Q(\theta, \hat{\theta}^j) = E_{x^m}[l_0(\theta; x, x^m | x, \hat{\theta}^j)]$.

3. *M*-step: Update $\hat{\theta}^{j+1} = \arg \max_{\theta} Q(\theta, \hat{\theta}^j)$.

4. Repeat 2 and 3 until convergence.

The convergence of the EM algorithm is based on the following lemmas.

Lemma 9.1 *If $f(x) - f(x_0) \geq g(x) - g(x_0)$ for any x and any x_0, then the maximum point of $g(x)$ is also the maximum point of $f(x)$.*

Proof 9.1 *Let x_m be the maximum point of g, then $g(x_m) \geq g(x)$ for all x. We have $f(x_m) \geq f(x)$ for all x. Therefore x_m is the maximum point of f.*

Lemma 9.2 *If $f(x) - f(x_0) \geq g(x) - g(x_0)$ for any x and a fixed point x_0. If x_0 is the maximum point of f, then x_0 is also the maximum point of g.*

Proof 9.2 *If this lemma is not true, let x' be the maximum point of g, and we have $g(x') \geq g(x_0)$. This leads to $f(x') - f(x_0) \geq g(x') - g(x_0) > 0$. Therefore x_0 is not the maximum point of f, which is a contradiction. This proves the validity of this lemma.*

Section 8.2 of Zangari et al. (1996) describes the filling in of missing data points using the EM algorithm and gives an example of imputing a missing data point in a time series.

9.12 Optimal Design of Experiment

In designing experiments one desires to make the most efficient use of limited testing resources, with the goal of maximizing the learned information with the minimum cost. In general there is a cost associated with gathering data; each data record has a cost associated with obtaining it. Experimental design is the methodology of identifying the optimal new data records to seek. Generally this requires the specification and iterative modification of a model as one seeks and acquires new data records. The nature of the model and the associated objective function determine the nature of the required optimization process to identify the new data to seek. Many model formulations can be reduced to examining the information or covariance matrix of the data. In optimality we desire to minimize the determinant of the information matrix.

The optimal design of experiment problem can be stated as such: select n data points from $m(m > n)$ data points such that the volume of the confidence region of the coefficients of the linear regression model built from the n data points is minimized. Here is an explanation of why the volume of the confidence region of the coefficients of the linear regression model has the following form

$$V \propto \left[\det \left(X^T X \right)^{-1} \right]^{1/2}. \tag{9.177}$$

We start with two facts for connecting this relationship:

1. In linear regression, the estimated coefficients are $\beta = (X^T X)^{-1}(X^T Y)$. The coefficients are normally distributed under the normality assumption: $B \sim N[\beta, \sigma^2(X^T X)^{-1}]$. Namely the covariance matrix of the coefficients is $\Sigma = \sigma^2(X^T X)^{-1}$.

2. In n-dimensional space, the multiple normal distribution function is $f(B) = \frac{1}{(2\pi)^{n/2}(\det \Sigma)^{1/2}} e^{-\frac{1}{2}(B-\beta)^T \Sigma^{-1}(B-\beta)}$. The volume of the confidence region of the coefficients (B), say 95% confidence level, is the volume of the n-dimensional ellipsoid $(B - \beta)^T \Sigma^{-1}(B - \beta) \leq a^2$.

If $n = 2$, it is an ellipse in general. By using the matrix decomposition,

$\Sigma = AA^T$, and defining $\xi = A^{-1}(B - \beta)$, the confidence region becomes $\xi^T \xi \leq a^2$. This is a regular n-dimensional sphere. Therefore the volume of the confidence region is

$$
\begin{aligned}
V &= \int_\Omega d^n B = \int_\Omega |\partial B / \partial \xi| \, d^n \xi = \det(A) \int_\Omega d^n \xi \\
&\sim \det(A) \, a^n \sim (\det \Sigma)^{1/2} \sim \left[\det \left(X^T X \right)^{-1} \right]^{1/2}.
\end{aligned}
\tag{9.178}
$$

The optimal design is based on this result: select n data points from $m(m > n)$ candidates, such that $\max \det(X^T X)$.

Chapter 10

Miscellaneous Topics

In this last chapter we discuss some particular relevant topics in other areas not covered in the previous chapters.

10.1 Multidimensional Scaling

Visualization of high-dimensional data is an interesting, useful yet challenging task. The approach of dimensionality reduction strives to find a lower dimensional space that captures all or most of the information that exisits in the higher dimensional space. Multidimensional scaling is a process whereby we seek an essentially information-preserving subspace of the original space. That is, we look for a lower dimensional space in which the problem becomes simpler or more clear, and still retains its essence. This discipline originated as a way to visualize higher-dimensional data, "projected" into lower dimensions, typically two, in such a way as the distances between all points was mostly preserved. The process has evolved into general dimensionality reduction methodology as well as being able to discover embedded, lower-dimensional nonlinear structures in which most of the data lies. Here we explore the general problem of finding a lower-dimensional space in which the data can be represented and the between-point distances is preserved as best as possible. For a more complete treatment on multidimensional scaling, refer to Cox and Cox (2000).

Given an $n \times n$ distance matrix, the metric or classical multidimensional scaling method finds the coordinates of n points in a p-dimensional Euclidean space. Note that the distance matrix itself does not tell the underlying dimension of the points. It could be from a two-, three- or higher-dimensional space.

Let $x_i = (x_{i1}, x_{i2}, ..., x_{ip})$ $(i = 1, 2, ..., n)$ be the coordinates of n points in a p-dimensional space. Since the distance matrix is translation invariant, we assume without loss of generality that the n points are centered, i.e., $\sum_{i=1}^{n} x_{ik} = 0$, $(k = 1, 2, ..., p)$. The distance matrix can be constructed by

$$d_{ij}^2 = (x_i - x_j)(x_i - x_j)^T = b_{ii} + b_{jj} - 2b_{ij}, \qquad (10.1)$$

where $b_{ij} = x_i x_j^T$. This is an equation in b_{ij} giving the distance matrix and can be solved by noting the following:

$$\frac{1}{n}\sum_{i=1}^{n} d_{ij}^2 = \frac{1}{n}\sum_{i=1}^{n} b_{ii} + b_{jj}, \tag{10.2}$$

$$\frac{1}{n}\sum_{j=1}^{n} d_{ij}^2 = \frac{1}{n}\sum_{j=1}^{n} b_{jj} + b_{ii}, \tag{10.3}$$

and

$$\frac{1}{n^2}\sum_{i,j=1}^{n} d_{ij}^2 = \frac{2}{n}\sum_{i=1}^{n} b_{ii}. \tag{10.4}$$

We have

$$b_{ij} = -\frac{1}{2}\left(d_{ij}^2 - \frac{1}{n}\sum_{i'=1}^{n} d_{i'j}^2 - \frac{1}{n}\sum_{j'=1}^{n} d_{ij'}^2 + \frac{1}{n^2}\sum_{i',j'=1}^{n} d_{i'j'}^2 \right). \tag{10.5}$$

Introduce a matrix $a_{ij} = -\frac{1}{2}d_{ij}^2$ and the notation of an index where a dot as an index represents the average of elements with respect to that index. We have

$$b_{ij} = a_{ij} - a_{i.} - a_{.j} + a_{..}, \tag{10.6}$$

which in matrix form, is

$$b = H\,a\,H \tag{10.7}$$

where $H = I - \frac{1}{n}11^T$. Define an $n \times p$ matrix of coordinates of n points:

$$X = \begin{bmatrix} x_1 \\ x_2 \\ \vdots \\ x_n \end{bmatrix} = \begin{bmatrix} x_{11} & \cdots & x_{1p} \\ x_{21} & \cdots & x_{2p} \\ \cdots & \cdots & \cdots \\ x_{n1} & \cdots & x_{np} \end{bmatrix}. \tag{10.8}$$

We have $b = XX^T$. Noting that

$$\mathrm{rank}(b) = \mathrm{rank}(XX^T) = \mathrm{rank}(X) = \min(n, p), \tag{10.9}$$

we find that the dimension of the underlying space is determined from the rank of the matrix b.

Since the matrix b is a symmetric matrix, it can be diagonalized in terms of eigenvectors and eigenvalues, $V = [v_1, v_2, ..., v_p]$ and $\Lambda = \mathrm{diag}(\lambda_1, \lambda_2, ..., \lambda_p)$,

$$b = V\Lambda V^T = \left(V\Lambda^{1/2}\right)\left(V\Lambda^{1/2}\right)^T. \tag{10.10}$$

Therefore we have $X = V\Lambda^{1/2}$. Finally, we have the $n \times p$ coordinate matrix

$$X = \left[\sqrt{\lambda_1}v_1, \sqrt{\lambda_2}v_2, ..., \sqrt{\lambda_p}v_p\right]. \tag{10.11}$$

Each column of X is a principal component vector scaled by the squared root of the corresponding eigenvalue. We can project the p-dimensional space into a two-dimensional or three-dimensional space.

Here we give a simple example to reconstruct a map from a table of flying mileages between 10 U.S. cities.

TABLE 10.1: The distances between 10 U.S. cities for the inputs for the classical multidimensional scaling

Distance	Atlanta	Chicago	Denver	Houston	LA	Miami	NY	SF	Seattle	D.C.
Atlanta	0	587	1,212	701	1,936	604	748	2,139	2,182	543
Chicago	587	0	920	940	1,745	1,188	713	1,858	1,737	597
Denver	1,212	920	0	879	831	1,726	1,631	949	1,021	1,494
Houston	701	940	879	0	1,374	968	1,420	1,645	1,891	1,220
LA	1,936	1,745	831	1,374	0	2,339	2,451	347	959	2,300
Miami	604	1,188	1,726	968	2,339	0	1,092	2,594	2,734	923
NY	748	713	1,631	1,420	2,451	1,092	0	2,571	2,408	205
SF	2,139	1,858	949	1,645	347	2,594	2,571	0	678	2,442
Seattle	2,182	1,737	1,021	1,891	959	2,734	2,408	678	0	2,329
D.C.	543	597	1,494	1,220	2,300	923	205	2,442	2,329	0

Using the "*cmds*()" function in DataMinerXL (refer to Appendix B), we find the first two columns of the constructed X

TABLE 10.2: Two-dimensional projection from the classical multidimensional scaling.

City	X_1	X_2
Atlanta	719	−143
Chicago	382	341
Denver	−482	25
Houston	161	−573
LA	−1,204	−390
Miami	1,134	−582
NY	1,072	519
SF	−1,421	−113
Seattle	−1,342	580
D.C.	980	335

If we plot (X_1, X_2) in two-dimensional coordinates, we recover the following map of 10 U.S. cities.

Finally, let's consider one interesting, atypical application of multidimensional scaling. We have a correlation matrix among variables and we want to examine the similarity of variables graphically. Define a distance matrix from the correlation matrix:

$$d_{ij}^2 = 2\left(1 - \rho_{ij}\right). \tag{10.12}$$

This definition is very intuitive. If the correlation of two variables is 1 then the distance is 0. If the correlation is 0 then the distance is $\sqrt{2}$. If the correlation

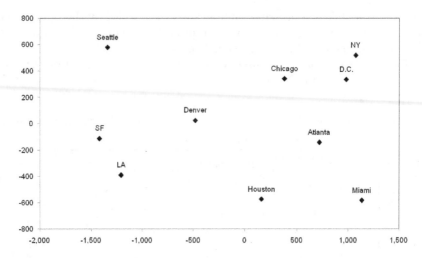

FIGURE 10.1: Two-dimensional projection by the classical multidimensional scaling from the distance matrix among 10 cities.

is -1 then the distance is 2. This truly measures the similarity of variables. Then we have the matrix a,

$$a_{ij} = -\frac{1}{2}d_{ij}^2 = \rho_{ij} - 1, \tag{10.13}$$

and the matrix b,

$$b_{ij} = \rho_{ij} - \rho_{i.} - \rho_{.j} + \rho, \tag{10.14}$$

or in matrix form $b = H\rho H$. Diagonalizing the matrix b as $b = V\Lambda V^T$, we have

$$X = \left[\sqrt{\lambda_1}v_1, \sqrt{\lambda_2}v_2, ...\right] \tag{10.15}$$

where $V = [v_1, v_2, ...]$ and $\Lambda = \text{diag}(\lambda_1, \lambda_2, ...)$ and eigenvalues are arranged in descending order. We can plot the most important two dimensions, $(\sqrt{\lambda_1}v_1, \sqrt{\lambda_2}v_2)$, to view the similarity of variables in two-dimensional space.

10.2   Simulation

A general definition of a model is an algorithmic connection between a set of inputs and a set of outputs. In this book we have been focusing on the subset of modeling that is data driven and statistically based, where a well-defined functional construct is asserted, consisting of a set of equations with free parameters. These free parameters are then set or adjusted via learning rules that operate on a set of data. Models can be supervised (an explicit target output), unsupervised, where there is no explicit output target and a different goal, for example to have some particular spanning property in input space. Models can be trained offline where the free parameters are found deterministically, perhaps optimally via a single pass through the data (linear regression is in this category). Models can be trained online where the optimal parameter values are iteratively and incrementally approached through training rules that operate on a single training record at a time, such as a neural network model.

There is another class of models that approach the functional relationship approximation in a different spirit, through a set of equations that as best as possible attempt to describe the dynamics of the process being modeled. This is the approach of simulation.

In simulation, typically evolutionary/relationship equations are written down *a priori*, through the detailed expert knowledge of the dynamics of the problem to be simulated. These dynamic equations are then approximately solved, typically through a numerical framework that allows a solution, such as discretization of differential equations. Frequently these simulation dynamic equations have parameters that are expert adjusted, typically guided by experience. Note: experience is in some ways similar to "data." Experience is the expert synthesis of lots of data typically over many years of careful observation and thinking, but may have imbedded bias simply because we are subjective, irrational humans!

In some cases these underlying evolutionary equations are well known and describe the system dynamics with very little error, such as in hydrodynamic simulations that numerically solve a system of partial differential equations in space and time. For decades we have solved systems of differential equations numerically, and many robust modeling solutions are based on such numerical approximations. Even in cases where the underlying dynamics is very well understood and defined, like fluid flow, complex computer simulations are subject to many kinds of error, from intrinsic numeric approximation problems to physical properties that deviate from the underlying assumptions (viscosity, turbulence, surface tension, etc.). With such complex computer simulations experts are constantly improving numerical algorithms and comparing simulations to benchmarks/exact solutions and experiments. One can certainly consider these as a class, perhaps the first well-developed class, of simulations.

Often these evolutionary equations are not well known or understood, or otherwise have large uncertainties because the dynamics lies substantially outside of a well-understood theoretical framework, such as in econometrics or when dealing with human behavior. In these instances one can still write down a set of system evolution equations, guided by expert knowledge and with some first principles guidance (such as the percentages/probabilities of all possible states summing to one). These somewhat heuristic dynamic equations have free parameters imbedded in them that should be guided by data as much as possible, but the data is frequently sparse or virtually nonexistent. Thus the practitioner has the latitude to set these parameters using judgment, and one typically examines the system behavior over a range of likely parameter values.

We describe here a few examples of these heuristic simulations of complex systems that the authors have worked with in projects across various industries.

Example 10.2.1 Agriculture

This simulation was designed to help a global agricultural and chemical products company better understand the dynamics of nonlinear feedback mechanisms in the adoption of new, genetically modified seed. The company's products included special seed for a variety of crops, where each seed was genetically designed to optimally interact with a combination of special fertilizer, pesticide, and herbicide. The company was interested in how these new seeds might be adopted by U.S. farmers, and how to best introduce and market these new products.

In this simulation we had a multistate dynamic system, with five different crops (corn, potatoes, soybeans, peas, and tomatoes), both regular and genetically modified, and each with its appropriately coupled fertilizer, herbicide, and pesticide. At the beginning of the growing season each artificial farmer in the simulation would select an acreage for each of the possible products, and at the end of the season there would be a certain yield for each crop for these choices. Farmers would then communicate, sharing results, which would then affect their choices for the next year.

The results showed nonlinear feedback mechanisms of new product adoption that helped guide the company in its marketing and pricing campaigns.

Example 10.2.2 Banking, Portfolio Level Simulation

In this complex simulator we modeled a bank at a portfolio level, where the entities are product lines: credit cards, mortgages, auto loans, checking/savings accounts, and installment loans. The operator of the simulator is the manager of this entire collection of product portfolios, and the time scale is monthly steps. The bank interacts in an economic environment, with evolving interest rates, unemployment rates, cross country trade balance and other economic time factors. The bank manager must make decisions at each monthly time step about how to respond to an evolving economy, passing through an economic crisis such as hyperinflation, massive unemployment, and/or cross border financial risk. The manager selects levels for credit quality, marketing efforts, treasury actions including hedging, makes decisions about product pricing, collections actions, and other high-level portfolio level decisions.

This particular simulator was built as part of a training class designed to take teams of senior bank country managers through a simulated economic crisis, with the goal of learning about complex interactions of conflicting decisions and the balance between short- and long-term thinking. This project was driven and sponsored by the CEO of this global financial institution who challenged us, saying: "The first time I went through a financial crisis I lost 700 million dollars. The second time I made 800 million dollars. How do I get my country managers through that first time experience without having to actually live through it?"

Example 10.2.3 Banking, Consumer Agent-based Simulation

Here we simulated a large consumer banking portfolio using many millions of artificial consumer agents, each of which could subscribe to a variety of financial products including credit cards, mortgages, auto loans, installment loans, checking/savings accounts, and CDs. Each artificial consumer had established characteristics in gender, age, income, wealth, revolve/transact behavior, and credit quality. Each consumer was individual with a randomized set of characteristics, but these characteristics were set by the multidimensional distributions of the actual, real product portfolios, with the multidimensional nature ensuring reasonable internal self-consistency within each artificial consumer. The combined portfolio of the artificial consumers was thus initiated to statistically represent the real portfolio of the actual global, multiproduct bank who was our client.

These millions of artificial consumers each evolved on a monthly level following a set of deterministic evolutionary rules with some stochastic components. Consumers spent, borrowed, paid, went delinquent, went bankrupt, moved, and died according to the measured probabilities in the real portfolios, along with the use of the usual statistical credit, attrition, and bankruptcy models. Interest rates could be set by a user and the portfolio would evolve and the resulting profitability could be assessed.

This simulator could be used by marketing managers to introduce new products and prices into the portfolio and to see the adoption and reaction to these actions. It could also be used by the overall business managers to assess the balance between marketing and credit actions.

Example 10.2.4 Large Company Organizational Simulation

We built a simulation of corporate dynamics for the CTO office of a large global company. Here the entities were people, and they had a collection of quantified characteristics. They had age, gender, education, skill levels, attitude, stress levels. They were interconnected by formal and informal connections, with quantified connection levels of trust, communication, coordination and commitment. There were dynamic rules around task evolution and people characteristic evolution. The goal of the simulator was to examine the emergence of positive or negative cycles of interaction that lead to high or low productivity.

These heuristic simulations are very problematic when the underlying dynamics are not that well known, particularly when dealing with human behavior or other large complex systems of many interacting parts (e.g., weather or agent-based simulations). There are assumptions compounded on assumptions, and first-principle simulations of these complex systems quickly become difficult. The simulated system is completely determined by the mathematical model asserted at the outset, and is generally not forced to fit a large volume of data as in a statistical model approach, usually because this data doesn't exist (otherwise, a statistical model would likely be built). Often some of the unknown, expert-adjusted parameters provide weights for conflicting phenomena, and the resulting effects are quite sensitive to the settings of these parameters.

Thus, expert-asserted simulations of complex systems are highly suspect in their quantitative results. They can be excellent guides for qualitative behavior, and can frequently produce plausible scenarios. In this way they are adequate for training and learning. However, expert simulations are, in general, not good predictors, and should be viewed with skepticism for predictions.

10.3 Odds Normalization and Score Transformation

It is a common desire that a developed score has a physical or absolute meaning with respect to odds. We then need to normalize scores to a given scale. There are some circumstances when score normalization, sometimes called score alignment, calibration, or odds normalization, is necessary.

If the modeling data set is not completely representative of the entire population there are two ways to remedy this during the modeling process: with weights or without weights. If weights are used, the weights should make the data set to be the same as the real population and no score alignment is then necessary. If no weights are used, then a score alignment is necessary after the model is built.

In a segmentation approach, there are multiple scores and each independent score is developed from each data set of each segment. In this case we need to combine multiple scorecards into a single score that all have the same meaning.

Usually for risk scores the relationship between the score and the odds is

$$\text{score} \sim \ln(\text{odds}). \tag{10.16}$$

We can set a score s_0 at a given odds r_0 and also set the incremental score change Δs. In this way, when the score increases Δs, the odds double. The following table shows this setting.

Score	Odds
s_0	r_0
$s_0 + \Delta s$	$2\, r_0$
$s_0 + 2\,\Delta s$	$4\, r_0$
$s_0 + 3\,\Delta s$	$8\, r_0$
...	...
s	r

From this table we can summarize the relationship as

$$s - s_0 = \alpha \log_2 (r/r_0). \tag{10.17}$$

When the score increases Δs, the odds double:

$$\Delta s = \alpha \log_2(2) = \alpha. \tag{10.18}$$

Therefore we have

$$s - s_0 = \Delta s \log_2 (r/r_0). \tag{10.19}$$

For example, let the odds be 12:1 when score is 680. If we require that the odds double when the score increases 20 points, we have

$$s = 680 + 20 \log_2 (r/12). \tag{10.20}$$

The procedure of score transformation is as follows:

1. Bin the raw scores into n (say 50) bins and then calculate the log-odds in each bin as shown in the following table.

2. Build a relationship between the log-odds and the raw score. This function should be as simple as possible:

$$\log_2 r = f(\hat{y}). \tag{10.21}$$

3. Plug this function into the equation mentioned above to obtain the aligned score.

Bin	Raw Score ($\hat{y}$)	Log-Odds ($\log_2 r$)
1		
2		
...		
N		

As a result we have the aligned, calibrated score. Continuing the example above,

$$s = 680 + 20\, f(\hat{y}(x)) - 20 \log_2 (12), \tag{10.22}$$

where $\hat{y}(x)$ is a raw score for the input data x.

10.4   Reject Inference

Generally a model is built on whatever data is available. Frequently the resulting model will be used on all new data observations, sometimes on data intrinsically outside of the model training set. This is the general model problem often referred to as reject inference.

A good example is a model to adjudicate the applications for a product or service, often simply called an application model. In an application model, applications are scored as they come "through the door." Some are accepted and others are rejected. A model is built on the accepted data sample because that is the only data whose output is known (e.g., did they eventually pay their bills?). However, the resulting model will be implemented and used to evaluate both the accepted and rejected (the through the door population). Thus the model needs to be made robust to handling this other category of incoming applications that it has never seen, those that were rejected.

A typical approach is to use some of these rejects in the model training process, and to do so one generally must infer the likely outcome of the rejects. That is, to include the rejected applications (whose outcomes are not known since they were not booked/accepted) in the model building process along with the accepted applications (whose outcome is known), one must *infer* what the outcome would have been for these rejected applications. Hence the term "reject inference."

A common approach is to first build a model in the standard way using the accepted population. Once this model has been established we can score the rejected applications to assign a predicted outcome to those rejected applications. The previously built model can now be retrained using this larger set of both accepted and rejected applications, and the model is adjusted somewhat.

The process could be iterative:

1. Build model on the accepts.

2. Score the rejects.

3. Rebuild model using all observations.

4. Go to 2 until sufficient convergence.

There is a fundamental logical fallacy to this commonly used approach. In essence, by assigning the model output to the rejects, one is using and therefore simply reinforcing the original model. The model will indeed adjust slightly as it then sees these reject records as new data, but it mostly just reaffirms the original model. As a result the model should be able to better handle this wider data set, the through the door population without strange results. While indeed the model is now more robust to this broader through the door population, no new information was gleaned from including these rejects.

The positive side of this approach is that the model has now seen the entire universe of applications it will be scoring when implemented, and has hopefully been made somewhat robust to this previously unseen, rejected population which it must be able to score. The negative of this approach is that one has statistically degraded the model in the sense that it is no longer the optimal model for the applications whose output is known and certain, since that original, optimal model has been modified via the reject inference process. There is currently no really good approach to this perennial problem, although this methodology that we describe here is almost always used, perhaps with small variant details (such as weighting the rejects in the model rebuild process).

10.5 Dempster–Shafer Theory of Evidence

Dempster–Shafer theory, introduced around 1968 by Arthur Dempster and Glenn Shafer, is an alternative approach to estimating future possibilities and can be considered a generalization of Bayes inference approaches. This alternative construct deals with calculations of functions of belief, plausibility, and ignorance, using set theory viewpoints. These constructed functions are not probabilities in the strict sense and thus have spawned a host of controversies and religious wars about the mathematical soundness of this alternative approach. Regardless, the Dempster–Shafer theory has established a foothold in a few niche applications such as interpreting medical data. While the approach has its structural limitations, it does indeed provide quantifiable objective measures of the future likelihood of outcomes. We must recognize that these alternative functions to be constructed are not probabilities and thus do not obey all the nice machinery of probability functions. Nevertheless, this approach yields useful results and in particular is a good construct when dealing with systems containing uncertainty.

10.5.1 Some Properties in Set Theory

Let A be a set and $P(A)$ be its power set, that is, the set whose elements are all possible subsets of the set A. The number of elements of A is $|A|$. For example, for $A = \{a, b, c\}$, $|A| = 3$,

$$P(A) = \{\{a, b, c\}, \{a, b\}, \{b, c\}, \{c, a\}, \{a\}, \{b\}, \{c\}, \phi\}, \qquad (10.23)$$

with ϕ being the empty set. $|P(A)| = 2^{|A|} = 2^3 = 8$. For any two sets we have

$$|A \cup B| = |A| + |B| - |A \cap B|. \qquad (10.24)$$

For any three sets we have

$$|A \cup B \cup C| = |A| + |B| + |C| - |A \cap B| - |B \cap C| - |C \cap A| + |A \cap B \cap C|. \quad (10.25)$$

This can be generalized to the n-sets case, and is called the principle of inclusion-exclusion:

$$|A_1 \cup A_2 \cup \cdots \cup A_n| = \sum_j |A_j| - \sum_{j<k} |A_j \cap A_k| + \cdots + (-1)^{n+1} |A_1 \cap A_2 \cap \cdots \cap A_n|.$$
$$(10.26)$$

Let $f(A)$ be any function of set A. We have the following two equalities:

$$\sum_{C \subseteq B \subseteq A} (-1)^{|B-C|} f(C) = f(A), \quad (10.27)$$

and

$$\sum_{C \subseteq B \subseteq A} (-1)^{|A-B|} f(C) = f(A). \quad (10.28)$$

In order to prove the first equality, note that for a given subset C, the summation over B is $\sum_{m=k}^{n} C_{n-k}^{m-k} \cdot (-1)^{m-k} = (1-1)^{n-k} = 0$, where $|A| = n, |B| = m$, and $|C| = k$. In the same manner, for the second equality, for a given subset C, the summation over B is $\sum_{m=k}^{n} C_{n-k}^{m-k} \cdot (-1)^{n-m} = (-1)^{n-k} \cdot (1-1)^{n-k} = 0$. In each equality, all items with proper subsets on the left-hand side are canceled out. This demonstrates the validity of the equalities.

10.5.2 Basic Probability Assignment, Belief Function, and Plausibility Function

Let X be a universal set of mutually exclusive alternatives. The Dempster Shafer theory of evidence assigns a belief mass m to every element in the power set. The basic probability assignment is a function

$$m : P(X) \to [0, 1] \quad (10.29)$$

such that $m(\phi) = 0$ and $\sum_{A \in P(X)} m(A) = 1$. Note that $m(A)$ only claims evidence on the set A and it does not claim anything on its subset. Therefore there is not any relationship among $m(a, b), m(a)$, and $m(b)$. It is important to note the fundamental difference between probability distribution functions and basic probability assignments: the former are defined on X, while the latter are defined on $P(X)$.

The belief function is a function

$$Bel : P(X) \to [0, 1] \quad (10.30)$$

such that $Bel(\phi) = 0, Bel(X) = 1$, and

$$Bel(A_1 \cup A_2 \cup \cdots \cup A_n) \geq \sum_j Bel(A_j) - \sum_{j<k} Bel(A_j \cap A_j) + \cdots$$
$$+ (-1)^{n+1} Bel(A_1 \cap A_2 \cap \cdots \cap A_n). \quad (10.31)$$

Property 10.1: *If $B \subseteq A$, then $Bel(B) \subseteq Bel(A)$.*

Note that $A = B \cup (A - B)$.

$$
\begin{aligned}
Bel(A) &= Bel(B \cup (A - B)) \\
&\geq Bel(B) + Bel(A - B) - Bel(B \cap (A - B)) \\
&= Bel(B) + Bel(A - B) \quad\quad (10.32) \\
&\geq Bel(B).
\end{aligned}
$$

Property 10.2: $Bel(A) + Bel(\bar{A}) \leq 1$.

Note that $X = A \cup \bar{A}$.

$$
\begin{aligned}
Bel(X) &= Bel(A \cup \bar{A}) \\
&\geq Bel(A) + Bel(\bar{A}) - Bel(A \cap \bar{A}) \quad\quad (10.33) \\
&= Bel(A) + Bel(\bar{A}).
\end{aligned}
$$

The belief function can be expressed in terms of the basic probability assignment:

$$Bel(A) = \sum_{B \subseteq A} m(B). \quad\quad (10.34)$$

Note that there are some subsets in $A \cup B$ with an element a from A but not from B, and an element b from B but not from A. The consequence is that the belief function does not satisfy the principle of inclusion-exclusion. By using the equality of set functions mentioned in the previous section we can express the basic probability assignment in terms of the belief function:

$$m(A) = \sum_{B \subseteq A} (-1)^{|A-B|} Bel(B). \quad\quad (10.35)$$

Associated with each belief function is a plausibility function defined by

$$Pl(A) = 1 - Bel(\bar{A}). \quad\quad (10.36)$$

This can also be expressed in terms of basic probability function:

$$Pl(A) = \sum_{A \cap B \neq \phi} m(B). \quad\quad (10.37)$$

Note that $Bel(A) + Bel(\bar{A}) \leq 1$, and we have $Bel(A) \leq Pl(A)$. From the expressions of Bel and Pl in terms of m, it is clear to see this inequality.

From the definition of $Bel(A)$, the plausibility function can be defined formally as a function:

$$Pl : P(X) \rightarrow [0, 1], \quad\quad (10.38)$$

such that $Pl(\phi) = 0, Pl(X) = 1$, and

$$Pl(A_1 \cup A_2 \cup \cdots \cup A_n) \leq \sum_j Pl(A_j) - \sum_{j<k} Pl(A_j \cap A_j) + \cdots$$
$$+ (-1)^{n+1} Pl(A_1 \cap A_2 \cap \cdots \cap A_n). \tag{10.39}$$

Now we define the ignorance (uncertainty) as the difference between Bel and Pl:

$$\text{Ignorance}(A) = Pl(A) - Bel(A) = \sum_{B \cap A \neq \phi, B \cap \bar{A} \neq \phi} m(B). \tag{10.40}$$

With $Bel(A)$ and $Pl(A)$, the poorly known probability $Pr(A)$ is in the interval $[Bel(A), Pl(A)]$. The basic probability assignment, belief function, and plausibility function are related to one another. Once knowing any one function, the other two functions can be determined from the first one. The relationship of belief function, plausibility function, ignorance (uncertainty), and probability function is showed in the following diagram:

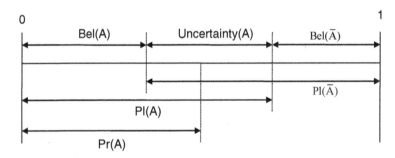

FIGURE 10.2: The relationship of belief function, plausibility function, ignorance (uncertainty), and probability function.

Here is an example showing that how this theory can help deal with uncertain information. Using probability theory to represent a system with uncertainty is generally not practical.

Example: A box contains 10 balls: 5 red, 3 green, 2 blue. The universal set is $X = \{r, g, b\}$. This is a system for which we have complete information. If we take a ball at random, the probability distribution is

$$Pr(r) = 0.5,$$
$$Pr(g) = 0.3, \tag{10.41}$$
$$Pr(b) = 0.2.$$

We understand this system completely, so we can quantify the distribution function completely.

TABLE 10.3: Basic probability assignment, belief function, and plausibility function for a system without complete information; probability function for a system with complete information.

Event	$\{r\}$	$\{g\}$	$\{b\}$	$\{r, g\}$	$\{r, b\}$	$\{g, b\}$	$\{r, g, b\}$
m	0.5	0.3	0.1	0	0	0	0.1
Bel	0.5	0.3	0.1	0.8	0.6	0.4	1
Pl	0.6	0.4	0.2	0.9	0.7	0.5	1
Probability given more evidence on x							
If x is red	0.6	0.3	0.1	0.9	0.7	0.4	1
If x is green	0.5	0.4	0.1	0.9	0.6	0.5	1
If x is blue	0.5	0.3	0.2	0.8	0.7	0.5	1

Now consider an example where we do not have complete information. A box contains 10 balls: 5 red, 3 green, 1 blue, and another ball (x) whose color is hidden from us (red, green, or blue). Then we can use the basic probability assignment to describe this system:

$$m(\{r\}) = 0.5,$$
$$m(\{g\}) = 0.3,$$
$$m(\{b\}) = 0.1, \tag{10.42}$$
$$m(\{r, g, b\}) = 0.1.$$

Bel and *Pl* can be calculated in terms of (10.34), (10.36), and (10.37), respectively, and are shown in the table. For example,

$$Bel(\{r, g\}) = m(\{r, g\}) + m(\{r\}) + m(\{g\}) = 0.5 + 0.3 = 0.8 \tag{10.43}$$

and

$$Pl(\{r, b\}) = 1 - Bel(\{g\}) = 1 - 0.3 = 0.7. \tag{10.44}$$

Once we have more information on unknown ball x, we can have the probability functions. It can be seen that, in any case, *Bel* and *Pl* provide the lower and upper boundaries of the distribution functions, respectively.

10.5.3 Dempster–Shafer's Rule of Combination

One of the advantages of the Dempster–Shafer construct is the practical way to combine information. Two evidences can be combined into stronger evidence. Dempster–Shafer's rule of combination is a convenient way to combine evidences. Note that from two evidences, represented in terms of the basic probability assignments m_1 and m_2, such that $\sum_B m_1(B) = 1$ and

$\sum_C m_2(C) = 1$, we have

$$
\begin{aligned}
1 &= \sum_B m_1(B) \cdot \sum_C m_2(C) = \sum_{B,C} m_1(B) \cdot m_2(C) \\
&= \sum_{B \cap C = \phi} m_1(B) \cdot m_2(C) + \sum_{A \neq \phi} \left[\sum_{B \cap C = A} m_1(B) \cdot m_2(C) \right].
\end{aligned}
\tag{10.45}
$$

Thus

$$
\sum_{A \neq \phi} \left[\frac{\displaystyle\sum_{B \cap C = A} m_1(B)\, m_2(C)}{1 - \displaystyle\sum_{B \cap C = \phi} m_1(B)\, m_2(C)} \right] = 1.
\tag{10.46}
$$

We can define the combination of basic probability assignments as

$$
m_{12}(A) = \frac{\displaystyle\sum_{B \cap C = A} m_1(B)\, m_2(C)}{1 - \displaystyle\sum_{B \cap C = \phi} m_1(B)\, m_2(C)}
\tag{10.47}
$$

for all $A \neq \phi$, and $m_{12}(\phi) = 0$. This satisfies $\sum_A m_{12}(A) = 1$. The following is an example of how to combine evidences.

Example: There has been a hit and run, and through license plate information there are three suspect vehicles: a silver Camry sedan, a red Sonata sedan, and an F-250 pickup truck. Thus X = {Camry, Sonata, Truck} $\equiv \{A, B, C\}$. Two police detectives interview witnesses, and get the following stories.

1. For the first detective, of 10 witnesses:

   - 5 think that they saw a sedan: $m_1(\{A, B\}) = 0.5$
   - 2 think that they saw a red vehicle: $m_1(\{B, C\}) = 0.2$
   - 3 express no opinion: $m_1(\{A, B, C\}) = 0.3$

2. For the second detecctive, of 10 witnesses:

   - 6 think that they saw a Camry: $m_2(\{A\}) = 0.6$
   - 4 express no opinion: $m_2(\{A, B, C\}) = 0.4$

Using the notation $0.5\{A, B\}$ to represent $m(\{A, B\}) = 0.5$, we can combine the evidences as follows.

$$
\begin{aligned}
&(0.5\{A, B\} + 0.2\{B, C\} + 0.3\{ABC\}) \cdot (0.6\{A\} + 0.4\{A, B, C\}) \\
&= 0.3\{A\} + 0.2\{A, B\} + 0.12\phi + 0.08\{B, C\} + 0.18\{A\} + 0.12\{A, B, C\} \\
&= 1.
\end{aligned}
\tag{10.48}
$$

TABLE 10.4: The combined evidences in terms of the basic probability assignment, belief function, and plausibility function.

Event	{A}	{B}	{C}	{A, B}	{A, C}	{B, C}	{A, B, C}
m_1	0	0	0	0.5	0	0.2	0.3
Bel_1	0	0	0	0.5	0	0.2	1
Pl_1	0.8	1	0.5	1	1	1	1
m_2	0.6	0	0	0	0	0	0.4
Bel_2	0.6	0	0	0.6	0.6	0	1
Pl_2	1	0.4	0.4	1	1	0.4	1
m_{12}	0.55	0	0	0.23	0	0.09	0.14
Bel_{12}	0.55	0	0	0.78	0.55	0.09	1
Pl_{12}	0.91	0.45	0.22	1	1	0.45	1

Therefore we have

$$\frac{0.48}{0.88}\{A\} + \frac{0.2}{0.88}\{A,B\} + \frac{0.08}{0.88}\{B,C\} + \frac{0.12}{0.88}\{A,B,C\} = 1. \qquad (10.49)$$

Then the basic probability assignments can be read from this equation

$$
\begin{aligned}
m_{12}(\{A\}) &= 0.48/0.88, \\
m_{12}(\{A,B\}) &= 0.2/0.88, \\
m_{12}(\{B,C\}) &= 0.08/0.88, \\
m_{12}(\{A,B,C\}) &= 0.12/0.88.
\end{aligned}
\qquad (10.50)
$$

Bel_{12} and Pl_{12} can be calculated from m_{12} in terms of (10.34), (10.36), and (10.37) as shown in last example. The complete description of the combined evidences in terms of the basic probability assignment, belief function, and plausibility function is shown in Table 10.4. It seems that our best choice using this combined evidence would be that the hit-and-run vehicle was the Camry.

10.5.4 Applications of Dempster–Shafer Theory of Evidence: Multiple Classifier Function

The Dempster–Shafer theory of evidence provides a framework to deal with a system with uncertain information. The general procedure is

1. Collect evidence

2. Combine evidence

3. Interpret evidence

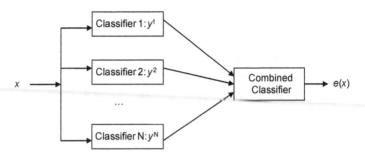

FIGURE 10.3: Multiple classifier function: Combine models using Dempster–Shafer theory.

This theory does not provide anything on how to identify and interpret evidence. Each step must be individually analyzed based on specifics on the problem.

Let's consider a problem described by Ng and Singh (1998) on how to combine multiple pattern classifiers into a single classifier so that the performance of the combined classifier is better than any single classifier. The following diagram shows the concept.

Each data point (x, y) belongs to one of K classes. Here the universal set X of mutually exclusive alternatives for the output y is $X = 1, 2, ..., K$. We construct N separate classifiers, where the output from the nth classifier $(n = 1, 2, ..., N)$ is a K-dimensional vector for each data input:

$$x \rightarrow y^n = f^n(x), \tag{10.51}$$

each y^n being a K-dimensional vector. We first calculate the evidence supporting that a data point belongs to class k from one of the classifiers n. Then we combine the evidence of class k from all the N classifiers using the Dempster–Shafer rule of combination. Let

$$r_k^n = \frac{\sum\limits_{x|y=k} y^n(x)}{\sum\limits_{y=k} 1} \tag{10.52}$$

be the center of all data points with $y = k$ in the K-dimensional space. The support function of class k is defined by using the Euclidean distance to this center:

$$s_k^n = 1 - \frac{1 + \|r_k^n - y^n\|^2}{1 + \sum\limits_{i=1}^{K} \|r_i^n - y^n\|^2}, \quad k = 1, 2, ..., K. \tag{10.53}$$

Then the support vector is written as

$$s^n = (s_1^n, s_2^n, ..., s_k^n, ..., s_K^n). \tag{10.54}$$

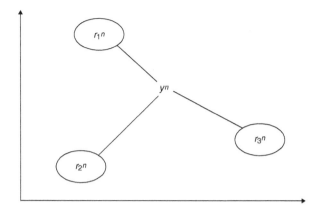

FIGURE 10.4: Multiple classifier function: The distances to the centers of the classes.

To support a data point belonging to class k, we observe that

- the larger s_k^n is, the stronger the support of belonging to class k, and

- the smaller s_i^n ($i \neq k$) is, the stronger the support of belonging to class k.

Now we can define K sets of evidences in terms of the basic probability assignments:

$$m_k(k) = s_k^n, \quad m_k(X) = 1 - s_k^n, \tag{10.55}$$

and

$$m_i(\bar{k}) = s_i^n, \quad m_i(X) = 1 - s_i^n, \quad i = 1, 2, \ldots, K, \quad \text{but} \quad i \neq k. \tag{10.56}$$

If we combine two evidences by using Dempster–Shafer's rule, $m_{i,j} = m_i \oplus m_j$ where $i \neq k$ and $j \neq k$, we have

$$m_{i,j}(\bar{k}) = 1 - (1 - s_i^n) \cdot (1 - s_j^n), \quad m_{i,j}(X) = (1 - s_i^n) \cdot (1 - s_j^n). \tag{10.57}$$

Recursively combining $K - 1$ evidences, $m_{\bar{k}} = m_1 \oplus \cdots \oplus m_{k-1} \oplus m_{k+1} \oplus \cdots \oplus m_K$, we have

$$m_{\bar{k}}(\bar{k}) = 1 - \prod_{i \neq k} (1 - s_i^n), \quad m_{\bar{k}}(X) = \prod_{i \neq k} (1 - s_i^n). \tag{10.58}$$

Finally, combining this with the first evidence, the focal elements are k, $\bar{k}$, X with

$$m_{k,\bar{k}}(k) = \frac{s_k^n \cdot \prod_{i \neq k} (1 - s_i^n)}{1 - s_k^n \cdot \left[1 - \prod_{i \neq k} (1 - s_i^n) \right]}. \tag{10.59}$$

The belief function will be $Bel(k) = m_{k,\bar{k}}(k)$. Now we can interpret $Bel(k)$, the evidence combined from K evidences, as the evidence for class k from classifier n:

$$e_k^n = \frac{s_k^n \cdot \prod_{i \neq k} (1 - s_i^n)}{1 - s_k^n \cdot \left[1 - \prod_{i \neq k} (1 - s_i^n)\right]}. \tag{10.60}$$

Finally, the total evidence for class k from all N classifiers is defined by

$$e_k = \sum_{n=1}^{N} e_k^n / N. \tag{10.61}$$

For each data point we can calculate the evidence of belonging to each of the possible classes:

$$e(x) = (e_1, e_2, ..., e_K). \tag{10.62}$$

A simple voting algorithm can be used to select the winner. The class with the maximum evidence indicates the class that the data point most likely belongs to.

Refer to the paper by Ng and Singh (1998) for the proof that the performance of the combined classifier is greater than or equal to the performance of any of the individual classifiers.

Appendix A

Useful Mathematical Relations

A.1 Information Inequality

Let $f(x)$ and $g(x)$ be two density functions in x. The following inequality holds

$$\int f(x) \ln g(x) dx \leq \int f(x) \ln f(x) dx \qquad (A.1)$$

with equality if and only if $f(x) = g(x)$ for all x. This can be easily proved by noting that $\ln x \geq 1 - 1/x$, and equality holds[1] if and only if $x = 1$. We have

$$\int f(x) \ln \left(\frac{f(x)}{g(x)} \right) dx \geq \int f(x) \left(1 - \frac{g(x)}{f(x)} \right) dx = \int \left(f(x) - g(x) \right) dx = 0 \qquad (A.2)$$

with equality if $f(x)/g(x) = 1$ for all x. For discrete density functions we have

$$I = \sum_\alpha f_\alpha \ln \left(f_\alpha / g_\alpha \right) \geq 0. \qquad (A.3)$$

It can be proved in the same way.

A.2 Relative Entropy

Let $p(x)$ and $q(x)$ be two population distributions in terms of a single variable x. The relative entropy or (symmetric) Kullback–Leibler distance between $p(x)$ and $q(x)$ is defined by

$$E[p, q] = \int dx [p(x) - q(x)] \cdot \ln \left(p(x)/q(x) \right) \qquad (A.4)$$

---

[1] It is much easier to see that $\ln x \leq x - 1$ from the shape of the curve of $\ln x$. By changing variable, $x \to 1/x$, we have $\ln x \geq 1 - 1/x$.

or, if x is discretized,

$$E[p, q] = \sum_i [p_i - q_i] \cdot \ln (p_i/q_i). \tag{A.5}$$

Because the signs of $p - q$ and $\ln(p/q)$ are always the same, it is obvious to see that the relative entropy is non-negative and is zero if and only if the distributions $p(x)$ and $q(x)$ are identical. For two Gaussian distributions, $N(\mu_1, \sigma_1^2)$ and $N(\mu_2, \sigma_2^2)$, with means μ_1, μ_2 and variances σ_1^2, σ_2^2, respectively, the relative entropy has an analytical expression

$$E[N(\mu_1, \sigma_1^2), N(\mu_2, \sigma_2^2)] = \frac{\left(\sigma_1^2 - \sigma_2^2\right)^2}{2\sigma_1^2\sigma_2^2} + \frac{\left(\sigma_1^2 + \sigma_2^2\right)}{2\sigma_1^2\sigma_2^2} \cdot (\mu_1 - \mu_2)^2. \tag{A.6}$$

It is an interesting exercise to derive this equation. In particular, for two Gaussian distributions with the same variance, the relative entropy has the simplified form

$$E[N(\mu_1, \sigma^2), N(\mu_2, \sigma^2)] = (\mu_1 - \mu_2)^2/\sigma^2. \tag{A.7}$$

This form is exactly the same as the objective function in Fisher's linear discriminant analysis.

A.3   Saddle-Point Method

Let's evaluate the integration in the limit

$$I(\alpha) = \int f(x) e^{\alpha g(x)} dx, \qquad \alpha \to \infty. \tag{A.8}$$

As $\alpha \to \infty$, the major contribution of this integration comes from the neighbor of the maximum point of $g(x)$, $g'(x_0) = 0$, $g''(x_0) < 0$. Expanding $f(x)$ and $g(x)$ around x_0 and letting $\Delta x = x - x_0$, we have

$$f(x)e^{\alpha g(x)} = \left[f(x_0) + f'(x_0)(\Delta x) + \tfrac{1}{2}f''(x_0)(\Delta x)^2 + ...\right]$$
$$\times e^{\alpha\left[g(x_0)+g'(x_0)(\Delta x)+\frac{1}{2!}g''(x_0)(\Delta x)^2+\frac{1}{3!}g^{(3)}(x_0)(\Delta x)^3+\frac{1}{4!}g^{(4)}(x_0)(\Delta x)^4+...\right]}. \tag{A.9}$$

Let $y = \sqrt{\alpha}(x - x_0)$. This becomes

$$f(x)e^{\alpha g(x)} = e^{\alpha g(x_0)+\frac{1}{2}g''(x_0)y^2}\left[f(x_0) + f'(x_0)\tfrac{y}{\sqrt{\alpha}} + \tfrac{1}{2!}f''(x_0)\tfrac{y^2}{\alpha} + ...\right]$$
$$\times e^{\frac{1}{3!}g^{(3)}(x_0)\frac{y^3}{\sqrt{\alpha}}+\frac{1}{4!}g^{(4)}(x_0)\frac{y^4}{\alpha}+...}. $$

$$\tag{A.10}$$

Noting that

$$e^{\frac{1}{3!}g^{(3)}(x_0)\frac{y^3}{\sqrt{\alpha}}+\frac{1}{4!}g^{(4)}(x_0)\frac{y^4}{\alpha}+\cdots} = 1 + \frac{1}{3!}g^{(3)}(x_0)\frac{y^3}{\sqrt{\alpha}} + \frac{1}{4!}g^{(4)}(x_0)\frac{y^4}{\alpha}$$
$$+ \frac{1}{72}\left(g^{(3)}(x_0)\right)^2\frac{y^6}{\alpha} + \cdots, \tag{A.11}$$

we have

$$f(x)e^{\alpha g(x)} = e^{\alpha g(x_0)+\frac{1}{2}g''(x_0)y^2}$$
$$\times \left\{ f + \frac{1}{4!}fg^{(4)}\frac{y^4}{\alpha} + \frac{1}{72}f\left(g^{(3)}\right)^2\frac{y^6}{\alpha} + \frac{1}{3!}f'g^{(3)}\frac{y^4}{\alpha} + \frac{1}{2!}f''\frac{y^2}{\alpha} + \cdots \right\}. \tag{A.12}$$

Using the integration

$$\int_{-\infty}^{\infty} e^{-\frac{1}{2}\beta y^2} y^{2n}\, dy = \sqrt{2\pi}(2n-1)!!\beta^{-\frac{2n+1}{2}}, \tag{A.13}$$

we have

$$\int f(x)\,e^{\alpha g(x)}dx = e^{\alpha g(x_0)}\sqrt{\frac{2\pi}{-\alpha g''(x_0)}} \times \left\{ f(x_0) + \frac{1}{\alpha}\left[\frac{1}{8}\cdot\frac{f(x_0)g^{(4)}(x_0)}{(g''(x_0))^2}\right.\right.$$
$$\left.\left. - \frac{5}{24}\cdot\frac{f(x_0)\left(g^{(3)}(x_0)\right)^2}{(g''(x_0))^3} + \frac{1}{2}\cdot\frac{f'(x_0)g^{(3)}(x_0)}{(g''(x_0))^2} - \frac{1}{2}\cdot\frac{f''(x_0)}{g''(x_0)}\right]\right\}. \tag{A.14}$$

In the next section we will give an example of using this expansion to prove Stirling's formula.

A.4   Stirling's Formula

The gamma function is defined by $\Gamma(x) \equiv \int_0^{\infty} t^{x-1}e^{-t}dt$ with the following properties: $\Gamma(x+1) = x\Gamma(x)$, $\Gamma(n+1) = n!$, and $\Gamma(1/2) = \sqrt{\pi}$. Stirling's formula is useful to estimate the function for large arguments:

$$\Gamma(x+1) = (x/e)^x\sqrt{2\pi x}\,[1+o(1)] \qquad x \to \infty. \tag{A.15}$$

We give a simple interpretation of Stirling's formula. By constructing an integral of the function $\ln(x)$ from 1 to n, we have

$$\int_1^n \ln x\, dx < \ln n! < \int_1^n \ln x\, dx + \ln n. \tag{A.16}$$

This leads to

$$n\ln n - (n-1) < \ln n! < (n+1)\ln n - (n-1). \tag{A.17}$$

Therefore we can write it as

$$\ln n! = (n + \alpha) \ln n - (n - 1) \tag{A.18}$$

where $0 < \alpha < 1$. Namely

$$n! = (n/e)^n \, n^\alpha \, e. \tag{A.19}$$

Making the approximation $\alpha \approx 0.5$ and $e \approx \sqrt{2\pi}$ we obtain Stirling's formula:

$$n! \approx (n/e)^n \sqrt{2\pi n}. \tag{A.20}$$

We can obtain a more accurate approximation from the saddle-point method discussed in the previous section. Note that

$$n! = \Gamma(n + 1) = \int_0^\infty t^n e^{-t} dt = \int_0^\infty e^{n \ln t - t} dt. \tag{A.21}$$

Let $t = nx$ and $g(x) = \ln x - x$, we have

$$n! = n^{n+1} \int_0^\infty e^{ng(x)} dx. \tag{A.22}$$

$g(x)$ is maximum at $x_0 = 1$. We immediately reach Stirling's formula to the order of $1/n$:

$$n! \approx (n/e)^n \sqrt{2\pi n} \left(1 + \frac{1}{12n}\right). \tag{A.23}$$

A.5 Convex Function and Jensen's Inequality

A function such as the quadratic function, x^2, is a convex function. In general it is defined as follows: A function $f : R^n \to R$ is a convex function if for any two points x and y, and $0 \le \alpha \le 1$, it satisfies the inequality:

$$f(\alpha x + (1 - \alpha)y) \le \alpha f(x) + (1 - \alpha)f(y). \tag{A.24}$$

This is called Jensen's inequality. How do we determine if a function is a convex function? The following three properties are equivalent to one another; use them to determine whether a function is a convex function:

1. $\nabla^2 f$ is positive semi-definite. In the one-dimensional case, $f'' \ge 0$.

2. $f(y) \ge f(x) + \nabla f(x) \cdot (y - x)$ for any x and y.

3. $f(\alpha x + (1 - \alpha)y) \le \alpha f(x) + (1 - \alpha)f(y)$.

To see the equivalence of 1 and 2 note that the third term in the Taylor expansion is $\frac{1}{2!}(y - x)^T \nabla^2 f(\xi)(y - x)$, and it follows immediately. To see the equivalence of 1 and 3, note that

$$f(x) \geq f(\alpha x + (1 - \alpha)y) + \nabla f(\alpha x + (1 - \alpha)y) \cdot (1 - \alpha)(x - y), \quad \text{(A.25)}$$

$$f(y) \geq f(\alpha x + (1 - \alpha)y) + \nabla f(\alpha x + (1 - \alpha)y) \cdot (-\alpha)(x - y), \quad \text{(A.26)}$$

so we have 3 from 1. From 3, the Taylor expansion at y shows that

$$f(\alpha x + (1-\alpha)y) = f(y) + \nabla f(y) \cdot \alpha(x-y) + \frac{1}{2!}\alpha^2(x - y)^T \nabla^2 f(\xi)(x-y), \quad \text{(A.27)}$$

$$\alpha f(x) + (1 - \alpha)f(y) = f(y) + \nabla f(y) \cdot \alpha(x - y) + \frac{1}{2!}\alpha(x - y)^T \nabla^2 f(\xi)(x - y). \quad \text{(A.28)}$$

When $x \to y$, $(x - y)^T \nabla^2 f(y)(x - y) \geq 0$. It is positive semi-definite.

Jensen's inequality can be generalized into multiple terms. By the method of induction we can prove that for $0 \leq \alpha_i \leq 1$, $\sum_i \alpha_i = 1$, we have

$$f\left(\sum_i \alpha_i x_i\right) \leq \sum_i \alpha_i f(x_i). \quad \text{(A.29)}$$

Let $p(x)$ be a distribution of x. Then we have

$$f\left(\sum_i p_i x_i\right) \leq \sum_i p_i f(x_i) \quad \text{(A.30)}$$

or in terms of expectation value, we have:

$$f(E[x]) \leq E[f(x)]. \quad \text{(A.31)}$$

The third property of the convex function is more general. It is still valid for non-smooth functions. For example, it is easy to see that $f(x) = \max(x, c)$ is a convex function. We then have

$$\max\left(\sum_i \alpha_i x_i, c\right) \leq \sum_i \alpha_i \max(x_i, c). \quad \text{(A.32)}$$

Analogously, $f(x) = \min(x, c)$ is a concave function. We have

$$\min\left(\sum_i \alpha_i x_i, c\right) \geq \sum_i \alpha_i \min(x_i, c). \quad \text{(A.33)}$$

Finally, here we give some applications of Jensen's inequality.

Lemma A.1 *The arithmetic mean is larger than the geometric mean:*

$$\frac{x_1 + x_2 + \ldots + x_n}{n} \geq (x_1 x_2 \ldots x_n)^{1/n}. \quad \text{(A.34)}$$

Proof A.1 *Note that* $-\ln(x)$ *is a convex function, and in terms of Jensen's inequality we have*

$$-\ln\left(\frac{x_1 + x_2 + \ldots + x_n}{n}\right) \le -\frac{1}{n}(\ln x_1 + \ln x_2 + \ldots + \ln x_n). \qquad (A.35)$$

Then the result immediately follows.

Lemma A.2 $f(x) = \left(\frac{a_1^x + a_2^x + \ldots + a_n^x}{n}\right)^{1/x}$ *is an increasing function of* x.

Proof A.2 *Defining* $g(x) = \ln f(x) = \frac{1}{x}\ln\left(\frac{a_1^x + a_2^x + \ldots + a_n^x}{n}\right)$, *we have*

$$g'(x) = \frac{1}{x^2}\frac{n}{\sum\limits_{i=1}^{n} a_i^x}\left(\frac{\sum\limits_{i=1}^{n} a_i^x \ln a_i^x}{n} - \frac{\sum\limits_{i=1}^{n} a_i^x}{n}\ln\frac{\sum\limits_{i=1}^{n} a_i^x}{n}\right). \qquad (A.36)$$

Note that $h(x) = x \ln x$ *is a convex function since* $h''(x) = 1/x > 0$. *Choose* $\alpha_i = 1/n$, $y_i = a_i^x$, *and from Jensen's inequality, we have*

$$\frac{1}{n}\sum_{i=1}^{n} a_i^x \ln\left(\frac{1}{n}\sum_{i=1}^{n} a_i^x\right) \le \frac{1}{n}\sum_{i=1}^{n} a_i^x \ln a_i^x. \qquad (A.37)$$

Therefore $g'(x) \ge 0$ *and* $f'(x) \ge 0$. *It is an increasing function of* x.

Some examples in increasing order are

$$f(-\infty) = \lim_{x \to -\infty}\left(\frac{a_1^x + a_2^x + \ldots + a_n^x}{n}\right)^{1/x} = \min(a_i) \qquad \text{Minimum}$$

$$f(-1) = \frac{1}{(a_1^{-1} + a_2^{-1} + \ldots + a_n^{-1})/n} \qquad \text{Harmonic mean}$$

$$f(0) = \lim_{x \to 0}\left(\frac{a_1^x + a_2^x + \ldots + a_n^x}{n}\right)^{1/x} = (a_1 a_2 \ldots a_n)^{1/n} \qquad \text{Geometric mean}$$

$$f(1) = \frac{a_1 + a_2 + \ldots + a_n}{n} \qquad \text{Arithmetic mean}$$

$$f(2) = \left(\frac{a_1^2 + a_2^2 + \ldots + a_n^2}{n}\right)^{1/2} \qquad \text{Squared mean}$$

$$f(\infty) = \lim_{x \to \infty}\left(\frac{a_1^x + a_2^x + \ldots + a_n^x}{n}\right)^{1/x} = \max(a_i) \qquad \text{Maximum}$$

Lemma A.3 *If* $f(0) = f(1) = 0$ *and* $f''(x) \ge 0$ *for all* $x \in [0, 1]$, *then* $f(x) \le 0$ *for all* $x \in [0, 1]$. *Further if there exists* x_0 $(x_0 \ne 0, 1)$ *such that* $f(x_0) = 0$ *then* $f(x) = 0$ *for all* $x \in [0, 1]$.

Proof A.3 *For any x, we can find an α such that*

$$f(x) \leq \alpha f(0) + (1 - \alpha)f(1) = 0. \tag{A.38}$$

For any points $x_1 < x_0$ and $x_2 > x_0$, we can find an α such that

$$f(x_0) \leq \alpha f(x_1) + (1 - \alpha)f(x_2). \tag{A.39}$$

Thus

$$\alpha f(x_1) + (1 - \alpha)f(x_2) \geq 0. \tag{A.40}$$

Since $f(x)$ is non-positive, we have $f(x) = 0$ for all x in $[0, 1]$.

This lemma is used in Section 5.3.4 to justify the validity of the entropy and the Gini index as the impurity measures.

Appendix B

DataMinerXL – Microsoft Excel
Add-In for Building Predictive Models

B.1   Overview

This appendix describes the DataMinerXL library, a Microsoft Excel add-in for building predictive models.

DataMinerXL is an add-in XLL, which is a DLL (Dynamic-Link Library) designed for Microsoft Excel. The algorithms in DataMinerXL library are implemented in C++. It serves as a core engine while Excel is focused on its role in creating a neat presentation or layout for input/output as a familiar user interface. By combining the strengths of both C++ and Excel, the calculation-intensive routines implemented in C++ are integrated into the convenient Excel environment. After the add-in is installed and loaded into Excel the functions in the add-in can be used exactly the same way as the built-in functions in Excel.

In this appendix we describe each function in DataMinerXL. In the last section we list Excel built-in statistical distribution functions for reference. The detailed descriptions of all functions, such as function arguments and return values, can be found in a separate document, "DataMinerXL – Microsoft Excel Add-in for Building Predictive Models," at the following website. You can find the description on how to install the add-in and some tips of using Excel at the same document. More information, such as how to download the add-in and sample spreadsheets can be found at this website:

www.DataMinerXL.com.

B.2   Utility Functions

version Displays the version number and build date/time of DataMinerXL library

function_list Lists all functions in DataMinerXL library

B.3   Data Manipulation Functions

variable_list Lists the variable names in an input data file

subset Gets a subset of a data table

data_save Saves a data table into a file

data_save_tex Saves a data table into a file in TEX format

data_load Loads a data table from a file

sort_file Sorts a data file given keys and orders

B.4   Basic Statistical Functions

ranks Creates 1-based ranks of data points given a column of data

ranks_from_file Creates 1-based ranks of data points given a data file

freq Creates frequency tables given a data table

freq_from_file Creates frequency tables given a data file

freq_2d Creates a frequency cross-table for two variables given a data table

freq_2d_from_file Creates a frequency cross-table for two variables given a data file

means Generates basic statistics: sum, average, standard deviation, minimum, and maximum given a data table

means_from_file Generates basic statistics: sum, average, standard deviation, minimum, and maximum given a data file

univariate Generates univariate statistics given a data table

univariate_from_file Generates univariate statistics given a data file

summary Generates descriptive statistics in classes given a data table

summary_from_file Generates descriptive statistics in classes given a data file

binning Creates equal interval binning given a column of data table

B.5   Modeling Functions for All Models

model_bin_eval Evaluates a binary target model given a column of actual values and a column of predicted values

model_bin_eval_from_file Evaluates a binary target model given a data file, a name of actual values, and a name of predicted values

model_cont_eval Evaluates a continuous target model given a column of actual values and a column of predicted values

model_cont_eval_from_file Evaluates a continuous target model given a data file, a name of actual values, and a name of predicted values

model_eval Evaluates model performance given a model and a data table

model_eval_from_file Evaluates model performance given a model and a data file

model_score Scores a population given a model and a data table

model_score_from_file Scores a population given a model and a data file

model_save_scoring_code Saves the scoring code of a given model to a file

B.6   Weight of Evidence Transformation Functions

woe_xcont_ybin Generates weight of evidence (WOE) of continous independent variables and a binary dependent variable given a data table

woe_xcont_ybin_from_file Generates weight of evidence (WOE) of continous independent variables and a binary dependent variable given a data file

woe_xcont_ycont Generates weight of evidence (WOE) of continous independent variables and a continous dependent variable given a data table

woe_xcont_ycont_from_file Generates weight of evidence (WOE) of continous independent variables and a continous dependent variable given a data file

woe_xcat_ybin Generates weight of evidence (WOE) of categorical independent variables and a binary dependent variable given a data table

woe_xcat_ybin_from_file Generates weight of evidence (WOE) of categorical independent variables and a binary dependent variable given a data file

woe_xcat_ycont Generates weight of evidence (WOE) of categorical independent variables and a continous dependent variable given a data table

woe_xcat_ycont_from_file Generates weight of evidence (WOE) of categorical independent variables and a continous dependent variable given a data file

woe_transform Performs weight of evidence (WOE) transformation given aWOE model and a data table

woe_transform_from_file Performs weight of evidence (WOE) transformation given a WOE model and a data file

B.7 Linear Regression Functions

linear_reg Builds a linear regression model given a data table

linear_reg_from_file Builds a linear regression model given a data file

linear_reg_forward_select Builds a linear regression model by forward selection given a data table

linear_reg_forward_select_from_file Builds a linear regression model by forward selection given a data file

linear_reg_score_from_coefs Scores a population from the coefficients of a linear regression model given a data table

linear_reg_piecewise Builds a two-segment piecewise linear regression model for each variable given a data table

linear_reg_piecewise_from_file Builds a two-segment piecewise linear regression model for each variable given a data file

B.8 Partial Least Squares Regression Functions

pls_reg Builds a partial least square regression model given a data table

pls_reg_from_file Builds a partial least square regression model given a data file

B.9 Logistic Regression Functions

logistic_reg Builds a logistic regression model given a data table

logistic_reg_from_file Builds a logistic regression model given a data file

logistic_reg_forward_select Builds a logistic regression model by forward selection given a data table

logistic_reg_forward_select_from_file Builds a logistic regression model by forward selection given a data file

logistic_reg_score_from_coefs Scores a population from the coefficients of a logistic regression model given a data table

B.10 Time Series Analysis Functions

ts_acf Calculates the autocorrealtion functions (ACF) given a data table

ts_pacf Calculates the partial autocorrealtion functions (ACF) given a data table

lowess Performs locally weighted scatterplot smoothing (lowess)

natural_cubic_spline Performs natural cubic spline

garch Estimates the parameters of GARCH(1, 1) (generalized autoregressive conditional heteroscedasticity) model

B.11 Naive Bayes Classifier Functions

naive_bayes_classifier Builds a naive Bayes classification model given a data table

naive_bayes_classifier_from_file Builds a naive Bayes classification model given a data file

B.12 Tree-Based Model Functions

tree Builds a regression or classification tree model given a data table

tree_from_file Builds a regression or classification tree model given a data file

tree_boosting_logistic_reg Builds a logistic boosting tree model given a data table

tree_boosting_logistic_reg_from_file Builds a logistic boosting tree model given a data file

tree_boosting_ls_reg Builds a least square boosting tree model given a data table

tree_boosting_ls_reg_from_file Builds a least square boosting tree model given a data file

B.13 Clustering and Segmentation Functions

k_means Performs K-means clustering analysis given a data table

k_means_from_file Performs K-means clustering analysis given a data file

cmds Performs classical multi-dimensional scaling

B.14 Neural Network Functions

neural_net Builds a neural network model given a data table

neural_net_from_file Builds a neural network model given a data file

B.15 Support Vector Machine Functions

svm Builds a support vector machine (SVM) model given a data table

svm_from_file Builds a support vector machine (SVM) model given a data file

B.16 Optimization Functions

linear_prog Solves a linear programming problem

quadratic_prog Solves a quadratic programming problem

B.17 Matrix Operation Functions

matrix_cov Computes the covariance matrix given a data table

matrix_cov_from_file Computes the covariance matrix given a data file

matrix_corr Computes the correlation matrix given a data table

matrix_corr_from_file Computes the correlation matrix given a data file

matrix_corr_from_cov Computes the correlation matrix from a covariance matrix

matrix_prod Computes the product of two matrices, one matrix could be a number

matrix_plus Computes the addition of two matrices with the same dimension

matrix_minus Computes the subtraction of two matrices with the same dimension

matrix_t Returns the transpose matrix of a matrix

matrix_inv Computes the inverse of a square matrix

matrix_pinv Computes the pseudoinverse of a matrix

matrix_solve Solves a system of linear equations $Ax = B$

matrix_chol Computes the Cholesky decomposition of a symmetric positive-definite matrix

matrix_sym_eigen Computes the eigenvalue-eigenvector pairs of a symmetric matrix

matrix_eigen Computes the eigenvalue-eigenvector pairs of a square real matrix

matrix_svd Computes the singular value decomposition (SVD) of a matrix

matrix_LU Computes the LU decomposition of a square matrix

matrix_QR Computes the QR decomposition of a square matrix

matrix_det Computes the determinant of a square matrix

matrix_random Generates a random matrix from the uniform distibution $U(0, 1)$ or a standard normal distribution $N(0, 1)$

B.18 Numerical Integration Functions

gauss_legendre Generates the abscissas and weights of the Gauss–Legendre n-point quadrature formula

gauss_laguerre Generates the abscissas and weights of the Gauss–Laguerre n-point quadrature formula

gauss_hermite Generates the abscissas and weights of the Gauss–Hermite n-point quadrature formula

---

B.19 Excel Built-in Statistical Distribution Functions

BETADIST Returns the beta cumulative distribution function

BETAINV Returns the inverse of the cumulative distribution function for a specified beta distribution

BINOMDIST Returns the individual term binomial distribution probability

CHIDIST Returns the one-tailed probability of the chi-squared distribution

CHIINV Returns the inverse of the one-tailed probability of the chi-squared distribution

CRITBINOM Returns the smallest value for which the cumulative binomial distribution is less than or equal to a criterion value

EXPONDIST Returns the exponential distribution

FDIST Returns the *F*-probability distribution

FINV Returns the inverse of the *F*-probability distribution

GAMMADIST Returns the gamma distribution

GAMMAINV Returns the inverse of the gamma cumulative distribution

HYPGEOMDIST Returns the hypergeometric distribution

LOGINV Returns the inverse of the lognormal distribution

LOGNORMDIST Returns the cumulative lognormal distribution

NEGBINOMDIST Returns the negative binomial distribution

NORMDIST Returns the normal cumulative distribution

NORMINV Returns the inverse of the normal cumulative distribution

NORMSDIST Returns the standard normal cumulative distribution

NORMSINV Returns the inverse of the standard normal cumulative distribution

POISSON Returns the Poisson distribution

TDIST Returns the Student's *t*-distribution

TINV Returns the inverse of the Student's *t*-distribution

WEIBULL Returns the Weibull distribution

Bibliography

[1] Beale, R. and Jackson, T. (1990), *Neural Computing: An Introduction*, Bristol, UK: Institute of Physics Publishing.

[2] Belsley, D.A., Kul, E., and Welsch, R.E. (1980), *Regression Diagnostics*, New York: John Wiley & Sons.

[3] Bishop, C. M. (2006), *Pattern Recognition and Machine Learning*, New York: Springer.

[4] Blinnikov, S. and Moessner, R. (1998), Expansions for nearly Gaussian distributions, em Astronomy and astrophysics Supplement series, 130: 193205.

[5] Boser, B. E., Guyon, I., and Vapnik, V. (1992), A training algorithm for optimal margin classifiers. *In Proceedings of the Fifth Annual Workshop on Computational Learning Theory*, 144–152. New York: ACM Press.

[6] Boyd, S. and Vandenberghe, L. (2004), *Convex Optimization*, Cambridge University Press, Cambridge.

[7] Breiman, L., Friedman, J., Olshen, R., and Stone, C. (1984), *Classification and Regression Trees*, Wadsworth.

[8] Brockwell, P. J. and Davis, R. A. (1991), *Time Series: Theory and Methods*, 2nd edition, New York: Springer-Verlag.

[9] Bronson, R. and Naadimuthu, G. (1997), *Schaum's Outlines of Theory and Problems of Operations Research*, 2nd edition, New York: McGraw-Hill.

[10] Chang, C.C. and Lin, C.J. (2011), LIBSVM : a library for support vector machines. *ACM Transactions on Intelligent Systems and Technology*, 2:27:1–27:27. Software available at http://www.csie.ntu.edu.tw/~cjlin/libsvm.

[11] Chatfield, C. (1996), *The Analysis of Time Series: An Introduction*, 5th edition, London: Chapman & Hall.

[12] Cornish, E. A. and Fisher, R. A. (1937), Moments and Cumulants in the Specification of Distributions. *Extrait de la Revue de l'Institute International de Statistique* 4, 1–14, 1937. Reprinted in Fisher, R. A. *Contributions to Mathematical Statistics*. New York: Wiley, 1950.

[13] Cortes, C. and Vapnik, V. (1995), Support-Vector Network. *Machine Learning*, 20:273–297.

[14] Cox, T. F. and Cox, M.A.A. (2000), *Multidimensional Scaling*, 2nd edition, Chapman & Hall/CRC.

[15] Drezner, Z. (1978), Computation of the Bivariate Normal Integral, *Mathematics of Computation*, 32, 277–279.

[16] Friedman, J. H. (1999), Stochastic Gradient Boosting. *Technical Report*, Dept. of Statistics, Stanford University, Stanford, CA.

[17] Friedman, J. H. (2001), Greedy Function Approximation: A Gradient Boosting Machine, *Annals of Statistics*, 29:5, 1189–1232.

[18] Greene, W. H. (1997), *Econometric Analysis*, 3rd edition, Upper Saddle River, NJ: Prentice-Hall.

[19] Hastie, T., Tibshirani, R., and Friedman, J. (2001), *The Elements of Statistical Learning: Data Mining, Inference, and Prediction*, New York: Springer.

[20] Hertz, J., Krogh, A., and Palmer, R. G. (1991), *Introduction to the Theory of Neural Computation*, Westview Press.

[21] Hock, W. and Schittkowski, K. (1981), *Test Examples for Nonlinear Programming Codes*, Lecture Notes in Economics and Mathematical Systems 187, New York: Springer-Verlag.

[22] Holt, C. C. (1957), Forecasting Seasonals and Trends by Exponentially Weighted Moving Averages, *International Journal of Forecasting*, 20:1

[23] Hosmer, D. W. and Lemeshow, S. (1989), *Applied Logistic Regression*, New York: John Wiley.

[24] Igel, C. and Husken, M. (2000), Improving the Rprop Learning Algorithm, *Proceedings of the Second International Symposium on Neural Computation, NC2000*, pp. 115–121, Zürich, Switzerland: ICSC Academic Press.

[25] Jaschke, S. (2002), The Cornish–Fisher-Expansion in the Context of Delta–Gamma-Normal Approximations, *J. Risk*, 4:4, 33–52.

[26] Johnson, R. A. and Wichern, D. W. (1992), *Applied Multivariate Statistical Analysis*, 3rd edition, Englewood Cliffs, NJ: Prentice-Hall.

[27] Lagarias, J. C., Reeds, J. A., Wright, M. H., and Wright, P. E. (1998), Convergence Properties of the Nelder-Mead Simplex Method in Low Dimensions, *SIAM Journal of Optimization*, 9:1, 112–147.

[28] Lemke, C.E. (1965), Bimatrix Equilibrium Points and Mathematical Programming, *Management Science*, 11, 681–689.

[29] Lewis, E. M. (1992), *An Introduction to Credit Scoring*, 2nd edition, San Raphael, CA: Fair, Isaac and Co. Inc.

[30] Lin, Y., Cunningham, G., and Coggeshall, S. (1996), Input Variable Identification – Fuzzy Curves and Fuzzy Surfaces, *Journal of Fuzzy Sets and Systems*, 82:1.

[31] Martens, H. and Naes, T. (1989), *Multivariate Calibration*, New York: Wiley.

[32] Matsumoto, M. and Nishimura, T., Mersenne Twister home page, http://www.math.sci.hiroshima-u.ac.jp/~m-mat/MT/emt.html.

[33] Mendel, J. M. (1995), Fuzzy Logic Systems for Engineering: A Tutorial, *Proceedings of the IEEE*, Vol. 83, No. 3, 345–377.

[34] Mersenne Twister, Wikipedia page on Mersenne Twister, http://en.wikipedia.org/wiki/Mersenne_twister.

[35] McCullagh, P. and Nelder, J.A. (1989), *Generalized Linear Models*, 2nd edition, London: Chapman & Hall.

[36] Monahan, J. F. (2001), *Numerical Methods of Statistics*, Cambridge: Cambridge University Press.

[37] Murty, K.G. (1988), *Linear Complementarity, Linear and Nonlinear Programming*, Berlin: Heldermann-Verlag. This book is available online: http://ioe.engin.umich.edu/people/fac/books/murty/ linear_complementarity_webbook/.

[38] Ng, G.S. and Singh, H. (1998), Democracy in Pattern Classifications: Combinations of Votes from Various Pattern Classifiers, *Artificial Intelligence in Engineering, Elsevier Science*, Vol. 12, No. 3, 189–204.

[39] Nocedal, J. and Wright, S.J. (1999), *Numerical Optimization*, Springer Series in Operations Research, New York: Springer-Verlag.

[40] Press, W.H., Teukolsky, S.A., Vetterling, W.T., Flannery, B.P. (1992), *Numerical Recipes in C: The Art of Scientific Computing*, 2nd edition, Cambridge: Cambridge University Press.

[41] Riedmiller, M. and Braun, H. (1993), A Direct Adaptive Method for Faster Backpropagation Learning: The RPROP Algorithm, *Proceedings of the IEEE International Conference on Neural Networks*, IEEE Press, pp. 586–591.

[42] Sankaran, M. (1959), On the Non-Central Chi-Square Distribution, *Biometrika*, 46, 235–237.

[43] Schittkowski, K. (1981a), The Nonlinear Programming Method of Wilson, Han, and Powell with an Augmented Lagrangian Type Line Search Function. Part 1: Convergence Analysis. *Numerical Mathematics*, 38, 83–114.

[44] Schittkowski, K. (1981b), The Nonlinear Programming Method of Wilson, Han, and Powell with an Augmented Lagrangian Type Line Search Function. Part 2: An Efficient Implementation with Linear Least Squares Subproblems. *Numerical Mathematics*, 38, 115–127.

[45] Schittkowski, K. (1983), On the Convergence of a Sequential Quadratic Programming Method with an Augmented Lagrangian Line Search Function, *Optimization*, Vol. 14, 197–216.

[46] Schittowski, K. (2002), *NLPQLP: A New Fortran Implementation of a Sequential Quadratic Programming Algorithm for Parallel Computing*: http://www.optimization-online.org/DB_HTML/2002/01/425.html.

[47] Sheskin, D. J. (2000), *Handbook of Parametric and Nonparametric Statistical Procedures*, 2nd edition, Boca Raton, FL: Chapman & Hall/CRC.

[48] Vapnik, V. (1998), *Statistical Learning Theory*, New York: Wiley.

[49] Wei, W. W. S. (1990), *Time Series Analysis, Univariate and Multivariate Methods*, Boston: Addison-Wesley.

[50] Winters, P. R. (1960), Forecasting Sales by Exponentially Weighted Moving Averages, *Management Science*, 6:3.

[51] Zangari, P. et al. (1996), *RiskMetrics Technical Document*, 4th edition, New York: RiskMetrics Group.

Index